THIRD EDITION

MongoDB: The Definitive Guide
Powerful and Scalable Data Storage

Shannon Bradshaw, Eoin Brazil, and
Kristina Chodorow

Beijing · Boston · Farnham · Sebastopol · Tokyo

MongoDB: The Definitive Guide

by Shannon Bradshaw, Eoin Brazil, and Kristina Chodorow

Copyright © 2020 Shannon Bradshaw and Eoin Brazil. All rights reserved.

Published by O'Reilly Media, Inc., 1005 Gravenstein Highway North, Sebastopol, CA 95472.

O'Reilly books may be purchased for educational, business, or sales promotional use. Online editions are also available for most titles (*http://oreilly.com*). For more information, contact our corporate/institutional sales department: 800-998-9938 or *corporate@oreilly.com*.

Editor: Nicole Taché
Production Editor: Kristen Brown
Copyeditor: Rachel Head
Proofreader: Christina Edwards

Indexer: Judith McConville
Interior Designer: David Futato
Cover Designer: Karen Montgomery
Illustrator: Rebecca Demarest

September 2010:   First Edition
May 2013:   Second Edition
December 2019:   Third Edition

Revision History for the Third Edition
2019-12-09: First Release

See *http://oreilly.com/catalog/errata.csp?isbn=9781491954461* for release details.

The O'Reilly logo is a registered trademark of O'Reilly Media, Inc. *MongoDB: The Definitive Guide*, the cover image, and related trade dress are trademarks of O'Reilly Media, Inc.

978-1-491-95446-1

[LSI]

This book is dedicated to our families for the time, space, and support they provided to make our work on this book possible and for their love.

For Anna, Sigourney, Graham, and Beckett. —Shannon

And for Gemma, Clodagh, and Bronagh. —Eoin

Table of Contents

Part I.   Introduction to MongoDB

Part II.   Designing Your Application

Part III. Replication

Part IV.   Sharding

Part V. Application Administration

Preface

How This Book Is Organized

This book is split up into six sections, covering development, administration, and deployment information.

Getting Started with MongoDB

In Chapter 1 we provide background on MongoDB: why it was created, the goals it is trying to accomplish, and why you might choose to use it for a project. We go into more detail in Chapter 2, which provides an introduction to the core concepts and vocabulary of MongoDB. Chapter 2 also provides a first look at working with MongoDB, getting you started with the database and the shell. The next two chapters cover the basic material that developers need to know to work with MongoDB. In Chapter 3, we describe how to perform those basic write operations, including how to do them with different levels of safety and speed. Chapter 4 explains how to find documents and create complex queries. This chapter also covers how to iterate through results and gives options for limiting, skipping, and sorting results.

Developing with MongoDB

Chapter 5 covers what indexing is and how to index your MongoDB collections. Chapter 6 explains how to use several special types of indexes and collections. Chapter 7 covers a number of techniques for aggregating data with MongoDB, including counting, finding distinct values, grouping documents, the aggregation framework, and writing these results to a collection. Chapter 8 introduces transactions: what they are, how best to use them for your application, and how to tune. Finally, this section finishes with a chapter on designing your application: Chapter 9 goes over tips for writing an application that works well with MongoDB.

Replication

The replication section starts with Chapter 10, which gives you a quick way to set up a replica set locally and covers many of the available configuration options. Chapter 11 then covers the various concepts related to replication. Chapter 12 shows how replication interacts with your application and Chapter 13 covers the administrative aspects of running a replica set.

Sharding

The sharding section starts in Chapter 14 with a quick local setup. Chapter 15 then gives an overview of the components of the cluster and how to set them up. Chapter 16 has advice on choosing a shard key for a variety of applications. Finally, Chapter 17 covers administering a sharded cluster.

Application Administration

The next two chapters cover many aspects of MongoDB administration from the perspective of your application. Chapter 18 discusses how to introspect what MongoDB is doing. Chapter 19 covers security in MongoDb and how to configure authentication as well as authorization for your deployment. Chapter 20 explains how MongoDB stores data durably.

Server Administration

The final section is focused on server administration. Chapter 21 covers common options when starting and stopping MongoDB. Chapter 22 discusses what to look for and how to read stats when monitoring. Chapter 23 describes how to take and restore backups for each type of deployment. Finally, Chapter 24 discusses a number of system settings to keep in mind when deploying MongoDB.

Appendixes

Appendix A explains MongoDB's versioning scheme and how to install it on Windows, OS X, and Linux. Appendix B details how MongoDB works internally: its storage engine, data format, and wire protocol.

Conventions Used in This Book

The following typographical conventions are used in this book:

Italic

    Indicates new terms, URLs, email addresses, collection names, database names, filenames, and file extensions.

Constant width

> Used for program listings, as well as within paragraphs to refer to program elements such as variable or function names, command-line utilities, environment variables, statements, and keywords.

Constant width bold

> Shows commands or other text that should be typed literally by the user.

Constant width italic

> Shows text that should be replaced with user-supplied values or by values determined by context.

 This element signifies a tip or suggestion.

 This element signifies a general note.

 This element indicates a warning or caution.

Using Code Examples

Supplemental material (code examples, exercises, etc.) is available for download at *https://github.com/mongodb-the-definitive-guide-3e/mongodb-the-definitive-guide-3e*.

If you have a technical question or a problem using the code examples, please send email to *bookquestions@oreilly.com*.

This book is here to help you get your job done. In general, if example code is offered with this book, you may use it in your programs and documentation. You do not need to contact us for permission unless you're reproducing a significant portion of the code. For example, writing a program that uses several chunks of code from this book does not require permission. Selling or distributing examples from O'Reilly books does require permission. Answering a question by citing this book and quoting example code does not require permission. Incorporating a significant amount of example code from this book into your product's documentation does require permission.

We appreciate, but generally do not require, attribution. An attribution usually includes the title, author, publisher, and ISBN. For example: "*MongoDB: The Definitive Guide*, Third Edition by Shannon Bradshaw, Eoin Brazil, and Kristina Chodorow (O'Reilly). Copyright 2020 Shannon Bradshaw and Eoin Brazil, 978-1-491-95446-1."

If you feel your use of code examples falls outside fair use or the permission given above, feel free to contact us at *permissions@oreilly.com*.

O'Reilly Online Learning

O'REILLY® For more than 40 years, O'Reilly Media has provided technology and business training, knowledge, and insight to help companies succeed.

Our unique network of experts and innovators share their knowledge and expertise through books, articles, conferences, and our online learning platform. O'Reilly's online learning platform gives you on-demand access to live training courses, in-depth learning paths, interactive coding environments, and a vast collection of text and video from O'Reilly and 200+ other publishers. For more information, please visit *http://oreilly.com*.

How to Contact Us

Please address comments and questions concerning this book to the publisher:

O'Reilly Media, Inc.
1005 Gravenstein Highway North
Sebastopol, CA 95472
800-998-9938 (in the United States or Canada)
707-829-0515 (international or local)
707-829-0104 (fax)

We have a web page for this book, where we list errata, examples, and any additional information. You can access this page at *https://oreil.ly/mongoDB_TDG_3e*.

Email *bookquestions@oreilly.com* to comment or ask technical questions about this book.

For more information about our books, courses, conferences, and news, see our website at *http://www.oreilly.com*.

Find us on Facebook: *http://facebook.com/oreilly*

Follow us on Twitter: *http://twitter.com/oreillymedia*

Watch us on YouTube: *http://www.youtube.com/oreillymedia*

## PART I

Introduction to MongoDB

## CHAPTER 1

Introduction

MongoDB is a powerful, flexible, and scalable general-purpose database. It combines the ability to scale out with features such as secondary indexes, range queries, sorting, aggregations, and geospatial indexes. This chapter covers the major design decisions that made MongoDB what it is.

Ease of Use

MongoDB is a *document-oriented* database, not a relational one. The primary reason for moving away from the relational model is to make scaling out easier, but there are some other advantages as well.

A document-oriented database replaces the concept of a "row" with a more flexible model, the "document." By allowing embedded documents and arrays, the document-oriented approach makes it possible to represent complex hierarchical relationships with a single record. This fits naturally into the way developers in modern object-oriented languages think about their data.

There are also no predefined schemas: a document's keys and values are not of fixed types or sizes. Without a fixed schema, adding or removing fields as needed becomes easier. Generally, this makes development faster as developers can quickly iterate. It is also easier to experiment. Developers can try dozens of models for the data and then choose the best one to pursue.

Designed to Scale

Dataset sizes for applications are growing at an incredible pace. Increases in available bandwidth and cheap storage have created an environment where even small-scale applications need to store more data than many databases were meant to handle. A terabyte of data, once an unheard-of amount of information, is now commonplace.

As the amount of data that developers need to store grows, developers face a difficult decision: how should they scale their databases? Scaling a database comes down to the choice between scaling up (getting a bigger machine) or scaling out (partitioning data across more machines). Scaling up is often the path of least resistance, but it has drawbacks: large machines are often very expensive, and eventually a physical limit is reached where a more powerful machine cannot be purchased at any cost. The alternative is to scale out: to add storage space or increase throughput for read and write operations, buy additional servers, and add them to your cluster. This is both cheaper and more scalable; however, it is more difficult to administer a thousand machines than it is to care for one.

MongoDB was designed to scale out. The document-oriented data model makes it easier to split data across multiple servers. MongoDB automatically takes care of balancing data and load across a cluster, redistributing documents automatically and routing reads and writes to the correct machines, as shown in Figure 1-1.

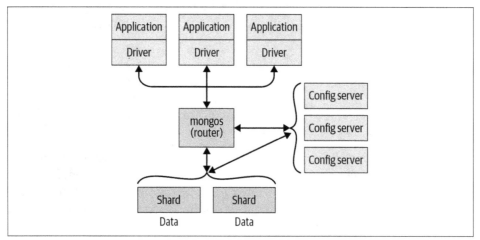

Figure 1-1. Scaling out MongoDB using sharding across multiple servers

The topology of a MongoDB cluster, or whether there is in fact a cluster rather than a single node at the other end of a database connection, is transparent to the application. This allows developers to focus on programming the application, not scaling it.

Likewise, if the topology of an existing deployment needs to change in order to, for example, scale to support greater load, the application logic can remain the same.

Rich with Features...

MongoDB is a general-purpose database, so aside from creating, reading, updating, and deleting data, it provides most of the features you would expect from a database management system and many others that set it apart. These include:

Indexing

> MongoDB supports generic secondary indexes and provides unique, compound, geospatial, and full-text indexing capabilities as well. Secondary indexes on hierarchical structures such as nested documents and arrays are also supported and enable developers to take full advantage of the ability to model in ways that best suit their applications.

Aggregation

> MongoDB provides an aggregation framework based on the concept of data processing pipelines. Aggregation pipelines allow you to build complex analytics engines by processing data through a series of relatively simple stages on the server side, taking full advantage of database optimizations.

Special collection and index types

> MongoDB supports time-to-live (TTL) collections for data that should expire at a certain time, such as sessions and fixed-size (capped) collections, for holding recent data, such as logs. MongoDB also supports partial indexes limited to only those documents matching a criteria filter in order to increase efficiency and reduce the amount of storage space required.

File storage

> MongoDB supports an easy-to-use protocol for storing large files and file metadata.

Some features common to relational databases are not present in MongoDB, notably complex joins. MongoDB supports joins in a very limited way through use of the $lookup aggregation operator introduced in the 3.2 release. In the 3.6 release, more complex joins are possible using multiple join conditions as well as unrelated subqueries. MongoDB's treatment of joins were architectural decisions to allow for greater scalability, because both of those features are difficult to provide efficiently in a distributed system.

…Without Sacrificing Speed

Performance is a driving objective for MongoDB, and has shaped much of its design. It uses opportunistic locking in its WiredTiger storage engine to maximize concurrency and throughput. It uses as much RAM as it can as its cache and attempts to automatically choose the correct indexes for queries. In short, almost every aspect of MongoDB was designed to maintain high performance.

Although MongoDB is powerful, incorporating many features from relational systems, it is not intended to do everything that a relational database does. For some functionality, the database server offloads processing and logic to the client side (handled either by the drivers or by a user's application code). Its maintenance of this streamlined design is one of the reasons MongoDB can achieve such high performance.

The Philosophy

Throughout this book, we will take the time to note the reasoning or motivation behind particular decisions made in the development of MongoDB. Through those notes we hope to share the philosophy behind MongoDB. The best way to summarize the MongoDB project, however, is by referencing its main focus—to create a full-featured data store that is scalable, flexible, and fast.

## CHAPTER 2

Getting Started

MongoDB is powerful but easy to get started with. In this chapter we'll introduce some of the basic concepts of MongoDB:

- A *document* is the basic unit of data for MongoDB and is roughly equivalent to a row in a relational database management system (but much more expressive).

- Similarly, a *collection* can be thought of as a table with a dynamic schema.

- A single instance of MongoDB can host multiple independent *databases*, each of which contains its own collections.

- Every document has a special key, "_id", that is unique within a collection.

- MongoDB is distributed with a simple but powerful tool called the *mongo shell*. The *mongo* shell provides built-in support for administering MongoDB instances and manipulating data using the MongoDB query language. It is also a fully functional JavaScript interpreter that enables users to create and load their own scripts for a variety of purposes.

Documents

At the heart of MongoDB is the *document*: an ordered set of keys with associated values. The representation of a document varies by programming language, but most languages have a data structure that is a natural fit, such as a map, hash, or dictionary. In JavaScript, for example, documents are represented as objects:

```
{"greeting" : "Hello, world!"}
```

This simple document contains a single key, "greeting", with a value of "Hello, world!". Most documents will be more complex than this simple one and often will contain multiple key/value pairs:

```
{"greeting" : "Hello, world!", "views" : 3}
```

As you can see, values in documents are not just "blobs." They can be one of several different data types (or even an entire embedded document—see "Embedded Documents" on page 19). In this example the value for `"greeting"` is a string, whereas the value for `"views"` is an integer.

The keys in a document are strings. Any UTF-8 character is allowed in a key, with a few notable exceptions:

- Keys must not contain the character `\0` (the null character). This character is used to signify the end of a key.

- The `.` and `$` characters have some special properties and should be used only in certain circumstances, as described in later chapters. In general, they should be considered reserved, and drivers will complain if they are used inappropriately.

MongoDB is type-sensitive and case-sensitive. For example, these documents are distinct:

```
{"count" : 5}
{"count" : "5"}
```

as are these:

```
{"count" : 5}
{"Count" : 5}
```

A final important thing to note is that documents in MongoDB cannot contain duplicate keys. For example, the following is not a legal document:

```
{"greeting" : "Hello, world!", "greeting" : "Hello, MongoDB!"}
```

Collections

A *collection* is a group of documents. If a document is the MongoDB analog of a row in a relational database, then a collection can be thought of as the analog to a table.

Dynamic Schemas

Collections have *dynamic schemas*. This means that the documents within a single collection can have any number of different "shapes." For example, both of the following documents could be stored in a single collection:

```
{"greeting" : "Hello, world!", "views": 3}
{"signoff": "Good night, and good luck"}
```

Note that the previous documents have different keys, different numbers of keys, and values of different types. Because any document can be put into any collection, the question often arises: "Why do we need separate collections at all?" With no need for separate schemas for different kinds of documents, why *should* we use more than one collection? There are several good reasons:

- Keeping different kinds of documents in the same collection can be a nightmare for developers and admins. Developers need to make sure that each query is only returning documents adhering to a particular schema or that the application code performing a query can handle documents of different shapes. If we're querying for blog posts, it's a hassle to weed out documents containing author data.

- It's much faster to get a list of collections than to extract a list of the types of documents in a collection. For example, if we had a "type" field in each document that specified whether the document was a "skim," "whole," or "chunky monkey," it would be much slower to find those three values in a single collection than to have three separate collections and query the correct collection.

- Grouping documents of the same kind together in the same collection allows for data locality. Getting several blog posts from a collection containing only posts will likely require fewer disk seeks than getting the same posts from a collection containing posts and author data.

- We begin to impose some structure on our documents when we create indexes. (This is especially true in the case of unique indexes.) These indexes are defined per collection. By putting only documents of a single type into the same collection, we can index our collections more efficiently.

There are sound reasons for creating a schema and for grouping related types of documents together. While not required by default, defining schemas for your application is good practice and can be enforced through the use of MongoDB's documentation validation functionality and object–document mapping libraries available for many programming languages.

Naming

A collection is identified by its name. Collection names can be any UTF-8 string, with a few restrictions:

- The empty string ("") is not a valid collection name.

- Collection names may not contain the character \0 (the null character), because this delineates the end of a collection name.

- You should not create any collections with names that start with *system.*, a prefix reserved for internal collections. For example, the *system.users* collection contains the database's users, and the *system.namespaces* collection contains information about all of the database's collections.

- User-created collections should not contain the reserved character $ in their names. The various drivers available for the database do support using $ in collection names because some system-generated collections contain it, but you should not use $ in a name unless you are accessing one of these collections.

Subcollections

One convention for organizing collections is to use namespaced subcollections separated by the . character. For example, an application containing a blog might have a collection named *blog.posts* and a separate collection named *blog.authors*. This is for organizational purposes only—there is no relationship between the *blog* collection (it doesn't even have to exist) and its "children."

Although subcollections do not have any special properties, they are useful and are incorporated into many MongoDB tools. For instance:

- GridFS, a protocol for storing large files, uses subcollections to store file metadata separately from content chunks (see Chapter 6 for more information about GridFS).
- Most drivers provide some syntactic sugar for accessing a subcollection of a given collection. For example, in the database shell, `db.blog` will give you the *blog* collection, and `db.blog.posts` will give you the *blog.posts* collection.

Subcollections are a good way to organize data in MongoDB for many use cases.

Databases

In addition to grouping documents by collection, MongoDB groups collections into *databases*. A single instance of MongoDB can host several databases, each grouping together zero or more collections. A good rule of thumb is to store all data for a single application in the same database. Separate databases are useful when storing data for several applications or users on the same MongoDB server.

Like collections, databases are identified by name. Database names can be any UTF-8 string, with the following restrictions:

- The empty string ("") is not a valid database name.
- A database name cannot contain any of these characters: /, \, ., ", *, <, >, :, |, ?, $, (a single space), or \0 (the null character). Basically, stick with alphanumeric ASCII.
- Database names are case-insensitive.
- Database names are limited to a maximum of 64 bytes.

Historically, prior to the use of the WiredTiger storage engine, database names became files on your filesystem. It is no longer the case. This explains why many of the previous restrictions exist in the first place.

There are also some reserved database names, which you can access but which have special semantics. These are as follows:

admin

The *admin* database plays a role in authentication and authorization. In addition, access to this database is required for some administrative operations. See Chapter 19 for more information about the *admin* database.

local

This database stores data specific to a single server. In replica sets, *local* stores data used in the replication process. The *local* database itself is never replicated. (See Chapter 10 for more information about replication and the local database.)

config

Sharded MongoDB clusters (see Chapter 14) use the *config* database to store information about each shard.

By concatenating a database name with a collection in that database you can get a fully qualified collection name, which is called a *namespace*. For instance, if you are using the *blog.posts* collection in the *cms* database, the namespace of that collection would be *cms.blog.posts*. Namespaces are limited to 120 bytes in length and, in practice, should be fewer than 100 bytes long. For more on namespaces and the internal representation of collections in MongoDB, see Appendix B.

Getting and Starting MongoDB

To start the server, run the *mongod* executable in the Unix command-line environment of your choice:

```
$ mongod
2016-04-27T22:15:55.871-0400 I CONTROL  [initandlisten] MongoDB starting :
pid=8680 port=27017 dbpath=/data/db 64-bit host=morty
2016-04-27T22:15:55.872-0400 I CONTROL  [initandlisten] db version v4.2.0
2016-04-27T22:15:55.872-0400 I CONTROL  [initandlisten] git version:
34e65e5383f7ea1726332cb175b73077ec4a1b02
2016-04-27T22:15:55.872-0400 I CONTROL  [initandlisten] allocator: system
2016-04-27T22:15:55.872-0400 I CONTROL  [initandlisten] modules: none
2016-04-27T22:15:55.872-0400 I CONTROL  [initandlisten] build environment:
2016-04-27T22:15:55.872-0400 I CONTROL  [initandlisten]     distarch: x86_64
2016-04-27T22:15:55.872-0400 I CONTROL  [initandlisten]     target_arch: x86_64
2016-04-27T22:15:55.872-0400 I CONTROL  [initandlisten] options: {}
2016-04-27T22:15:55.889-0400 I JOURNAL  [initandlisten]
journal dir=/data/db/journal
2016-04-27T22:15:55.889-0400 I JOURNAL  [initandlisten] recover :
```

```
no journal files
present, no recovery needed
2016-04-27T22:15:55.909-0400 I JOURNAL  [durability] Durability thread started
2016-04-27T22:15:55.909-0400 I JOURNAL  [journal writer] Journal writer thread
started
2016-04-27T22:15:55.909-0400 I CONTROL  [initandlisten]
2016-04-27T22:15:56.777-0400 I NETWORK  [HostnameCanonicalizationWorker]
Starting hostname canonicalization worker
2016-04-27T22:15:56.778-0400 I FTDC     [initandlisten] Initializing full-time
diagnostic data capture with directory '/data/db/diagnostic.data'
2016-04-27T22:15:56.779-0400 I NETWORK  [initandlisten] waiting for connections
on port 27017
```

If you're on Windows, run this:

```
> mongod.exe
```

For detailed information on installing MongoDB on your system, see Appendix A or the appropriate installation tutorial (*https://oreil.ly/5WP5e*) in the MongoDB documentation.

When run with no arguments, *mongod* will use the default data directory, */data/db/* (or *\data\db* on the current volume on Windows). If the data directory does not already exist or is not writable, the server will fail to start. It is important to create the data directory (e.g., mkdir -p /data/db/) and to make sure your user has permission to write to the directory before starting MongoDB.

On startup, the server will print some version and system information and then begin waiting for connections. By default MongoDB listens for socket connections on port 27017. The server will fail to start if that port is not available—the most common cause of this is another instance of MongoDB that is already running.

You should always secure your *mongod* instances. See Chapter 19 for more information on securing MongoDB.

You can safely stop *mongod* by typing Ctrl-C in the command-line-environment from which you launched the *mongod* server.

For more information on starting or stopping MongoDB, see Chapter 21.

Introduction to the MongoDB Shell

MongoDB comes with a JavaScript shell that allows interaction with a MongoDB instance from the command line. The shell is useful for performing administrative functions, inspecting a running instance, or just exploring MongoDB. The *mongo* shell is a crucial tool for using MongoDB. We'll use it extensively throughout the rest of the text.

Running the Shell

To start the shell, run the *mongo* executable:

```
$ mongo
MongoDB shell version: 4.2.0
connecting to: test
>
```

The shell automatically attempts to connect to a MongoDB server running on the local machine on startup, so make sure you start *mongod* before starting the shell.

The shell is a full-featured JavaScript interpreter, capable of running arbitrary JavaScript programs. To illustrate this, let's perform some basic math:

```
> x = 200;
200
> x / 5;
40
```

We can also leverage all of the standard JavaScript libraries:

```
> Math.sin(Math.PI / 2);
1
> new Date("20109/1/1");
ISODate("2019-01-01T05:00:00Z")
> "Hello, World!".replace("World", "MongoDB");
Hello, MongoDB!
```

We can even define and call JavaScript functions:

```
> function factorial (n) {
... if (n <= 1) return 1;
... return n * factorial(n - 1);
... }
> factorial(5);
120
```

Note that you can create multiline commands. The shell will detect whether the JavaScript statement is complete when you press Enter. If the statement is not complete, the shell will allow you to continue writing it on the next line. Pressing Enter three times in a row will cancel the half-formed command and get you back to the > prompt.

A MongoDB Client

Although the ability to execute arbitrary JavaScript is useful, the real power of the shell lies in the fact that it is also a standalone MongoDB client. On startup, the shell connects to the *test* database on a MongoDB server and assigns this database connection to the global variable db. This variable is the primary access point to your MongoDB server through the shell.

To see the database to which db is currently assigned, type in db and hit Enter:

```
> db
test
```

The shell contains some add-ons that are not valid JavaScript syntax but were implemented because of their familiarity to users of SQL shells. The add-ons do not provide any extra functionality, but they are nice syntactic sugar. For instance, one of the most important operations is selecting which database to use:

```
> use video
switched to db video
```

Now if you look at the db variable, you can see that it refers to the *video* database:

```
> db
video
```

Because this is a JavaScript shell, typing a variable name will cause the name to be evaluated as an expression. The value (in this case, the database name) is then printed.

You may access collections from the db variable. For example:

```
> db.movies
```

returns the *movies* collection in the current database. Now that we can access a collection in the shell, we can perform almost any database operation.

Basic Operations with the Shell

We can use the four basic operations, create, read, update, and delete (CRUD), to manipulate and view data in the shell.

Create

The insertOne function adds a document to a collection. For example, suppose we want to store a movie. First, we'll create a local variable called movie that is a JavaScript object representing our document. It will have the keys "title", "director", and "year" (the year it was released):

```
> movie = {"title" : "Star Wars: Episode IV - A New Hope",
... "director" : "George Lucas",
... "year" : 1977}
{
        "title" : "Star Wars: Episode IV - A New Hope",
        "director" : "George Lucas",
        "year" : 1977
}
```

This object is a valid MongoDB document, so we can save it to the *movies* collection using the insertOne method:

```
> db.movies.insertOne(movie)
{
        "acknowledged" : true,
        "insertedId" : ObjectId("5721794b349c32b32a012b11")
}
```

The movie has been saved to the database. We can see it by calling find on the collection:

```
> db.movies.find().pretty()
{
        "_id" : ObjectId("5721794b349c32b32a012b11"),
        "title" : "Star Wars: Episode IV - A New Hope",
        "director" : "George Lucas",
        "year" : 1977
}
```

We can see that an "_id" key was added and that the other key/value pairs were saved as we entered them. The reason for the sudden appearance of the "_id" field is explained at the end of this chapter.

Read

find and findOne can be used to query a collection. If we just want to see one document from a collection, we can use findOne:

```
> db.movies.findOne()
{
        "_id" : ObjectId("5721794b349c32b32a012b11"),
        "title" : "Star Wars: Episode IV - A New Hope",
        "director" : "George Lucas",
        "year" : 1977
}
```

find and findOne can also be passed criteria in the form of a query document. This will restrict the documents matched by the query. The shell will automatically display up to 20 documents matching a find, but more can be fetched. (See Chapter 4 for more information on querying.)

Update

If we would like to modify our post, we can use `updateOne`. `updateOne` takes (at least) two parameters: the first is the criteria to find which document to update, and the second is a document describing the updates to make. Suppose we decide to enable reviews for the movie we created earlier. We'll need to add an array of reviews as the value for a new key in our document.

To perform the update, we'll need to use an update operator, `set`:

```
> db.movies.updateOne({title : "Star Wars: Episode IV - A New Hope"},
... {$set : {reviews: []}})
WriteResult({"nMatched": 1, "nUpserted": 0, "nModified": 1})
```

Now the document has a `"reviews"` key. If we call `find` again, we can see the new key:

```
> db.movies.find().pretty()
{
        "_id" : ObjectId("5721794b349c32b32a012b11"),
        "title" : "Star Wars: Episode IV - A New Hope",
        "director" : "George Lucas",
        "year" : 1977,
        "reviews" : [ ]
}
```

See "Updating Documents" on page 35 for detailed information on updating documents.

Delete

`deleteOne` and `deleteMany` permanently delete documents from the database. Both methods take a filter document specifying criteria for the removal. For example, this would remove the movie we just created:

```
> db.movies.deleteOne({title : "Star Wars: Episode IV - A New Hope"})
```

Use `deleteMany` to delete all documents matching a filter.

Data Types

The beginning of this chapter covered the basics of what a document is. Now that you are up and running with MongoDB and can try things in the shell, this section will dive a little deeper. MongoDB supports a wide range of data types as values in documents. In this section, we'll outline all the supported types.

Basic Data Types

Documents in MongoDB can be thought of as "JSON-like" in that they are conceptually similar to objects in JavaScript. JSON (*http://www.json.org*) is a simple represen-

---

tation of data: the specification can be described in about one paragraph (the website proves it) and lists only six data types. This is a good thing in many ways: it's easy to understand, parse, and remember. On the other hand, JSON's expressive capabilities are limited because the only types are null, boolean, numeric, string, array, and object.

Although these types allow for an impressive amount of expressivity, there are a couple of additional types that are crucial for most applications, especially when working with a database. For example, JSON has no date type, which makes working with dates even more annoying than it usually is. There is a number type, but only one—there is no way to differentiate floats and integers, never mind any distinction between 32-bit and 64-bit numbers. There is no way to represent other commonly used types, either, such as regular expressions or functions.

MongoDB adds support for a number of additional data types while keeping JSON's essential key/value–pair nature. Exactly how values of each type are represented varies by language, but this is a list of the commonly supported types and how they are represented as part of a document in the shell. The most common types are:

Null
> The null type can be used to represent both a null value and a nonexistent field:

> ```
> {"x" : null}
> ```

Boolean
> There is a boolean type, which can be used for the values `true` and `false`:

> ```
> {"x" : true}
> ```

Number
> The shell defaults to using 64-bit floating-point numbers. Thus, these numbers both look "normal" in the shell:

> ```
> {"x" : 3.14}
> ```
> ```
> {"x" : 3}
> ```

> For integers, use the `NumberInt` or `NumberLong` classes, which represent 4-byte or 8-byte signed integers, respectively.

> ```
> {"x" : NumberInt("3")}
> {"x" : NumberLong("3")}
> ```

String
> Any string of UTF-8 characters can be represented using the string type:

> ```
> {"x" : "foobar"}
> ```

Date
> MongoDB stores dates as 64-bit integers representing milliseconds since the Unix epoch (January 1, 1970). The time zone is not stored:

```
{"x" : new Date()}
```

Regular expression

Queries can use regular expressions using JavaScript's regular expression syntax:

```
{"x" : /foobar/i}
```

Array

Sets or lists of values can be represented as arrays:

```
{"x" : ["a", "b", "c"]}
```

Embedded document

Documents can contain entire documents embedded as values in a parent document:

```
{"x" : {"foo" : "bar"}}
```

Object ID

An object ID is a 12-byte ID for documents:

```
{"x" : ObjectId()}
```

See the section "_id and ObjectIds" on page 20 for details.

There are also a few less common types that you may need, including:

Binary data

Binary data is a string of arbitrary bytes. It cannot be manipulated from the shell. Binary data is the only way to save non-UTF-8 strings to the database.

Code

MongoDB also makes it possible to store arbitrary JavaScript in queries and documents:

```
{"x" : function() { /* ... */ }}
```

Finally, there are a few types that are mostly used internally (or superseded by other types). These will be described in the text as needed.

For more information on MongoDB's data format, see Appendix B.

Dates

In JavaScript, the Date class is used for MongoDB's date type. When creating a new Date object, always call new Date(), not just Date(). Calling the constructor as a function (i.e., not including new) returns a string representation of the date, not an actual Date object. This is not MongoDB's choice; it is how JavaScript works. If you are not careful to always use the Date constructor, you can end up with a mishmash of strings and dates. Strings do not match dates and vice versa, so this can cause problems with removing, updating, querying...pretty much everything.

For a full explanation of JavaScript's `Date` class and acceptable formats for the constructor, see section 15.9 of the ECMAScript specification (*http://www.ecma-international.org*).

Dates in the shell are displayed using local time zone settings. However, dates in the database are just stored as milliseconds since the epoch, so they have no time zone information associated with them. (Time zone information could, of course, be stored as the value for another key.)

Arrays

Arrays are values that can be used interchangeably for both ordered operations (as though they were lists, stacks, or queues) and unordered operations (as though they were sets).

In the following document, the key `"things"` has an array value:

```
{"things" : ["pie", 3.14]}
```

As you can see from this example, arrays can contain different data types as values (in this case, a string and a floating-point number). In fact, array values can be any of the supported value types for normal key/value pairs, even nested arrays.

One of the great things about arrays in documents is that MongoDB "understands" their structure and knows how to reach inside of arrays to perform operations on their contents. This allows us to query on arrays and build indexes using their contents. For instance, in the previous example, MongoDB can query for all documents where `3.14` is an element of the `"things"` array. If this is a common query, you can even create an index on the `"things"` key to improve the query's speed.

MongoDB also allows atomic updates that modify the contents of arrays, such as reaching into the array and changing the value `"pie"` to pi. We'll see more examples of these types of operations throughout the text.

Embedded Documents

A document can be used as the value for a key. This is called an *embedded document*. Embedded documents can be used to organize data in a more natural way than just a flat structure of key/value pairs.

For example, if we have a document representing a person and want to store that person's address, we can nest this information in an embedded `"address"` document:

```
{
    "name" : "John Doe",
    "address" : {
        "street" : "123 Park Street",
        "city" : "Anytown",
```

```
            "state" : "NY"
        }
    }
```

The value for the "address" key in this example is an embedded document with its own key/value pairs for "street", "city", and "state".

As with arrays, MongoDB "understands" the structure of embedded documents and is able to reach inside them to build indexes, perform queries, or make updates.

We'll discuss schema design in-depth later, but even from this basic example we can begin to see how embedded documents can change the way we work with data. In a relational database, the previous document would probably be modeled as two sepa-rate rows in two different tables (*people* and *addresses*). With MongoDB we can embed the "address" document directly within the "person" document. Thus, when used properly, embedded documents can provide a more natural representation of information.

The flip side of this is that there can be more data repetition with MongoDB. Suppose *addresses* was a separate table in a relational database and we needed to fix a typo in an address. When we did a join with *people* and *addresses*, we'd get the updated address for everyone who shares it. With MongoDB, we'd need to fix the typo in each person's document.

_id and ObjectIds

Every document stored in MongoDB must have an "_id" key. The "_id" key's value can be any type, but it defaults to an ObjectId. In a single collection, every document must have a unique value for "_id", which ensures that every document in a collec-tion can be uniquely identified. That is, if you had two collections, each one could have a document where the value for "_id" was 123. However, neither collection could contain more than one document with an "_id" of 123.

ObjectIds

ObjectId is the default type for "_id". The ObjectId class is designed to be light-weight, while still being easy to generate in a globally unique way across different machines. MongoDB's distributed nature is the main reason why it uses ObjectIds as opposed to something more traditional, like an autoincrementing primary key: it is difficult and time-consuming to synchronize autoincrementing primary keys across multiple servers. Because MongoDB was designed to be a distributed database, it was important to be able to generate unique identifiers in a sharded environment.

ObjectIds use 12 bytes of storage, which gives them a string representation that is 24 hexadecimal digits: 2 digits for each byte. This causes them to appear larger than they are, which makes some people nervous. It's important to note that even though an

ObjectId is often represented as a giant hexadecimal string, the string is actually twice as long as the data being stored.

If you create multiple new ObjectIds in rapid succession, you can see that only the last few digits change each time. In addition, a couple of digits in the middle of the ObjectId will change if you space the creations out by a couple of seconds. This is because of the manner in which ObjectIds are created. The 12 bytes of an ObjectId are generated as follows:

0	1	2	3	4	5	6	7	8	9	10	11
Timestamp	Random	Counter (random start value)									

The first four bytes of an ObjectId are a timestamp in seconds since the epoch. This provides a couple of useful properties:

- The timestamp, when combined with the next five bytes (which will be described in a moment), provides uniqueness at the granularity of a second.

- Because the timestamp comes first, ObjectIds will sort in *rough* insertion order. This is not a strong guarantee but does have some nice properties, such as making ObjectIds efficient to index.

- In these four bytes exists an implicit timestamp of when each document was created. Most drivers expose a method for extracting this information from an ObjectId.

Because the current time is used in ObjectIds, some users worry that their servers will need to have synchronized clocks. Although synchronized clocks are a good idea for other reasons (see "Synchronizing Clocks" on page 462), the actual timestamp doesn't matter to ObjectIds, only that it is often new (once per second) and increasing.

The next five bytes of an ObjectId are a random value. The final three bytes are a counter that starts with a random value to avoid generating colliding ObjectIds on different machines.

These first nine bytes of an ObjectId therefore guarantee its uniqueness across machines and processes for a single second. The last three bytes are simply an incrementing counter that is responsible for uniqueness within a second in a single process. This allows for up to 256^3 (16,777,216) unique ObjectIds to be generated *per process* in a single second.

Autogeneration of _id

As stated earlier, if there is no `"_id"` key present when a document is inserted, one will be automatically added to the inserted document. This can be handled by the MongoDB server but will generally be done by the driver on the client side.

Using the MongoDB Shell

This section covers how to use the shell as part of your command-line toolkit, customize it, and use some of its more advanced functionality.

Although we connected to a local *mongod* instance above, you can connect your shell to any MongoDB instance that your machine can reach. To connect to a *mongod* on a different machine or port, specify the hostname, port, and database when starting the shell:

```
$ mongo some-host:30000/myDB
MongoDB shell version: 4.2.0
connecting to: some-host:30000/myDB
>
```

db will now refer to *some-host:30000*'s myDB database.

Sometimes it is handy to not connect to a *mongod* at all when starting the *mongo* shell. If you start the shell with `--nodb`, it will start up without attempting to connect to anything:

```
$ mongo --nodb
MongoDB shell version: 4.2.0
>
```

Once started, you can connect to a *mongod* at your leisure by running new Mongo(`"hostname"`):

```
> conn = new Mongo("some-host:30000")
connection to some-host:30000
> db = conn.getDB("myDB")
myDB
```

After these two commands, you can use db normally. You can use these commands to connect to a different database or server at any time.

Tips for Using the Shell

Because *mongo* is simply a JavaScript shell, you can get a great deal of help for it by simply looking up JavaScript documentation online. For MongoDB-specific functionality, the shell includes built-in help that can be accessed by typing **help**:

```
> help
    db.help()                       help on db methods
    db.mycoll.help()                help on collection methods
    sh.help()                       sharding helpers
    ...

    show dbs                        show database names
    show collections                show collections in current database
    show users                      show users in current database
    ...
```

Database-level help is provided by db.help() and collection-level help by db.foo.help().

A good way of figuring out what a function is doing is to type it without the parentheses. This will print the JavaScript source code for the function. For example, if you are curious about how the update function works or cannot remember the order of parameters, you can do the following:

```
> db.movies.updateOne
function (filter, update, options) {
    var opts = Object.extend({}, options || {});

    // Check if first key in update statement contains a $
    var keys = Object.keys(update);
    if (keys.length == 0) {
        throw new Error("the update operation document must contain at
        least one atomic operator");
    }
    ...
```

Running Scripts with the Shell

In addition to using the shell interactively, you can also pass the shell JavaScript files to execute. Simply pass in your scripts at the command line:

```
$ mongo script1.js script2.js script3.js
MongoDB shell version: 4.2.1
connecting to: mongodb://127.0.0.1:27017
MongoDB server version: 4.2.1

loading file: script1.js
I am script1.js
loading file: script2.js
I am script2.js
loading file: script3.js
I am script3.js
...
```

The *mongo* shell will execute each script listed and exit.

If you want to run a script using a connection to a nondefault host/port *mongod*, specify the address first, then the script(s):

```
$ mongo server-1:30000/foo --quiet script1.js script2.js script3.js
```

This would execute the three scripts with db set to the *foo* database on *server-1:30000*.

You can print to stdout in scripts (as the preceding scripts did) using the `print` function. This allows you to use the shell as part of a pipeline of commands. If you're planning to pipe the output of a shell script to another command, use the `--quiet` option to prevent the "MongoDB shell version v4.2.0" banner from printing.

You can also run scripts from within the interactive shell using the `load` function:

```
> load("script1.js")
I am script1.js
true
>
```

Scripts have access to the db variable (as well as any other global). However, shell helpers such as `use db` or `show collections` do not work from files. There are valid JavaScript equivalents to each of these, as shown in Table 2-1.

Table 2-1. JavaScript equivalents to shell helpers

Helper	Equivalent
use video	db.getSisterDB("video")
show dbs	db.getMongo().getDBs()
show collections	db.getCollectionNames()

You can also use scripts to inject variables into the shell. For example, you could have a script that simply initializes helper functions that you commonly use. The following script, for instance, may be helpful for Part III and Part IV. It defines a function, `con nectTo`, that connects to the locally running database on the given port and sets db to that connection:

```
// defineConnectTo.js

/**
 * Connect to a database and set db.
 */
var connectTo = function(port, dbname) {
    if (!port) {
        port = 27017;
    }

    if (!dbname) {
        dbname = "test";
    }
```

```
    db = connect("localhost:"+port+"/"+dbname);
    return db;
};
```

If you load this script in the shell, connectTo is now defined:

```
> typeof connectTo
undefined
> load('defineConnectTo.js')
> typeof connectTo
function
```

In addition to adding helper functions, you can use scripts to automate common tasks and administrative activities.

By default, the shell will look in the directory that you started the shell in (use pwd() to see what directory that is). If the script is not in your current directory, you can give the shell a relative or absolute path to it. For example, if you wanted to put your shell scripts in *~/my-scripts*, you could load *defineConnectTo.js* with load("/home/myUser/my-scripts/defineConnectTo.js"). Note that load cannot resolve ~.

You can use run to run command-line programs from the shell. You can pass arguments to the function as parameters:

```
> run("ls", "-l", "/home/myUser/my-scripts/")
sh70352| -rw-r--r--  1 myUser myUser 2012-12-13 13:15 defineConnectTo.js
sh70532| -rw-r--r--  1 myUser myUser 2013-02-22 15:10 script1.js
sh70532| -rw-r--r--  1 myUser myUser 2013-02-22 15:12 script2.js
sh70532| -rw-r--r--  1 myUser myUser 2013-02-22 15:13 script3.js
```

This is of limited use, generally, as the output is formatted oddly and it doesn't support pipes.

Creating a .mongorc.js

If you have frequently loaded scripts, you might want to put them in your *.mongorc.js* file. This file is run whenever you start up the shell.

For example, suppose you would like the shell to greet you when you log in. Create a file called *.mongorc.js* in your home directory, and then add the following lines to it:

```
// .mongorc.js

var compliment = ["attractive", "intelligent", "like Batman"];
var index = Math.floor(Math.random()*3);

print("Hello, you're looking particularly "+compliment[index]+" today!");
```

Then, when you start the shell, you'll see something like:

```
$ mongo
MongoDB shell version: 4.2.1
connecting to: test
Hello, you're looking particularly like Batman today!
>
```

More practically, you can use this script to set up any global variables you'd like to use, alias long names to shorter ones, and override built-in functions. One of the most common uses for *.mongorc.js* is to remove some of the more "dangerous" shell helpers. You can override functions like dropDatabase or deleteIndexes with no-ops or undefine them altogether:

```
var no = function() {
    print("Not on my watch.");
};

// Prevent dropping databases
db.dropDatabase = DB.prototype.dropDatabase = no;

// Prevent dropping collections
DBCollection.prototype.drop = no;

// Prevent dropping an index
DBCollection.prototype.dropIndex = no;

// Prevent dropping indexes
DBCollection.prototype.dropIndexes = no;
```

Now if you try to call any of these functions, it will simply print an error message. Note that this technique does not protect you against malicious users; it can only help with fat-fingering.

You can disable loading your *.mongorc.js* by using the --norc option when starting the shell.

Customizing Your Prompt

The default shell prompt can be overridden by setting the prompt variable to either a string or a function. For example, if you are running a query that takes minutes to complete, you may want to have a prompt that displays the current time so you can see when the last operation finished:

```
prompt = function() {
    return (new Date())+"> ";
};
```

Another handy prompt might show the current database you're using:

```
prompt = function() {
    if (typeof db == 'undefined') {
        return '(nodb)> ';
    }

    // Check the last db operation
    try {
        db.runCommand({getLastError:1});
    }
    catch (e) {
        print(e);
    }

    return db+"> ";
};
```

Note that prompt functions should return strings and be very cautious about catching exceptions: it can be extremely confusing if your prompt turns into an exception!

In general, your prompt function should include a call to `getLastError`. This catches errors on writes and reconnects you automatically if the shell gets disconnected (e.g., if you restart *mongod*).

The *.mongorc.js* file is a good place to set your prompt if you want to always use a custom one (or set up a couple of custom prompts that you can switch between in the shell).

Editing Complex Variables

The multiline support in the shell is somewhat limited: you cannot edit previous lines, which can be annoying when you realize that the first line has a typo and you're currently working on line 15. Thus, for larger blocks of code or objects, you may want to edit them in an editor. To do so, set the `EDITOR` variable in the shell (or in your environment, but since you're already in the shell…):

```
> EDITOR="/usr/bin/emacs"
```

Now, if you want to edit a variable, you can say *edit varname*—for example:

```
> var wap = db.books.findOne({title: "War and Peace"});
> edit wap
```

When you're done making changes, save and exit the editor. The variable will be parsed and loaded back into the shell.

Add `EDITOR="/path/to/editor";` to your *.mongorc.js* file and you won't have to worry about setting it again.

Inconvenient Collection Names

Fetching a collection with the db.*collectionName* syntax almost always works, unless the collection name is a reserved word or is an invalid JavaScript property name.

For example, suppose we are trying to access the *version* collection. We cannot say db.version because db.version is a method on db (it returns the version of the running MongoDB server):

```
> db.version
function () {
    return this.serverBuildInfo().version;
}
```

To actually access the *version* collection, you must use the getCollection function:

```
> db.getCollection("version");
test.version
```

This can also be used for collection names with characters that aren't valid JavaScript property names, such as *foo-bar-baz* and *123abc* (JavaScript property names can only contain letters, numbers, $ and _, and cannot start with a number).

Another way of getting around invalid properties is to use array-access syntax. In JavaScript, x.y is identical to x['y']. This means that subcollections can be accessed using variables, not just literal names. Thus, if you needed to perform some operation on every *blog* subcollection, you could iterate through them with something like this:

```
var collections = ["posts", "comments", "authors"];

for (var i in collections) {
    print(db.blog[collections[i]]);
}
```

instead of this:

```
print(db.blog.posts);
print(db.blog.comments);
print(db.blog.authors);
```

Note that you cannot do db.blog.i, which would be interpreted as test.blog.i, not test.blog.posts. You must use the db.blog[i] syntax for i to be interpreted as a variable.

You can use this technique to access awkwardly named collections:

```
> var name = "@#&!"
> db[name].find()
```

Attempting to query db.@#&! would be illegal, but db[name] would work.

## CHAPTER 3

Creating, Updating, and Deleting Documents

This chapter covers the basics of moving data into and out of the database, including the following:

- Adding new documents to a collection
- Removing documents from a collection
- Updating existing documents
- Choosing the correct level of safety versus speed for all of these operations

Inserting Documents

Inserts are the basic method for adding data to MongoDB. To insert a single document, use the collection's `insertOne` method:

```
> db.movies.insertOne({"title" : "Stand by Me"})
```

`insertOne` will add an `"_id"` key to the document (if you do not supply one) and store the document in MongoDB.

insertMany

If you need to insert multiple documents into a collection, you can use `insertMany`. This method enables you to pass an array of documents to the database. This is far more efficient because your code will not make a round trip to the database for each document inserted, but will insert them in bulk.

In the shell, you can try this out as follows:

```
> db.movies.drop()
true
> db.movies.insertMany([{"title" : "Ghostbusters"},
...                        {"title" : "E.T."},
...                        {"title" : "Blade Runner"}]);
{
    "acknowledged" : true,
    "insertedIds" : [
        ObjectId("572630ba11722fac4b6b4996"),
        ObjectId("572630ba11722fac4b6b4997"),
        ObjectId("572630ba11722fac4b6b4998")
    ]
}
> db.movies.find()
{ "_id" : ObjectId("572630ba11722fac4b6b4996"), "title" : "Ghostbusters" }
{ "_id" : ObjectId("572630ba11722fac4b6b4997"), "title" : "E.T." }
{ "_id" : ObjectId("572630ba11722fac4b6b4998"), "title" : "Blade Runner" }
```

Sending dozens, hundreds, or even thousands of documents at a time can make inserts significantly faster.

insertMany is useful if you are inserting multiple documents into a single collection. If you are just importing raw data (e.g., from a data feed or MySQL), there are command-line tools like *mongoimport* that can be used instead of a batch insert. On the other hand, it is often handy to munge data before saving it to MongoDB (converting dates to the date type or adding a custom "_id", for example). In such cases insertMany can be used for importing data, as well.

Current versions of MongoDB do not accept messages longer than 48 MB, so there is a limit to how much can be inserted in a single batch insert. If you attempt to insert more than 48 MB, many drivers will split up the batch insert into multiple 48 MB batch inserts. Check your driver documentation for details.

When performing a bulk insert using insertMany, if a document halfway through the array produces an error of some type, what happens depends on whether you have opted for ordered or unordered operations. As the second parameter to insertMany you may specify an options document. Specify true for the key "ordered" in the options document to ensure documents are inserted in the order they are provided. Specify false and MongoDB may reorder the inserts to increase performance. Ordered inserts is the default if no ordering is specified. For ordered inserts, the array passed to insertMany defines the insertion order. If a document produces an insertion error, no documents beyond that point in the array will be inserted. For unordered inserts, MongoDB will attempt to insert all documents, regardless of whether some insertions produce errors.

In this example, because ordered inserts is the default, only the first two documents will be inserted. The third document will produce an error, because you cannot insert two documents with the same "_id":

```
> db.movies.insertMany([
... {"_id" : 0, "title" : "Top Gun"},
... {"_id" : 1, "title" : "Back to the Future"},
... {"_id" : 1, "title" : "Gremlins"},
... {"_id" : 2, "title" : "Aliens"}])
2019-04-22T12:27:57.278-0400 E QUERY    [js] BulkWriteError: write
error at item 2 in bulk operation :
BulkWriteError({
    "writeErrors" : [
        {
            "index" : 2,
            "code" : 11000,
            "errmsg" : "E11000 duplicate key error collection:
            test.movies index: _id_ dup key: { _id: 1.0 }",
            "op" : {
                "_id" : 1,
                "title" : "Gremlins"
            }
        }
    ],
    "writeConcernErrors" : [ ],
    "nInserted" : 2,
    "nUpserted" : 0,
    "nMatched" : 0,
    "nModified" : 0,
    "nRemoved" : 0,
    "upserted" : [ ]
})
BulkWriteError@src/mongo/shell/bulk_api.js:367:48
BulkWriteResult/this.toError@src/mongo/shell/bulk_api.js:332:24
Bulk/this.execute@src/mongo/shell/bulk_api.js:1186:23
DBCollection.prototype.insertMany@src/mongo/shell/crud_api.js:314:5
@(shell):1:1
```

If instead we specify unordered inserts, the first, second, and fourth documents in the array are inserted. The only insert that fails is the third document, again because of a duplicate "_id" error:

```
> db.movies.insertMany([
... {"_id" : 3, "title" : "Sixteen Candles"},
... {"_id" : 4, "title" : "The Terminator"},
... {"_id" : 4, "title" : "The Princess Bride"},
... {"_id" : 5, "title" : "Scarface"}],
... {"ordered" : false})
2019-05-01T17:02:25.511-0400 E QUERY    [thread1] BulkWriteError: write
error at item 2 in bulk operation :
BulkWriteError({
  "writeErrors" : [
    {
      "index" : 2,
      "code" : 11000,
      "errmsg" : "E11000 duplicate key error index: test.movies.$_id_
```

```
      dup key: { : 4.0 }",
      "op" : {
        "_id" : 4,
        "title" : "The Princess Bride"
      }
    }
  ],
  "writeConcernErrors" : [ ],
  "nInserted" : 3,
  "nUpserted" : 0,
  "nMatched" : 0,
  "nModified" : 0,
  "nRemoved" : 0,
  "upserted" : [ ]
})
BulkWriteError@src/mongo/shell/bulk_api.js:367:48
BulkWriteResult/this.toError@src/mongo/shell/bulk_api.js:332:24
Bulk/this.execute@src/mongo/shell/bulk_api.js:1186.23
DBCollection.prototype.insertMany@src/mongo/shell/crud_api.js:314:5
@(shell):1:1
```

If you study these examples closely, you might note that the output of these two calls
to insertMany hints that other operations besides simply inserts might be supported
for bulk writes. While insertMany does not support operations other than insert,
MongoDB does support a Bulk Write API that enables you to batch together a number of operations of different types in one call. While that is beyond the scope of this
chapter, you can read about the Bulk Write API (*https://docs.mongodb.org/manual/
core/bulk-write-operations/*) in the MongoDB documentation.

Insert Validation

MongoDB does minimal checks on data being inserted: it checks the document's
basic structure and adds an "_id" field if one does not exist. One of the basic structure checks is size: all documents must be smaller than 16 MB. This is a somewhat
arbitrary limit (and may be raised in the future); it is mostly intended to prevent bad
schema design and ensure consistent performance. To see the Binary JSON (BSON)
size, in bytes, of the document *doc*, run Object.bsonsize(*doc*) from the shell.

To give you an idea of how much data 16 MB is, the entire text of *War and Peace* is
just 3.14 MB.

These minimal checks also mean that it is fairly easy to insert invalid data (if you are
trying to). Thus, you should only allow trusted sources, such as your application
servers, to connect to the database. All of the MongoDB drivers for major languages
(and most of the minor ones, too) do check for a variety of invalid data (documents
that are too large, contain non-UTF-8 strings, or use unrecognized types) before
sending anything to the database.

insert

In versions of MongoDB prior to 3.0, `insert` was the primary method for inserting documents into MongoDB. MongoDB drivers introduced a new CRUD API at the same time as the MongoDB 3.0 server release. As of MongoDB 3.2 the *mongo* shell also supports this API, which includes `insertOne` and `insertMany` as well as several other methods. The goal of the current CRUD API is to make the semantics of all CRUD operations consistent and clear across the drivers and the shell. While methods such as `insert` are still supported for backward compatibility, they should not be used in applications going forward. You should instead prefer `insertOne` and `insert Many` for creating documents.

Removing Documents

Now that there's data in our database, let's delete it. The CRUD API provides `deleteOne` and `deleteMany` for this purpose. Both of these methods take a filter document as their first parameter. The filter specifies a set of criteria to match against in removing documents. To delete the document with the `"_id"` value of 4, we use `deleteOne` in the *mongo* shell as illustrated here:

```
> db.movies.find()
{ "_id" : 0, "title" : "Top Gun"}
{ "_id" : 1, "title" : "Back to the Future"}
{ "_id" : 3, "title" : "Sixteen Candles"}
{ "_id" : 4, "title" : "The Terminator"}
{ "_id" : 5, "title" : "Scarface"}
> db.movies.deleteOne({"_id" : 4})
{ "acknowledged" : true, "deletedCount" : 1 }
> db.movies.find()
{ "_id" : 0, "title" : "Top Gun"}
{ "_id" : 1, "title" : "Back to the Future"}
{ "_id" : 3, "title" : "Sixteen Candles"}
{ "_id" : 5, "title" : "Scarface"}
```

In this example, we used a filter that could only match one document since `"_id"` values are unique in a collection. However, we can also specify a filter that matches multiple documents in a collection. In this case, `deleteOne` will delete the first document found that matches the filter. Which document is found first depends on several factors, including the order in which the documents were inserted, what updates were made to the documents (for some storage engines), and what indexes are specified. As with any database operation, be sure you know what effect your use of `deleteOne` will have on your data.

To delete all the documents that match a filter, use `deleteMany`:

```
> db.movies.find()
{ "_id" : 0, "title" : "Top Gun", "year" : 1986 }
{ "_id" : 1, "title" : "Back to the Future", "year" : 1985 }
{ "_id" : 3, "title" : "Sixteen Candles", "year" : 1984 }
{ "_id" : 4, "title" : "The Terminator", "year" : 1984 }
{ "_id" : 5, "title" : "Scarface", "year" : 1983 }
> db.movies.deleteMany({"year" : 1984})
{ "acknowledged" : true, "deletedCount" : 2 }
> db.movies.find()
{ "_id" : 0, "title" : "Top Gun", "year" : 1986 }
{ "_id" : 1, "title" : "Back to the Future", "year" : 1985 }
{ "_id" : 5, "title" : "Scarface", "year" : 1983 }
```

As a more realistic use case, suppose you want to remove every user from the *mailing.list* collection where the value for "opt-out" is true:

```
> db.mailing.list.deleteMany({"opt-out" : true})
```

In versions of MongoDB prior to 3.0, remove was the primary method for deleting documents. MongoDB drivers introduced the deleteOne and deleteMany methods at the same time as the MongoDB 3.0 server release, and the shell began supporting these methods in MongoDB 3.2. While remove is still supported for backward compatibility, you should use deleteOne and deleteMany in your applications. The current CRUD API provides a cleaner set of semantics and, especially for multidocument operations, helps application developers avoid a couple of common pitfalls with the previous API.

drop

It is possible to use deleteMany to remove all documents in a collection:

```
> db.movies.find()
{ "_id" : 0, "title" : "Top Gun", "year" : 1986 }
{ "_id" : 1, "title" : "Back to the Future", "year" : 1985 }
{ "_id" : 3, "title" : "Sixteen Candles", "year" : 1984 }
{ "_id" : 4, "title" : "The Terminator", "year" : 1984 }
{ "_id" : 5, "title" : "Scarface", "year" : 1983 }
> db.movies.deleteMany({})
{ "acknowledged" : true, "deletedCount" : 5 }
> db.movies.find()
```

Removing documents is usually a fairly quick operation. However, if you want to clear an entire collection, it is faster to drop it:

```
> db.movies.drop()
true
```

and then recreate any indexes on the empty collection.

Once data has been removed, it is gone forever. There is no way to undo a delete or drop operation or recover deleted documents, except, of course, by restoring a previously backed up version of the data. See Chapter 23 for a detailed discussion of MongoDB backup and restore.

Updating Documents

Once a document is stored in the database, it can be changed using one of several update methods: updateOne, updateMany, and replaceOne. updateOne and update Many each take a filter document as their first parameter and a modifier document, which describes changes to make, as the second parameter. replaceOne also takes a filter as the first parameter, but as the second parameter replaceOne expects a document with which it will replace the document matching the filter.

Updating a document is atomic: if two updates happen at the same time, whichever one reaches the server first will be applied, and then the next one will be applied. Thus, conflicting updates can safely be sent in rapid-fire succession without any documents being corrupted: the last update will "win." The Document Versioning pattern (see "Schema Design Patterns" on page 208) is worth considering if you don't want the default behavior.

Document Replacement

replaceOne fully replaces a matching document with a new one. This can be useful to do a dramatic schema migration (see Chapter 9 for scheme migration strategies). For example, suppose we are making major changes to a user document, which looks like the following:

```
{
    "_id" : ObjectId("4b2b9f67a1f631733d917a7a"),
    "name" : "joe",
    "friends" : 32,
    "enemies" : 2
}
```

We want to move the "friends" and "enemies" fields to a "relationships" subdocument. We can change the structure of the document in the shell and then replace the database's version with a replaceOne:

```
> var joe = db.users.findOne({"name" : "joe"});
> joe.relationships = {"friends" : joe.friends, "enemies" : joe.enemies};
{
    "friends" : 32,
    "enemies" : 2
}
> joe.username = joe.name;
"joe"
> delete joe.friends;
true
> delete joe.enemies;
```

```
true
> delete joe.name;
true
> db.users.replaceOne({"name" : "joe"}, joe);
```

Now, doing a findOne shows that the structure of the document has been updated:

```
{
    "_id" : ObjectId("4b2b9f67a1f631733d917a7a"),
    "username" : "joe",
    "relationships" : {
        "friends" : 32,
        "enemies" : 2
    }
}
```

A common mistake is matching more than one document with the criteria and then creating a duplicate "_id" value with the second parameter. The database will throw an error for this, and no documents will be updated.

For example, suppose we create several documents with the same value for "name", but we don't realize it:

```
> db.people.find()
{"_id" : ObjectId("4b2b9f67a1f631733d917a7b"), "name" : "joe", "age" : 65}
{"_id" : ObjectId("4b2b9f67a1f631733d917a7c"), "name" : "joe", "age" : 20}
{"_id" : ObjectId("4b2b9f67a1f631733d917a7d"), "name" : "joe", "age" : 49}
```

Now, if it's Joe #2's birthday, we want to increment the value of his "age" key, so we might say this:

```
> joe = db.people.findOne({"name" : "joe", "age" : 20});
{
    "_id" : ObjectId("4b2b9f67a1f631733d917a7c"),
    "name" : "joe",
    "age" : 20
}
> joe.age++;
> db.people.replaceOne({"name" : "joe"}, joe);
E11001 duplicate key on update
```

What happened? When you do the update, the database will look for a document matching {"name" : "joe"}. The first one it finds will be the 65-year-old Joe. It will attempt to replace that document with the one in the joe variable, but there's already a document in this collection with the same "_id". Thus, the update will fail, because "_id" values must be unique. The best way to avoid this situation is to make sure that your update always specifies a unique document, perhaps by matching on a key like "_id". For the preceding example, this would be the correct update to use:

```
> db.people.replaceOne({"_id" : ObjectId("4b2b9f67a1f631733d917a7c")}, joe)
```

Using "_id" for the filter will also be efficient since"_id" values form the basis for the primary index of a collection. We'll cover primary and secondary indexes and how indexing affects updates and other operations more in Chapter 5.

Using Update Operators

Usually only certain portions of a document need to be updated. You can update specific fields in a document using atomic *update operators*. Update operators are special keys that can be used to specify complex update operations, such as altering, adding, or removing keys, and even manipulating arrays and embedded documents.

Suppose we're keeping website analytics in a collection and want to increment a counter each time someone visits a page. We can use update operators to do this increment atomically. Each URL and its number of page views is stored in a document that looks like this:

```
{
    "_id" : ObjectId("4b253b067525f35f94b60a31"),
    "url" : "www.example.com",
    "pageviews" : 52
}
```

Every time someone visits a page, we can find the page by its URL and use the "$inc" modifier to increment the value of the "pageviews" key:

```
> db.analytics.updateOne({"url" : "www.example.com"},
... {"$inc" : {"pageviews" : 1}})
{ "acknowledged" : true, "matchedCount" : 1, "modifiedCount" : 1 }
```

Now, if we do a findOne, we see that "pageviews" has increased by one:

```
> db.analytics.findOne()
{
    "_id" : ObjectId("4b253b067525f35f94b60a31"),
    "url" : "www.example.com",
    "pageviews" : 53
}
```

When using operators, the value of "_id" cannot be changed. (Note that "_id" *can* be changed by using whole-document replacement.) Values for any other key, including other uniquely indexed keys, can be modified.

Getting started with the "$set" modifier

"$set" sets the value of a field. If the field does not yet exist, it will be created. This can be handy for updating schemas or adding user-defined keys. For example, suppose you have a simple user profile stored as a document that looks something like the following:

```
> db.users.findOne()
{
    "_id" : ObjectId("4b253b067525f35f94b60a31"),
    "name" : "joe",
    "age" : 30,
    "sex" : "male",
    "location" : "Wisconsin"
}
```

This is a pretty bare-bones user profile. If the user wanted to store his favorite book in his profile, he could add it using "$set":

```
> db.users.updateOne({"_id" : ObjectId("4b253b067525f35f94b60a31")},
... {"$set" : {"favorite book" : "War and Peace"}})
```

Now the document will have a "favorite book" key:

```
> db.users.findOne()
{
    "_id" : ObjectId("4b253b067525f35f94b60a31"),
    "name" : "joe",
    "age" : 30,
    "sex" : "male",
    "location" : "Wisconsin",
    "favorite book" : "War and Peace"
}
```

If the user decides that he actually enjoys a different book, "$set" can be used again to change the value:

```
> db.users.updateOne({"name" : "joe"},
... {"$set" : {"favorite book" : "Green Eggs and Ham"}})
```

"$set" can even change the type of the key it modifies. For instance, if our fickle user decides that he actually likes quite a few books, he can change the value of the "favor ite book" key into an array:

```
> db.users.updateOne({"name" : "joe"},
... {"$set" : {"favorite book" :
...    ["Cat's Cradle", "Foundation Trilogy", "Ender's Game"]}})
```

If the user realizes that he actually doesn't like reading, he can remove the key altogether with "$unset":

```
> db.users.updateOne({"name" : "joe"},
... {"$unset" : {"favorite book" : 1}})
```

Now the document will be the same as it was at the beginning of this example.

You can also use "$set" to reach in and change embedded documents:

```
> db.blog.posts.findOne()
{
    "_id" : ObjectId("4b253b067525f35f94b60a31"),
```

```
        "title" : "A Blog Post",
        "content" : "...",
        "author" : {
            "name" : "joe",
            "email" : "joe@example.com"
        }
    }
> db.blog.posts.updateOne({"author.name" : "joe"},
... {"$set" : {"author.name" : "joe schmoe"}})

> db.blog.posts.findOne()
{
    "_id" : ObjectId("4b253b067525f35f94b60a31"),
    "title" : "A Blog Post",
    "content" : "...",
    "author" : {
        "name" : "joe schmoe",
        "email" : "joe@example.com"
    }
}
```

You must always use a $-modifier for adding, changing, or removing keys. A common error people make when starting out is to try to set the value of a key to some other value by doing an update that resembles this:

```
> db.blog.posts.updateOne({"author.name" : "joe"},
... {"author.name" : "joe schmoe"})
```

This will result in an error. The update document must contain update operators. Previous versions of the CRUD API did not catch this type of error. Earlier update methods would simply complete a whole document replacement in such situations. It is this type of pitfall that led to the creation of a new CRUD API.

Incrementing and decrementing

The "$inc" operator can be used to change the value for an existing key or to create a new key if it does not already exist. It's useful for updating analytics, karma, votes, or anything else that has a changeable, numeric value.

Suppose we are creating a game collection where we want to save games and update scores as they change. When a user starts playing, say, a game of pinball, we can insert a document that identifies the game by name and the user playing it:

```
> db.games.insertOne({"game" : "pinball", "user" : "joe"})
```

When the ball hits a bumper, the game should increment the player's score. Since points in pinball are given out pretty freely, let's say that the base unit of points a player can earn is 50. We can use the "$inc" modifier to add 50 to the player's score:

```
> db.games.updateOne({"game" : "pinball", "user" : "joe"},
... {"$inc" : {"score" : 50}})
```

If we look at the document after this update, we'll see the following:

```
> db.games.findOne()
{
    "_id" : ObjectId("4b2d75476cc613d5ee930164"),
    "game" : "pinball",
    "user" : "joe",
    "score" : 50
}
```

The `"score"` key did not already exist, so it was created by `"$inc"` and set to the increment amount: 50.

If the ball lands in a "bonus" slot, we want to add 10,000 to the score. We can do this by passing a different value to `"$inc"`:

```
> db.games.updateOne({"game" : "pinball", "user" : "joe"},
... {"$inc" : {"score" : 10000}})
```

Now if we look at the game, we'll see the following:

```
> db.games.findOne()
{
    "_id" : ObjectId("4b2d75476cc613d5ee930164"),
    "game" : "pinball",
    "user" : "joe",
    "score" : 10050
}
```

The `"score"` key existed and had a numeric value, so the server added 10,000 to it.

`"$inc"` is similar to `"$set"`, but it is designed for incrementing (and decrementing) numbers. `"$inc"` can be used only on values of type integer, long, double, or decimal. If it is used on any other type of value, it will fail. This includes types that many languages will automatically cast into numbers, like nulls, booleans, or strings of numeric characters:

```
> db.strcounts.insert({"count" : "1"})
WriteResult({ "nInserted" : 1 })
> db.strcounts.update({}, {"$inc" : {"count" : 1}})
WriteResult({
  "nMatched" : 0,
  "nUpserted" : 0,
  "nModified" : 0,
  "writeError" : {
    "code" : 16837,
    "errmsg" : "Cannot apply $inc to a value of non-numeric type.
    {_id: ObjectId('5726c0d36855a935cb57a659')} has the field 'count' of
    non-numeric type String"
  }
})
```

Also, the value of the "$inc" key must be a number. You cannot increment by a string, array, or other nonnumeric value. Doing so will give a "Modifier "$inc" allowed for numbers only" error message. To modify other types, use "$set" or one of the following array operators.

Array operators

An extensive class of update operators exists for manipulating arrays. Arrays are common and powerful data structures: not only are they lists that can be referenced by index, but they can also double as sets.

Adding elements. "$push" adds elements to the end of an array if the array exists and creates a new array if it does not. For example, suppose that we are storing blog posts and want to add a "comments" key containing an array. We can push a comment onto the nonexistent "comments" array, which will create the array and add the comment:

```
> db.blog.posts.findOne()
{
    "_id" : ObjectId("4b2d75476cc613d5ee930164"),
    "title" : "A blog post",
    "content" : "..."
}
> db.blog.posts.updateOne({"title" : "A blog post"},
... {"$push" : {"comments" :
...     {"name" : "joe", "email" : "joe@example.com",
...      "content" : "nice post."}}})
{ "acknowledged" : true, "matchedCount" : 1, "modifiedCount" : 1 }
> db.blog.posts.findOne()
{
    "_id" : ObjectId("4b2d75476cc613d5ee930164"),
    "title" : "A blog post",
    "content" : "...",
    "comments" : [
        {
            "name" : "joe",
            "email" : "joe@example.com",
            "content" : "nice post."
        }
    ]
}
```

Now, if we want to add another comment, we can simply use "$push" again:

```
> db.blog.posts.updateOne({"title" : "A blog post"},
... {"$push" : {"comments" :
...     {"name" : "bob", "email" : "bob@example.com",
...      "content" : "good post."}}})
{ "acknowledged" : true, "matchedCount" : 1, "modifiedCount" : 1 }
> db.blog.posts.findOne()
{
```

```
    "_id" : ObjectId("4b2d75476cc613d5ee930164"),
    "title" : "A blog post",
    "content" : "...",
    "comments" : [
        {
            "name" : "joe",
            "email" : "joe@example.com",
            "content" : "nice post."
        },
        {
            "name" : "bob",
            "email" : "bob@example.com",
            "content" : "good post."
        }
    ]
}
```

This is the "simple" form of "push", but you can use it for more complex array operations as well. The MongoDB query language provides modifiers for some operators,
including "$push". You can push multiple values in one operation using the "$each"
modifer for "$push":

```
> db.stock.ticker.updateOne({"_id" : "GOOG"},
... {"$push" : {"hourly" : {"$each" : [562.776, 562.790, 559.123]}}})
```

This would push three new elements onto the array.

If you only want the array to grow to a certain length, you can use the "$slice"
modifier with "$push" to prevent an array from growing beyond a certain size, effec-
tively making a "top N" list of items:

```
> db.movies.updateOne({"genre" : "horror"},
... {"$push" : {"top10" : {"$each" : ["Nightmare on Elm Street", "Saw"],
...                         "$slice" : -10}}})
```

This example limits the array to the last 10 elements pushed.

If the array is smaller than 10 elements (after the push), all elements will be kept. If
the array is larger than 10 elements, only the last 10 elements will be kept. Thus,
"$slice" can be used to create a queue in a document.

Finally, you can apply the "$sort" modifier to "$push" operations before trimming:

```
> db.movies.updateOne({"genre" : "horror"},
... {"$push" : {"top10" : {"$each" : [{"name" : "Nightmare on Elm Street",
...                                    "rating" : 6.6},
...                                   {"name" : "Saw", "rating" : 4.3}],
...                         "$slice" : -10,
...                         "$sort" : {"rating" : -1}}}})
```

This will sort all of the objects in the array by their "rating" field and then keep the first 10. Note that you must include "$each"; you cannot just "$slice" or "$sort" an array with "$push".

Using arrays as sets. You might want to treat an array as a set, only adding values if they are not present. This can be done using "$ne" in the query document. For example, to push an author onto a list of citations, but only if they aren't already there, use the following:

```
> db.papers.updateOne({"authors cited" : {"$ne" : "Richie"}},
... {$push : {"authors cited" : "Richie"}})
```

This can also be done with "$addToSet", which is useful for cases where "$ne" won't work or where "$addToSet" describes what is happening better.

For example, suppose you have a document that represents a user. You might have a set of email addresses that they have added:

```
> db.users.findOne({"_id" : ObjectId("4b2d75476cc613d5ee930164")})
{
    "_id" : ObjectId("4b2d75476cc613d5ee930164"),
    "username" : "joe",
    "emails" : [
        "joe@example.com",
        "joe@gmail.com",
        "joe@yahoo.com"
    ]
}
```

When adding another address, you can use "$addToSet" to prevent duplicates:

```
> db.users.updateOne({"_id" : ObjectId("4b2d75476cc613d5ee930164")},
... {"$addToSet" : {"emails" : "joe@gmail.com"}})
{ "acknowledged" : true, "matchedCount" : 1, "modifiedCount" : 0 }
> db.users.findOne({"_id" : ObjectId("4b2d75476cc613d5ee930164")})
{
    "_id" : ObjectId("4b2d75476cc613d5ee930164"),
    "username" : "joe",
    "emails" : [
        "joe@example.com",
        "joe@gmail.com",
        "joe@yahoo.com",
    ]
}
> db.users.updateOne({"_id" : ObjectId("4b2d75476cc613d5ee930164")},
... {"$addToSet" : {"emails" : "joe@hotmail.com"}})
{ "acknowledged" : true, "matchedCount" : 1, "modifiedCount" : 1 }
> db.users.findOne({"_id" : ObjectId("4b2d75476cc613d5ee930164")})
{
    "_id" : ObjectId("4b2d75476cc613d5ee930164"),
    "username" : "joe",
```

```
    "emails" : [
        "joe@example.com",
        "joe@gmail.com",
        "joe@yahoo.com",
        "joe@hotmail.com"
    ]
}
```

You can also use "$addToSet" in conjunction with "$each" to add multiple unique values, which cannot be done with the "$ne"/"$push" combination. For instance, you could use these operators if the user wanted to add more than one email address:

```
> db.users.updateOne({"_id" : ObjectId("4b2d75476cc613d5ee930164")},
... {"$addToSet" : {"emails" : {"$each" :
...    ["joe@php.net", "joe@example.com", "joe@python.org"]}}})
{ "acknowledged" : true, "matchedCount" : 1, "modifiedCount" : 1 }
> db.users.findOne({"_id" : ObjectId("4b2d75476cc613d5ee930164")})
{
    "_id" : ObjectId("4b2d75476cc613d5ee930164"),
    "username" : "joe",
    "emails" : [
        "joe@example.com",
        "joe@gmail.com",
        "joe@yahoo.com",
        "joe@hotmail.com"
        "joe@php.net"
        "joe@python.org"
    ]
}
```

Removing elements. There are a few ways to remove elements from an array. If you want to treat the array like a queue or a stack, you can use "$pop", which can remove elements from either end. {"$pop" : {"key" : 1}} removes an element from the end of the array. {"$pop" : {"key" : -1}} removes it from the beginning.

Sometimes an element should be removed based on specific criteria, rather than its position in the array. "$pull" is used to remove elements of an array that match the given criteria. For example, suppose we have a list of things that need to be done, but not in any specific order:

```
> db.lists.insertOne({"todo" : ["dishes", "laundry", "dry cleaning"]})
```

If we do the laundry first, we can remove it from the list with the following:

```
> db.lists.updateOne({}, {"$pull" : {"todo" : "laundry"}})
```

Now if we do a find, we'll see that there are only two elements remaining in the array:

```
> db.lists.findOne()
{
    "_id" : ObjectId("4b2d75476cc613d5ee930164"),
    "todo" : [
```

```
        "dishes",
        "dry cleaning"
    ]
}
```

Pulling removes all matching documents, not just a single match. If you have an array that looks like [1, 1, 2, 1] and pull 1, you'll end up with a single-element array, [2].

Array operators can be used only on keys with array values. For example, you cannot push onto an integer or pop off of a string. Use "$set" or "$inc" to modify scalar values.

Positional array modifications. Array manipulation becomes a little trickier when you have multiple values in an array and want to modify some of them. There are two ways to manipulate values in arrays: by position or by using the position operator (the $ character).

Arrays use 0-based indexing, and elements can be selected as though their index were a document key. For example, suppose we have a document containing an array with a few embedded documents, such as a blog post with comments:

```
> db.blog.posts.findOne()
{
    "_id" : ObjectId("4b329a216cc613d5ee930192"),
    "content" : "...",
    "comments" : [
        {
            "comment" : "good post",
            "author" : "John",
            "votes" : 0
        },
        {
            "comment" : "i thought it was too short",
            "author" : "Claire",
            "votes" : 3
        },
        {
            "comment" : "free watches",
            "author" : "Alice",
            "votes" : -5
        },
        {
            "comment" : "vacation getaways",
            "author" : "Lynn",
            "votes" : -7
        }
    ]
}
```

If we want to increment the number of votes for the first comment, we can say the following:

```
> db.blog.updateOne({"post" : post_id},
... {"$inc" : {"comments.0.votes" : 1}})
```

In many cases, though, we don't know what index of the array to modify without querying for the document first and examining it. To get around this, MongoDB has a positional operator, $, that figures out which element of the array the query document matched and updates that element. For example, if we have a user named John who updates his name to Jim, we can replace it in the comments by using the positional operator:

```
> db.blog.updateOne({"comments.author" : "John"},
... {"$set" : {"comments.$.author" : "Jim"}})
```

The positional operator updates only the first match. Thus, if John had left more than one comment, his name would be changed only for the first comment he left.

Updates using array filters. MongoDB 3.6 introduced another option for updating individual array elements: `arrayFilters`. This option enables us to modify array elements matching particular critera. For example, if we want to hide all comments with five or more down votes, we can do something like the following:

```
db.blog.updateOne(
    {"post" : post_id },
    { $set: { "comments.$[elem].hidden" : true } },
    {
       arrayFilters: [ { "elem.votes": { $lte: -5 } } ]
    }
)
```

This command defines `elem` as the identifier for each matching element in the "com ments" array. If the `votes` value for the comment identified by `elem` is less than or equal to `-5`, we will add a field called `"hidden"` to the `"comments"` document and set its value to `true`.

Upserts

An *upsert* is a special type of update. If no document is found that matches the filter, a new document will be created by combining the criteria and updated documents. If a matching document is found, it will be updated normally. Upserts can be handy because they can eliminate the need to "seed" your collection: you can often have the same code create and update documents.

Let's go back to our example that records the number of views for each page of a website. Without an upsert, we might try to find the URL and increment the number of views or create a new document if the URL doesn't exist. If we were to write this out as a JavaScript program it might look something like the following:

```
// check if we have an entry for this page
blog = db.analytics.findOne({url : "/blog"})

// if we do, add one to the number of views and save
if (blog) {
  blog.pageviews++;
  db.analytics.save(blog);
}
// otherwise, create a new document for this page
else {
  db.analytics.insertOne({url : "/blog", pageviews : 1})
}
```

This means we are making a round trip to the database, plus sending an update or insert, every time someone visits a page. If we are running this code in multiple processes, we are also subject to a race condition where more than one document can be inserted for a given URL.

We can eliminate the race condition and cut down the amount of code by just sending an upsert to the database (the third parameter to `updateOne` and `updateMany` is an options document that enables us to specify this):

```
> db.analytics.updateOne({"url" : "/blog"}, {"$inc" : {"pageviews" : 1}},
... {"upsert" : true})
```

This line does exactly what the previous code block does, except it's faster and atomic! The new document is created by using the criteria document as a base and applying any modifier documents to it.

For example, if you do an upsert that matches a key and increments to the value of that key, the increment will be applied to the match:

```
> db.users.updateOne({"rep" : 25}, {"$inc" : {"rep" : 3}}, {"upsert" : true})
WriteResult({
    "acknowledged" : true,
    "matchedCount" : 0,
    "modifiedCount" : 0,
    "upsertedId" : ObjectId("5a93b07aaea1cb8780a4cf72")
})
> db.users.findOne({"_id" : ObjectId("5727b2a7223502483c7f3acd")} )
{ "_id" : ObjectId("5727b2a7223502483c7f3acd"), "rep" : 28 }
```

The upsert creates a new document with a `"rep"` of 25 and then increments that by 3, giving us a document where `"rep"` is 28. If the upsert option were not specified, `{"rep" : 25}` would not match any documents, so nothing would happen.

If we run the upsert again (with the criterion {"rep" : 25}), it will create another new document. This is because the criterion does not match the only document in the collection. (Its "rep" is 28.)

Sometimes a field needs to be set when a document is created, but not changed on subsequent updates. This is what "$setOnInsert" is for. "$setOnInsert" is an operator that only sets the value of a field when the document is being inserted. Thus, we could do something like this:

```
> db.users.updateOne({}, {"$setOnInsert" : {"createdAt" : new Date()}},
... {"upsert" : true})
{
    "acknowledged" : true,
    "matchedCount" : 0,
    "modifiedCount" : 0,
    "upsertedId" : ObjectId("5727b4ac223502483c7f3ace")
}
> db.users.findOne()
{
    "_id" : ObjectId("5727b4ac223502483c7f3ace"),
    "createdAt" : ISODate("2016-05-02T20:12:28.640Z")
}
```

If we run this update again, it will match the existing document, nothing will be inserted, and so the "createdAt" field will not be changed:

```
> db.users.updateOne({}, {"$setOnInsert" : {"createdAt" : new Date()}},
... {"upsert" : true})
{ "acknowledged" : true, "matchedCount" : 1, "modifiedCount" : 0 }
> db.users.findOne()
{
    "_id" : ObjectId("5727b4ac223502483c7f3ace"),
    "createdAt" : ISODate("2016-05-02T20:12:28.640Z")
}
```

Note that you generally do not need to keep a "createdAt" field, as ObjectIds contain a timestamp of when the document was created. However, "$setOnInsert" can be useful for creating padding, initializing counters, and for collections that do not use ObjectIds.

The save shell helper

save is a shell function that lets you insert a document if it doesn't exist and update it if it does. It takes one argument: a document. If the document contains an "_id" key, save will do an upsert. Otherwise, it will do an insert. save is really just a convenience function so that programmers can quickly modify documents in the shell:

```
> var x = db.testcol.findOne()
> x.num = 42
```

```
> db.testcol.save(x)
```

Without **save**, the last line would have been more cumbersome:

```
db.testcol.replaceOne({"_id" : x._id}, x)
```

Updating Multiple Documents

So far in this chapter we have used **updateOne** to illustrate update operations. **updateOne** updates only the first document found that matches the filter criteria. If there are more matching documents, they will remain unchanged. To modify all of the documents matching a filter, use **updateMany**. **updateMany** follows the same semantics as **updateOne** and takes the same parameters. The key difference is in the number of documents that might be changed.

updateMany provides a powerful tool for performing schema migrations or rolling out new features to certain users. Suppose, for example, we want to give a gift to every user who has a birthday on a certain day. We can use **updateMany** to add a **"gift"** to their accounts. For example:

```
> db.users.insertMany([
... {birthday: "10/13/1978"},
... {birthday: "10/13/1978"},
... {birthday: "10/13/1978"}])
{
    "acknowledged" : true,
    "insertedIds" : [
        ObjectId("5727d6fc6855a935cb57a65b"),
        ObjectId("5727d6fc6855a935cb57a65c"),
        ObjectId("5727d6fc6855a935cb57a65d")
    ]
}
> db.users.updateMany({"birthday" : "10/13/1978"},
... {"$set" : {"gift" : "Happy Birthday!"}})
{ "acknowledged" : true, "matchedCount" : 3, "modifiedCount" : 3 }
```

The call to **updateMany** adds a **"gift"** field to each of the three documents we inserted into the *users* collection immediately before.

Returning Updated Documents

For some use cases it is important to return the document modified. In earlier versions of MongoDB, **findAndModify** was the method of choice in such situations. It is handy for manipulating queues and performing other operations that need get-and-set–style atomicity. However, **findAndModify** is prone to user error because it's a complex method combining the functionality of three different types of operations: delete, replace, and update (including upserts).

MongoDB 3.2 introduced three new collection methods to the shell to accommodate the functionality of findAndModify, but with semantics that are easier to learn and remember: findOneAndDelete, findOneAndReplace, and findOneAndUpdate. The primary difference between these methods and, for example, updateOne is that they enable you to atomically get the value of a modified document. MongoDB 4.2 extended findOneAndUpdate to accept an aggregation pipeline for the update. The pipeline can consist of the following stages: $addFields and its alias $set, $project and its alias $unset, and $replaceRoot and its alias $replaceWith.

Suppose we have a collection of processes run in a certain order. Each is represented with a document that has the following form:

```
{
    "_id" : ObjectId(),
    "status" : "state",
    "priority" : N
}
```

"status" is a string that can be "READY", "RUNNING", or "DONE". We need to find the job with the highest priority in the "READY" state, run the process function, and then update the status to "DONE". We might try querying for the ready processes, sorting by priority, and updating the status of the highest-priority process to mark it as "RUNNING". Once we have processed it, we update the status to "DONE". This looks something like the following:

```
var cursor = db.processes.find({"status" : "READY"});
ps = cursor.sort({"priority" : -1}).limit(1).next();
db.processes.updateOne({"_id" : ps._id}, {"$set" : {"status" : "RUNNING"}});
do_something(ps);
db.processes.updateOne({"_id" : ps._id}, {"$set" : {"status" : "DONE"}});
```

This algorithm isn't great because it is subject to a race condition. Suppose we have two threads running. If one thread (call it A) retrieved the document and another thread (call it B) retrieved the same document before A had updated its status to "RUNNING", then both threads would be running the same process. We can avoid this by checking the result as part of the update query, but this becomes complex:

```
var cursor = db.processes.find({"status" : "READY"});
cursor.sort({"priority" : -1}).limit(1);
while ((ps = cursor.next()) != null) {
    var result = db.processes.updateOne({"_id" : ps._id, "status" : "READY"},
                            {"$set" : {"status" : "RUNNING"}});

    if (result.modifiedCount === 1) {
        do_something(ps);
        db.processes.updateOne({"_id" : ps._id}, {"$set" : {"status" : "DONE"}});
        break;
    }
    cursor = db.processes.find({"status" : "READY"});
```

```
        cursor.sort({"priority" : -1}).limit(1);
}
```

Also, depending on timing, one thread may end up doing all the work while another
thread uselessly trails it. Thread A could always grab the process, and then B would
try to get the same process, fail, and leave A to do all the work.

Situations like this are perfect for `findOneAndUpdate`. `findOneAndUpdate` can return
the item and update it in a single operation. In this case, it looks like the following:

```
> db.processes.findOneAndUpdate({"status" : "READY"},
... {"$set" : {"status" : "RUNNING"}},
... {"sort" : {"priority" : -1}})
{
    "_id" : ObjectId("4b3e7a18005cab32be6291f7"),
    "priority" : 1,
    "status" : "READY"
}
```

Notice that the status is still `"READY"` in the returned document because the
`findOneAndUpdate` method defaults to returning the state of the document before it
was modified. It will return the updated document if we set the `"returnNewDocu
ment"` field in the options document to `true`. An options document is passed as the
third parameter to `findOneAndUpdate`:

```
> db.processes.findOneAndUpdate({"status" : "READY"},
... {"$set" : {"status" : "RUNNING"}},
... {"sort" : {"priority" : -1},
...  "returnNewDocument": true})
{
    "_id" : ObjectId("4b3e7a18005cab32be6291f7"),
    "priority" : 1,
    "status" : "RUNNING"
}
```

Thus, the program becomes the following:

```
ps = db.processes.findOneAndUpdate({"status" : "READY"},
                                   {"$set" : {"status" : "RUNNING"}},
                                   {"sort" : {"priority" : -1},
                                    "returnNewDocument": true})
do_something(ps)
db.process.updateOne({"_id" : ps._id}, {"$set" : {"status" : "DONE"}})
```

In addition to this one, there are two other methods you should be aware of.
`findOneAndReplace` takes the same parameters and returns the document matching
the filter either before or after the replacement, depending on the value of `returnNew
Document`. `findOneAndDelete` is similar except it does not take an update document
as a parameter and has a subset of the options of the other two methods. `findOneAnd
Delete` returns the deleted document.

## CHAPTER 4

Querying

This chapter looks at querying in detail. The main areas covered are as follows:

- You can query for ranges, set inclusion, inequalities, and more by using $ conditionals.

- Queries return a database cursor, which lazily returns batches of documents as you need them.

- There are a lot of metaoperations you can perform on a cursor, including skipping a certain number of results, limiting the number of results returned, and sorting results.

Introduction to find

The find method is used to perform queries in MongoDB. Querying returns a subset of documents in a collection, from no documents at all to the entire collection. Which documents get returned is determined by the first argument to find, which is a document specifying the query criteria.

An empty query document (i.e., {}) matches everything in the collection. If find isn't given a query document, it defaults to {}. For example, the following:

```
> db.c.find()
```

matches every document in the collection c (and returns these documents in batches).

When we start adding key/value pairs to the query document, we begin restricting our search. This works in a straightforward way for most types: numbers match numbers, booleans match booleans, and strings match strings. Querying for a simple type is as easy as specifying the value that you are looking for. For example, to find all documents where the value for "age" is 27, we can add that key/value pair to the query document:

```
> db.users.find({"age" : 27})
```

If we have a string we want to match, such as a "username" key with the value "joe", we use that key/value pair instead:

```
> db.users.find({"username" : "joe"})
```

Multiple conditions can be strung together by adding more key/value pairs to the query document, which gets interpreted as "*condition1* AND *condition2* AND ... AND *conditionN*." For instance, to get all users who are 27-year-olds with the user-name "joe," we can query for the following:

```
> db.users.find({"username" : "joe", "age" : 27})
```

Specifying Which Keys to Return

Sometimes you do not need all of the key/value pairs in a document returned. If this is the case, you can pass a second argument to find (or findOne) specifying the keys you want. This reduces both the amount of data sent over the wire and the time and memory used to decode documents on the client side.

For example, if you have a user collection and you are interested only in the "username" and "email" keys, you could return just those keys with the following query:

```
> db.users.find({}, {"username" : 1, "email" : 1})
{
    "_id" : ObjectId("4ba0f0dfd22aa494fd523620"),
    "username" : "joe",
    "email" : "joe@example.com"
}
```

As you can see from the previous output, the "_id" key is returned by default, even if it isn't specifically requested.

You can also use this second parameter to exclude specific key/value pairs from the results of a query. For instance, you may have documents with a variety of keys, and the only thing you know is that you never want to return the "fatal_weakness" key:

```
> db.users.find({}, {"fatal_weakness" : 0})
```

This can also prevent "_id" from being returned:

```
> db.users.find({}, {"username" : 1, "_id" : 0})
{
    "username" : "joe",
}
```

Limitations

There are some restrictions on queries. The value of a query document must be a constant as far as the database is concerned. (It can be a normal variable in your own code.) That is, it cannot refer to the value of another key in the document. For example, if we were keeping inventory and we had both "in_stock" and "num_sold" keys, we couldn't compare their values by querying the following:

```
> db.stock.find({"in_stock" : "this.num_sold"}) // doesn't work
```

There are ways to do this (see "$where Queries" on page 65), but you will usually get better performance by restructuring your document slightly, such that a "normal" query will suffice. In this example, we could instead use the keys "initial_stock" and "in_stock". Then, every time someone buys an item, we decrement the value of the "in_stock" key by one. Finally, we can do a simple query to check which items are out of stock:

```
> db.stock.find({"in_stock" : 0})
```

Query Criteria

Queries can go beyond the exact matching described in the previous section; they can match more complex criteria, such as ranges, OR-clauses, and negation.

Query Conditionals

"$lt", "$lte", "$gt", and "$gte" are all comparison operators, corresponding to <, <=, >, and >=, respectively. They can be combined to look for a range of values. For example, to look for users who are between the ages of 18 and 30, we can do this:

```
> db.users.find({"age" : {"$gte" : 18, "$lte" : 30}})
```

This would find all documents where the "age" field was greater than or equal to 18 AND less than or equal to 30.

These types of range queries are often useful for dates. For example, to find people who registered before January 1, 2007, we can do this:

```
> start = new Date("01/01/2007")
> db.users.find({"registered" : {"$lt" : start}})
```

Depending on how you create and store dates, an exact match might be less useful, since dates are stored with millisecond precision. Often you want a whole day, week, or month, making a range query necessary.

To query for documents where a key's value is not equal to a certain value, you must use another conditional operator, "$ne", which stands for "not equal." If you want to find all users who do not have the username "joe," you can query for them using this:

```
> db.users.find({"username" : {"$ne" : "joe"}})
```

"$ne" can be used with any type.

OR Queries

There are two ways to do an OR query in MongoDB. "$in" can be used to query for a variety of values for a single key. "$or" is more general; it can be used to query for any of the given values across multiple keys.

If you have more than one possible value to match for a single key, use an array of criteria with "$in". For instance, suppose we're running a raffle and the winning ticket numbers are 725, 542, and 390. To find all three of these documents, we can construct the following query:

```
> db.raffle.find({"ticket_no" : {"$in" : [725, 542, 390]}})
```

"$in" is very flexible and allows you to specify criteria of different types as well as values. For example, if we are gradually migrating our schema to use usernames instead of user ID numbers, we can query for either by using this:

```
> db.users.find({"user_id" : {"$in" : [12345, "joe"]}})
```

This matches documents with a "user_id" equal to 12345 and documents with a "user_id" equal to "joe".

If "$in" is given an array with a single value, it behaves the same as directly matching the value. For instance, {ticket_no : {$in : [725]}} matches the same documents as {ticket_no : 725}.

The opposite of "$in" is "$nin", which returns documents that don't match any of the criteria in the array. If we want to return all of the people who didn't win anything in the raffle, we can query for them with this:

```
> db.raffle.find({"ticket_no" : {"$nin" : [725, 542, 390]}})
```

This query returns everyone who did not have tickets with those numbers.

"$in" gives you an OR query for a single key, but what if we need to find documents where "ticket_no" is 725 or "winner" is true? For this type of query, we'll need to use the "$or" conditional. "$or" takes an array of possible criteria. In the raffle case, using "$or" would look like this:

```
> db.raffle.find({"$or" : [{"ticket_no" : 725}, {"winner" : true}]})
```

"$or" can contain other conditionals. If, for example, we want to match any of the three "ticket_no" values or the "winner" key, we can use this:

```
> db.raffle.find({"$or" : [{"ticket_no" : {"$in" : [725, 542, 390]}},
...                        {"winner" : true}]})
```

With a normal AND-type query, you want to narrow down your results as far as possible in as few arguments as possible. OR-type queries are the opposite: they are most efficient if the first arguments match as many documents as possible.

While `"$or"` will always work, use `"$in"` whenever possible as the query optimizer handles it more efficiently.

$not

`"$not"` is a metaconditional: it can be applied on top of any other criteria. As an example, let's consider the modulus operator, `"$mod"`. `"$mod"` queries for keys whose values, when divided by the first value given, have a remainder of the second value:

```
> db.users.find({"id_num" : {"$mod" : [5, 1]}})
```

The previous query returns users with `"id_num"`s of 1, 6, 11, 16, and so on. If we want, instead, to return users with `"id_num"`s of 2, 3, 4, 5, 7, 8, 9, 10, 12, etc., we can use `"$not"`:

```
> db.users.find({"id_num" : {"$not" : {"$mod" : [5, 1]}}})
```

`"$not"` can be particularly useful in conjunction with regular expressions to find all documents that don't match a given pattern (regular expression usage is described in the section "Regular Expressions" on page 58).

Type-Specific Queries

As covered in Chapter 2, MongoDB has a wide variety of types that can be used in a document. Some of these types have special behavior when querying.

null

`null` behaves a bit strangely. It does match itself, so if we have a collection with the following documents:

```
> db.c.find()
{ "_id" : ObjectId("4ba0f0dfd22aa494fd523621"), "y" : null }
{ "_id" : ObjectId("4ba0f0dfd22aa494fd523622"), "y" : 1 }
{ "_id" : ObjectId("4ba0f148d22aa494fd523623"), "y" : 2 }
```

we can query for documents whose `"y"` key is `null` in the expected way:

```
> db.c.find({"y" : null})
{ "_id" : ObjectId("4ba0f0dfd22aa494fd523621"), "y" : null }
```

However, `null` also matches "does not exist." Thus, querying for a key with the value `null` will return all documents lacking that key:

```
> db.c.find({"z" : null})
{ "_id" : ObjectId("4ba0f0dfd22aa494fd523621"), "y" : null }
```

```
{ "_id" : ObjectId("4ba0f0dfd22aa494fd523622"), "y" : 1 }
{ "_id" : ObjectId("4ba0f148d22aa494fd523623"), "y" : 2 }
```

If we only want to find keys whose value is null, we can check that the key is null and exists using the "$exists" conditional:

```
> db.c.find({"z" : {"$eq" : null, "$exists" : true}})
```

Regular Expressions

"$regex" provides regular expression capabilities for pattern matching strings in queries. Regular expressions are useful for flexible string matching. For example, if we want to find all users with the name "Joe" or "joe," we can use a regular expression to do case-insensitive matching:

```
> db.users.find( {"name" : {"$regex" : /joe/i } })
```

Regular expression flags (e.g., i) are allowed but not required. If we want to match not only various capitalizations of "joe," but also "joey," we can continue to improve our regular expression:

```
> db.users.find({"name" : /joey?/i})
```

MongoDB uses the Perl Compatible Regular Expression (PCRE) library to match regular expressions; any regular expression syntax allowed by PCRE is allowed in MongoDB. It is a good idea to check your syntax with the JavaScript shell before using it in a query to make sure it matches what you think it matches.

 MongoDB can leverage an index for queries on prefix regular expressions (e.g., /^joey/). Indexes *cannot* be used for case-insensitive searches (/^joey/i). A regular expression is a "prefix expression" when it starts with either a caret (^) or a left anchor (\A). If the regular expression uses a case-sensitive query, then if an index exists for the field, the matches can be conducted against values in the index. If it also is a prefix expression, then the search can be limited to the values within the range created by that prefix from the index.

Regular expressions can also match themselves. Very few people insert regular expressions into the database, but if you insert one, you can match it with itself:

```
> db.foo.insertOne({"bar" : /baz/})
> db.foo.find({"bar" : /baz/})
{
    "_id" : ObjectId("4b23c3ca7525f35f94b60a2d"),
    "bar" : /baz/
}
```

Querying Arrays

Querying for elements of an array is designed to behave the way querying for scalars does. For example, if the array is a list of fruits, like this:

```
> db.food.insertOne({"fruit" : ["apple", "banana", "peach"]})
```

the following query will successfully match the document:

```
> db.food.find({"fruit" : "banana"})
```

We can query for it in much the same way as we would if we had a document that looked like the (illegal) document {"fruit" : "apple", "fruit" : "banana", "fruit" : "peach"}.

"$all"

If you need to match arrays by more than one element, you can use "$all". This allows you to match a list of elements. For example, suppose we create a collection with three elements:

```
> db.food.insertOne({"_id" : 1, "fruit" : ["apple", "banana", "peach"]})
> db.food.insertOne({"_id" : 2, "fruit" : ["apple", "kumquat", "orange"]})
> db.food.insertOne({"_id" : 3, "fruit" : ["cherry", "banana", "apple"]})
```

Then we can find all documents with both "apple" and "banana" elements by querying with "$all":

```
> db.food.find({fruit : {$all : ["apple", "banana"]}})
{"_id" : 1, "fruit" : ["apple", "banana", "peach"]}
{"_id" : 3, "fruit" : ["cherry", "banana", "apple"]}
```

Order does not matter. Notice "banana" comes before "apple" in the second result. Using a one-element array with "$all" is equivalent to not using "$all". For instance, {fruit : {$all : ['apple']}} will match the same documents as {fruit : 'apple'}.

You can also query by exact match using the entire array. However, exact match will not match a document if any elements are missing or superfluous. For example, this will match the first of our three documents:

```
> db.food.find({"fruit" : ["apple", "banana", "peach"]})
```

But this will not:

```
> db.food.find({"fruit" : ["apple", "banana"]})
```

and neither will this:

```
> db.food.find({"fruit" : ["banana", "apple", "peach"]})
```

If you want to query for a specific element of an array, you can specify an index using the syntax *key.index*:

```
> db.food.find({"fruit.2" : "peach"})
```

Arrays are always 0-indexed, so this would match the third array element against the string "peach".

"$size"

A useful conditional for querying arrays is "$size", which allows you to query for arrays of a given size. Here's an example:

```
> db.food.find({"fruit" : {"$size" : 3}})
```

One common query is to get a range of sizes. "$size" cannot be combined with another $ conditional (in this example, "$gt"), but this query can be accomplished by adding a "size" key to the document. Then, every time you add an element to the array, increment the value of "size". If the original update looked like this:

```
> db.food.update(criteria, {"$push" : {"fruit" : "strawberry"}})
```

it can simply be changed to this:

```
> db.food.update(criteria,
... {"$push" : {"fruit" : "strawberry"}, "$inc" : {"size" : 1}})
```

Incrementing is extremely fast, so any performance penalty is negligible. Storing documents like this allows you to do queries such as this:

```
> db.food.find({"size" : {"$gt" : 3}})
```

Unfortunately, this technique doesn't work as well with the "$addToSet" operator.

"$slice"

As mentioned earlier in this chapter, the optional second argument to find specifies the keys to be returned. The special "$slice" operator can be used to return a subset of elements for an array key.

For example, suppose we had a blog post document and we wanted to return the first 10 comments:

```
> db.blog.posts.findOne(criteria, {"comments" : {"$slice" : 10}})
```

Alternatively, if we wanted the last 10 comments, we could use –10:

```
> db.blog.posts.findOne(criteria, {"comments" : {"$slice" : -10}})
```

"$slice" can also return pages in the middle of the results by taking an offset and the number of elements to return:

```
> db.blog.posts.findOne(criteria, {"comments" : {"$slice" : [23, 10]}})
```

This would skip the first 23 elements and return the 24th through 33rd. If there were fewer than 33 elements in the array, it would return as many as possible.

Unless otherwise specified, all keys in a document are returned when `"$slice"` is used. This is unlike the other key specifiers, which suppress unmentioned keys from being returned. For instance, if we had a blog post document that looked like this:

```
{
    "_id" : ObjectId("4b2d75476cc613d5ee930164"),
    "title" : "A blog post",
    "content" : "...",
    "comments" : [
        {
            "name" : "joe",
            "email" : "joe@example.com",
            "content" : "nice post."
        },
        {
            "name" : "bob",
            "email" : "bob@example.com",
            "content" : "good post."
        }
    ]
}
```

and we did a `"$slice"` to get the last comment, we'd get this:

```
> db.blog.posts.findOne(criteria, {"comments" : {"$slice" : -1}})
{
    "_id" : ObjectId("4b2d75476cc613d5ee930164"),
    "title" : "A blog post",
    "content" : "...",
    "comments" : [
        {
            "name" : "bob",
            "email" : "bob@example.com",
            "content" : "good post."
        }
    ]
}
```

Both `"title"` and `"content"` are still returned, even though they weren't explicitly included in the key specifier.

Returning a matching array element

`"$slice"` is helpful when you know the index of the element, but sometimes you want whichever array element matched your criteria. You can return the matching element with the $ operator. Given the previous blog example, you could get Bob's comment back with:

```
> db.blog.posts.find({"comments.name" : "bob"}, {"comments.$" : 1})
{
    "_id" : ObjectId("4b2d75476cc613d5ee930164"),
    "comments" : [
```

```
        {
            "name" : "bob",
            "email" : "bob@example.com",
            "content" : "good post."
        }
    ]
}
```

Note that this only returns the first match for each document: if Bob had left multiple comments on this post, only the first one in the `"comments"` array would be returned.

Array and range query interactions

Scalars (nonarray elements) in documents must match each clause of a query's criteria. For example, if you queried for `{"x" : {"$gt" : 10, "$lt" : 20}}`, `"x"` would have to be both greater than 10 and less than 20. However, if a document's `"x"` field is an array, the document matches if there is an element of `"x"` that matches each part of the criteria *but each query clause can match a different array element.*

The best way to understand this behavior is to see an example. Suppose we have the following documents:

```
{"x" : 5}
{"x" : 15}
{"x" : 25}
{"x" : [5, 25]}
```

If we wanted to find all documents where `"x"` is between 10 and 20, we might naively structure a query as `db.test.find({"x" : {"$gt" : 10, "$lt" : 20}})` and expect to get back one document: `{"x" : 15}`. However, running this, we get two:

```
> db.test.find({"x" : {"$gt" : 10, "$lt" : 20}})
{"x" : 15}
{"x" : [5, 25]}
```

Neither 5 nor 25 is between 10 and 20, but the document is returned because 25 matches the first clause (it is greater than 10) and 5 matches the second clause (it is less than 20).

This makes range queries against arrays essentially useless: a range will match any multielement array. There are a couple of ways to get the expected behavior.

First, you can use `"$elemMatch"` to force MongoDB to compare both clauses with a single array element. However, the catch is that `"$elemMatch"` won't match nonarray elements:

```
> db.test.find({"x" : {"$elemMatch" : {"$gt" : 10, "$lt" : 20}}})
> // no results
```

The document `{"x" : 15}` no longer matches the query, because the `"x"` field is not an array. That said, you should have a good reason for mixing array and scalar values in a field. Many uses cases do not require mixing. For those, `"$elemMatch"` provides a good solution for range queries on array elements.

If you have an index over the field that you're querying on (see Chapter 5), you can use `min` and `max` to limit the index range traversed by the query to your `"$gt"` and `"$lt"` values:

```
> db.test.find({"x" : {"$gt" : 10, "$lt" : 20}}).min({"x" : 10}).max({"x" : 20})
{"x" : 15}
```

Now this will only traverse the index from 10 to 20, missing the 5 and 25 entries. You can only use `min` and `max` when you have an index on the field you are querying for, though, and you must pass all fields of the index to `min` and `max`.

Using `min` and `max` when querying for ranges over documents that may include arrays is generally a good idea. The index bounds for a `"$gt"`/`"$lt"` query over an array is inefficient. It basically accepts any value, so it will search every index entry, not just those in the range.

Querying on Embedded Documents

There are two ways of querying for an embedded document: querying for the whole document or querying for its individual key/value pairs.

Querying for an entire embedded document works identically to a normal query. For example, if we have a document that looks like this:

```
{
    "name" : {
        "first" : "Joe",
        "last" : "Schmoe"
    },
    "age" : 45
}
```

we can query for someone named Joe Schmoe with the following:

```
> db.people.find({"name" : {"first" : "Joe", "last" : "Schmoe"}})
```

However, a query for a full subdocument must exactly match the subdocument. If Joe decides to add a middle name field, suddenly this query won't work anymore; it doesn't match the entire embedded document! This type of query is also order-sensitive: `{"last" : "Schmoe", "first" : "Joe"}` would not be a match.

If possible, it's usually a good idea to query for just a specific key or keys of an embedded document. Then, if your schema changes, all of your queries won't suddenly break because they're no longer exact matches. You can query for embedded keys using dot notation:

```
> db.people.find({"name.first" : "Joe", "name.last" : "Schmoe"})
```

Now, if Joe adds more keys, this query will still match his first and last names.

This dot notation is the main difference between query documents and other document types. Query documents can contain dots, which mean "reach into an embedded document." Dot notation is also the reason that documents to be inserted cannot contain the . character. Oftentimes people run into this limitation when trying to save URLs as keys. One way to get around it is to always perform a global replace before inserting or after retrieving, substituting a character that isn't legal in URLs for the dot character.

Embedded document matches can get a little tricky as the document structure gets more complicated. For example, suppose we are storing blog posts and we want to find comments by Joe that were scored at least a 5. We could model the post as follows:

```
> db.blog.find()
{
    "content" : "...",
    "comments" : [
        {
            "author" : "joe",
            "score" : 3,
            "comment" : "nice post"
        },
        {
            "author" : "mary",
            "score" : 6,
            "comment" : "terrible post"
        }
    ]
}
```

Now, we can't query using db.blog.find({"comments" : {"author" : "joe", "score" : {"$gte" : 5}}}). Embedded document matches have to match the whole document, and this doesn't match the "comment" key. It also wouldn't work to do db.blog.find({"comments.author" : "joe", "comments.score" : {"$gte" : 5}}), because the author criterion could match a different comment than the score criterion. That is, it would return the document shown above: it would match "author" : "joe" in the first comment and "score" : 6 in the second comment.

To correctly group criteria without needing to specify every key, use "$elemMatch". This vaguely named conditional allows you to partially specify criteria to match a single embedded document in an array. The correct query looks like this:

```
> db.blog.find({"comments" : {"$elemMatch" :
... {"author" : "joe", "score" : {"$gte" : 5}}}})
```

"$elemMatch" allows you to "group" your criteria. As such, it's only needed when you have more than one key you want to match on in an embedded document.

$where Queries

Key/value pairs are a fairly expressive way to query, but there are some queries that they cannot represent. For queries that cannot be done any other way, there are "$where" clauses, which allow you to execute arbitrary JavaScript as part of your query. This allows you to do (almost) anything within a query. For security, use of "$where" clauses should be highly restricted or eliminated. End users should never be allowed to execute arbitrary "$where" clauses.

The most common case for using "$where" is to compare the values for two keys in a document. For instance, suppose we have documents that look like this:

```
> db.foo.insertOne({"apple" : 1, "banana" : 6, "peach" : 3})
> db.foo.insertOne({"apple" : 8, "spinach" : 4, "watermelon" : 4})
```

We'd like to return documents where any two of the fields are equal. For example, in the second document, "spinach" and "watermelon" have the same value, so we'd like that document returned. It's unlikely MongoDB will ever have a $ conditional for this, so we can use a "$where" clause to do it with JavaScript:

```
> db.foo.find({"$where" : function () {
... for (var current in this) {
...     for (var other in this) {
...         if (current != other && this[current] == this[other]) {
...             return true;
...         }
...     }
... }
... return false;
... }});
```

If the function returns true, the document will be part of the result set; if it returns false, it won't be.

"$where" queries should not be used unless strictly necessary: they are much slower than regular queries. Each document has to be converted from BSON to a JavaScript object and then run through the "$where" expression. Indexes cannot be used to satisfy a "$where" either. Hence, you should use "$where" only when there is no other way of doing the query. You can cut down on the penalty by using other query filters in combination with "$where". If possible, an index will be used to filter based on the non-$where clauses; the "$where" expression will be used only to fine-tune the results. MongoDB 3.6 added the $expr operator which allows the use of aggregation expressions with the MongoDB query language. It is faster than $where as it does not execute JavaScript and is recommended as a replacement to this operator where possible.

Another way of doing complex queries is to use one of the aggregation tools, which are covered in Chapter 7.

Cursors

The database returns results from find using a *cursor*. The client-side implementations of cursors generally allow you to control a great deal about the eventual output of a query. You can limit the number of results, skip over some number of results, sort results by any combination of keys in any direction, and perform a number of other powerful operations.

To create a cursor with the shell, put some documents into a collection, do a query on them, and assign the results to a local variable (variables defined with "var" are local). Here, we create a very simple collection and query it, storing the results in the cursor variable:

```
> for(i=0; i<100; i++) {
...     db.collection.insertOne({x : i});
... }
> var cursor = db.collection.find();
```

The advantage of doing this is that you can look at one result at a time. If you store the results in a global variable or no variable at all, the MongoDB shell will automatically iterate through and display the first couple of documents. This is what we've been seeing up until this point, and it is often the behavior you want for seeing what's in a collection but not doing actual programming with the shell.

To iterate through the results, you can use the next method on the cursor. You can use hasNext to check whether there is another result. A typical loop through result looks like the following:

```
> while (cursor.hasNext()) {
...     obj = cursor.next();
...     // do stuff
... }
```

cursor.hasNext() checks that the next result exists, and cursor.next() fetches it.

The cursor class also implements JavaScript's iterator interface, so you can use it in a forEach loop:

```
> var cursor = db.people.find();
> cursor.forEach(function(x) {
...     print(x.name);
... });
adam
matt
zak
```

When you call find, the shell does not query the database immediately. It waits until you start requesting results to send the query, which allows you to chain additional options onto a query before it is performed. Almost every method on a cursor object returns the cursor itself, so that you can chain options in any order. For instance, all of the following are equivalent:

```
> var cursor = db.foo.find().sort({"x" : 1}).limit(1).skip(10);
> var cursor = db.foo.find().limit(1).sort({"x" : 1}).skip(10);
> var cursor = db.foo.find().skip(10).limit(1).sort({"x" : 1});
```

At this point, the query has not been executed yet. All of these functions merely build the query. Now, suppose we call the following:

```
> cursor.hasNext()
```

At this point, the query will be sent to the server. The shell fetches the first 100 results or first 4 MB of results (whichever is smaller) at once so that the next calls to next or hasNext will not have to make trips to the server. After the client has run through the first set of results, the shell will again contact the database and ask for more results with a getMore request. getMore requests basically contain an identifier for the cursor and ask the database if there are any more results, returning the next batch if there are. This process continues until the cursor is exhausted and all results have been returned.

Limits, Skips, and Sorts

The most common query options are limiting the number of results returned, skipping a number of results, and sorting. All these options must be added before a query is sent to the database.

To set a limit, chain the limit function onto your call to find. For example, to only return three results, use this:

```
> db.c.find().limit(3)
```

If there are fewer than three documents matching your query in the collection, only the number of matching documents will be returned; limit sets an upper limit, not a lower limit.

skip works similarly to limit:

```
> db.c.find().skip(3)
```

This will skip the first three matching documents and return the rest of the matches. If there are fewer than three documents in your collection, it will not return any documents.

sort takes an object: a set of key/value pairs where the keys are key names and the values are the sort directions. The sort direction can be 1 (ascending) or –1 (descending). If multiple keys are given, the results will be sorted in that order. For instance, to sort the results by "username" ascending and "age" descending, we do the following:

```
> db.c.find().sort({username : 1, age : -1})
```

These three methods can be combined. This is often handy for pagination. For example, suppose that you are running an online store and someone searches for *mp3*. If you want 50 results per page sorted by price from high to low, you can do the following:

```
> db.stock.find({"desc" : "mp3"}).limit(50).sort({"price" : -1})
```

If that person clicks Next Page to see more results, you can simply add a skip to the query, which will skip over the first 50 matches (which the user already saw on page 1):

```
> db.stock.find({"desc" : "mp3"}).limit(50).skip(50).sort({"price" : -1})
```

However, large skips are not very performant; there are suggestions for how to avoid them in the next section.

Comparison order

MongoDB has a hierarchy as to how types compare. Sometimes you will have a single key with multiple types: for instance, integers and booleans, or strings and nulls. If you do a sort on a key with a mix of types, there is a predefined order that they will be sorted in. From least to greatest value, this ordering is as follows:

1. Minimum value
2. Null
3. Numbers (integers, longs, doubles, decimals)
4. Strings
5. Object/document
6. Array
7. Binary data
8. Object ID
9. Boolean
10. Date
11. Timestamp
12. Regular expression
13. Maximum value

Avoiding Large Skips

Using `skip` for a small number of documents is fine. But for a large number of results, `skip` can be slow, since it has to find and then discard all the skipped results. Most databases keep more metadata in the index to help with skips, but MongoDB does not yet support this, so large skips should be avoided. Often you can calculate the results of the next query based on the previous one.

Paginating results without skip

The easiest way to do pagination is to return the first page of results using `limit` and then return each subsequent page as an offset from the beginning:

```
> // do not use: slow for large skips
> var page1 = db.foo.find(criteria).limit(100)
> var page2 = db.foo.find(criteria).skip(100).limit(100)
> var page3 = db.foo.find(criteria).skip(200).limit(100)
...
```

However, depending on your query, you can usually find a way to paginate without skips. For example, suppose we want to display documents in descending order based on "date". We can get the first page of results with the following:

```
> var page1 = db.foo.find().sort({"date" : -1}).limit(100)
```

Then, assuming the date is unique, we can use the "date" value of the last document as the criterion for fetching the next page:

```
var latest = null;

// display first page
while (page1.hasNext()) {
    latest = page1.next();
    display(latest);
}

// get next page
var page2 = db.foo.find({"date" : {"$lt" : latest.date}});
page2.sort({"date" : -1}).limit(100);
```

Now the query does not need to include a skip.

Finding a random document

One fairly common problem is how to get a random document from a collection. The naive (and slow) solution is to count the number of documents and then do a `find`, skipping a random number of documents between zero and the size of the collection:

```
> // do not use
> var total = db.foo.count()
> var random = Math.floor(Math.random()*total)
> db.foo.find().skip(random).limit(1)
```

It is actually highly inefficient to get a random element this way: you have to do a count (which can be expensive if you are using criteria), and skipping large numbers of elements can be time-consuming.

It takes a little forethought, but if you know you'll be looking up a random element in a collection, there's a much more efficient way to do so. The trick is to add an extra random key to each document when it is inserted. For instance, if we're using the shell, we could use the `Math.random()` function (which creates a random number between 0 and 1):

```
> db.people.insertOne({"name" : "joe", "random" : Math.random()})
> db.people.insertOne({"name" : "john", "random" : Math.random()})
> db.people.insertOne({"name" : "jim", "random" : Math.random()})
```

Now, when we want to find a random document from the collection, we can calculate a random number and use that as a query criterion, instead of using `skip`:

```
> var random = Math.random()
> result = db.people.findOne({"random" : {"$gt" : random}})
```

There is a slight chance that `random` will be greater than any of the `"random"` values in the collection, and no results will be returned. We can guard against this by simply returning a document in the other direction:

```
> if (result == null) {
...       result = db.people.findOne({"random" : {"$lte" : random}})
... }
```

If there aren't any documents in the collection, this technique will end up returning `null`, which makes sense.

This technique can be used with arbitrarily complex queries; just make sure to have an index that includes the random key. For example, if we want to find a random plumber in California, we can create an index on `"profession"`, `"state"`, and `"random"`:

```
> db.people.ensureIndex({"profession" : 1, "state" : 1, "random" : 1})
```

This allows us to quickly find a random result (see Chapter 5 for more information on indexing).

Immortal Cursors

There are two sides to a cursor: the client-facing cursor and the database cursor that the client-side one represents. We have been talking about the client-side one up until now, but we are going to take a brief look at what's happening on the server.

On the server side, a cursor takes up memory and resources. Once a cursor runs out of results or the client sends a message telling it to die, the database can free the resources it was using. Freeing these resources lets the database use them for other things, which is good, so we want to make sure that cursors can be freed quickly (within reason).

There are a couple of conditions that can cause the death (and subsequent cleanup) of a cursor. First, when a cursor finishes iterating through the matching results, it will clean itself up. Another way is that, when a cursor goes out of scope on the client side, the drivers send the database a special message to let it know that it can kill that cursor. Finally, even if the user hasn't iterated through all the results and the cursor is still in scope, after 10 minutes of inactivity, a database cursor will automatically "die." This way, if a client crashes or is buggy, MongoDB will not be left with thousands of open cursors.

This "death by timeout" is usually the desired behavior: very few applications expect their users to sit around for minutes at a time waiting for results. However, sometimes you might know that you need a cursor to last for a long time. In that case, many drivers have implemented a function called immortal, or a similar mechanism, which tells the database not to time out the cursor. If you turn off a cursor's timeout, you must iterate through all of its results or kill it to make sure it gets closed. Otherwise, it will sit around in the database hogging resources until the server is restarted.

## PART II

Designing Your Application

## CHAPTER 5

Indexes

This chapter introduces MongoDB indexes. Indexes enable you to perform queries efficiently. They're an important part of application development and are even required for certain types of queries. In this chapter we will cover:

- What indexes are and why you'd want to use them
- How to choose which fields to index
- How to enforce and evaluate index usage
- Administrative details on creating and removing indexes

As you'll see, choosing the right indexes for your collections is critical to performance.

Introduction to Indexes

A database index is similar to a book's index. Instead of looking through the whole book, the database takes a shortcut and just looks at an ordered list with references to the content. This allows MongoDB to query orders of magnitude faster.

A query that does not use an index is called a *collection scan*, which means that the server has to "look through the whole book" to find a query's results. This process is basically what you'd do if you were looking for information in a book without an index: you'd start at page 1 and read through the whole thing. In general, you want to avoid making the server do collection scans because the process is very slow for large collections.

Let's look at an example. To get started, we'll create a collection with 1 million docu-ments in it (or 10 million or 100 million, if you have the patience):

```
> for (i=0; i<1000000; i++) {
...         db.users.insertOne(
...             {
...                 "i" : i,
...                 "username" : "user"+i,
...                 "age" : Math.floor(Math.random()*120),
...                 "created" : new Date()
...             }
...         );
... }
```

Then we'll look at the differences in performance for queries on this collection, first
without an index and then with an index.

If we do a query on this collection, we can use the `explain` command to see what
MongoDB is doing when it executes the query. The preferred way to use the `explain`
command is through the cursor helper method that wraps this command. The
`explain` cursor method provides information on the execution of a variety of CRUD
operations. This method may be run in several verbosity modes. We'll look at `execu
tionStats` mode since this helps us understand the effect of using an index to satisfy
queries. Try querying on a specific username to see an example:

```
> db.users.find({"username": "user101"}).explain("executionStats")
{
    "queryPlanner" : {
        "plannerVersion" : 1,
        "namespace" : "test.users",
        "indexFilterSet" : false,
        "parsedQuery" : {
            "username" : {
                "$eq" : "user101"
            }
        },
        "winningPlan" : {
            "stage" : "COLLSCAN",
            "filter" : {
                "username" : {
                    "$eq" : "user101"
                }
            },
            "direction" : "forward"
        },
        "rejectedPlans" : [ ]
    },
    "executionStats" : {
        "executionSuccess" : true,
        "nReturned" : 1,
        "executionTimeMillis" : 419,
        "totalKeysExamined" : 0,
        "totalDocsExamined" : 1000000,
        "executionStages" : {
```

```
            "stage" : "COLLSCAN",
            "filter" : {
                "username" : {
                    "$eq" : "user101"
                }
            },
            "nReturned" : 1,
            "executionTimeMillisEstimate" : 375,
            "works" : 1000002,
            "advanced" : 1,
            "needTime" : 1000000,
            "needYield" : 0,
            "saveState" : 7822,
            "restoreState" : 7822,
            "isEOF" : 1,
            "invalidates" : 0,
            "direction" : "forward",
            "docsExamined" : 1000000
        }
    },
    "serverInfo" : {
        "host" : "eoinbrazil-laptop-osx",
        "port" : 27017,
        "version" : "4.0.12",
        "gitVersion" : "5776e3cbf9e7afe86e6b29e22520ffb6766e95d4"
    },
    "ok" : 1
}
```

"explain Output" on page 116 will explain the output fields; for now you can ignore almost all of them. For this example, we want to look at the nested document that is the value of the "executionStats" field. In this document, "totalDocsExamined" is the number of documents MongoDB looked at while trying to satisfy the query, which, as you can see, is every document in the collection. That is, MongoDB had to look through every field in every document. This took nearly half a second to accomplish on my laptop (the "executionTimeMillis" field shows the number of milliseconds it took to execute the query).

The "nReturned" field of the "executionStats" document shows the number of results returned: 1, which makes sense because there is only one user with the username "user101". Note that MongoDB had to look through every document in the collection for matches because it did not know that usernames are unique.

To enable MongoDB to respond to queries efficiently, all query patterns in your application should be supported by an index. By query patterns, we simply mean the different types of questions your application asks of the database. In this example, we queried the *users* collection by username. That is an example of a specific query pattern. In many applications, a single index will support several query patterns. We will discuss tailoring indexes to query patterns in a later section.

Creating an Index

Now let's try creating an index on the `"username"` field. To create an index, we'll use the `createIndex` collection method:

```
> db.users.createIndex({"username" : 1})
{
    "createdCollectionAutomatically" : false,
    "numIndexesBefore" : 1,
    "numIndexesAfter" : 2,
    "ok" : 1
}
```

Creating the index should take no longer than a few seconds, unless you made your collection especially large. If the `createIndex` call does not return after a few seconds, run `db.currentOp()` (in a different shell) or check your *mongod*'s log to see the index build's progress.

Once the index build is complete, try repeating the original query:

```
> db.users.find({"username": "user101"}).explain("executionStats")
{
    "queryPlanner" : {
        "plannerVersion" : 1,
        "namespace" : "test.users",
        "indexFilterSet" : false,
        "parsedQuery" : {
            "username" : {
                "$eq" : "user101"
            }
        },
        "winningPlan" : {
            "stage" : "FETCH",
            "inputStage" : {
                "stage" : "IXSCAN",
                "keyPattern" : {
                    "username" : 1
                },
                "indexName" : "username_1",
                "isMultiKey" : false,
                "multiKeyPaths" : {
                    "username" : [ ]
                },
                "isUnique" : false,
                "isSparse" : false,
                "isPartial" : false,
                "indexVersion" : 2,
                "direction" : "forward",
                "indexBounds" : {
                    "username" : [
                        "[\"user101\", \"user101\"]"
                    ]
```

```
                }
            }
        },
        "rejectedPlans" : [ ]
    },
    "executionStats" : {
        "executionSuccess" : true,
        "nReturned" : 1,
        "executionTimeMillis" : 1,
        "totalKeysExamined" : 1,
        "totalDocsExamined" : 1,
        "executionStages" : {
            "stage" : "FETCH",
            "nReturned" : 1,
            "executionTimeMillisEstimate" : 0,
            "works" : 2,
            "advanced" : 1,
            "needTime" : 0,
            "needYield" : 0,
            "saveState" : 0,
            "restoreState" : 0,
            "isEOF" : 1,
            "invalidates" : 0,
            "docsExamined" : 1,
            "alreadyHasObj" : 0,
            "inputStage" : {
                "stage" : "IXSCAN",
                "nReturned" : 1,
                "executionTimeMillisEstimate" : 0,
                "works" : 2,
                "advanced" : 1,
                "needTime" : 0,
                "needYield" : 0,
                "saveState" : 0,
                "restoreState" : 0,
                "isEOF" : 1,
                "invalidates" : 0,
                "keyPattern" : {
                    "username" : 1
                },
                "indexName" : "username_1",
                "isMultiKey" : false,
                "multiKeyPaths" : {
                    "username" : [ ]
                },
                "isUnique" : false,
                "isSparse" : false,
                "isPartial" : false,
                "indexVersion" : 2,
                "direction" : "forward",
                "indexBounds" : {
                    "username" : [
```

```
                    "[\"user101\", \"user101\"]"
                ]
            },
            "keysExamined" : 1,
            "seeks" : 1,
            "dupsTested" : 0,
            "dupsDropped" : 0,
            "seenInvalidated" : 0
        }
    }
},
"serverInfo" : {
    "host" : "eoinbrazil-laptop-osx",
    "port" : 27017,
    "version" : "4.0.12",
    "gitVersion" : "5776e3cbf9e7afe86e6b29e22520ffb6766e95d4"
},
"ok" : 1
}
```

This `explain` output is more complex, but for now you can continue to ignore all the fields other than `"nReturned"`, `"totalDocsExamined"`, and `"executionTimeMillis"` in the `"executionStats"` nested document. As you can see, the query is now almost instantaneous and, even better, has a similar runtime when querying, for example, for any username:

```
> db.users.find({"username": "user999999"}).explain("executionStats")
```

An index can make a dramatic difference in query times. However, indexes have their price: write operations (inserts, updates, and deletes) that modify an indexed field will take longer. This is because in addition to updating the document, MongoDB has to update indexes when your data changes. Typically, the tradeoff is worth it. The tricky part becomes figuring out which fields to index.

> MongoDB's indexes work almost identically to typical relational database indexes, so if you are familiar with those, you can just skim this section for syntax specifics.

To choose which fields to create indexes for, look through your frequent queries and queries that need to be fast and try to find a common set of keys from those. For instance, in the preceding example, we were querying on `"username"`. If that were a particularly common query or were becoming a bottleneck, indexing `"username"` would be a good choice. However, if this were an unusual query or one that's only done by administrators who don't care how long it takes, it would not be a good choice for indexing.

Introduction to Compound Indexes

The purpose of an index is to make your queries as efficient as possible. For many query patterns it is necessary to build indexes based on two or more keys. For example, an index keeps all of its values in a sorted order, so it makes sorting documents by the indexed key much faster. However, an index can only help with sorting if it is a prefix of the sort. For example, the index on "username" wouldn't help much for this sort:

```
> db.users.find().sort({"age" : 1, "username" : 1})
```

This sorts by "age" and then "username", so a strict sorting by "username" isn't terribly helpful. To optimize this sort, you could make an index on "age" *and* "username":

```
> db.users.createIndex({"age" : 1, "username" : 1})
```

This is called a *compound index* and is useful if your query has multiple sort directions or multiple keys in the criteria. A compound index is an index on more than one field.

Suppose we have a *users* collection that looks something like this, if we run a query with no sorting (called natural order):

```
> db.users.find({}, {"_id" : 0, "i" : 0, "created" : 0})
{ "username" : "user0", "age" : 69 }
{ "username" : "user1", "age" : 50 }
{ "username" : "user2", "age" : 88 }
{ "username" : "user3", "age" : 52 }
{ "username" : "user4", "age" : 74 }
{ "username" : "user5", "age" : 104 }
{ "username" : "user6", "age" : 59 }
{ "username" : "user7", "age" : 102 }
{ "username" : "user8", "age" : 94 }
{ "username" : "user9", "age" : 7 }
{ "username" : "user10", "age" : 80 }
...
```

If we index this collection by {"age" : 1, "username" : 1}, the index will have a form we can represent as follows:

```
[0, "user100020"] -> 8623513776
[0, "user1002"] -> 8599246768
[0, "user100388"] -> 8623560880
...
[0, "user100414"] -> 8623564208
[1, "user100113"] -> 8623525680
[1, "user100280"] -> 8623547056
[1, "user100551"] -> 8623581744
...
[1, "user100626"] -> 8623591344
[2, "user100191"] -> 8623535664
```

```
[2, "user100195"] -> 8623536176
[2, "user100197"] -> 8623536432
...
```

Each index entry contains an age and a username and points to a record identifier. A record identifier is used internally by the storage engine to locate the data for a document. Note that "age" fields are ordered to be strictly ascending and, within each age, usernames are also in ascending order. In this example dataset, each age has approximately 8,000 usernames associated with it. Here we've included only those necessary to convey the general idea.

The way MongoDB uses this index depends on the type of query you're doing. These are the three most common ways:

`db.users.find({"age" : 21}).sort({"username" : -1})`

This is an equality query, which searches for a single value. There may be multiple documents with that value. Due to the second field in the index, the results are already in the correct order for the sort: MongoDB can start with the last match for `{"age" : 21}` and traverse the index in order:

```
[21, "user100154"] -> 8623530928
[21, "user100266"] -> 8623545264
[21, "user100270"] -> 8623545776
[21, "user100285"] -> 8623547696
[21, "user100349"] -> 8623555888
...
```

This type of query is very efficient: MongoDB can jump directly to the correct age and doesn't need to sort the results because traversing the index returns the data in the correct order.

Note that sort direction doesn't matter: MongoDB can traverse the index in either direction.

`db.users.find({"age" : {"$gte" : 21, "$lte" : 30}})`

This is a range query, which looks for documents matching multiple values (in this case, all ages between 21 and 30). MongoDB will use the first key in the index, "age", to return the matching documents, like so:

```
[21, "user100154"] -> 8623530928
[21, "user100266"] -> 8623545264
[21, "user100270"] -> 8623545776
...
[21, "user999390"] -> 8765250224
[21, "user999407"] -> 8765252400
[21, "user999600"] -> 8765277104
[22, "user100017"] -> 8623513392
...
[29, "user999861"] -> 8765310512
```

```
[30, "user100098"] -> 8623523760
[30, "user100155"] -> 8623531056
[30, "user100168"] -> 8623532720
...
```

In general, if MongoDB uses an index for a query it will return the resulting documents in index order.

```
db.users.find({"age" : {"$gte" : 21, "$lte" : 30}}).sort({"username" :
1})
```

This is a multivalue query, like the previous one, but this time it has a sort. As before, MongoDB will use the index to match the criteria. However, the index doesn't return the usernames in sorted order and the query requested that the results be sorted by username. This means MongoDB will need to sort the results in memory before returning them, rather than simply traversing an index in which the documents are already sorted in the desired order. This type of query is usually less efficient as a consequence.

Of course, the speed depends on how many results match your criteria: if your result set is only a couple of documents MongoDB won't have much work to do to sort them, but if there are more results it will be slower or may not work at all. If you have more than 32 MB of results MongoDB will just error out, refusing to sort that much data:

```
Error: error: {
    "ok" : 0,
    "errmsg" : "Executor error during find command: OperationFailed:
Sort operation used more than the maximum 33554432 bytes of RAM. Add
an index, or specify a smaller limit.",
    "code" : 96,
    "codeName" : "OperationFailed"
}
```

> If you need to avoid this error, then you must create an index supporting the sort operation (*https://docs.mongodb.com/manual/refer ence/method/cursor.sort/index.html#sort-index-use*) or use `sort` in conjunction with `limit` to reduce the results to below 32 MB.

One other index you can use in the last example is the same keys in reverse order: {"username" : 1, "age" : 1}. MongoDB will then traverse all the index entries, but in the order you want them back in. It will pick out the matching documents using the "age" part of the index:

```
[user0, 4]
[user1, 67]
[user10, 11]
[user100, 92]
[user1000, 10]
[user10000, 31]
[user100000, 21] -> 8623511216
[user100001, 52]
[user100002, 69]
[user100003, 27] -> 8623511600
[user100004, 22] -> 8623511728
[user100005, 95]
...
```

This is good in that it does not require any giant in-memory sorts. However, it does have to scan the entire index to find all the matches. Putting the sort key first is generally a good strategy when designing compound indexes. As we'll see shortly, this is one of several best practices when considering how to construct compound indexes with consideration for equality queries, multivalue queries, and sorting.

How MongoDB Selects an Index

Now let's take a look at how MongoDB chooses an index to satisfy a query. Let's imagine we have five indexes. When a query comes in, MongoDB looks at the query's *shape*. The shape has to do with what fields are being searched on and additional information, such as whether or not there is a sort. Based on that information, the system identifies a set of candidate indexes that it might be able to use in satisfying the query.

Let's assume we have a query come in, and three of our five indexes are identified as candidates for this query. MongoDB will then create three query plans, one for each of these indexes, and run the query in three parallel threads, each using a different index. The objective here is to see which one is able to return results the fastest.

Visually, we can think of this as a race, as pictured in Figure 5-1. The idea here is that the first query plan to reach a goal state is the winner. But more importantly, going forward it will be selected as the index to use for queries that have that same query shape. The plans are raced against each other for a period (referred to as the trial period), after which the results of each race are used to calculate the overall winning plan.

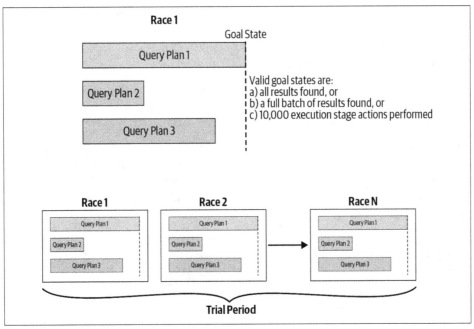

Figure 5-1. How the MongoDB Query Planner selects an index, visualized as a race

To win the race, a query thread must be the first to either return all the query results or return a trial number of results in sort order. The sort order portion of this is important given how expensive it is to perform in-memory sorts.

The real value of racing several query plans against one another is that for subsequent queries that have the same query shape, the MongoDB server will know which index to select. The server maintains a cache of query plans. A winning plan is stored in the cache for future use for queries of that shape. Over time, as a collection changes and as the indexes change, eventually a query plan might be evicted from the cache and MongoDB will, again, experiment with possible query plans to find the one that works best for the current collection and set of indexes. Other events that will lead to plans being evicted from the cache are if we rebuild a given index, add or drop an index, or explicitly clear the plan cache. Finally, the query plan cache does not survive a restart of a *mongod* process.

Using Compound Indexes

In the previous sections, we've been using compound indexes, which are indexes with more than one key in them. Compound indexes are a little more complicated to think about than single-key indexes, but they are very powerful. This section covers them in more depth.

Here, we will walk through an example that gives you an idea of the type of thinking you need to do when you are designing compound indexes. The goal is for our read and write operations to be as efficient as possible—but as with so many things, this requires some upfront thinking and some experimentation.

To be sure we get the right indexes in place, it is necessary to test our indexes under some real-world workloads and make adjustments from there. However, there are some best practices we can apply as we design our indexes.

First, we need to consider the selectivity of the index. We are interested in the degree to which, for a given query pattern, the index is going to minimize the number of records scanned. We need to consider selectivity in light of all operations necessary to satisfy a query, and sometimes make tradeoffs. We will need to consider, for example, how sorts are handled.

Let's look at an example. For this, we will use a student dataset containing approximately one million records. Documents in this dataset resemble the following:

```
{
    "_id" : ObjectId("585d817db4743f74e2da067c"),
    "student_id" : 0,
    "scores" : [
    {
        "type" : "exam",
        "score" : 38.05000060199827
    },
    {
        "type" : "quiz",
        "score" : 79.45079445008987
    },
    {
        "type" : "homework",
        "score" : 74.50150548699534
    },
    {
        "type" : "homework",
        "score" : 74.68381684615845
    }
    ],
    "class_id" : 127
}
```

We will begin with two indexes and look at how MongoDB uses these indexes (or doesn't) in order to satisfy queries. These two indexes are created as follows:

```
> db.students.createIndex({"class_id": 1})
> db.students.createIndex({student_id: 1, class_id: 1})
```

In working with this dataset, we will consider the following query, because it illustrates several of the issues that we have to think about in designing our indexes:

```
> db.students.find({student_id:{$gt:500000}, class_id:54})
...              .sort({student_id:1})
...              .explain("executionStats")
```

Note that in this query we are requesting all records with an ID greater than 500,000, so about half of the records. We are also constraining the search to records for the class with ID 54. There are about 500 classes represented in this dataset. Finally, we are sorting in ascending order based on "student_id". Note that this is the same field on which we are doing a multivalue query. Throughout this example we will look at the execution stats that the explain method provides to illustrate how MongoDB will handle this query.

If we run the query, the output of the explain method tells us how MongoDB used indexes to satisfy it:

```
{
  "queryPlanner": {
    "plannerVersion": 1,
    "namespace": "school.students",
    "indexFilterSet": false,
    "parsedQuery": {
      "$and": [
        {
          "class_id": {
            "$eq": 54
          }
        },
        {
          "student_id": {
            "$gt": 500000
          }
        }
      ]
    },
    "winningPlan": {
      "stage": "FETCH",
      "inputStage": {
        "stage": "IXSCAN",
        "keyPattern": {
          "student_id": 1,
          "class_id": 1
        },
        "indexName": "student_id_1_class_id_1",
        "isMultiKey": false,
        "multiKeyPaths": {
          "student_id": [ ],
          "class_id": [ ]
        },
        "isUnique": false,
        "isSparse": false,
        "isPartial": false,
```

```
      "indexVersion": 2,
      "direction": "forward",
      "indexBounds": {
        "student_id": [
          "(500000.0, inf.0]"
        ],
        "class_id": [
          "[54.0, 54.0]"
        ]
      }
    }
  },
  "rejectedPlans": [
    {
      "stage": "SORT",
      "sortPattern": {
        "student_id": 1
      },
      "inputStage": {
        "stage": "SORT_KEY_GENERATOR",
        "inputStage": {
          "stage": "FETCH",
          "filter": {
            "student_id": {
              "$gt": 500000
            }
          },
          "inputStage": {
            "stage": "IXSCAN",
            "keyPattern": {
              "class_id": 1
            },
            "indexName": "class_id_1",
            "isMultiKey": false,
            "multiKeyPaths": {
              "class_id": [ ]
            },
            "isUnique": false,
            "isSparse": false,
            "isPartial": false,
            "indexVersion": 2,
            "direction": "forward",
            "indexBounds": {
              "class_id": [
                "[54.0, 54.0]"
              ]
            }
          }
        }
      }
    }
  ]
```

```
    },
    "executionStats": {
      "executionSuccess": true,
      "nReturned": 9903,
      "executionTimeMillis": 4325,
      "totalKeysExamined": 850477,
      "totalDocsExamined": 9903,
      "executionStages": {
        "stage": "FETCH",
        "nReturned": 9903,
        "executionTimeMillisEstimate": 3485,
        "works": 850478,
        "advanced": 9903,
        "needTime": 840574,
        "needYield": 0,
        "saveState": 6861,
        "restoreState": 6861,
        "isEOF": 1,
        "invalidates": 0,
        "docsExamined": 9903,
        "alreadyHasObj": 0,
        "inputStage": {
          "stage": "IXSCAN",
          "nReturned": 9903,
          "executionTimeMillisEstimate": 2834,
          "works": 850478,
          "advanced": 9903,
          "needTime": 840574,
          "needYield": 0,
          "saveState": 6861,
          "restoreState": 6861,
          "isEOF": 1,
          "invalidates": 0,
          "keyPattern": {
            "student_id": 1,
            "class_id": 1
          },
          "indexName": "student_id_1_class_id_1",
          "isMultiKey": false,
          "multiKeyPaths": {
            "student_id": [ ],
            "class_id": [ ]
          },
          "isUnique": false,
          "isSparse": false,
          "isPartial": false,
          "indexVersion": 2,
          "direction": "forward",
          "indexBounds": {
            "student_id": [
              "(500000.0, inf.0]"
            ],
```

```
          "class_id": [
            "[54.0, 54.0]"
          ]
        },
        "keysExamined": 850477,
        "seeks": 840575,
        "dupsTested": 0,
        "dupsDropped": 0,
        "seenInvalidated": 0
      }
    }
  },
  "serverInfo": {
    "host": "SGB-MBP.local",
    "port": 27017,
    "version": "3.4.1",
    "gitVersion": "5e103c4f5583e2566a45d740225dc250baacfbd7"
  },
  "ok": 1
}
```

As with most data output from MongoDB, the `explain` output is JSON. Let's look first at the bottom half of this output, which is almost entirely the execution stats. The `"executionStats"` field contains statistics that describe the completed query execution for the winning query plan. We will look at query plans and the query plan output from `explain` a little later.

Within `"executionStats"`, first we will look at `"totalKeysExamined"`. This is how many keys within the index MongoDB walked through in order to generate the result set. We can compare `"totalKeysExamined"` to `"nReturned"` to get a sense for how much of the index MongoDB had to traverse in order to find just the documents matching the query. In this case, 850,477 index keys were examined in order to locate the 9,903 matching documents.

This means that the index used in order to satisfy this query was not very selective. This is further emphasized by the fact that this query took more than 4.3 seconds to run, as indicated by the `"executionTimeMillis"` field. Selectivity is one of our key objectives when we are designing an index, so let's figure out where we went wrong with the existing indexes for this query.

Near the top of the `explain` output is the winning query plan (see the field `"winning Plan"`). A query plan describes the steps MongoDB used to satisfy a query. This is, in JSON form, the specific outcome of racing a couple of different query plans against one another. In particular, we are interested in what indexes were used and whether MongoDB had to do an in-memory sort. Below the winning plan are the rejected plans. We'll look at both.

In this case, the winning plan used a compound index based on `"student_id"` and `"class_id"`. This is evident in the following portion of the `explain` output:

```
"winningPlan": {
  "stage": "FETCH",
  "inputStage": {
    "stage": "IXSCAN",
    "keyPattern": {
      "student_id": 1,
      "class_id": 1
    },
```

The `explain` output presents the query plan as a tree of stages. A stage can have one or more input stages, depending on how many child stages it has. An input stage provides the documents or index keys to its parent. In this case, there was one input stage, an index scan, and that scan provided the record IDs for documents matching the query to its parent, the `"FETCH"` stage. The `"FETCH"` stage, then, will retrieve the documents themselves and return them in batches as the client requests them.

The losing query plan—there is only one—would have used an index based on `"class_id"` but then it would have had to do an in-memory sort. That is what the following portion of this particular query plan means. When you see a `"SORT"` stage in a query plan, it means that MongoDB would have been unable to sort the result set in the database using an index and instead would have had to do an in-memory sort:

```
"rejectedPlans": [
  {
    "stage": "SORT",
    "sortPattern": {
      "student_id": 1
    },
```

For this query, the index that won is one that was able to return sorted output. To win it only had to reach a trial number of sorted result documents. For the other plan to win, that query thread would have had to return the entire result set (nearly 10,000 documents) first, since those would then need to be sorted in memory.

The issue here is one of selectivity. The multivalue query we are running specifies a broad range of `"student_id"` values, because it's requesting records for which the `"student_id"` is greater than 500,000. That's about half the records in our collection. Here again, for convenience, is the query we are running:

```
> db.students.find({student_id:{$gt:500000}, class_id:54})
...           .sort({student_id:1})
...           .explain("executionStats")
```

Now, I'm sure you can see where we are headed here. This query contains both a multivalue portion and an equality portion. The equality portion is that we are asking for all records in which `"class_id"` is equal to 54. There are only about 500 classes in this dataset, and while there are a large number of students with grades in those classes, `"class_id"` would serve as a much more selective basis on which to execute this query. It is this value that constrains our result set to just under 10,000 records rather than the approximately 850,000 that were identified by the multivalue portion of this query.

In other words, it would be better, given the indexes we have, if we were to use the index based on just `"class_id"`—the one in the losing query plan. MongoDB provides two ways of forcing the database to use a particular index. However, I cannot stress strongly enough that you should use these ways of overriding what would be the outcome of the query planner with caution. These are not techniques you should use in a production deployment.

The cursor `hint` method enables us to specify a particular index to use, either by specifying its shape or its name. An index filter uses a query shape, which is a combination of a query, sort, and projection specification. The `planCacheSetFilter` function can be used with an index filter to limit the query optimizer to only considering indexes specified in the index filter. If an index filter exists for a query shape, MongoDB will ignore `hint`. Index filters only persist for the duration of the *mongod* server process; they do not persist after shutdown.

If we change our query slightly to use `hint`, as in the following example, the `explain` output will be quite different:

```
> db.students.find({student_id:{$gt:500000}, class_id:54})
...              .sort({student_id:1})
...              .hint({class_id:1})
...              .explain("executionStats")
```

The resulting output shows that we are now down from having scanned roughly 850,000 index keys to just about 20,000 in order to get to our result set of just under 10,000. In addition, the execution time is only 272 milliseconds rather than the 4.3 seconds we saw with the query plan using the other index:

```
{
  "queryPlanner": {
    "plannerVersion": 1,
    "namespace": "school.students",
    "indexFilterSet": false,
    "parsedQuery": {
      "$and": [
        {
          "class_id": {
            "$eq": 54
          }
        },
        {
          "student_id": {
            "$gt": 500000
```

```
          }
        }
      ]
    },
    "winningPlan": {
      "stage": "SORT",
      "sortPattern": {
        "student_id": 1
      },
      "inputStage": {
        "stage": "SORT_KEY_GENERATOR",
        "inputStage": {
          "stage": "FETCH",
          "filter": {
            "student_id": {
              "$gt": 500000
            }
          },
          "inputStage": {
            "stage": "IXSCAN",
            "keyPattern": {
              "class_id": 1
            },
            "indexName": "class_id_1",
            "isMultiKey": false,
            "multiKeyPaths": {
              "class_id": [ ]
            },
            "isUnique": false,
            "isSparse": false,
            "isPartial": false,
            "indexVersion": 2,
            "direction": "forward",
            "indexBounds": {
              "class_id": [
                "[54.0, 54.0]"
              ]
            }
          }
        }
      }
    },
    "rejectedPlans": [ ]
  },
  "executionStats": {
    "executionSuccess": true,
    "nReturned": 9903,
    "executionTimeMillis": 272,
    "totalKeysExamined": 20076,
    "totalDocsExamined": 20076,
    "executionStages": {
      "stage": "SORT",
```

```
"nReturned": 9903,
"executionTimeMillisEstimate": 248,
"works": 29982,
"advanced": 9903,
"needTime": 20078,
"needYield": 0,
"saveState": 242,
"restoreState": 242,
"isEOF": 1,
"invalidates": 0,
"sortPattern": {
  "student_id": 1
},
"memUsage": 2386623,
"memLimit": 33554432,
"inputStage": {
  "stage": "SORT_KEY_GENERATOR",
  "nReturned": 9903,
  "executionTimeMillisEstimate": 203,
  "works": 20078,
  "advanced": 9903,
  "needTime": 10174,
  "needYield": 0,
  "saveState": 242,
  "restoreState": 242,
  "isEOF": 1,
  "invalidates": 0,
  "inputStage": {
    "stage": "FETCH",
    "filter": {
      "student_id": {
        "$gt": 500000
      }
    },
    "nReturned": 9903,
    "executionTimeMillisEstimate": 192,
    "works": 20077,
    "advanced": 9903,
    "needTime": 10173,
    "needYield": 0,
    "saveState": 242,
    "restoreState": 242,
    "isEOF": 1,
    "invalidates": 0,
    "docsExamined": 20076,
    "alreadyHasObj": 0,
    "inputStage": {
      "stage": "IXSCAN",
      "nReturned": 20076,
      "executionTimeMillisEstimate": 45,
      "works": 20077,
      "advanced": 20076,
```

```
        "needTime": 0,
        "needYield": 0,
        "saveState": 242,
        "restoreState": 242,
        "isEOF": 1,
        "invalidates": 0,
        "keyPattern": {
          "class_id": 1
        },
        "indexName": "class_id_1",
        "isMultiKey": false,
        "multiKeyPaths": {
          "class_id": [ ]
        },
        "isUnique": false,
        "isSparse": false,
        "isPartial": false,
        "indexVersion": 2,
        "direction": "forward",
        "indexBounds": {
          "class_id": [
            "[54.0, 54.0]"
          ]
        },
        "keysExamined": 20076,
        "seeks": 1,
        "dupsTested": 0,
        "dupsDropped": 0,
        "seenInvalidated": 0
      }
     }
    }
   }
  },
  "serverInfo": {
    "host": "SGB-MBP.local",
    "port": 27017,
    "version": "3.4.1",
    "gitVersion": "5e103c4f5583e2566a45d740225dc250baacfbd7"
  },
  "ok": 1
}
```

However, what we really want to see is "nReturned" very close to "totalKeysExa
mined". In addition, we would like avoid having to use hint in order to more efficiently execute this query. The way to address both of these concerns is to design a
better index.

A better index for the query pattern in question is one based on "class_id" and "stu
dent_id", in that order. With "class_id" as the prefix, we are using the equality filter in our query to restrict the keys considered within the index. This is the most

selective component of our query, and therefore effectively constrains the number of keys MongoDB needs to consider to satisfy this query. We can build this index as follows:

```
> db.students.createIndex({class_id:1, student_id:1})
```

While not true for absolutely every dataset, in general you should design compound indexes such that fields on which you will be using equality filters come before those on which your application will use multivalue filters.

With our new index in place, if we rerun our query, this time no hinting is required and we can see from the "executionStats" field in the explain output that we have a fast query (37 milliseconds) for which the number of results returned ("nReturned") is equal to the number of keys scanned in the index ("totalKeysExamined"). We can also see that this is due to the fact that the "executionStages", which reflect the winning query plan, contain an index scan that makes use of the new index we created:

```
...
"executionStats": {
  "executionSuccess": true,
  "nReturned": 9903,
  "executionTimeMillis": 37,
  "totalKeysExamined": 9903,
  "totalDocsExamined": 9903,
  "executionStages": {
    "stage": "FETCH",
    "nReturned": 9903,
    "executionTimeMillisEstimate": 36,
    "works": 9904,
    "advanced": 9903,
    "needTime": 0,
    "needYield": 0,
    "saveState": 81,
    "restoreState": 81,
    "isEOF": 1,
    "invalidates": 0,
    "docsExamined": 9903,
    "alreadyHasObj": 0,
    "inputStage": {
      "stage": "IXSCAN",
      "nReturned": 9903,
      "executionTimeMillisEstimate": 0,
      "works": 9904,
      "advanced": 9903,
      "needTime": 0,
      "needYield": 0,
      "saveState": 81,
      "restoreState": 81,
      "isEOF": 1,
      "invalidates": 0,
```

```
      "keyPattern": {
        "class_id": 1,
        "student_id": 1
      },
      "indexName": "class_id_1_student_id_1",
      "isMultiKey": false,
      "multiKeyPaths": {
        "class_id": [ ],
        "student_id": [ ]
      },
      "isUnique": false,
      "isSparse": false,
      "isPartial": false,
      "indexVersion": 2,
      "direction": "forward",
      "indexBounds": {
        "class_id": [
          "[54.0, 54.0]"
        ],
        "student_id": [
          "(500000.0, inf.0]"
        ]
      },
      "keysExamined": 9903,
      "seeks": 1,
      "dupsTested": 0,
      "dupsDropped": 0,
      "seenInvalidated": 0
    }
  }
},
```

Considering what we know about how indexes are built, you can probably see why this works. The [class_id, student_id] index is composed of key pairs such as the following. Since the student IDs are ordered within these key pairs, in order to satisfy our sort MongoDB simply needs to walk all the key pairs beginning with the first one for class_id 54:

```
...
[53, 999617]
[53, 999780]
[53, 999916]
[54, 500001]
[54, 500009]
[54, 500048]
...
```

In considering the design of a compound index, we need to know how to address equality filters, multivalue filters, and sort components of common query patterns that will make use of the index. It is necessary to consider these three factors for all compound indexes, and if you design your index to balance these concerns correctly, you will get the best performance out of MongoDB for your queries. While we've addressed all three factors for our example query with the [class_id, student_id] index, the query as written represents a special case of the compound index problem because we're sorting on one of the fields we are also filtering on.

To remove the special-case nature of this example, let's sort on final grade instead, changing our query to the following:

```
> db.students.find({student_id:{$gt:500000}, class_id:54})
...           .sort({final_grade:1})
...           .explain("executionStats")
```

If we run this query and look at the explain output, we see that we're now doing an in-memory sort. While the query is still fast at only 136 milliseconds, it is an order of magnitude slower than when sorting on "student_id", because we are now doing an in-memory sort. We can see that we are doing an in-memory sort because the winning query plan now contains a "SORT" stage:

```
...
"executionStats": {
  "executionSuccess": true,
  "nReturned": 9903,
  "executionTimeMillis": 136,
  "totalKeysExamined": 9903,
  "totalDocsExamined": 9903,
  "executionStages": {
    "stage": "SORT",
    "nReturned": 9903,
    "executionTimeMillisEstimate": 36,
    "works": 19809,
    "advanced": 9903,
    "needTime": 9905,
    "needYield": 0,
    "saveState": 315,
    "restoreState": 315,
    "isEOF": 1,
    "invalidates": 0,
    "sortPattern": {
      "final_grade": 1
    },
    "memUsage": 2386623,
    "memLimit": 33554432,
    "inputStage": {
      "stage": "SORT_KEY_GENERATOR",
      "nReturned": 9903,
      "executionTimeMillisEstimate": 24,
      "works": 9905,
      "advanced": 9903,
      "needTime": 1,
      "needYield": 0,
      "saveState": 315,
```

```
      "restoreState": 315,
      "isEOF": 1,
      "invalidates": 0,
      "inputStage": {
        "stage": "FETCH",
        "nReturned": 9903,
        "executionTimeMillisEstimate": 24,
        "works": 9904,
        "advanced": 9903,
        "needTime": 0,
        "needYield": 0,
        "saveState": 315,
        "restoreState": 315,
        "isEOF": 1,
        "invalidates": 0,
        "docsExamined": 9903,
        "alreadyHasObj": 0,
        "inputStage": {
          "stage": "IXSCAN",
          "nReturned": 9903,
          "executionTimeMillisEstimate": 12,
          "works": 9904,
          "advanced": 9903,
          "needTime": 0,
          "needYield": 0,
          "saveState": 315,
          "restoreState": 315,
          "isEOF": 1,
          "invalidates": 0,
          "keyPattern": {
            "class_id": 1,
            "student_id": 1
          },
          "indexName": "class_id_1_student_id_1",
          "isMultiKey": false,
          "multiKeyPaths": {
            "class_id": [ ],
            "student_id": [ ]
          },
          "isUnique": false,
          "isSparse": false,
          "isPartial": false,
          "indexVersion": 2,
          "direction": "forward",
          "indexBounds": {
            "class_id": [
              "[54.0, 54.0]"
            ],
            "student_id": [
              "(500000.0, inf.0]"
            ]
          },
```

```
            "keysExamined": 9903,
            "seeks": 1,
            "dupsTested": 0,
            "dupsDropped": 0,
            "seenInvalidated": 0
          }
        }
      }
    }
  },
  ...
```

If we can avoid an in-memory sort with a better index design, we should. This will allow us to scale more easily with respect to dataset size and system load.

But to do that, we are going to have to make a tradeoff. This is commonly the case when designing compound indexes.

As is so often necessary for compound indexes, in order to avoid an in-memory sort we need to examine more keys than the number of documents we return. To use the index to sort, MongoDB needs to be able to walk the index keys in order. This means that we need to include the sort field among the compound index keys.

The keys in our new compound index should be ordered as follows: [class_id, final_grade, student_id]. Note that we include the sort component immediately after the equality filter, but before the multivalue filter. This index will very selectively narrow the set of keys considered for this query. Then, by walking the key triplets matching the equality filter in this index, MongoDB can identify the records that match the multivalue filter and those records will be ordered properly by final grade in ascending order.

This compound index forces MongoDB to examine keys for more documents than will end up being in our result set. However, by using the index to ensure we have sorted documents, we save execution time. We can construct the new index using the following command:

```
> db.students.createIndex({class_id:1, final_grade:1, student_id:1})
```

Now, if we once again issue our query:

```
> db.students.find({student_id:{$gt:500000}, class_id:54})
...            .sort({final_grade:1})
...            .explain("executionStats")
```

we get the following "executionStats" in the output from explain. This will vary depending on your hardware and what else is going on in the system, but you can see that the winning plan no longer includes an in-memory sort. It is instead using the index we just created to satisfy the query, including the sort:

```
"executionStats": {
  "executionSuccess": true,
  "nReturned": 9903,
  "executionTimeMillis": 42,
  "totalKeysExamined": 9905,
  "totalDocsExamined": 9903,
  "executionStages": {
    "stage": "FETCH",
    "nReturned": 9903,
    "executionTimeMillisEstimate": 34,
    "works": 9905,
    "advanced": 9903,
    "needTime": 1,
    "needYield": 0,
    "saveState": 82,
    "restoreState": 82,
    "isEOF": 1,
    "invalidates": 0,
    "docsExamined": 9903,
    "alreadyHasObj": 0,
    "inputStage": {
      "stage": "IXSCAN",
      "nReturned": 9903,
      "executionTimeMillisEstimate": 24,
      "works": 9905,
      "advanced": 9903,
      "needTime": 1,
      "needYield": 0,
      "saveState": 82,
      "restoreState": 82,
      "isEOF": 1,
      "invalidates": 0,
      "keyPattern": {
        "class_id": 1,
        "final_grade": 1,
        "student_id": 1
      },
      "indexName": "class_id_1_final_grade_1_student_id_1",
      "isMultiKey": false,
      "multiKeyPaths": {
        "class_id": [ ],
        "final_grade": [ ],
        "student_id": [ ]
      },
      "isUnique": false,
      "isSparse": false,
      "isPartial": false,
      "indexVersion": 2,
      "direction": "forward",
      "indexBounds": {
        "class_id": [
          "[54.0, 54.0]"
```

```
      ],
      "final_grade": [
        "[MinKey, MaxKey]"
      ],
      "student_id": [
        "(500000.0, inf.0]"
      ]
    },
    "keysExamined": 9905,
    "seeks": 2,
    "dupsTested": 0,
    "dupsDropped": 0,
    "seenInvalidated": 0
   }
  }
},
```

This section has provided a concrete example of some best practices for designing compound indexes. While these guidelines do not hold for every situation, they do for most and should be the first ideas you consider when constructing a compound index.

To recap, when designing a compound index:

- Keys for equality filters should appear first.
- Keys used for sorting should appear before multivalue fields.
- Keys for multivalue filters should appear last.

Design your compound index using these guidelines and then test it under real-world workloads for the range of query patterns your index is designed to support.

Choosing key directions

So far, all of our index entries have been sorted in ascending, or least-to-greatest, order. However, if you need to sort on two (or more) criteria, you may need to have index keys go in different directions. For example, going back to our earlier example with the *users* collection, suppose we wanted to sort the collection by age from youngest to oldest and by name from Z–A. Our previous indexes would not be very efficient for this problem: within each age group users were sorted by username in ascending order (A–Z, not Z–A). The compound indexes we've been using so far do not hold the values in any useful order for getting "age" ascending and "username" descending.

To optimize compound sorts in different directions, we need to use an index with matching directions. In this example, we could use {"age" : 1, "username" : -1}, which would organize the data as follows:

```
[21, user999600] -> 8765277104
[21, user999407] -> 8765252400
[21, user999390] -> 8765250224
...
[21, user100270] -> 8623545776
[21, user100266] -> 8623545264
[21, user100154] -> 8623530928
...
[30, user100168] -> 8623532720
[30, user100155] -> 8623531056
[30, user100098] -> 8623523760
```

The ages are arranged from youngest to oldest, and within each age, the usernames are sorted from Z to A (or rather 9 to 0, given our usernames).

If our application also needed to optimize sorting by {"age" : 1, "username" : 1}, we would have to create a second index with those directions. To figure out which directions to use for an index, simply match the directions your sort is using. Note that inverse indexes (multiplying each direction by −1) are equivalent: {"age" : 1, "username" : -1} suits the same queries that {"age" : -1, "username" : 1} does.

Index direction only really matters when you're sorting based on multiple criteria. If you're only sorting by a single key, MongoDB can just as easily read the index in the opposite order. For example, if you had a sort on {"age" : -1} and an index on {"age" : 1}, MongoDB could optimize it just as well as if you had an index on {"age" : -1} (so don't create both!). The direction only matters for multikey sorts.

Using covered queries

In the preceding examples, the index was always used to find the correct document and then follow a pointer back to fetch the actual document. However, if your query is only looking for the fields that are included in the index, it does not need to fetch the document. When an index contains all the values requested by a query, the query is considered to be *covered*. Whenever practical, use covered queries in preference to going back to documents. You can make your working set much smaller that way.

To make sure a query can use the index only, you should use projections (which limit the fields returned to only those specified in your query; see "Specifying Which Keys to Return" on page 54) to avoid returning the "_id" field (unless it is part of the index). You may also have to index fields that you aren't querying on, so you should balance your need for faster queries with the overhead this will add on writes.

If you run explain on a covered query, the result has an "IXSCAN" stage that is *not* a descendant of a "FETCH" stage, and in the "executionStats", the value of "totalDoc sExamined" is 0.

Implicit indexes

Compound indexes can do "double duty" and act like different indexes for different queries. If we have an index on {"age" : 1, "username" : 1}, the "age" field is sorted identically to the way it would be if we had an index on just {"age" : 1}. Thus, the compound index can be used the way an index on {"age" : 1} by itself would be.

This can be generalized to as many keys as necessary: if an index has *N* keys, you get a "free" index on any prefix of those keys. For example, if we have an index that looks like {"a": 1, "b": 1, "c": 1, ..., "z": 1}, we effectively have indexes on {"a": 1}, {"a": 1, "b" : 1}, {"a": 1, "b": 1, "c": 1}, and so on.

Note that this doesn't hold for *any* subset of keys: queries that would use the index {"b": 1} or {"a": 1, "c": 1} (for example) will not be optimized. Only queries that can use a prefix of the index can take advantage of it.

How $ Operators Use Indexes

Some queries can use indexes more efficiently than others; some queries cannot use indexes at all. This section covers how various query operators are handled by MongoDB.

Inefficient operators

In general, negation is inefficient. "$ne" queries can use an index, but not very well. They must look at all the index entries other than the one specified by "$ne", so they basically have to scan the entire index. For example, for a collection with an index on the field named "i", here are the index ranges traversed for such a query:

```
db.example.find({"i" : {"$ne" : 3}}).explain()
{
    "queryPlanner" : {
        ...,
        "parsedQuery" : {
            "i" : {
                "$ne" : "3"
            }
        },
        "winningPlan" : {
            {
                ...,
                "indexBounds" : {
                    "i" : [
                        [
                            {
                                "$minElement" : 1
                            },
                            3
```

```
                           ],
                           [
                                3,
                                {
                                     "$maxElement" : 1
                                }
                           ]
                       ]
                     }
                 }
              },
              "rejectedPlans" : [ ]
           },
           "serverInfo" : {
               ...,
           }
       }
```

This query looks at all index entries less than 3 and all index entries greater than 3. This can be efficient if a large swath of your collection is 3, but otherwise it must check almost everything.

"$not" can sometimes use an index but often does not know how. It can reverse basic ranges ({"*key*" : {"$lt" : 7}} becomes {"*key*" : {"$gte" : 7}}) and regular expressions. However, most other queries with "$not" will fall back to doing a table scan. "$nin" always uses a table scan.

If you need to perform one of these types of queries quickly, figure out if there's another clause that you could add to the query that could use an index to filter the result set down to a small number of documents before MongoDB attempts to do nonindexed matching.

Ranges

Compound indexes can help MongoDB efficiently execute queries with multiple clauses. When designing an index with multiple fields, put fields that will be used in exact matches first (e.g., "x" : 1) and ranges last (e.g., "y": {"$gt" : 3, "$lt" : 5}). This allows the query to find an exact value for the first index key and then search within that for a second index range. For example, suppose we were querying for a specific age and a range of usernames using an {"age" : 1, "username" : 1} index. We would get fairly exact index bounds:

```
> db.users.find({"age" : 47, "username" :
... {"$gt" : "user5", "$lt" : "user8"}}).explain('executionStats')
{
    "queryPlanner" : {
        "plannerVersion" : 1,
        "namespace" : "test.users",
        "indexFilterSet" : false,
```

```
"parsedQuery" : {
    "$and" : [
        {
            "age" : {
                "$eq" : 47
            }
        },
        {
            "username" : {
                "$lt" : "user8"
            }
        },
        {
            "username" : {
                "$gt" : "user5"
            }
        }
    ]
},
"winningPlan" : {
    "stage" : "FETCH",
    "inputStage" : {
        "stage" : "IXSCAN",
        "keyPattern" : {
            "age" : 1,
            "username" : 1
        },
        "indexName" : "age_1_username_1",
        "isMultiKey" : false,
        "multiKeyPaths" : {
            "age" : [ ],
            "username" : [ ]
        },
        "isUnique" : false,
        "isSparse" : false,
        "isPartial" : false,
        "indexVersion" : 2,
        "direction" : "forward",
        "indexBounds" : {
            "age" : [
                "[47.0, 47.0]"
            ],
            "username" : [
                "(\"user5\", \"user8\")"
            ]
        }
    }
},
"rejectedPlans" : [
    {
        "stage" : "FETCH",
        "filter" : {
```

```
                "age" : {
                    "$eq" : 47
                }
            },
            "inputStage" : {
                "stage" : "IXSCAN",
                "keyPattern" : {
                    "username" : 1
                },
                "indexName" : "username_1",
                "isMultiKey" : false,
                "multiKeyPaths" : {
                    "username" : [ ]
                },
                "isUnique" : false,
                "isSparse" : false,
                "isPartial" : false,
                "indexVersion" : 2,
                "direction" : "forward",
                "indexBounds" : {
                    "username" : [
                        "(\"user5\", \"user8\")"
                    ]
                }
            }
        }
    ]
},
"executionStats" : {
    "executionSuccess" : true,
    "nReturned" : 2742,
    "executionTimeMillis" : 5,
    "totalKeysExamined" : 2742,
    "totalDocsExamined" : 2742,
    "executionStages" : {
        "stage" : "FETCH",
        "nReturned" : 2742,
        "executionTimeMillisEstimate" : 0,
        "works" : 2743,
        "advanced" : 2742,
        "needTime" : 0,
        "needYield" : 0,
        "saveState" : 23,
        "restoreState" : 23,
        "isEOF" : 1,
        "invalidates" : 0,
        "docsExamined" : 2742,
        "alreadyHasObj" : 0,
        "inputStage" : {
            "stage" : "IXSCAN",
            "nReturned" : 2742,
            "executionTimeMillisEstimate" : 0,
```

```
        "works" : 2743,
        "advanced" : 2742,
        "needTime" : 0,
        "needYield" : 0,
        "saveState" : 23,
        "restoreState" : 23,
        "isEOF" : 1,
        "invalidates" : 0,
        "keyPattern" : {
            "age" : 1,
            "username" : 1
        },
        "indexName" : "age_1_username_1",
        "isMultiKey" : false,
        "multiKeyPaths" : {
            "age" : [ ],
            "username" : [ ]
        },
        "isUnique" : false,
        "isSparse" : false,
        "isPartial" : false,
        "indexVersion" : 2,
        "direction" : "forward",
        "indexBounds" : {
            "age" : [
                "[47.0, 47.0]"
            ],
            "username" : [
                "(\"user5\", \"user8\")"
            ]
        },
        "keysExamined" : 2742,
        "seeks" : 1,
        "dupsTested" : 0,
        "dupsDropped" : 0,
        "seenInvalidated" : 0
            }
        }
    },
    "serverInfo" : {
        "host" : "eoinbrazil-laptop-osx",
        "port" : 27017,
        "version" : "4.0.12",
        "gitVersion" : "5776e3cbf9e7afe86e6b29e22520ffb6766e95d4"
    },
    "ok" : 1
}
```

The query goes directly to "age" : 47 and then searches within that for usernames between "user5" and "user8".

Conversely, suppose we use an index on {"username" : 1, "age" : 1}. This changes the query plan, as the query must look at all users between "user5" and "user8" and pick out the ones with "age" : 47:

```
> db.users.find({"age" : 47, "username" : {"$gt" : "user5", "$lt" : "user8"}})
                .explain('executionStats')
{
    "queryPlanner" : {
        "plannerVersion" : 1,
        "namespace" : "test.users",
        "indexFilterSet" : false,
        "parsedQuery" : {
            "$and" : [
                {
                    "age" : {
                        "$eq" : 47
                    }
                },
                {
                    "username" : {
                        "$lt" : "user8"
                    }
                },
                {
                    "username" : {
                        "$gt" : "user5"
                    }
                }
            ]
        },
        "winningPlan" : {
            "stage" : "FETCH",
            "filter" : {
                "age" : {
                    "$eq" : 47
                }
            },
            "inputStage" : {
                "stage" : "IXSCAN",
                "keyPattern" : {
                    "username" : 1
                },
                "indexName" : "username_1",
                "isMultiKey" : false,
                "multiKeyPaths" : {
                    "username" : [ ]
                },
                "isUnique" : false,
                "isSparse" : false,
                "isPartial" : false,
                "indexVersion" : 2,
                "direction" : "forward",
```

```
            "indexBounds" : {
                "username" : [
                    "(\"user5\", \"user8\")"
                ]
            }
        }
    },
    "rejectedPlans" : [
        {
            "stage" : "FETCH",
            "inputStage" : {
                "stage" : "IXSCAN",
                "keyPattern" : {
                    "username" : 1,
                    "age" : 1
                },
                "indexName" : "username_1_age_1",
                "isMultiKey" : false,
                "multiKeyPaths" : {
                    "username" : [ ],
                    "age" : [ ]
                },
                "isUnique" : false,
                "isSparse" : false,
                "isPartial" : false,
                "indexVersion" : 2,
                "direction" : "forward",
                "indexBounds" : {
                    "username" : [
                        "(\"user5\", \"user8\")"
                    ],
                    "age" : [
                        "[47.0, 47.0]"
                    ]
                }
            }
        }
    ]
},
"executionStats" : {
    "executionSuccess" : true,
    "nReturned" : 2742,
    "executionTimeMillis" : 369,
    "totalKeysExamined" : 333332,
    "totalDocsExamined" : 333332,
    "executionStages" : {
        "stage" : "FETCH",
        "filter" : {
            "age" : {
                "$eq" : 47
            }
        },
```

```
            "nReturned" : 2742,
            "executionTimeMillisEstimate" : 312,
            "works" : 333333,
            "advanced" : 2742,
            "needTime" : 330590,
            "needYield" : 0,
            "saveState" : 2697,
            "restoreState" : 2697,
            "isEOF" : 1,
            "invalidates" : 0,
            "docsExamined" : 333332,
            "alreadyHasObj" : 0,
            "inputStage" : {
                "stage" : "IXSCAN",
                "nReturned" : 333332,
                "executionTimeMillisEstimate" : 117,
                "works" : 333333,
                "advanced" : 333332,
                "needTime" : 0,
                "needYield" : 0,
                "saveState" : 2697,
                "restoreState" : 2697,
                "isEOF" : 1,
                "invalidates" : 0,
                "keyPattern" : {
                    "username" : 1
                },
                "indexName" : "username_1",
                "isMultiKey" : false,
                "multiKeyPaths" : {
                    "username" : [ ]
                },
                "isUnique" : false,
                "isSparse" : false,
                "isPartial" : false,
                "indexVersion" : 2,
                "direction" : "forward",
                "indexBounds" : {
                    "username" : [
                        "(\"user5\", \"user8\")"
                    ]
                },
                "keysExamined" : 333332,
                "seeks" : 1,
                "dupsTested" : 0,
                "dupsDropped" : 0,
                "seenInvalidated" : 0
            }
        }
    },
    "serverInfo" : {
        "host" : "eoinbrazil-laptop-osx",
```

```
                "port" : 27017,
                "version" : "4.0.12",
                "gitVersion" : "5776e3cbf9e7afe86e6b29e22520ffb6766e95d4"
        },
        "ok" : 1
}
```

This forces MongoDB to scan 100 times the number of index entries as using the previous index would. Using two ranges in a query basically always forces this less-
efficient query plan.

OR queries

As of this writing, MongoDB can only use one index per query. That is, if you create
one index on {"x" : 1} and another index on {"y" : 1} and then do a query on
{"x" : 123, "y" : 456}, MongoDB will use one of the indexes you created, not
both. The only exception to this rule is "$or". "$or" can use one index per "$or"
clause, as "$or" performs two queries and then merges the results:

```
db.foo.find({"$or" : [{"x" : 123}, {"y" : 456}]}).explain()
{
    "queryPlanner" : {
        "plannerVersion" : 1,
        "namespace" : "foo.foo",
        "indexFilterSet" : false,
        "parsedQuery" : {
            "$or" : [
                {
                    "x" : {
                        "$eq" : 123
                    }
                },
                {
                    "y" : {
                        "$eq" : 456
                    }
                }
            ]
        },
        "winningPlan" : {
            "stage" : "SUBPLAN",
            "inputStage" : {
                "stage" : "FETCH",
                "inputStage" : {
                    "stage" : "OR",
                    "inputStages" : [
                        {
                            "stage" : "IXSCAN",
                            "keyPattern" : {
                                "x" : 1
                            },
```

```
                    "indexName" : "x_1",
                    "isMultiKey" : false,
                    "multiKeyPaths" : {
                        "x" : [ ]
                    },
                    "isUnique" : false,
                    "isSparse" : false,
                    "isPartial" : false,
                    "indexVersion" : 2,
                    "direction" : "forward",
                    "indexBounds" : {
                        "x" : [
                            "[123.0, 123.0]"
                        ]
                    }
                },
                {
                    "stage" : "IXSCAN",
                    "keyPattern" : {
                        "y" : 1
                    },
                    "indexName" : "y_1",
                    "isMultiKey" : false,
                    "multiKeyPaths" : {
                        "y" : [ ]
                    },
                    "isUnique" : false,
                    "isSparse" : false,
                    "isPartial" : false,
                    "indexVersion" : 2,
                    "direction" : "forward",
                    "indexBounds" : {
                        "y" : [
                            "[456.0, 456.0]"
                        ]
                    }
                }
            ]
          }
        }
      },
      "rejectedPlans" : [ ]
    },
    "serverInfo" : {
    ...,
    },
    "ok" : 1
}
```

As you can see, this `explain` required two separate queries on the two indexes (as indicated by the two `"IXSCAN"` stages). In general, doing two queries and merging the results is much less efficient than doing a single query; thus, whenever possible, prefer "$in" to "$or".

If you must use an "$or", keep in mind that MongoDB needs to look through the results of both queries and remove any duplicates (documents that matched more than one "$or" clause).

When running "$in" queries there is no way, other than sorting, to control the order of documents returned. For example, {"x" : {"$in" : [1, 2, 3]}} will return documents in the same order as {"x" : {"$in" : [3, 2, 1]}}.

Indexing Objects and Arrays

MongoDB allows you to reach into your documents and create indexes on nested fields and arrays. Embedded object and array fields can be combined with top-level fields in compound indexes, and although they are special in some ways, they mostly behave the way "normal" index fields behave.

Indexing embedded docs

Indexes can be created on keys in embedded documents in the same way that they are created on normal keys. If we had a collection where each document represented a user, we might have an embedded document that described each user's location:

```
{
    "username" : "sid",
    "loc" : {
        "ip" : "1.2.3.4",
        "city" : "Springfield",
        "state" : "NY"
    }
}
```

We could put an index on one of the subfields of "loc", say "loc.city", to speed up queries using that field:

```
> db.users.createIndex({"loc.city" : 1})
```

You can go as deep as you'd like with these: you could index "x.y.z.w.a.b.c" (and so on) if you wanted.

Note that indexing the embedded document itself ("loc") has very different behavior than indexing a field of that embedded document ("loc.city"). Indexing the entire subdocument will only help queries that are querying for the entire subdocument. The query optimizer could only use an index on "loc" for queries that described the whole subdocument with fields in the correct order (e.g., db.users.find({"loc" : {"ip" : "123.456.789.000", "city" : "Shelbyville", "state" : "NY"}})). It could not use the index for queries that looked like db.users.find({"loc.city" : "Shelbyville"}).

Indexing arrays

You can also index arrays, which allows you to use the index to search for specific array elements efficiently.

Suppose we have a collection of blog posts where each document is a post. Each post has a "comments" field, which is an array of "comment" subdocuments. If we wanted to be able to find the most recently commented-on blog posts, we could create an index on the "date" key in the array of embedded "comments" documents of our blog post collection:

```
> db.blog.createIndex({"comments.date" : 1})
```

Indexing an array creates an index entry for each element of the array, so if a post had 20 comments, it would have 20 index entries. This makes array indexes more expensive than single-value ones: for a single insert, update, or remove, every array entry might have to be updated (potentially thousands of index entries).

Unlike the "loc" example in the previous section, you cannot index an entire array as a single entity: indexing an array field indexes each element of the array, not the array itself.

Indexes on array elements do not keep any notion of position: you cannot use an index for a query that is looking for a specific array element, such as "comments.4".

You can, incidentally, index a specific array entry, as in:

```
> db.blog.createIndex({"comments.10.votes": 1})
```

However, this index would only be useful for queries for exactly the 11th array element (arrays start at index 0).

Only one field in an index entry can be from an array. This is to avoid the explosive number of index entries you'd get from multiple multikey indexes: every possible pair of elements would have to be indexed, causing indexes to be $n*m$ entries per document. For example, suppose we had an index on {"x" : 1, "y" : 1}:

```
> // x is an array - legal
> db.multi.insert({"x" : [1, 2, 3], "y" : 1})
>
> // y is an array - still legal
> db.multi.insert({"x" : 1, "y" : [4, 5, 6]})
>
> // x and y are arrays - illegal!
> db.multi.insert({"x" : [1, 2, 3], "y" : [4, 5, 6]})
cannot index parallel arrays [y] [x]
```

Were MongoDB to index the final example, it would have to create index entries for {"x" : 1, "y" : 4}, {"x" : 1, "y" : 5}, {"x" : 1, "y" : 6}, {"x" : 2, "y" : 4}, {"x" : 2, "y" : 5}, {"x" : 2, "y" : 6}, {"x" : 3, "y" : 4}, {"x" : 3, "y" : 5}, and {"x" : 3, "y" : 6} (and these arrays are only three elements long).

Multikey index implications

If any document has an array field for the indexed key, the index immediately is flagged as a multikey index. You can see whether an index is multikey from explain's output: if a multikey index was used, the "isMultikey" field will be true. Once an index has been flagged as multikey, it can never be un-multikeyed, even if all of the documents containing arrays in that field are removed. The only way to un-multikey it is to drop and recreate it.

Multikey indexes may be a bit slower than non-multikey indexes. Many index entries can point at a single document, so MongoDB may need to do some deduplication before returning results.

Index Cardinality

Cardinality refers to how many distinct values there are for a field in a collection. Some fields, such as "gender" or "newsletter opt-out", might only have two possible values, which is considered a very low cardinality. Others, such as "username" or "email", might have a unique value for every document in the collection, which is high cardinality. Still others fall somewhere in between, such as "age" or "zip code".

In general, the greater the cardinality of a field, the more helpful an index on that field can be. This is because the index can quickly narrow the search space to a much smaller result set. For a low-cardinality field, an index generally cannot eliminate as many possible matches.

For example, suppose we had an index on "gender" and were looking for women named Susan. We could only narrow down the result space by approximately 50% before referring to individual documents to look up "name". Conversely, if we indexed by "name", we could immediately narrow down our result set to the tiny fraction of users named Susan, and then we could refer to those documents to check the gender.

As a rule of thumb, try to create indexes on high-cardinality keys or at least put high-cardinality keys first in compound indexes (before low-cardinality keys).

explain Output

As you've seen, explain gives you lots of information about your queries. It's one of the most important diagnostic tools there is for slow queries. You can find out which indexes are being used and how by looking at a query's "explain" output. For any query, you can add a call to explain at the end (the way you would add a sort or limit, but explain must be the last call).

There are two types of explain output that you'll see most commonly: for indexed and nonindexed queries. Special index types may create slightly different query plans, but most fields should be similar. Also, sharding returns a conglomerate of explains (as covered in Chapter 14), as it runs the query on multiple servers.

The most basic type of explain is on a query that doesn't use an index. You can tell that a query doesn't use an index because it uses a "COLLSCAN".

The output of an explain on a query that uses an index varies, but in the simplest case it looks something like this if we add an index on imdb.rating:

```
> db.users.find({"age" : 42}).explain('executionStats')
{
    "queryPlanner" : {
        "plannerVersion" : 1,
        "namespace" : "test.users",
        "indexFilterSet" : false,
        "parsedQuery" : {
            "age" : {
                "$eq" : 42
            }
        },
        "winningPlan" : {
            "stage" : "FETCH",
            "inputStage" : {
                "stage" : "IXSCAN",
                "keyPattern" : {
                    "age" : 1,
                    "username" : 1
                },
                "indexName" : "age_1_username_1",
                "isMultiKey" : false,
                "multiKeyPaths" : {
                    "age" : [ ],
                    "username" : [ ]
                },
                "isUnique" : false,
                "isSparse" : false,
                "isPartial" : false,
                "indexVersion" : 2,
                "direction" : "forward",
                "indexBounds" : {
                    "age" : [
                        "[42.0, 42.0]"
                    ],
                    "username" : [
                        "[MinKey, MaxKey]"
```

```
                    ]
                }
            }
        },
        "rejectedPlans" : [ ]
    },
    "executionStats" : {
        "executionSuccess" : true,
        "nReturned" : 8449,
        "executionTimeMillis" : 15,
        "totalKeysExamined" : 8449,
        "totalDocsExamined" : 8449,
        "executionStages" : {
            "stage" : "FETCH",
            "nReturned" : 8449,
            "executionTimeMillisEstimate" : 10,
            "works" : 8450,
            "advanced" : 8449,
            "needTime" : 0,
            "needYield" : 0,
            "saveState" : 66,
            "restoreState" : 66,
            "isEOF" : 1,
            "invalidates" : 0,
            "docsExamined" : 8449,
            "alreadyHasObj" : 0,
            "inputStage" : {
                "stage" : "IXSCAN",
                "nReturned" : 8449,
                "executionTimeMillisEstimate" : 0,
                "works" : 8450,
                "advanced" : 8449,
                "needTime" : 0,
                "needYield" : 0,
                "saveState" : 66,
                "restoreState" : 66,
                "isEOF" : 1,
                "invalidates" : 0,
                "keyPattern" : {
                    "age" : 1,
                    "username" : 1
                },
                "indexName" : "age_1_username_1",
                "isMultiKey" : false,
                "multiKeyPaths" : {
                    "age" : [ ],
                    "username" : [ ]
                },
                "isUnique" : false,
                "isSparse" : false,
                "isPartial" : false,
                "indexVersion" : 2,
```

```
                "direction" : "forward",
                "indexBounds" : {
                    "age" : [
                        "[42.0, 42.0]"
                    ],
                    "username" : [
                        "[MinKey, MaxKey]"
                    ]
                },
                "keysExamined" : 8449,
                "seeks" : 1,
                "dupsTested" : 0,
                "dupsDropped" : 0,
                "seenInvalidated" : 0
            }
        }
    },
    "serverInfo" : {
        "host" : "eoinbrazil-laptop-osx",
        "port" : 27017,
        "version" : "4.0.12",
        "gitVersion" : "5776e3cbf9e7afe86e6b29e22520ffb6766e95d4"
    },
    "ok" : 1
}
```

This output first tells you what index was used: `imdb.rating`. Next is how many documents were actually returned as a result: `"nReturned"`. Note that this doesn't necessarily reflect how much work MongoDB did to answer the query (i.e., how many indexes and documents it had to search). `"totalKeysExamined"` reports the number of index entries scanned while `"totalDocsExamined"` indicates how many documents were scanned. The number of documents scanned is reflected in `"nscannedObjects"`.

The output also shows that there were no `rejectedPlans` and that it used a bounded search on the index within the value 42.0.

`"executionTimeMillis"` reports how fast the query was executed, from the server receiving the request to when it sent a response. However, it may not always be the number you are looking for. If MongoDB tried multiple query plans, `"executionTimeMillis"` will reflect how long it took all of them to run, not the one chosen as the best.

Now that you know the basics, here is a breakdown of some of the more important fields in more detail:

`"isMultiKey" : false`
    If this query used a multikey index (see "Indexing Objects and Arrays" on page 114).

`"nReturned" : 8449`

The number of documents returned by the query.

`"totalDocsExamined" : 8449`

The number of times MongoDB had to follow an index pointer to the actual document on disk. If the query contains criteria that are not part of the index or requests fields that aren't contained in the index, MongoDB must look up the document each index entry points to.

`"totalKeysExamined" : 8449`

The number of index entries looked at, if an index was used. If this was a table scan, it is the number of documents examined.

`"stage" : "IXSCAN"`

If MongoDB was able to fulfill this query using an index; if not `"COLSCAN"` would indicate it had to perform a collection scan to fulfill the query.

In this example, MongoDB found all matching documents using the index, which we know because `"totalKeysExamined"` is the same as `"totalDocsExamined"`. However, the query was told to return every field in the matching documents and the index only contained the `"age"` and `"username"` fields.

`"needYield" : 0`

The number of times this query yielded (paused) to allow a write request to proceed. If there are writes waiting to go, queries will periodically release their lock and allow them to continue. On this system, there were no writes waiting so the query never yielded.

`"executionTimeMillis" : 15`

The number of milliseconds it took the database to execute the query. The lower this number is, the better.

`"indexBounds" : {...}`

A description of how the index was used, giving ranges of the index traversed. In this example, as the first clause in the query was an exact match, the index only needed to look at that value: 42. The second index key was a free variable, because the query didn't specify any restrictions to it. Thus, the database looked for values between negative infinity (`"$minElement" : 1`) and infinity (`"$maxElement" : 1`) for usernames within `"age" : 42`.

Let's take a look at a slightly more complicated example. Suppose you have an index on `{"username" : 1, "age" : 1}` and an index on `{"age" : 1, "username" : 1}`. What happens if you query for `"username"` and `"age"`? Well, it depends on the query:

```
> db.users.find({"age" : {$gt : 10}, "username" : "user2134"}).explain()
{
```

```
"queryPlanner" : {
    "plannerVersion" : 1,
    "namespace" : "test.users",
    "indexFilterSet" : false,
    "parsedQuery" : {
        "$and" : [
            {
                "username" : {
                    "$eq" : "user2134"
                }
            },
            {
                "age" : {
                    "$gt" : 10
                }
            }
        ]
    },
    "winningPlan" : {
        "stage" : "FETCH",
        "filter" : {
            "age" : {
                "$gt" : 10
            }
        },
        "inputStage" : {
            "stage" : "IXSCAN",
            "keyPattern" : {
                "username" : 1
            },
            "indexName" : "username_1",
            "isMultiKey" : false,
            "multiKeyPaths" : {
                "username" : [ ]
            },
            "isUnique" : false,
            "isSparse" : false,
            "isPartial" : false,
            "indexVersion" : 2,
            "direction" : "forward",
            "indexBounds" : {
                "username" : [
                    "[\"user2134\", \"user2134\"]"
                ]
            }
        }
    },
    "rejectedPlans" : [
        {
            "stage" : "FETCH",
            "inputStage" : {
                "stage" : "IXSCAN",
```

```
                    "keyPattern" : {
                        "age" : 1,
                        "username" : 1
                    },
                    "indexName" : "age_1_username_1",
                    "isMultiKey" : false,
                    "multiKeyPaths" : {
                        "age" : [ ],
                        "username" : [ ]
                    },
                    "isUnique" : false,
                    "isSparse" : false,
                    "isPartial" : false,
                    "indexVersion" : 2,
                    "direction" : "forward",
                    "indexBounds" : {
                        "age" : [
                            "(10.0, inf.0]"
                        ],
                        "username" : [
                            "[\"user2134\", \"user2134\"]"
                        ]
                    }
                }
            }
        }
    ]
},
"serverInfo" : {
    "host" : "eoinbrazil-laptop-osx",
    "port" : 27017,
    "version" : "4.0.12",
    "gitVersion" : "5776e3cbf9e7afe86e6b29e22520ffb6766e95d4"
},
"ok" : 1
}
```

We are querying for an exact match on "username" and a range of values for "age", so the database chooses to use the {"username" : 1, "age" : 1} index, reversing the terms of the query. If, on the other hand, we query for an exact age and a range of names, MongoDB will use the other index:

```
> db.users.find({"age" : 14, "username" : /.*/}).explain()
{
    "queryPlanner" : {
        "plannerVersion" : 1,
        "namespace" : "test.users",
        "indexFilterSet" : false,
        "parsedQuery" : {
            "$and" : [
                {
                    "age" : {
                        "$eq" : 14
```

```
                }
            },
            {
                "username" : {
                    "$regex" : ".*"
                }
            }
        ]
    },
    "winningPlan" : {
        "stage" : "FETCH",
        "inputStage" : {
            "stage" : "IXSCAN",
            "filter" : {
                "username" : {
                    "$regex" : ".*"
                }
            },
            "keyPattern" : {
                "age" : 1,
                "username" : 1
            },
            "indexName" : "age_1_username_1",
            "isMultiKey" : false,
            "multiKeyPaths" : {
                "age" : [ ],
                "username" : [ ]
            },
            "isUnique" : false,
            "isSparse" : false,
            "isPartial" : false,
            "indexVersion" : 2,
            "direction" : "forward",
            "indexBounds" : {
                "age" : [
                    "[14.0, 14.0]"
                ],
                "username" : [
                    "[\"\", {})",
                    "[/.*/, /.*/]"
                ]
            }
        }
    },
    "rejectedPlans" : [
        {
            "stage" : "FETCH",
            "filter" : {
                "age" : {
                    "$eq" : 14
                }
            },
```

```
                "inputStage" : {
                    "stage" : "IXSCAN",
                    "filter" : {
                        "username" : {
                            "$regex" : ".*"
                        }
                    },
                    "keyPattern" : {
                        "username" : 1
                    },
                    "indexName" : "username_1",
                    "isMultiKey" : false,
                    "multiKeyPaths" : {
                        "username" : [ ]
                    },
                    "isUnique" : false,
                    "isSparse" : false,
                    "isPartial" : false,
                    "indexVersion" : 2,
                    "direction" : "forward",
                    "indexBounds" : {
                        "username" : [
                            "[\"\", {})",
                            "[/.*/, /.*/]"
                        ]
                    }
                }
            }
        }
    ]
    },
    "serverInfo" : {
        "host" : "eoinbrazil-laptop-osx",
        "port" : 27017,
        "version" : "4.0.12",
        "gitVersion" : "5776e3cbf9e7afe86e6b29e22520ffb6766e95d4"
    },
    "ok" : 1
}
```

If you find that Mongo is using different indexes than you want it to for a query, you can force it to use a certain index by using hint. For instance, if you want to make sure MongoDB uses the {"username" : 1, "age" : 1} index on the previous query, you could say the following:

```
> db.users.find({"age" : 14, "username" : /.*/}).hint({"username" : 1, "age" : 1})
```

If a query is not using the index that you want it to and you use a hint to change it, run an explain on the hinted query before deploying. If you force MongoDB to use an index on a query that it does not know how to use an index for, you could end up making the query less efficient than it was without the index.

When Not to Index

Indexes are most effective at retrieving small subsets of data, and some types of queries are faster without indexes. Indexes become less and less efficient as you need to get larger percentages of a collection because using an index requires two lookups: one to look at the index entry and one following the index's pointer to the document. A collection scan only requires one: looking at the document. In the worst case (returning all of the documents in a collection) using an index would take twice as many lookups and would generally be significantly slower than a collection scan.

Unfortunately, there isn't a hard-and-fast rule about when an index helps and when it hinders as it really depends on the size of your data, indexes, documents, and average result set (Table 5-1). As a rule of thumb, an index often speeds things up if the query is returning 30% or more of the collection. However, this number can vary from 2% to 60%. Table 5-1 summarizes the conditions in which indexes or collection scans tend to work better.

Table 5-1. Properties that affect the effectiveness of indexes

Indexes often work well for	Collection scans often work well for
Large collections	Small collections
Large documents	Small documents
Selective queries	Nonselective queries

Let's say we have an analytics system that collects statistics. Our application queries the system for all documents for a given account to generate a nice graph of all data from an hour ago to the beginning of time:

```
> db.entries.find({"created_at" : {"$lt" : hourAgo}})
```

We index `"created_at"` to speed up this query.

When we first launch, the result set is tiny and the query returns instantly. But after a couple of weeks, it starts being a lot of data, and after a month this query is already taking too long to run.

For most applications, this is probably the "wrong" query: do you really want a query that's returning most of your dataset? Most applications, particularly those with large datasets, do not. However, there are some legitimate cases where you may want most or all of your data. For example, you might be exporting this data to a reporting system or using it for a batch job. In these cases, you would like to return this large proportion of the dataset as fast as possible.

Types of Indexes

There are a few index options you can specify when building an index that change the way the index behaves. The most common variations are described in the following sections, and more advanced or special-case options are described in the next chapter.

Unique Indexes

Unique indexes guarantee that each value will appear at most once in the index. For example, if you want to make sure no two documents can have the same value in the "username" key, you can create a unique index with a partialFilterExpression for only documents with a firstname field (more on this option later in the chapter):

```
> db.users.createIndex({"firstname" : 1},
... {"unique" : true, "partialFilterExpression":{
    "firstname": {$exists: true } } } )
{
    "createdCollectionAutomatically" : false,
    "numIndexesBefore" : 3,
    "numIndexesAfter" : 4,
    "ok" : 1
}
```

For example, suppose you tried to insert the following documents in the *users* collection:

```
> db.users.insert({firstname: "bob"})
WriteResult({ "nInserted" : 1 })
> db.users.insert({firstname: "bob"})
WriteResult({
  "nInserted" : 0,
  "writeError" : {
    "code" : 11000,
    "errmsg" : "E11000 duplicate key error collection: test.users index:
            firstname_1 dup key: { : \"bob\" }"
  }
})
```

If you check the collection, you'll see that only the first "bob" was stored. Throwing duplicate key exceptions is not very efficient, so use the unique constraint for the occasional duplicate, not to filter out zillions of duplicates a second.

A unique index that you are probably already familiar with is the index on "_id", which is automatically created whenever you create a collection. This is a normal unique index (aside from the fact that it cannot be dropped, as other unique indexes can be).

If a key does not exist, the index stores its value as null for that document. This means that if you create a unique index and try to insert more than one document that is missing the indexed field, the inserts will fail because you already have a document with a value of null. See "Partial Indexes" on page 128 for advice on handling this.

In some cases a value won't be indexed. Index buckets are of limited size and if an index entry exceeds it, it just won't be included in the index. This can cause confusion as it makes a document "invisible" to queries that use the index. Prior to MongoDB 4.2, a field was required to be smaller than 1,024 bytes to be included in an index. In MongoDB 4.2 and later, this constraint was removed. MongoDB does not return any sort of error or warning if a document's fields cannot be indexed due to size. This means that keys longer than 8 KB will not be subject to the unique index constraints: you can insert identical 8 KB strings, for example.

Compound unique indexes

You can also create a compound unique index. If you do this, individual keys can have the same values, but the combination of values across all keys in an index entry can appear in the index at most once.

For example, if we had a unique index on {"username" : 1, "age" : 1}, the following inserts would be legal:

```
> db.users.insert({"username" : "bob"})
> db.users.insert({"username" : "bob", "age" : 23})
> db.users.insert({"username" : "fred", "age" : 23})
```

However, attempting to insert a second copy of any of these documents would cause a duplicate key exception.

GridFS, the standard method for storing large files in MongoDB (see "Storing Files with GridFS" on page 156), uses a compound unique index. The collection that holds the file content has a unique index on {"files_id" : 1, "n" : 1}, which allows documents that look like (in part) the following:

```
{"files_id" : ObjectId("4b23c3ca7525f35f94b60a2d"), "n" : 1}
{"files_id" : ObjectId("4b23c3ca7525f35f94b60a2d"), "n" : 2}
{"files_id" : ObjectId("4b23c3ca7525f35f94b60a2d"), "n" : 3}
{"files_id" : ObjectId("4b23c3ca7525f35f94b60a2d"), "n" : 4}
```

Note that all of the values for "files_id" are the same, but "n" is different.

Dropping duplicates

If you attempt to build a unique index on an existing collection, it will fail to build if there are any duplicate values:

```
> db.users.createIndex({"age" : 1}, {"unique" : true})
WriteResult({
    "nInserted" : 0,
    "writeError" : {
        "code" : 11000,
        "errmsg" : "E11000 duplicate key error collection:
                   test.users index: age_1 dup key: { : 12 }"
    }
})
```

Generally, you'll need to process your data (the aggregation framework can help) and figure out where the duplicates are and what to do with them.

Partial Indexes

As mentioned in the previous section, unique indexes count `null` as a value, so you cannot have a unique index with more than one document missing the key. However, there are lots of cases where you may want the unique index to be enforced only if the key exists. If you have a field that may or may not exist but must be unique when it does, you can combine the `"unique"` option with the `"partial"` option.

 Partial indexes in MongoDB are only created on a subset of the data. This is unlike sparse indexes on relational databases, which create fewer index entries pointing to a block of data—however, all blocks of data will have an associated sparse index entry in RDBMS.

To create a partial index, include the `"partialFilterExpression"` option. Partial indexes represent a superset of the functionality offered by sparse indexes, with a document representing the filter expression you wish to create it on. For example, if providing an email address was optional but, if provided, should be unique, we could do:

```
> db.users.ensureIndex({"email" : 1}, {"unique" : true, "partialFilterExpression" :
... { email: { $exists: true } }})
```

Partial indexes do not necessarily have to be unique. To make a nonunique partial index, simply do not include the `"unique"` option.

One thing to be aware of is that the same query can return different results depending on whether or not it uses the partial index. For example, suppose we have a collection where most of the documents have `"x"` fields, but one does not:

```
> db.foo.find()
{ "_id" : 0 }
{ "_id" : 1, "x" : 1 }
{ "_id" : 2, "x" : 2 }
{ "_id" : 3, "x" : 3 }
```

When we do a query on "x", it will return all matching documents:

```
> db.foo.find({"x" : {"$ne" : 2}})
{ "_id" : 0 }
{ "_id" : 1, "x" : 1 }
{ "_id" : 3, "x" : 3 }
```

If we create a partial index on "x", the "_id" : 0 document won't be included in the index. So now if we query on "x", MongoDB will use the index and not return the {"_id" : 0} document:

```
> db.foo.find({"x" : {"$ne" : 2}})
{ "_id" : 1, "x" : 1 }
{ "_id" : 3, "x" : 3 }
```

You can use hint to force it to do a table scan if you need documents with missing fields.

Index Administration

As shown in the previous section, you can create new indexes using the createIndex function. An index only needs to be created once per collection. If you try to create the same index again, nothing will happen.

All of the information about a database's indexes is stored in the *system.indexes* collection. This is a reserved collection, so you cannot modify its documents or remove documents from it. You can manipulate it only through the createIndex, createIndexes, and dropIndexes database commands.

When you create an index, you can see its metainformation in *system.indexes*. You can also run db.*collectionName*.getIndexes() to see information about all the indexes on a given collection:

```
> db.students.getIndexes()
[
    {
        "v" : 2,
        "key" : {
            "_id" : 1
        },
        "name" : "_id_",
        "ns" : "school.students"
    },
    {
        "v" : 2,
        "key" : {
            "class_id" : 1
        },
        "name" : "class_id_1",
        "ns" : "school.students"
```

```
    },
    {
    "v" : 2,
    "key" : {
        "student_id" : 1,
        "class_id" : 1
    },
    "name" : "student_id_1_class_id_1",
    "ns" : "school.students"
    }
]
```

The important fields are "key" and "name". The key can be used for hinting and other places where an index must be specified. This is a place where field order matters: an index on {"class_id" : 1, "student_id" : 1} is not the same as an index on {"student_id" : 1, "class_id" : 1}. The index name is used as an identifier for a lot of administrative index operations, such as dropIndexes. Whether or not the index is multikey is not specified in its spec.

The "v" field is used internally for index versioning. If you have any indexes that do not have at least a "v" : 1 field, they are being stored in an older, less efficient format. You can upgrade them by ensuring that you're running at least MongoDB version 2.0 and dropping and rebuilding the indexes.

Identifying Indexes

Each index in a collection has a name that uniquely identifies that index and is used by the server to delete or manipulate it. Index names are, by default, *key name1_dir1_keyname2_dir2_..._keynameN_dirN*, where *keynameX* is the index's key and *dirX* is the index's direction (1 or -1). This can get unwieldy if indexes contain more than a couple of keys, so you can specify your own name as one of the options to createIndex:

```
> db.soup.createIndex({"a" : 1, "b" : 1, "c" : 1, ..., "z" : 1},
... {"name" : "alphabet"})
```

There is a limit to the number of characters in an index name, so complex indexes may need custom names to be created. A call to getLastError will show if the index creation succeeded or why it didn't.

Changing Indexes

As your application grows and changes, you may find that your data or queries have changed and that indexes that used to work well no longer do. You can remove unneeded indexes using the dropIndex command:

```
> db.people.dropIndex("x_1_y_1")
{ "nIndexesWas" : 3, "ok" : 1 }
```

Use the "name" field from the index description to specify which index to drop.

Building new indexes is time-consuming and resource-intensive. Prior to version 4.2, MongoDB will build an index as fast as possible, blocking all reads and writes on a database until the index build has finished. If you would like your database to remain somewhat responsive to reads and writes, use the "background" option when building an index. This forces the index build to occasionally yield to other operations, but may still have a severe impact on your application (see "Building Indexes" on page 283 for more information). Background indexing is also much slower than foreground indexing. MongoDB version 4.2 introduced a new approach, the hybrid index build. It only holds the exclusive lock at the beginning and end of the index build. The rest of the build process yields to interleaving read and write operations. This replaces both the foreground and the background index build type in MongoDB 4.2.

If you have the choice, creating indexes on existing documents is slightly faster than creating the index first and then inserting all documents.

There is more on the operational aspects of building indexes in Chapter 19.

## CHAPTER 6

Special Index and Collection Types

This chapter covers the special collections and index types MongoDB has available, including:

- Capped collections for queue-like data
- TTL indexes for caches
- Full-text indexes for simple string searching
- Geospatial indexes for 2D and spherical geometries
- GridFS for storing large files

Geospatial Indexes

MongoDB has two types of geospatial indexes: 2dsphere and 2d. 2dsphere indexes work with spherical geometries that model the surface of the earth based on the WGS84 datum. This datum models the surface of the earth as an oblate spheroid, meaning that there is some flattening at the poles. Distance calculations using 2sphere indexes, therefore, take the shape of the earth into account and provide a more accurate treatment of distance between, for example, two cities, than do 2d indexes. Use 2d indexes for points stored on a two-dimensional plane.

2dsphere allows you to specify geometries for points, lines, and polygons in the Geo-JSON format (*http://www.geojson.org/*). A point is given by a two-element array, representing [*longitude, latitude*]:

```
{
    "name" : "New York City",
    "loc" : {
        "type" : "Point",
        "coordinates" : [50, 2]
    }
}
```

A line is given by an array of points:

```
{
    "name" : "Hudson River",
    "loc" : {
        "type" : "LineString",
        "coordinates" : [[0,1], [0,2], [1,2]]
    }
}
```

A polygon is specified the same way a line is (an array of points), but with a different "type":

```
{
    "name" : "New England",
    "loc" : {
        "type" : "Polygon",
        "coordinates" : [[0,1], [0,2], [1,2]]
    }
}
```

The field that we are naming, "loc" in this example, can be called anything, but the field names in the embedded object are specified by GeoJSON and cannot be changed.

You can create a geospatial index using the "2dsphere" type with createIndex:

```
> db.openStreetMap.createIndex({"loc" : "2dsphere"})
```

To create a 2dsphere index, pass a document to createIndex that specifies the field containing geometries you want to index for the collection in question and specify "2dsphere" as the value.

Types of Geospatial Queries

There are three types of geospatial queries that you can perform: intersection, within, and nearness. You specify what you're looking for as a GeoJSON object that looks like {"$geometry" : geoJsonDesc}.

For example, you can find documents that intersect the query's location using the "$geoIntersects" operator:

```
> var eastVillage = {
... "type" : "Polygon",
... "coordinates" : [
... [
...     [ -73.9732566, 40.7187272 ],
...     [ -73.9724573, 40.7217745 ],
...     [ -73.9717144, 40.7250025 ],
...     [ -73.9714435, 40.7266002 ],
...     [ -73.975735, 40.7284702 ],
...     [ -73.9803565, 40.7304255 ],
...     [ -73.9825505, 40.7313605 ],
...     [ -73.9887732, 40.7339641 ],
...     [ -73.9907554, 40.7348137 ],
...     [ -73.9914581, 40.7317345 ],
...     [ -73.9919248, 40.7311674 ],
...     [ -73.9904979, 40.7305556 ],
...     [ -73.9907017, 40.7298849 ],
...     [ -73.9908171, 40.7297751 ],
...     [ -73.9911416, 40.7286592 ],
...     [ -73.9911943, 40.728492 ],
...     [ -73.9914313, 40.7277405 ],
...     [ -73.9914635, 40.7275759 ],
...     [ -73.9916003, 40.7271124 ],
...     [ -73.9915386, 40.727088 ],
...     [ -73.991788, 40.7263908 ],
...     [ -73.9920616, 40.7256489 ],
...     [ -73.9923298, 40.7248907 ],
...     [ -73.9925954, 40.7241427 ],
...     [ -73.9863029, 40.7222237 ],
...     [ -73.9787659, 40.719947 ],
...     [ -73.9772317, 40.7193229 ],
...     [ -73.9750886, 40.7188838 ],
...     [ -73.9732566, 40.7187272 ]
... ]
... ]}
> db.openStreetMap.find(
... {"loc" : {"$geoIntersects" : {"$geometry" : eastVillage}}})
```

This would find all point-, line-, and polygon-containing documents that had a point in the East Village in New York City.

You can use "$geoWithin" to query for things that are completely contained in an area (for instance, "What restaurants are in the East Village?"):

```
> db.openStreetMap.find({"loc" : {"$geoWithin" : {"$geometry" : eastVillage}}})
```

Unlike our first query, this will not return things that merely pass through the East Village (such as streets) or partially overlap it (such as a polygon describing Manhattan).

Finally, you can query for nearby locations with `"$near"`:

```
> db.openStreetMap.find({"loc" : {"$near" : {"$geometry" : eastVillage}}})
```

Note that `"$near"` is the only geospatial operator that implies a sort: results from `"$near"` are always returned in order of distance, from closest to farthest.

Using Geospatial Indexes

MongoDB's geospatial indexing allows you to efficiently execute spatial queries on a collection that contains geospatial shapes and points. To showcase the capabilities of geospatial features and compare different approaches, we will go through the process of writing queries for a simple geospatial application. We'll go a little deeper into a few concepts central to geospatial indexes and then demonstrate their use with `"$geo Within"`, `"$geoIntersects"`, and `"$geoNear"`.

Suppose we are designing a mobile application to help users find restaurants in New York City. The application must:

- Determine the neighborhood the user is currently in.

- Show the number of restaurants in that neighborhood.

- Find restaurants within a specified distance.

We will use a `2dsphere` index to query on this spherical geometry data.

2D versus spherical geometry in queries

Geospatial queries can use either spherical or 2D (flat) geometries, depending on both the query and the type of index in use. Table 6-1 shows what kind of geometry each geospatial operator uses.

Table 6-1. Query types and geometries in MongoDB

Query type	Geometry type
$near (GeoJSON point, 2dsphere index)	Spherical
$near (legacy coordinates, 2d index)	Flat
$geoNear (GeoJSON point, 2dsphere index)	Spherical
$geoNear (legacy coordinates, 2d index)	Flat
$nearSphere (GeoJSON point, 2dsphere index)	Spherical
$nearSphere (legacy coordinates, 2d index)[a]	Spherical
$geoWithin : { $geometry: ... }	Spherical

Query type	Geometry type
$geoWithin: { $box: ... }	Flat
$geoWithin: { $polygon: ... }	Flat
$geoWithin : { $center: ... }	Flat
$geoWithin : { $centerSphere: ... }	Spherical
$geoIntersects	Spherical

^a Use GeoJSON points instead.

Note also that 2d indexes support both flat geometries and distance-only calculations on spheres (i.e., using $nearSphere). However, queries using spherical geometries will be more performant and accurate with a 2dsphere index.

Note also that the $geoNear operator is an aggregation operator. The aggregation framework is discussed in Chapter 7. In addition to the $near query operation, the $geoNear aggregation operator and the special command geoNear enable us to query for nearby locations. Keep in mind that the $near query operator will not work on collections that are distributed using sharding, MongoDB's scaling solution (see Chapter 15).

The geoNear command and the $geoNear aggregation operator require that a collection have at most one 2dsphere index and at most one 2d index, whereas geospatial query operators (e.g., $near and $geoWithin) permit collections to have multiple geospatial indexes.

The geospatial index restriction for the geoNear command and the $geoNear aggregation operator exists because neither the geoNear command nor the $geoNear syntax includes the location field. As such, index selection among multiple 2d indexes or 2dsphere indexes is ambiguous.

No such restriction applies for geospatial query operators; these operators take a location field, eliminating the ambiguity.

Distortion

Spherical geometry will appear distorted when visualized on a map due to the nature of projecting a three-dimensional sphere, such as the earth, onto a flat plane.

For example, take the specification of the spherical square defined by the longitude, latitude points (0,0), (80,0), (80,80), and (0,80). Figure 6-1 depicts the area covered by this region.

Figure 6-1. The spherical square defined by the points (0,0), (80,0), (80, 80), and (0,80)

Searching for restaurants

In this example, we will work with neighborhood (*https://oreil.ly/rpGna*) and restaurant (*https://oreil.ly/JXYd-*) datasets based in New York City. You can download the example datasets from GitHub.

We can import the datasets into our database using the `mongoimport` tool as follows:

```
$ mongoimport <path to neighborhoods.json> -c neighborhoods
$ mongoimport <path to restaurants.json> -c restaurants
```

We can create a 2dsphere index on each collection using the createIndex command in the *mongo* shell (*https://oreil.ly/NMUhn*):

```
> db.neighborhoods.createIndex({location:"2dsphere"})
> db.restaurants.createIndex({location:"2dsphere"})
```

Exploring the data

We can get a sense for the schema used for documents in these collections with a couple of quick queries in the *mongo* shell:

```
> db.neighborhoods.find({name: "Clinton"})
{
  "_id": ObjectId("55cb9c666c522cafdb053a4b"),
  "geometry": {
    "coordinates": [
      [
        [-73.99,40.77],
        .

        .
        .

        [-73.99,40.77],
        [-73.99,40.77]]
      ]
    ],
    "type": "Polygon"
  },
  "name": "Clinton"
}

> db.restaurants.find({name: "Little Pie Company"})
{
  "_id": ObjectId("55cba2476c522cafdb053dea"),
  "location": {
    "coordinates": [
      -73.99331699999999,
      40.7594404
    ],
    "type": "Point"
  },
  "name": "Little Pie Company"
}
```

The neighborhood document in the previous code corresponds to the area of New York City shown in Figure 6-2.

Figure 6-2. The Hell's Kitchen (Clinton) neighborhood of New York City

The bakery corresponds to the location shown in Figure 6-3.

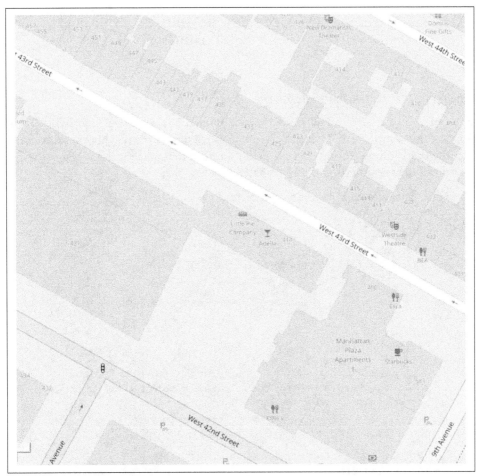

Figure 6-3. The Little Pie Company at 424 West 43rd Street

Finding the current neighborhood

Assuming the user's mobile device can give a reasonably accurate location user, it is simple to find the user's current neighborhood with $geoIntersects.

Suppose the user is located at −73.93414657 longitude and 40.82302903 latitude. To find the current neighborhood (Hell's Kitchen), we can specify a point using the special $geometry field in GeoJSON format:

```
> db.neighborhoods.findOne({geometry:{$geoIntersects:{$geometry:{type:"Point",
... coordinates:[-73.93414657,40.82302903]}}}})
```

This query will return the following result:

```
{
  "_id":ObjectId("55cb9c666c522cafdb053a68"),
```

```
    "geometry":{
      "type":"Polygon",
      "coordinates":[[[-73.93383000695911,40.81949109558767],...]]},
      "name":"Central Harlem North-Polo Grounds"
}
```

Finding all restaurants in the neighborhood

We can also query to find all restaurants contained in a given neighborhood. To do
so, we can execute the following in the *mongo* shell to find the neighborhood containing the user, and then count the restaurants within that neighborhood. For example,
to find all the restaurants in the Hell's Kitchen neighborhood:

```
> var neighborhood = db.neighborhoods.findOne({
  geometry: {
    $geoIntersects: {
      $geometry: {
        type: "Point",
        coordinates: [-73.93414657,40.82302903]
      }
    }
  }
});

> db.restaurants.find({
    location: {
      $geoWithin: {
        // Use the geometry from the neighborhood object we retrieved above
        $geometry: neighborhood.geometry
      }
    }
  },
  // Project just the name of each matching restaurant
  {name: 1, _id: 0});
```

This query will tell you that there are 127 restaurants in the requested neighborhood
that have the following names:

```
{
  "name": "White Castle"
}
{
  "name": "Touch Of Dee'S"
}
{
  "name": "Mcdonald'S"
}
{
  "name": "Popeyes Chicken & Biscuits"
}
{
  "name": "Make My Cake"
```

```
  }
  {
    "name": "Manna Restaurant Ii"
  }
  ...
  {
    "name": "Harlem Coral Llc"
  }
```

Finding restaurants within a distance

To find restaurants within a specified distance of a point, you can use either "$geoWi
thin" with "$centerSphere" to return results in unsorted order, or "$nearSphere"
with "$maxDistance" if you need results sorted by distance.

To find restaurants within a circular region, use "$geoWithin" with "$center
Sphere". "$centerSphere" is a MongoDB-specific syntax to denote a circular region
by specifying the center and the radius in radians. "$geoWithin" does not return the
documents in any specific order, so it might return the furthest documents first.

The following will find all restaurants within five miles of the user:

```
> db.restaurants.find({
  location: {
    $geoWithin: {
      $centerSphere: [
        [-73.93414657,40.82302903],
        5/3963.2
      ]
    }
  }
})
```

"$centerSphere"'s second argument accepts the radius in radians. The query con-
verts the distance to radians by dividing by the approximate equatorial radius of the
earth, 3963.2 miles.

Applications can use "$centerSphere" without having a geospatial index. However,
geospatial indexes support much faster queries than the unindexed equivalents. Both
2dsphere and 2d geospatial indexes support "$centerSphere".

You may also use "$nearSphere" and specify a "$maxDistance" term in meters. This
will return all restaurants within five miles of the user in sorted order from nearest to
farthest:

```
> var METERS_PER_MILE = 1609.34;
db.restaurants.find({
  location: {
    $nearSphere: {
      $geometry: {
        type: "Point",
```

```
      coordinates: [-73.93414657,40.82302903]
    },
    $maxDistance: 5*METERS_PER_MILE
  }
 }
});
```

Compound Geospatial Indexes

As with other types of indexes, you can combine geospatial indexes with other fields
to optimize more complex queries. A possible query mentioned earlier was: "What
restaurants are in Hell's Kitchen?" Using only a geospatial index, we could narrow the
field to everything in Hell's Kitchen, but narrowing it down to only "restaurants" or
"pizza" would require another field in the index:

```
> db.openStreetMap.createIndex({"tags" : 1, "location" : "2dsphere"})
```

Then we can quickly find a pizza place in Hell's Kitchen:

```
> db.openStreetMap.find({"loc" : {"$geoWithin" :
... {"$geometry" : hellsKitchen.geometry}},
... "tags" : "pizza"})
```

We can have the "vanilla" index field either before or after the "2dsphere" field,
depending on whether we'd like to filter by the vanilla field or the location first.
Choose whichever is more selective (i.e., will filter out more results as the first index
term).

2d Indexes

For nonspherical maps (videogame maps, time series data, etc.) you can use a "2d"
index instead of "2dsphere":

```
> db.hyrule.createIndex({"tile" : "2d"})
```

2d indexes assume a perfectly flat surface, instead of a sphere. Thus, 2d indexes
should not be used with spheres unless you don't mind massive distortion around the
poles.

Documents should use a two-element array for their "2d" indexed field. The elements
in this array should reflect the longitude and lattitude coordinates, respectively. A
sample document might look like this:

```
{
    "name" : "Water Temple",
    "tile" : [ 32, 22 ]
}
```

Do not use a 2d index if you plan to store GeoJSON data—they can only index points.
You can store an array of points, but it will be stored as exactly that: an array of

---

points, not a line. This is an important distinction for `"$geoWithin"` queries, in particular. If you store a street as an array of points, the document will match `"$geoWithin"` if one of those points is within the given shape. However, the line created by those points might not be wholly contained in the shape.

By default, 2d indexes assume that your values are going to range from −180 to 180. If you are expecting larger or smaller bounds, you can specify what the minimum and maximum values will be as options to `createIndex`:

```
> db.hyrule.createIndex({"light-years" : "2d"}, {"min" : -1000, "max" : 1000})
```

This will create a spatial index calibrated for a 2,000 × 2,000 square.

2d indexes support the `"$geoWithin"`, `"$nearSphere"`, and `"$near"` query selectors. Use `"$geoWithin"` to query for points within a shape defined on a flat surface. `"$geoWithin"` can query for all points within a rectangle, polygon, circle, or sphere; it uses the `"$geometry"` operator to specify the GeoJSON object. Returning to our grid indexed as follows:

```
> db.hyrule.createIndex({"tile" : "2d"})
```

the following queries for documents within a rectangle defined by [10, 10] at the bottom-left corner and by [100, 100] at the top-right corner:

```
> db.hyrule.find({
    tile: {
      $geoWithin: {
        $box: [[10, 10], [100, 100]]
      }
    }
})
```

`$box` takes a two-element array: the first element specifies the coordinates of the lower-left corner and the second element the upper right.

To query for documents that are within the circle centered on [−17 , 20.5] and with a radius of 25 we can issue the following command:

```
> db.hyrule.find({
    tile: {
      $geoWithin: {
        $center: [[-17, 20.5] , 25]
      }
    }
})
```

The following query returns all documents with coordinates that exist within the polygon defined by [0, 0], [3, 6], and [6 , 0]:

```
> db.hyrule.find({
    tile: {
      $geoWithin: {
```

```
        $polygon: [[0, 0], [3, 6], [6, 0]]
      }
    }
})
```

You specify a polygon as an array of points. The final point in the list will be "connected to" the first point to form the polygon. This example would locate all documents containing points within the given triangle.

MongoDB also supports rudimentary spherical queries on flat 2d indexes for legacy reasons. In general, spherical calculations should use a 2dsphere index, as described in "2D versus spherical geometry in queries" on page 136. However, to query for legacy coordinate pairs within a sphere, use "$geoWithin" with the "$centerSphere" operator. Specify an array that contains:

- The grid coordinates of the circle's center point
- The circle's radius measured in radians

For example:

```
> db.hyrule.find({
    loc: {
      $geoWithin: {
        $centerSphere: [[88, 30], 10/3963.2]
      }
    }
})
```

To query for nearby points, use "$near". Proximity queries return the documents with coordinate pairs closest to the defined point and sort the results by distance. This finds all of the documents in the *hyrule* collection in order by distance from the point (20, 21):

```
> db.hyrule.find({"tile" : {"$near" : [20, 21]}})
```

A default limit of 100 documents is applied if no limit is specified. If you don't need that many results, you should set a limit to conserve server resources. For example, the following code returns the 10 documents nearest to (20, 21):

```
> db.hyrule.find({"tile" : {"$near" : [20, 21]}}).limit(10)
```

Indexes for Full Text Search

text indexes in MongoDB support full-text search requirements. This type of text index should not be confused with the MongoDB Atlas Full-Text Search Indexes, which utilize Apache Lucene for additional text search capabilities when compared to MongoDB text indexes. Use a text index if your application needs to enable users to submit keyword queries that should match titles, descriptions, and text in other fields within a collection.

In previous chapters, we've queried for strings using exact matches and regular expressions, but these techniques have some limitations. Searching a large block of text for a regular expression is slow, and it's tough to take morphology (e.g., that "entry" should match "entries") and other challenges presented by human language into account. text indexes give you the ability to search text quickly and provide support for common search engine requirements such as language-appropriate tokenization, stop words, and stemming.

text indexes require a number of keys proportional to the words in the fields being indexed. As a consequence, creating a text index can consume a large amount of system resources. You should create such an index at a time when it will not negatively impact the performance of your application for users or build the index in the background, if possible. To ensure good performance, as with all indexes, you should also take care that any text index you create fits in RAM. See Chapter 19 for more information on creating indexes with minimal impact on your application.

Writes to a collection require that all indexes are updated. If you are using text search, strings will be tokenized and stemmed and the index updated in, potentially, many places. For this reason, writes involving text indexes are usually more expensive than writes to single-field, compound, or even multikey indexes. Thus, you will tend to see poorer write performance on text-indexed collections than on others. They will also slow down data movement if you are sharding: all text must be reindexed when it is migrated to a new shard.

Creating a Text Index

Suppose we have a collection of Wikipedia articles that we want to index. To run a search over the text, we first need to create a text index. The following call to crea teIndex will create the index based on the terms in both the "title" and "body" fields:

```
> db.articles.createIndex({"title": "text",
                           "body" : "text"})
```

This is not like a "normal" compound index where there is an ordering on the keys. By default, each field is given equal consideration in a text index. You can control the relative importance MongoDB attaches to each field by specifying weights:

```
> db.articles.createIndex({"title": "text",
                           "body": "text"},
                          {"weights" : {
                               "title" : 3,
                               "body" : 2}})
```

This would weight the "title" field at a ratio of 3:2 in comparison to the "body" field.

You cannot change field weights after index creation (without dropping the index and recreating it), so you may want to play with weights on a sample dataset before creating the index on your production data.

For some collections, you may not know which fields a document will contain. You can create a full-text index on all string fields in a document by creating an index on "$**"—this not only indexes all top-level string fields, but also searches embedded documents and arrays for string fields:

```
> db.articles.createIndex({"$**" : "text"})
```

Text Search

Use the "$text" query operator to perform text searches on a collection with a text index. "$text" will tokenize the search string using whitespace and most punctuation as delimiters, and perform a logical OR of all such tokens in the search string. For example, you could use the following query to find all articles containing any of the terms "impact," "crater," or "lunar." Note that because our index is based on terms in both the title and body of an article, this query will match documents in which those terms are found in either field. For the purposes of this example, we will project the title so that we can fit more results on the page:

```
> db.articles.find({"$text": {"$search": "impact crater lunar"}},
                   {title: 1}
                   ).limit(10)
{ "_id" : "170375", "title" : "Chengdu" }
{ "_id" : "34331213", "title" : "Avengers vs. X-Men" }
{ "_id" : "498834", "title" : "Culture of Tunisia" }
{ "_id" : "602564", "title" : "ABC Warriors" }
{ "_id" : "40255", "title" : "Jupiter (mythology)" }
{ "_id" : "80356", "title" : "History of Vietnam" }
{ "_id" : "22483", "title" : "Optics" }
{ "_id" : "8919057", "title" : "Characters in The Legend of Zelda series" }
{ "_id" : "20767983", "title" : "First inauguration of Barack Obama" }
{ "_id" : "17845285", "title" : "Kushiel's Mercy" }
```

You can see that the results with our initial query are not terribly relevant. As with all technologies, it's important to have a good grasp of how text indexes work in MongoDB in order to use them effectively. In this case, there are two problems with the way we've issued the query. The first is that our query is pretty broad, given that MongoDB issues the query using a logical OR of "impact," "crater," and "lunar." The second problem is that, by default, a text search does not sort the results by relevance.

We can begin to address the problem of the query itself by using a phrase in our query. You can search for exact phrases by wrapping them in double quotes. For example, the following will find all documents containing the phrase "impact crater." Possibly surprising is that MongoDB will issue this query as "impact crater" AND "lunar":

```
> db.articles.find({$text: {$search: "\"impact crater\" lunar"}},
                    {title: 1}
                    ).limit(10)
{ "_id" : "2621724", "title" : "Schjellerup (crater)" }
{ "_id" : "2622075", "title" : "Steno (lunar crater)" }
{ "_id" : "168118", "title" : "South Pole-Aitken basin" }
{ "_id" : "1509118", "title" : "Jackson (crater)" }
{ "_id" : "10096822", "title" : "Victoria Island structure" }
{ "_id" : "968071", "title" : "Buldhana district" }
{ "_id" : "780422", "title" : "Puchezh-Katunki crater" }
{ "_id" : "28088964", "title" : "Svedberg (crater)" }
{ "_id" : "780628", "title" : "Zeleny Gai crater" }
{ "_id" : "926711", "title" : "Fracastorius (crater)" }
```

To make sure the semantics of this are clear, let's look at an expanded example. For the following query, MongoDB will issue the query as "impact crater" AND ("lunar" OR "meteor"). MongoDB performs a logical AND of the phrase with the individual terms in the search string and a logical OR of the individual terms with one another:

```
> db.articles.find({$text: {$search: "\"impact crater\" lunar meteor"}},
                    {title: 1}
                    ).limit(10)
```

If you want to issue a logical AND between individual terms in a query, treat each term as a phrase by wrapping it in quotes. The following query will return documents containing "impact crater" AND "lunar" AND "meteor":

```
> db.articles.find({$text: {$search: "\"impact crater\" \"lunar\" \"meteor\""}},
                    {title: 1}
                    ).limit(10)
{ "_id" : "168118", "title" : "South Pole-Aitken basin" }
{ "_id" : "330593", "title" : "Giordano Bruno (crater)" }
{ "_id" : "421051", "title" : "Opportunity (rover)" }
{ "_id" : "2693649", "title" : "Pascal Lee" }
{ "_id" : "275128", "title" : "Tektite" }
{ "_id" : "14594455", "title" : "Beethoven quadrangle" }
{ "_id" : "266344", "title" : "Space debris" }
{ "_id" : "2137763", "title" : "Wegener (lunar crater)" }
{ "_id" : "929164", "title" : "Dawes (lunar crater)" }
{ "_id" : "24944", "title" : "Plate tectonics" }
```

Now that you have a better understanding of using phrases and logical ANDs in your queries, let's return to the problem of the results not being sorted by relevance. While the preceding results are certainly relevant, this is mostly due to the fairly strict query we've issued. We can do better by sorting for relevance.

Text queries cause some metadata to be associated with each query result. The metadata is not displayed in the query results unless we explicitly project it using the $meta operator. So, in addition to the title, we will project the relevance score calculated for each document. The relevance score is stored in the metadata field named "textScore". For this example, we'll return to our query of "impact crater" AND "lunar":

```
> db.articles.find({$text: {$search: "\"impact crater\" lunar"}},
                   {title: 1, score: {$meta: "textScore"}}
                   ).limit(10)
{"_id": "2621724", "title": "Schjellerup (crater)", "score": 2.852987132352941}
{"_id": "2622075", "title": "Steno (lunar crater)", "score": 2.4766639610389607}
{"_id": "168118", "title": "South Pole-Aitken basin", "score": 2.980198136295181}
{"_id": "1509118", "title": "Jackson (crater)", "score": 2.3419137286324787}
{"_id": "10096822", "title": "Victoria Island structure",
 "score": 1.782051282051282}
{"_id": "968071", "title": "Buldhana district", "score": 1.6279783393501805}
{"_id": "780422", "title": "Puchezh-Katunki crater", "score": 1.9295977011494254}
{"_id": "28088964", "title": "Svedberg (crater)", "score": 2.497767857142857}
{"_id": "780628", "title": "Zeleny Gai crater", "score": 1.4866071428571428}
{"_id": "926711", "title": "Fracastorius (crater)", "score": 2.7511877111486487}
```

Now you can see the relevance score projected with the title for each result. Note that they are not sorted. To sort the results in order of relevance score, we must add a call to sort, again using $meta to specify the "textScore" field value. Note that we must use the same field name in our sort as we used in our projection. In this case, we used the field name "score" for the relevance score value displayed in our search results. As you can see, the results are now sorted in decreasing order of relevance:

```
> db.articles.find({$text: {$search: "\"impact crater\" lunar"}},
                   {title: 1, score: {$meta: "textScore"}}
                   ).sort({score: {$meta: "textScore"}}).limit(10)
{"_id": "1621514", "title": "Lunar craters", "score": 3.1655242042922014}
{"_id": "14580008", "title": "Kuiper quadrangle", "score": 3.0847527829208814}
{"_id": "1019830", "title": "Shackleton (crater)", "score": 3.076471119932001}
{"_id": "2096232", "title": "Geology of the Moon", "score": 3.064981949458484}
{"_id": "927269", "title": "Messier (crater)", "score": 3.0638183133686008}
{"_id": "206589", "title": "Lunar geologic timescale", "score": 3.062029540854157}
{"_id": "14536060", "title": "Borealis quadrangle", "score": 3.0573010719646687}
{"_id": "14609586", "title": "Michelangelo quadrangle",
 "score": 3.057224063486582}
{"_id": "14568465", "title": "Shakespeare quadrangle",
 "score": 3.0495256481056443}
{"_id": "275128", "title": "Tektite", "score" : 3.0378807169646915}
```

Text search is also available in the aggregation pipeline. We discuss the aggregation pipeline in Chapter 7.

Optimizing Full-Text Search

There are a couple of ways to optimize full-text searches. If you can first narrow your search results by other criteria, you can create a compound index with a prefix of those criteria and then the full-text fields:

```
> db.blog.createIndex({"date" : 1, "post" : "text"})
```

This is referred to as *partitioning* the full-text index, as it breaks it into several smaller trees based on `"date"` (in this example). This makes full-text searches for a specific date or date range much faster.

You can also use a postfix of other criteria to cover queries with the index. For example, if we were only returning the `"author"` and `"post"` fields, we could create a compound index on both:

```
> db.blog.createIndex({"post" : "text", "author" : 1})
```

These prefix and postfix forms can be combined:

```
> db.blog.createIndex({"date" : 1, "post" : "text", "author" : 1})
```

Searching in Other Languages

When a document is inserted (or the index is first created), MongoDB looks at the index's fields and stems each word, reducing it to an essential unit. However, different languages stem words in different ways, so you must specify what language the index or document is in. `text` indexes allow a `"default_language"` option to be specified, which defaults to `"english"` but can be set to a number of other languages (see the online documentation (*https://oreil.ly/eUt0Z*) for an up-to-date list).

For example, to create a French-language index, we could say:

```
> db.users.createIndex({"profil" : "text",
                         "intérêts" : "text"},
                        {"default_language" : "french"})
```

Then French would be used for stemming, unless otherwise specified. You can, on a per-document basis, specify another stemming language by having a `"language"` field that describes the document's language:

```
> db.users.insert({"username" : "swedishChef",
... "profile" : "Bork de bork", language : "swedish"})
```

Capped Collections

"Normal" collections in MongoDB are created dynamically and automatically grow in size to fit additional data. MongoDB also supports a different type of collection, called a *capped collection*, which is created in advance and is fixed in size (see Figure 6-4).

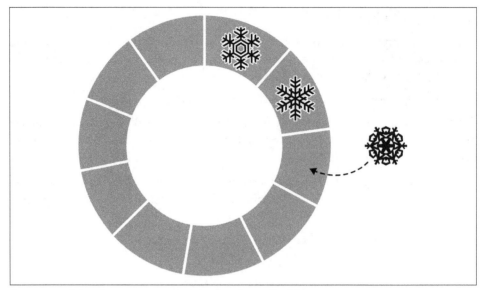

Figure 6-4. New documents are inserted at the end of the queue

Having fixed-size collections brings up an interesting question: what happens when we try to insert into a capped collection that is already full? The answer is that capped collections behave like circular queues: if we're out of space, the oldest document will be deleted, and the new one will take its place (see Figure 6-5). This means that capped collections automatically age out the oldest documents as new documents are inserted.

Certain operations are not allowed on capped collections. Documents cannot be removed or deleted (aside from the automatic age-out described earlier), and updates that would cause documents to grow in size are disallowed. By preventing these two operations, we guarantee that documents in a capped collection are stored in insertion order and that there is no need to maintain a free list for space from removed documents.

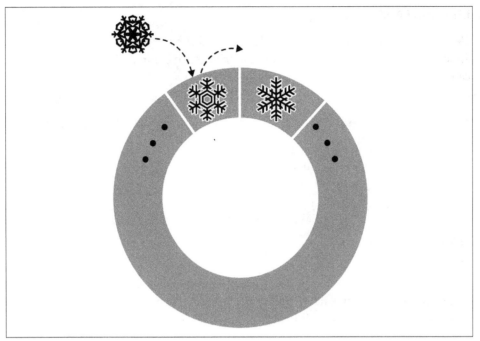

Figure 6-5. When the queue is full, the oldest element will be replaced by the newest

Capped collections have a different access pattern than most MongoDB collections: data is written sequentially over a fixed section of disk. This makes them tend to perform writes quickly on spinning disks, especially if they can be given their own disk (so as not to be "interrupted" by other collections' random writes).

In general, MongoDB TTL indexes are recommended over capped collections because they perform better with the WiredTiger storage engine. TTL indexes expire and remove data from normal collections based on the value of a date-typed field and a TTL value for the index. These are covered in more depth later in this chapter.

 Capped collections cannot be sharded. If an update or a replacement operation changes the document size in a capped collection, the operation will fail.

Capped collections tend to be useful for logging, although they lack flexibility: you cannot control when data ages out, other than setting a size when you create the collection.

Creating Capped Collections

Unlike normal collections, capped collections must be explicitly created before they are used. To create a capped collection, use the `create` command. From the shell, this can be done using `createCollection`:

```
> db.createCollection("my_collection", {"capped" : true, "size" : 100000});
```

The previous command creates a capped collection, *my_collection*, that has a fixed size of 100,000 bytes.

`createCollection` can also specify a limit on the number of documents in a capped collection:

```
> db.createCollection("my_collection2",
                      {"capped" : true, "size" : 100000, "max" : 100});
```

You could use this to keep, say, the latest 10 news articles or limit a user to 1,000 documents.

Once a capped collection has been created, it cannot be changed (it must be dropped and recreated if you wish to change its properties). Thus, you should think carefully about the size of a large collection before creating it.

> When limiting the number of documents in a capped collection, you must specify a size limit as well. Age-out will be based on whichever limit is reached first: it can neither hold more than `"max"` documents nor take up more than `"size"` space.

Another option for creating a capped collection is to convert an existing regular collection into a capped collection. This can be done using the `convertToCapped` command—in the following example, we convert the *test* collection to a capped collection of 10,000 bytes:

```
> db.runCommand({"convertToCapped" : "test", "size" : 10000});
{ "ok" : true }
```

There is no way to "uncap" a capped collection (other than dropping it).

Tailable Cursors

Tailable cursors are a special type of cursor that are not closed when their results are exhausted. They were inspired by the `tail -f` command and, similar to that command, will continue fetching output for as long as possible. Because the cursors do not die when they run out of results, they can continue to fetch new results as documents are added to the collection. Tailable cursors can be used only on capped collections, since insert order is not tracked for normal collections. For the vast majority of uses, change streams, covered in Chapter 16, are recommended over tailable cursors as they offer vastly more control and configuration plus they work with normal collections.

Tailable cursors are often used for processing documents as they are inserted onto a "work queue" (the capped collection). Because tailable cursors will time out after 10 minutes of no results, it is important to include logic to requery the collection if they die. The *mongo* shell does not allow you to use tailable cursors, but using one in PHP looks something like the following:

```php
$cursor = $collection->find([], [
    'cursorType' => MongoDB\Operation\Find::TAILABLE_AWAIT,
    'maxAwaitTimeMS' => 100,
]);


while (true) {
    if ($iterator->valid()) {
        $document = $iterator->current();
        printf("Consumed document created at: %s\n", $document->createdAt);
    }

    $iterator->next();
}
```

The cursor will process results or wait for more results to arrive until it times out or someone kills the query operation.

Time-To-Live Indexes

As mentioned in the previous section, capped collections give you limited control over when their contents are overwritten. If you need a more flexible age-out system, TTL indexes allow you to set a timeout for each document. When a document reaches a preconfigured age, it will be deleted. This type of index is useful for caching use cases such as session storage.

You can create a TTL index by specifying the "expireAfterSeconds" option in the second argument to createIndex:

```
> // 24-hour timeout
> db.sessions.createIndex({"lastUpdated" : 1}, {"expireAfterSeconds" : 60*60*24})
```

This creates a TTL index on the "lastUpdated" field. If a document's "lastUpdated" field exists and is a date, the document will be removed once the server time is "expireAfterSeconds" seconds ahead of the document's time.

To prevent an active session from being removed, you can update the "lastUpdated" field to the current time whenever there is activity. Once "lastUpdated" is 24 hours old, the document will be removed.

MongoDB sweeps the TTL index once per minute, so you should not depend on to-the-second granularity. You can change the "expireAfterSeconds" using the coll Mod command:

```
> db.runCommand( {"collMod" : "someapp.cache" , "index" : { "keyPattern" :
... {"lastUpdated" : 1} , "expireAfterSeconds" : 3600 } } );
```

You can have multiple TTL indexes on a given collection. They cannot be compound indexes but can be used like "normal" indexes for the purposes of sorting and query optimization.

Storing Files with GridFS

GridFS is a mechanism for storing large binary files in MongoDB. There are several reasons why you might consider using GridFS for file storage:

- Using GridFS can simplify your stack. If you're already using MongoDB, you might be able to use GridFS instead of a separate tool for file storage.

- GridFS will leverage any existing replication or autosharding that you've set up for MongoDB, so getting failover and scale-out for file storage is easier.

- GridFS can alleviate some of the issues that certain filesystems can exhibit when being used to store user uploads. For example, GridFS does not have issues with storing large numbers of files in the same directory.

There are some downsides, too:

- Performance is slower. Accessing files from MongoDB will not be as fast as going directly through the filesystem.

- You can only modify documents by deleting them and resaving the whole thing. MongoDB stores files as multiple documents, so it cannot lock all of the chunks in a file at the same time.

GridFS is generally best when you have large files you'll be accessing in a sequential fashion that won't be changing much.

Getting Started with GridFS: mongofiles

The easiest way to try out GridFS is by using the *mongofiles* utility. *mongofiles* is included with all MongoDB distributions and can be used to upload, download, list, search for, or delete files in GridFS.

As with any of the other command-line tools, run mongofiles --help to see the options available for *mongofiles*.

The following session shows how to use *mongofiles* to upload a file from the filesystem to GridFS, list all of the files in GridFS, and download a file that we've previously uploaded:

```
$ echo "Hello, world" > foo.tx
$ mongofiles put foo.txt
2019-10-30T10:12:06.588+0000  connected to: localhost
2019-10-30T10:12:06.588+0000  added file: foo.txt
$  mongofiles list
2019-10-30T10:12:41.603+0000  connected to: localhost
foo.txt 13
$ rm foo.txt
$ mongofiles get foo.txt
2019-10-30T10:13:23.948+0000  connected to: localhost
2019-10-30T10:13:23.955+0000  finished writing to foo.txt
$ cat foo.txt
Hello, world
```

In the previous example, we perform three basic operations using *mongofiles*: put, list, and get. The put operation takes a file in the filesystem and adds it to GridFS. list will list any files that have been added to GridFS. get does the inverse of put: it takes a file from GridFS and writes it to the filesystem. *mongofiles* also supports two other operations: search for finding files in GridFS by filename and delete for removing a file from GridFS.

Working with GridFS from the MongoDB Drivers

All the client libraries have GridFS APIs. For example, with PyMongo (the Python driver for MongoDB) you can perform the same series of operations (this assumes Python 3 and a locally running *mongod* on port 27017) as we did with *mongofiles* as follows:

```
>>> import pymongo
>>> import gridfs
>>> client = pymongo.MongoClient()
>>> db = client.test
>>> fs = gridfs.GridFS(db)
>>> file_id = fs.put(b"Hello, world", filename="foo.txt")
>>> fs.list()
['foo.txt']
>>> fs.get(file_id).read()
b'Hello, world'
```

The API for working with GridFS from PyMongo is very similar to that of *mongofiles*: you can easily perform the basic put, get, and list operations. Almost all the MongoDB drivers follow this basic pattern for working with GridFS, while often exposing more advanced functionality as well. For driver-specific information on GridFS, please check out the documentation for the specific driver you're using.

Under the Hood

GridFS is a lightweight specification for storing files that is built on top of normal MongoDB documents. The MongoDB server actually does almost nothing to "special-case" the handling of GridFS requests; all the work is handled by the client-side drivers and tools.

The basic idea behind GridFS is that we can store large files by splitting them up into *chunks* and storing each chunk as a separate document. Because MongoDB supports storing binary data in documents, we can keep the storage overhead for chunks to a minimum. In addition to storing each chunk of a file, we store a single document that groups the chunks together and contains metadata about the file.

The chunks for GridFS are stored in their own collection. By default chunks will use the collection *fs.chunks*, but this can be overridden. Within the chunks collection the structure of the individual documents is pretty simple:

```
{
    "_id" : ObjectId("..."),
    "n" : 0,
    "data" : BinData("..."),
    "files_id" : ObjectId("...")
}
```

Like any other MongoDB document, a chunk has its own unique "_id". In addition, it has a couple of other keys:

"files_id"
: The "_id" of the file document that contains the metadata for the file this chunk is from

"n"
: The chunk's position in the file, relative to the other chunks

"data"
: The bytes in this chunk of the file

The metadata for each file is stored in a separate collection, which defaults to *fs.files*. Each document in the files collection represents a single file in GridFS and can contain any custom metadata that should be associated with that file. In addition to any user-defined keys, there are a couple of keys that are mandated by the GridFS specification:

"_id"
: A unique ID for the file—this is what will be stored in each chunk as the value for the "files_id" key.

"length"

The total number of bytes making up the content of the file.

"chunkSize"

The size of each chunk comprising the file, in bytes. The default is 255 KB, but this can be adjusted if needed.

"uploadDate"

A timestamp representing when this file was stored in GridFS.

"md5"

An MD5 checksum of this file's contents, generated on the server side.

Of all the required keys, perhaps the most interesting (or least self-explanatory) is "md5". The value for "md5" is generated by the MongoDB server using the filemd5 command, which computes the MD5 checksum of the uploaded chunks. This means that users can check the value of the "md5" key to ensure that a file was uploaded correctly.

As mentioned previously, you are not limited to the required fields in *fs.files*: feel free to keep any other file metadata in this collection as well. You might want to keep information such as download count, MIME type, or user rating with a file's metadata.

Once you understand the underlying GridFS specification, it becomes trivial to implement features that the driver you're using might not provide helpers for. For example, you can use the distinct command to get a list of unique filenames stored in GridFS:

```
> db.fs.files.distinct("filename")
[ "foo.txt" , "bar.txt" , "baz.txt" ]
```

This allows your application a great deal of flexibility in loading and collecting information about files. We'll change direction slightly in the next chapter, as we introduce the aggregation framework. It offers a range of data analytic tools to process the data in your database.

## CHAPTER 7

Introduction to the Aggregation Framework

Many applications require data analysis of one form or another. MongoDB provides powerful support for running analytics natively using the aggregation framework. In this chapter, we introduce this framework and some of the fundamental tools it provides. We'll cover:

- The aggregation framework
- Aggregation stages
- Aggregation expressions
- Aggregation accumulators

In the next chapter we'll dive deeper and look at more advanced aggregation features, including the ability to perform joins across collections.

Pipelines, Stages, and Tunables

The aggregation framework is a set of analytics tools within MongoDB that allow you to do analytics on documents in one or more collections.

The aggregation framework is based on the concept of a pipeline. With an aggregation pipeline we take input from a MongoDB collection and pass the documents from that collection through one or more stages, each of which performs a different operation on its inputs (Figure 7-1). Each stage takes as input whatever the stage before it produced as output. The inputs and outputs for all stages are documents—a stream of documents, if you will.

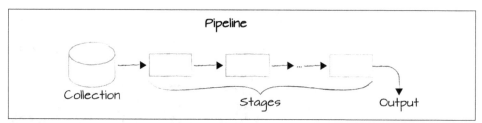

Figure 7-1. The aggregation pipeline

If you're familiar with pipelines in a Linux shell, such as bash, this is a very similar idea. Each stage has a specific job that it does. It expects a specific form of document and produces a specific output, which is itself a stream of documents. At the end of the pipeline we get access to the output, in much the same way that we would by executing a find query. That is, we get a stream of documents back that we can then use to do additional work, whether it's creating a report of some kind, generating a website, or some other type of task.

Now, let's dive in a little deeper and consider the individual stages. An individual stage of an aggregation pipeline is a data processing unit. It takes in a stream of input documents one at a time, processes each document one at a time, and produces an output stream of documents one at a time (Figure 7-2).

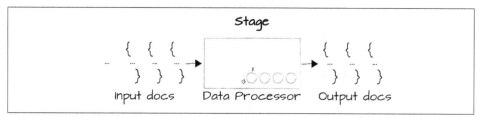

Figure 7-2. Stages of the aggregation pipeline

Each stage provides a set of knobs, or *tunables*, that we can control to parameterize the stage to perform whatever task we're interested in doing. A stage performs a generic, general-purpose task of some kind, and we parameterize the stage for the particular collection that we're working with and exactly what we would like that stage to do with those documents.

These tunables typically take the form of operators that we can supply that will modify fields, perform arithmetic operations, reshape documents, or do some sort of accumulation task or a variety of other things.

Before we start looking at some concrete examples, there's one more aspect of pipelines that is especially important to keep in mind as you begin to work with them. Frequently, we want to include the same type of stage multiple times within a single pipeline (Figure 7-3). For example, we may want to perform an initial filter so that we don't have to pass the entire collection into our pipeline. Later, following some additional processing, we might then want to filter further, applying a different set of criteria.

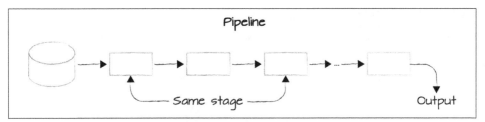

Figure 7-3. Repeated stages in the aggregation pipeline

To recap, pipelines work with MongoDB collections. They're composed of stages, each of which does a different data processing task on its input and produces documents as output to be passed to the next stage. Finally, at the end of the processing, a pipeline produces output that we can then do something with in our application or that we can send to a collection for later use. In many cases, in order to perform the analysis we need to do, we will include the same type of stage multiple times within an individual pipeline.

Getting Started with Stages: Familiar Operations

To get started developing aggregation pipelines, we will look at building some pipelines that involve operations that are already familiar to you. For this we will look at the *match*, *project*, *sort*, *skip*, and *limit* stages.

To work through these aggregation examples, we will use a collection of company data. The collection has a number of fields that specify details about the companies, such as name, a short description of the company, and when the company was founded.

There are also fields describing the rounds of funding a company has gone through, important milestones for the company, whether or not the company has been through an initial public offering (IPO), and, if so, the details of the IPO. Here's an example document containing data on Facebook, Inc.:

```
{
  "_id" : "52cdef7c4bab8bd675297d8e",
  "name" : "Facebook",
  "category_code" : "social",
  "founded_year" : 2004,
  "description" : "Social network",
  "funding_rounds" : [{
      "id" : 4,
      "round_code" : "b",
      "raised_amount" : 27500000,
```

```
        "raised_currency_code" : "USD",
        "funded_year" : 2006,
        "investments" : [
          {
            "company" : null,
            "financial_org" : {
              "name" : "Greylock Partners",
              "permalink" : "greylock"
            },
            "person" : null
          },
          {
            "company" : null,
            "financial_org" : {
              "name" : "Meritech Capital Partners",
              "permalink" : "meritech-capital-partners"
            },
            "person" : null
          },
          {
            "company" : null,
            "financial_org" : {
              "name" : "Founders Fund",
              "permalink" : "founders-fund"
            },
            "person" : null
          },
          {
            "company" : null,
            "financial_org" : {
              "name" : "SV Angel",
              "permalink" : "sv-angel"
            },
            "person" : null
          }
        ]
      },
      {
        "id" : 2197,
        "round_code" : "c",
        "raised_amount" : 15000000,
        "raised_currency_code" : "USD",
        "funded_year" : 2008,
        "investments" : [
          {
            "company" : null,
            "financial_org" : {
              "name" : "European Founders Fund",
              "permalink" : "european-founders-fund"
            },
            "person" : null
          }
```

```
      ]
   }],
   "ipo" : {
     "valuation_amount" : NumberLong("104000000000"),
     "valuation_currency_code" : "USD",
     "pub_year" : 2012,
     "pub_month" : 5,
     "pub_day" : 18,
     "stock_symbol" : "NASDAQ:FB"
   }
 }
```

As our first aggregation example, let's do a simple filter looking for all companies that were founded in 2004:

```
db.companies.aggregate([
    {$match: {founded_year: 2004}},
])
```

This is equivalent to the following operation using find:

```
db.companies.find({founded_year: 2004})
```

Now let's add a project stage to our pipeline to reduce the output to just a few fields per document. We'll exclude the "_id" field, but include "name" and "founded_year". Our pipeline will be as follows:

```
db.companies.aggregate([
  {$match: {founded_year: 2004}},
  {$project: {
    _id: 0,
    name: 1,
    founded_year: 1
  }}
])
```

If we run this, we get output that looks like the following:

```
{"name": "Digg", "founded_year": 2004 }
{"name": "Facebook", "founded_year": 2004 }
{"name": "AddThis", "founded_year": 2004 }
{"name": "Veoh", "founded_year": 2004 }
{"name": "Pando Networks", "founded_year": 2004 }
{"name": "Jobster", "founded_year": 2004 }
{"name": "AllPeers", "founded_year": 2004 }
{"name": "blinkx", "founded_year": 2004 }
{"name": "Yelp", "founded_year": 2004 }
{"name": "KickApps", "founded_year": 2004 }
{"name": "Flickr", "founded_year": 2004 }
{"name": "FeedBurner", "founded_year": 2004 }
{"name": "Dogster", "founded_year": 2004 }
{"name": "Sway", "founded_year": 2004 }
{"name": "Loomia", "founded_year": 2004 }
{"name": "Redfin", "founded_year": 2004 }
```

```
{"name": "Wink", "founded_year": 2004 }
{"name": "Techmeme", "founded_year": 2004 }
{"name": "Eventful", "founded_year": 2004 }
{"name": "Oodle", "founded_year": 2004 }
...
```

Let's unpack this aggregation pipeline in a little more detail. The first thing you will notice is that we're using the `aggregate` method. This is the method we call when we want to run an aggregation query. To aggregate, we pass in an aggregation pipeline. A pipeline is an array with documents as elements. Each of the documents must stipulate a particular stage operator. In this example, we have a pipeline that has two stages: a match stage for filtering and a project stage with which we're limiting the output to just two fields per document.

The match stage filters against the collection and passes the resulting documents to the project stage one at a time. The project stage then performs its operation, reshaping the documents, and passes the output out of the pipeline and back to us.

Now let's extend our pipeline a bit further to include a limit stage. We're going to match using the same query, but we'll limit our result set to five and then project out the fields we want. For simplicity, let's limit our output to just the names of each company:

```
db.companies.aggregate([
  {$match: {founded_year: 2004}},
  {$limit: 5},
  {$project: {
    _id: 0,
    name: 1}}
])
```

The result is as follows:

```
{"name": "Digg"}
{"name": "Facebook"}
{"name": "AddThis"}
{"name": "Veoh"}
{"name": "Pando Networks"}
```

Note that we've constructed this pipeline so that we limit before the project stage. If we ran the project stage first and then the limit, as in the following query, we would get exactly the same results, but we'd have to pass hundreds of documents through the project stage before finally limiting the results to five:

```
db.companies.aggregate([
  {$match: {founded_year: 2004}},
  {$project: {
    _id: 0,
    name: 1}},
  {$limit: 5}
])
```

Regardless of what types of optimizations the MongoDB query planner might be capable of in a given release, you should always consider the efficiency of your aggregation pipeline. Ensure that you are limiting the number of documents that need to be passed on from one stage to another as you build your pipeline.

This requires careful consideration of the entire flow of documents through a pipeline. In the case of the preceding query, we're only interested in the first five documents that match our query, regardless of how they are sorted, so it's perfectly fine to limit as our second stage.

However, if the order matters, then we'll need to sort before the limit stage. Sorting works in a manner similar to what we have seen already, except that in the aggregation framework, we specify sort as a stage within a pipeline as follows (in this case, we will sort by name in ascending order):

```
db.companies.aggregate([
    { $match: { founded_year: 2004 } },
    { $sort: { name: 1} },
    { $limit: 5 },
    { $project: {
        _id: 0,
        name: 1 } }
])
```

We get the following result from our *companies* collection:

```
{"name": "1915 Studios"}
{"name": "1Scan"}
{"name": "2GeeksinaLab"}
{"name": "2GeeksinaLab"}
{"name": "2threads"}
```

Note that we're looking at a different set of five companies now, getting instead the first five documents in alphanumeric order by name.

Finally, let's take a look at including a skip stage. Here, we sort first, then skip the first 10 documents and again limit our result set to 5 documents:

```
db.companies.aggregate([
    {$match: {founded_year: 2004}},
    {$sort: {name: 1}},
    {$skip: 10},
    {$limit: 5},
    {$project: {
        _id: 0,
        name: 1}},
])
```

Let's review our pipeline one more time. We have five stages. First, we're filtering the *companies* collection, looking only for documents where the "founded_year" is 2004. Then we're sorting based on the name in ascending order, skipping the first 10 matches, and limiting our end results to 5. Finally, we pass those five documents on to the project stage, where we reshape the documents such that our output documents contain just the company name.

Here, we've looked at constructing pipelines using stages that perform operations that should already be familiar to you. These operations are provided in the aggregation framework because they are necessary for the types of analytics that we'll want to accomplish using stages discussed in later sections. As we move through the rest of this chapter, we will take a deep dive into the other operations that the aggregation framework provides.

Expressions

As we move deeper into our discussion of the aggregation framework, it is important to have a sense of the different types of expressions available for use as you construct aggregation pipelines. The aggregation framework supports many different classes of expressions:

- *Boolean* expressions allow us to use AND, OR, and NOT expressions.
- *Set* expressions allow us to work with arrays as sets. In particular, we can get the intersection or union of two or more sets. We can also take the difference of two sets and perform a number of other set operations.
- *Comparison* expressions enable us to express many different types of range filters.
- *Arithmetic* expressions enable us to calculate the ceiling, floor, natural log, and log, as well as perform simple arithmetic operations like multiplication, division, addition, and subtraction. We can even do more complex operations, such as calculating the square root of a value.
- *String* expressions allow us to concatenate, find substrings, and perform operations having to do with case and text search operations.
- *Array* expressions provide a lot of power for manipulating arrays, including the ability to filter array elements, slice an array, or just take a range of values from a specific array.
- *Variable* expressions, which we won't dive into too deeply, allow us to work with literals, expressions for parsing date values, and conditional expressions.
- *Accumulators* provide the ability to calculate sums, descriptive statistics, and many other types of values.

$project

Now we're going to take a deeper dive into the project stage and reshaping documents, exploring the types of reshaping operations that should be most common in the applications that you develop. We have seen some simple projections in aggregation pipelines, and now we'll take a look at some that are a little more complex.

First, let's look at promoting nested fields. In the following pipeline, we are doing a match:

```
db.companies.aggregate([
  {$match: {"funding_rounds.investments.financial_org.permalink": "greylock" }},
  {$project: {
    _id: 0,
    name: 1,
    ipo: "$ipo.pub_year",
    valuation: "$ipo.valuation_amount",
    funders: "$funding_rounds.investments.financial_org.permalink"
  }}
]).pretty()
```

As an example of the relevant fields for documents in our *companies* collection, let's again look at a portion of the Facebook document:

```
{
  "_id" : "52cdef7c4bab8bd675297d8e",
  "name" : "Facebook",
  "category_code" : "social",
  "founded_year" : 2004,
  "description" : "Social network",
  "funding_rounds" : [{
    "id" : 4,
    "round_code" : "b",
    "raised_amount" : 27500000,
    "raised_currency_code" : "USD",
    "funded_year" : 2006,
    "investments" : [
      {
        "company" : null,
        "financial_org" : {
          "name" : "Greylock Partners",
          "permalink" : "greylock"
        },
        "person" : null
      },
      {
        "company" : null,
        "financial_org" : {
          "name" : "Meritech Capital Partners",
          "permalink" : "meritech-capital-partners"
        },
        "person" : null
```

```
      },
      {
        "company" : null,
        "financial_org" : {
          "name" : "Founders Fund",
          "permalink" : "founders-fund"
        },
        "person" : null
      },
      {
        "company" : null,
        "financial_org" : {
          "name" : "SV Angel",
          "permalink" : "sv-angel"
        },
        "person" : null
      }
    ]
  },
  {
    "id" : 2197,
    "round_code" : "c",
    "raised_amount" : 15000000,
    "raised_currency_code" : "USD",
    "funded_year" : 2008,
    "investments" : [
      {
        "company" : null,
        "financial_org" : {
          "name" : "European Founders Fund",
          "permalink" : "european-founders-fund"
        },
        "person" : null
      }
    ]
  }],
  "ipo" : {
    "valuation_amount" : NumberLong("104000000000"),
    "valuation_currency_code" : "USD",
    "pub_year" : 2012,
    "pub_month" : 5,
    "pub_day" : 18,
    "stock_symbol" : "NASDAQ:FB"
  }
}
```

Going back to our match:

```
db.companies.aggregate([
  {$match: {"funding_rounds.investments.financial_org.permalink": "greylock" }},
  {$project: {
    _id: 0,
    name: 1,
```

```
      ipo: "$ipo.pub_year",
      valuation: "$ipo.valuation_amount",
      funders: "$funding_rounds.investments.financial_org.permalink"
   }}
]).pretty()
```

we are filtering for all companies that had a funding round in which Greylock Partners participated. The permalink value, "greylock", is the unique identifier for such
documents. Here is another view of the Facebook document with just the relevant
fields displayed:

```
{
   ...
   "name" : "Facebook",
   ...
   "funding_rounds" : [{
      ...
      "investments" : [{
         ...
         "financial_org" : {
            "name" : "Greylock Partners",
            "permalink" : "greylock"
         },
         ...
      },
      {
         ...
         "financial_org" : {
            "name" : "Meritech Capital Partners",
            "permalink" : "meritech-capital-partners"
         },
         ...
      },
      {
         ...
         "financial_org" : {
            "name" : "Founders Fund",
            "permalink" : "founders-fnd"
         },
         ...
      },
      {
         "company" : null,
         "financial_org" : {
            "name" : "SV Angel",
            "permalink" : "sv-angel"
         },
         ...
      }],
      ...
   }],
   {
```

```
  ...
  "investments" : [{
    ...
    "financial_org" : {
      "name" : "European Founders Fund",
      "permalink" : "european-founders-fund"
    },
    ...
  }]
}],
"ipo" : {
  "valuation_amount" : NumberLong("104000000000"),
  "valuation_currency_code" : "USD",
  "pub_year" : 2012,
  "pub_month" : 5,
  "pub_day" : 18,
  "stock_symbol" : "NASDAQ:FB"
}
}
```

The project stage we have defined in this aggregation pipeline will suppress the "_id" and include the "name". It will also promote some nested fields. This project uses dot notation to express field paths that reach into the "ipo" field and the "fund ing_rounds" field to select values from those nested documents and arrays. This project stage will make those the values of top-level fields in the documents it produces as output, as shown here:

```
{
  "name" : "Digg",
  "funders" : [
    [
      "greylock",
      "omidyar-network"
    ],
    [
      "greylock",
      "omidyar-network",
      "floodgate",
      "sv-angel"
    ],
    [
      "highland-capital-partners",
      "greylock",
      "omidyar-network",
      "svb-financial-group"
    ]
  ]
}
{
  "name" : "Facebook",
  "ipo" : 2012,
  "valuation" : NumberLong("104000000000"),
```

```
    "funders" : [
      [
        "accel-partners"
      ],
      [
        "greylock",
        "meritech-capital-partners",
        "founders-fund",
        "sv-angel"
      ],
      ...
      [
        "goldman-sachs",
        "digital-sky-technologies-fo"
      ]
    ]
  }
  {
    "name" : "Revision3",
    "funders" : [
      [
        "greylock",
        "sv-angel"
      ],
      [
        "greylock"
      ]
    ]
  }
  ...
```

In the output, each document has a "name" field and a "funders" field. For those companies that have gone through an IPO, the "ipo" field contains the year the company went public and the "valuation" field contains the value of the company at the time of the IPO. Note that in all of these documents, these are top-level fields and the values for those fields were promoted from nested documents and arrays.

The $ character used to specify the values for ipo, valuation, and funders in our project stage indicates that the values should be interpreted as field paths and used to select the value that should be projected for each field, respectively.

One thing you might have noticed is that we're seeing multiple values printed out for funders. In fact, we're seeing an array of arrays. Based on our review of the Facebook example document, we know that all of the funders are listed within an array called "investments". Our stage specifies that we want to project the financial_org.permalink value for each entry in the "investments" array, for every funding round. So, an array of arrays of funders' names is built up.

In later sections we will look at how to perform arithmetic and other operations on strings, dates, and a number of other value types to project documents of all shapes and sizes. Just about the only thing we can't do from a project stage is change the data type for a value.

$unwind

When working with array fields in an aggregation pipeline, it is often necessary to include one or more unwind stages. This allows us to produce output such that there is one output document for each element in a specified array field.

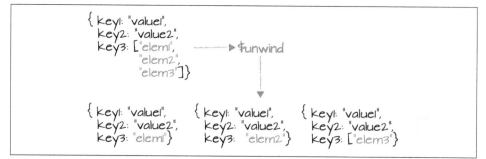

Figure 7-4. $unwind takes an array from the input document and creates an output document for each element in that array

In the example in Figure 7-4, we have an input document that has three keys and their corresponding values. The third key has as its value an array with three elements. $unwind if run on this type of input document and configured to unwind the key3 field will produce documents that look like those shown at the bottom of Figure 7-4. The thing that might not be intuitive to you about this is that in each of these output documents there will be a key3 field, but that field will contain a single value rather than an array value, and there will be a separate document for each one of the elements that were in this array. In other words, if there were 10 elements in the array, the unwind stage would produce 10 output documents.

Let's go back to our *companies* example, and take a look at the use of an unwind stage. We'll start with the following aggregation pipeline. Note that in this pipeline, as in the previous section, we are simply matching on a specific funder and promoting values from embedded funding_rounds documents using a project stage:

```
db.companies.aggregate([
  {$match: {"funding_rounds.investments.financial_org.permalink": "greylock"} },
  {$project: {
    _id: 0,
    name: 1,
    amount: "$funding_rounds.raised_amount",
    year: "$funding_rounds.funded_year"
  }}
])
```

Once again, here's an example of the data model for documents in this collection:

```
{
  "_id" : "52cdef7c4bab8bd675297d8e",
  "name" : "Facebook",
  "category_code" : "social",
  "founded_year" : 2004,
  "description" : "Social network",
  "funding_rounds" : [{
      "id" : 4,
      "round_code" : "b",
      "raised_amount" : 27500000,
      "raised_currency_code" : "USD",
      "funded_year" : 2006,
      "investments" : [
        {
          "company" : null,
          "financial_org" : {
            "name" : "Greylock Partners",
            "permalink" : "greylock"
          },
          "person" : null
        },
        {
          "company" : null,
          "financial_org" : {
            "name" : "Meritech Capital Partners",
            "permalink" : "meritech-capital-partners"
          },
          "person" : null
        },
        {
          "company" : null,
          "financial_org" : {
            "name" : "Founders Fund",
            "permalink" : "founders-fund"
          },
          "person" : null
        },
        {
          "company" : null,
          "financial_org" : {
            "name" : "SV Angel",
            "permalink" : "sv-angel"
          },
          "person" : null
        }
      ]
    },
    {
      "id" : 2197,
      "round_code" : "c",
      "raised_amount" : 15000000,
```

```
              "raised_currency_code" : "USD",
              "funded_year" : 2008,
              "investments" : [
                {
                  "company" : null,
                  "financial_org" : {
                    "name" : "European Founders Fund",
                    "permalink" : "european-founders-fund"
                  },
                  "person" : null
                }
              ]
            }],
          "ipo" : {
            "valuation_amount" : NumberLong("104000000000"),
            "valuation_currency_code" : "USD",
            "pub_year" : 2012,
            "pub_month" : 5,
            "pub_day" : 18,
            "stock_symbol" : "NASDAQ:FB"
          }
        }
```

Our aggregation query will produce results such as the following:

```
{
  "name" : "Digg",
  "amount" : [
    8500000,
    2800000,
    28700000,
    5000000
  ],
  "year" : [
    2006,
    2005,
    2008,
    2011
  ]
}
{
  "name" : "Facebook",
  "amount" : [
    500000,
    12700000,
    27500000,
    ...
```

The query produces documents that have arrays for both "amount" and "year", because we're accessing the "raised_amount" and "funded_year" for every element in the "funding_rounds" array.

To fix this, we can include an unwind stage before our project stage in this aggregation pipeline, and parameterize this by specifying that it is the "funding_rounds"
array that should be unwound (Figure 7-5).

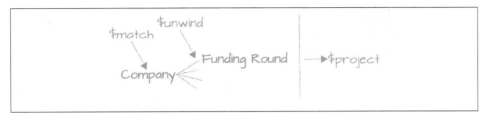

*Figure 7-5. The outline of our aggregation pipeline so far, matching for "greylock" then
unwinding the "funding_rounds", and finally projecting out the name, amount, and year
for each of the funding rounds*

Returning again to our Facebook example, we can see that for each funding round
there is a "raised_amount" field and a "funded_year" field.

The unwind stage will produce an output document for each element of the "fund
ing_rounds" array. In this example our values are strings, but regardless of the type
of value, the unwind stage will produce an output document for each one. Here's the
updated aggregation query:

```
db.companies.aggregate([
  { $match: {"funding_rounds.investments.financial_org.permalink": "greylock"} },
  { $unwind: "$funding_rounds" },
  { $project: {
    _id: 0,
    name: 1,
    amount: "$funding_rounds.raised_amount",
    year: "$funding_rounds.funded_year"
  } }
])
```

The unwind stage produces an exact copy of every one of the documents that it
receives as input. All the fields will have the same key and value, with the exception of
the "funding_rounds" field. Rather than being an array of "funding_rounds" documents, instead it will have a value that is a single document, which corresponds to an
individual funding round:

```
{"name": "Digg", "amount": 8500000, "year": 2006 }
{"name": "Digg", "amount": 2800000, "year": 2005 }
{"name": "Digg", "amount": 28700000, "year": 2008 }
{"name": "Digg", "amount": 5000000, "year": 2011 }
{"name": "Facebook", "amount": 500000, "year": 2004 }
{"name": "Facebook", "amount": 12700000, "year": 2005 }
{"name": "Facebook", "amount": 27500000, "year": 2006 }
{"name": "Facebook", "amount": 240000000, "year": 2007 }
{"name": "Facebook", "amount": 60000000, "year": 2007 }
```

```
{"name": "Facebook", "amount": 15000000, "year": 2008 }
{"name": "Facebook", "amount": 100000000, "year": 2008 }
{"name": "Facebook", "amount": 60000000, "year": 2008 }
{"name": "Facebook", "amount": 200000000, "year": 2009 }
{"name": "Facebook", "amount": 210000000, "year": 2010 }
{"name": "Facebook", "amount": 1500000000, "year": 2011 }
{"name": "Revision3", "amount": 1000000, "year": 2006 }
{"name": "Revision3", "amount": 8000000, "year": 2007 }
...
```

Now let's add an additional field to our output documents. In doing so, we'll actually identify a small problem with this aggregation pipeline as currently written:

```
db.companies.aggregate([
  { $match: {"funding_rounds.investments.financial_org.permalink": "greylock"} },
  { $unwind: "$funding_rounds" },
  { $project: {
    _id: 0,
    name: 1,
    funder: "$funding_rounds.investments.financial_org.permalink",
    amount: "$funding_rounds.raised_amount",
    year: "$funding_rounds.funded_year"
  } }
])
```

In adding the "funder" field we now have a field path value that will access the "investments" field of the "funding_rounds" embedded document that it gets from the unwind stage and, for the financial organization, selects the permalink value. Note that this is very similar to what we're doing in our match filter. Let's have a look at our output:

```
{
  "name" : "Digg",
  "funder" : [
    "greylock",
    "omidyar-network"
  ],
  "amount" : 8500000,
  "year" : 2006
}
{
  "name" : "Digg",
  "funder" : [
    "greylock",
    "omidyar-network",
    "floodgate",
    "sv-angel"
  ],
  "amount" : 2800000,
  "year" : 2005
}
{
```

```
      "name" : "Digg",
      "funder" : [
        "highland-capital-partners",
        "greylock",
        "omidyar-network",
        "svb-financial-group"
      ],
      "amount" : 28700000,
      "year" : 2008
  }
  ...
  {
      "name" : "Farecast",
      "funder" : [
        "madrona-venture-group",
        "wrf-capital"
      ],
      "amount" : 1500000,
      "year" : 2004
  }
  {
      "name" : "Farecast",
      "funder" : [
        "greylock",
        "madrona-venture-group",
        "wrf-capital"
      ],
      "amount" : 7000000,
      "year" : 2005
  }
  {
      "name" : "Farecast",
      "funder" : [
        "greylock",
        "madrona-venture-group",
        "par-capital-management",
        "pinnacle-ventures",
        "sutter-hill-ventures",
        "wrf-capital"
      ],
      "amount" : 12100000,
      "year" : 2007
  }
```

To understand what we're seeing here, we need to go back to our document and look
at the "investments" field.

The "funding_rounds.investments" field is itself an array. Multiple funders can participate in each funding round, so "investments" will list every one of those funders.
Looking at the results, as we originally saw with the "raised_amount" and "fun

ded_year" fields, we're now seeing an array for "funder" because "investments" is an array-valued field.

Another problem is that because of the way we've written our pipeline, many documents are passed to the project stage that represent funding rounds that Greylock did not participate in. We can see this by looking at the funding rounds for Farecast. This problem stems from the fact that our match stage selects all companies where Greylock participated in at least one funding round. If we are interested in considering only those funding rounds in which Greylock actually participated, we need to figure out a way to filter differently.

One possibility is to reverse the order of our unwind and match stages—that is to say, do the unwind first and then do the match. This guarantees that we will only match documents coming out of the unwind stage. But in thinking through this approach, it quickly becomes clear that, with unwind as the first stage, we would be doing a scan through the entire collection.

For efficiency, we want to match as early as possible in our pipeline. This enables the aggregation framework to make use of indexes, for example. So, in order to select only those funding rounds in which Greylock participated, we can include a second match stage:

```
db.companies.aggregate([
  { $match: {"funding_rounds.investments.financial_org.permalink": "greylock"} },
  { $unwind: "$funding_rounds" },
  { $match: {"funding_rounds.investments.financial_org.permalink": "greylock"} },
  { $project: {
    _id: 0,
    name: 1,
    individualFunder: "$funding_rounds.investments.person.permalink",
    fundingOrganization: "$funding_rounds.investments.financial_org.permalink",
    amount: "$funding_rounds.raised_amount",
    year: "$funding_rounds.funded_year"
  } }
])
```

This pipeline will first filter for companies where Greylock participated in at least one funding round. It will then unwind the funding rounds and filter again, so that only documents that represent funding rounds that Greylock actually participated in will be passed on to the project stage.

As mentioned at the beginning of this chapter, it is often the case that we need to include multiple stages of the same type. This is a good example: we're filtering to reduce the number of documents that we're looking at initially by narrowing down our set of documents for consideration to those for which Greylock participated in at least one funding round. Then, through our unwind stage, we end up with a number of documents that represent funding rounds from companies that Greylock did, in fact, fund, but individual funding rounds that Greylock did not participate in. We can get rid of all the funding rounds we're not interested in by simply including another filter, using a second match stage.

Array Expressions

Now let's turn our attention to array expressions. As part of our deep dive, we'll take a look at using array expressions in project stages.

The first expression we'll examine is a filter expression. A filter expression selects a subset of the elements in an array based on filter criteria.

Working again with our *companies* dataset, we'll match using the same criteria for funding rounds in which Greylock participated. Take a look at the rounds field in this pipeline:

```
db.companies.aggregate([
  { $match: {"funding_rounds.investments.financial_org.permalink": "greylock"} },
  { $project: {
    _id: 0,
    name: 1,
    founded_year: 1,
    rounds: { $filter: {
      input: "$funding_rounds",
      as: "round",
      cond: { $gte: ["$$round.raised_amount", 100000000] } } } }
  } },
  { $match: {"rounds.investments.financial_org.permalink": "greylock" } },
]).pretty()
```

The rounds field uses a filter expression. The $filter operator is designed to work with array fields and specifies the options we must supply. The first option to $filter is input. For input, we simply specify an array. In this case, we use a field path specifier to identify the "funding_rounds" array found in documents in our *companies* collection. Next, we specify the name we'd like to use for this "funding_rounds" array throughout the rest of our filter expression. Then, as the third option, we need to specify a condition. The condition should provide criteria used to filter whatever array we've provided as input, selecting a subset. In this case, we're filtering such that we only select elements where the "raised_amount" for a "funding_round" is greater than or equal to 100 million.

In specifying the condition, we've made use of $$. We use $$ to reference a variable defined within the expression we're working in. The as clause defines a variable within our filter expression. This variable has the name "round" because that's what we labeled it in the as clause. This is to disambiguate a reference to a variable from a field path. In this case, our comparison expression takes an array of two values and will return true if the first value provided is greater than or equal to the second value.

Now let's consider what documents the project stage of this pipeline will produce, given this filter. The output documents will have "name", "founded_year", and "rounds" fields. The values for "rounds" will be arrays composed of the elements that match our filter condition: that the raised amount is greater than $100,000,000.

In the match stage that follows, as we did previously, we will simply filter the input documents for those that were funded in some way by Greylock. Documents output by this pipeline will resemble the following:

```
{
  "name" : "Dropbox",
  "founded_year" : 2007,
  "rounds" : [
    {
      "id" : 25090,
      "round_code" : "b",
      "source_description" :
        "Dropbox Raises $250M In Funding, Boasts 45 Million Users",
      "raised_amount" : 250000000,
      "raised_currency_code" : "USD",
      "funded_year" : 2011,
      "investments" : [
        {
          "financial_org" : {
            "name" : "Index Ventures",
            "permalink" : "index-ventures"
          }
        },
        {
          "financial_org" : {
            "name" : "RIT Capital Partners",
            "permalink" : "rit-capital-partners"
          }
        },
        {
          "financial_org" : {
            "name" : "Valiant Capital Partners",
            "permalink" : "valiant-capital-partners"
          }
        },
        {
          "financial_org" : {
            "name" : "Benchmark",
            "permalink" : "benchmark-2"
          }
        },
        {
          "company" : null,
          "financial_org" : {
            "name" : "Goldman Sachs",
            "permalink" : "goldman-sachs"
```

```
        },
        "person" : null
      },
      {
        "financial_org" : {
          "name" : "Greylock Partners",
          "permalink" : "greylock"
        }
      },
      {
        "financial_org" : {
          "name" : "Institutional Venture Partners",
          "permalink" : "institutional-venture-partners"
        }
      },
      {
        "financial_org" : {
          "name" : "Sequoia Capital",
          "permalink" : "sequoia-capital"
        }
      },
      {
        "financial_org" : {
          "name" : "Accel Partners",
          "permalink" : "accel-partners"
        }
      },
      {
        "financial_org" : {
          "name" : "Glynn Capital Management",
          "permalink" : "glynn-capital-management"
        }
      },
      {
        "financial_org" : {
          "name" : "SV Angel",
          "permalink" : "sv-angel"
        }
      }
    ]
  }
]
}
```

Only the "rounds" array items for which the raised amount exceeds $100,000,000 will pass through the filter. In the case of Dropbox, there is just one round that meets that criterion. You have a lot of flexibility in how you set up filter expressions, but this is the basic form and provides a concrete example of a use case for this particular array expression.

Next, let's look at the array element operator. We'll continue working with funding rounds, but in this case we simply want to pull out the first round and the last round. We might be interested, for example, in seeing when these rounds occurred or in comparing their amounts. These are things we can do with date and arithmetic expressions, as we'll see in the next section.

The $arrayElemAt operator enables us to select an element at a particular slot within an array. The following pipeline provides an example of using $arrayElemAt:

```
db.companies.aggregate([
  { $match: { "founded_year": 2010 } },
  { $project: {
    _id: 0,
    name: 1,
    founded_year: 1,
    first_round: { $arrayElemAt: [ "$funding_rounds", 0 ] },
    last_round: { $arrayElemAt: [ "$funding_rounds", -1 ] }
  } }
]).pretty()
```

Note the syntax for using $arrayElemAt within a project stage. We define a field that we want projected out and as the value specify a document with $arrayElemAt as the field name and a two-element array as the value. The first element should be a field path that specifies the array field we want to select from. The second element identifies the slot within that array that we want. Remember that arrays are 0-indexed.

In many cases, the length of an array is not readily available. To select array slots starting from the end of the array, use negative integers. The last element in an array is identified with -1.

A simple output document for this aggregation pipeline would resemble the following:

```
{
  "name" : "vufind",
  "founded_year" : 2010,
  "first_round" : {
    "id" : 19876,
    "round_code" : "angel",
    "source_url" : "",
    "source_description" : "",
    "raised_amount" : 250000,
    "raised_currency_code" : "USD",
    "funded_year" : 2010,
    "funded_month" : 9,
    "funded_day" : 1,
    "investments" : [ ]
  },
  "last_round" : {
    "id" : 57219,
    "round_code" : "seed",
```

```
        "source_url" : "",
        "source_description" : "",
        "raised_amount" : 500000,
        "raised_currency_code" : "USD",
        "funded_year" : 2012,
        "funded_month" : 7,
        "funded_day" : 1,
        "investments" : [ ]
    }
}
```

Related to $arrayElemAt is the $slice expression. This allows us to return not just one but multiple items from an array in sequence, beginning with a particular index:

```
db.companies.aggregate([
  { $match: { "founded_year": 2010 } },
  { $project: {
    _id: 0,
    name: 1,
    founded_year: 1,
    early_rounds: { $slice: [ "$funding_rounds", 1, 3 ] }
  } }
]).pretty()
```

Here, again with the funding_rounds array, we begin at index 1 and take three elements from the array. Perhaps we know that in this dataset the first funding round isn't all that interesting, or we simply want some early ones but not the very first one.

Filtering and selecting individual elements or slices of arrays are among the more common operations we need to perform on arrays. Probably the most common, however, is determining an array's size or length. To do this we can use the $size operator:

```
db.companies.aggregate([
  { $match: { "founded_year": 2004 } },
  { $project: {
    _id: 0,
    name: 1,
    founded_year: 1,
    total_rounds: { $size: "$funding_rounds" }
  } }
]).pretty()
```

When used in a project stage, a $size expression will simply provide a value that is the number of elements in the array.

In this section, we've explored some of the most common array expressions. There are many more, and the list grows with each release. Please review the Aggregation Pipeline Quick Reference in the MongoDB documentation (*https://oreil.ly/ZtUES*) for a summary of all expressions that are available.

Accumulators

At this point, we've covered a few different types of expressions. Next, let's look at what accumulators the aggregation framework has to offer. Accumulators are essentially another type of expression, but we think about them in their own class because they calculate values from field values found in multiple documents.

Accumulators the aggregation framework provides enable us to perform operations such as summing all values in a particular field ($sum), calculating an average ($avg), etc. We also consider $first and $last to be accumulators because these consider values in all documents that pass through the stage in which they are used. $max and $min are two more examples of accumulators that consider a stream of documents and save just one of the values they see. We can use $mergeObjects to combine multiple documents into a single document.

We also have accumulators for arrays. We can $push values onto an array as documents pass through a pipeline stage. $addToSet is very similar to $push except that it ensures no duplicate values are included in the resulting array.

Then there are some expressions for calculating descriptive statistics—for example, for calculating the standard deviation of a sample and of a population. Both work with a stream of documents that pass through a pipeline stage.

Prior to MongoDB 3.2, accumulators were available only in the group stage. MongoDB 3.2 introduced the ability to access a subset of accumulators within the project stage. The primary difference between the accumulators in the group stage and the project stage is that in the project stage accumulators such as $sum and $avg must operate on arrays within a single document, whereas accumulators in the group stage, as we'll see in a later section, provide you with the ability to perform calculations on values across multiple documents.

That's a quick overview of accumulators to provide some context and set the stage for our deep dive into examples.

Using Accumulators in Project Stages

We'll begin with an example of using an accumulator in a project stage. Note that our match stage filters for documents that contain a "funding_rounds" field and for which the funding_rounds array is not empty:

```
db.companies.aggregate([
  { $match: { "funding_rounds": { $exists: true, $ne: [ ]} } },
  { $project: {
    _id: 0,
    name: 1,
    largest_round: { $max: "$funding_rounds.raised_amount" }
```

```
    } }
  ])
```

Because the value for $funding_rounds is an array within each company document, we can use an accumulator. Remember that in project stages accumulators must work on an array-valued field. In this case, we're able to do something pretty cool here. We are easily identifying the largest value in an array by reaching into an embedded document within that array and projecting the max value in the output documents:

```
{ "name" : "Wetpaint", "largest_round" : 25000000 }
{ "name" : "Digg", "largest_round" : 28700000 }
{ "name" : "Facebook", "largest_round" : 1500000000 }
{ "name" : "Omnidrive", "largest_round" : 800000 }
{ "name" : "Geni", "largest_round" : 10000000 }
{ "name" : "Twitter", "largest_round" : 400000000 }
{ "name" : "StumbleUpon", "largest_round" : 17000000 }
{ "name" : "Gizmoz", "largest_round" : 6500000 }
{ "name" : "Scribd", "largest_round" : 13000000 }
{ "name" : "Slacker", "largest_round" : 40000000 }
{ "name" : "Lala", "largest_round" : 20000000 }
{ "name" : "eBay", "largest_round" : 6700000 }
{ "name" : "MeetMoi", "largest_round" : 2575000 }
{ "name" : "Joost", "largest_round" : 45000000 }
{ "name" : "Babelgum", "largest_round" : 13200000 }
{ "name" : "Plaxo", "largest_round" : 9000000 }
{ "name" : "Cisco", "largest_round" : 2500000 }
{ "name" : "Yahoo!", "largest_round" : 4800000 }
{ "name" : "Powerset", "largest_round" : 12500000 }
{ "name" : "Technorati", "largest_round" : 10520000 }
...
```

As another example, let's use the $sum accumulator to calculate the total funding for each company in our collection:

```
db.companies.aggregate([
  { $match: { "funding_rounds": { $exists: true, $ne: [ ]} } },
  { $project: {
    _id: 0,
    name: 1,
    total_funding: { $sum: "$funding_rounds.raised_amount" }
  } }
])
```

This is just a taste of what you can do using accumulators in project stages. Again, you're encouraged to review the Aggregation Pipeline Quick Reference in the MongoDB docs (*https://oreil.ly/SZiFx*) for a complete overview of the accumulator expressions available.

Introduction to Grouping

Historically, accumulators were the province of the group stage in the MongoDB aggregation framework. The group stage performs a function that is similar to the SQL GROUP BY command. In a group stage, we can aggregate together values from multiple documents and perform some type of aggregation operation on them, such as calculating an average. Let's take a look at an example:

```
db.companies.aggregate([
  { $group: {
    _id: { founded_year: "$founded_year" },
    average_number_of_employees: { $avg: "$number_of_employees" }
  } },
  { $sort: { average_number_of_employees: -1 } }

])
```

Here, we're using a group stage to aggregate together all companies based on the year they were founded, then calculate the average number of employees for each year. The output for this pipeline resembles the following:

```
{ "_id" : { "founded_year" : 1847 }, "average_number_of_employees" : 405000 }
{ "_id" : { "founded_year" : 1896 }, "average_number_of_employees" : 388000 }
{ "_id" : { "founded_year" : 1933 }, "average_number_of_employees" : 320000 }
{ "_id" : { "founded_year" : 1915 }, "average_number_of_employees" : 186000 }
{ "_id" : { "founded_year" : 1903 }, "average_number_of_employees" : 171000 }
{ "_id" : { "founded_year" : 1865 }, "average_number_of_employees" : 125000 }
{ "_id" : { "founded_year" : 1921 }, "average_number_of_employees" : 107000 }
{ "_id" : { "founded_year" : 1835 }, "average_number_of_employees" : 100000 }
{ "_id" : { "founded_year" : 1952 }, "average_number_of_employees" : 92900 }
{ "_id" : { "founded_year" : 1946 }, "average_number_of_employees" : 91500 }
{ "_id" : { "founded_year" : 1947 }, "average_number_of_employees" : 88510.5 }
{ "_id" : { "founded_year" : 1898 }, "average_number_of_employees" : 80000 }
{ "_id" : { "founded_year" : 1968 }, "average_number_of_employees" : 73550 }
{ "_id" : { "founded_year" : 1957 }, "average_number_of_employees" : 70055 }
{ "_id" : { "founded_year" : 1969 }, "average_number_of_employees" : 67635.1 }
{ "_id" : { "founded_year" : 1928 }, "average_number_of_employees" : 51000 }
{ "_id" : { "founded_year" : 1963 }, "average_number_of_employees" : 50503 }
{ "_id" : { "founded_year" : 1959 }, "average_number_of_employees" : 47432.5 }
{ "_id" : { "founded_year" : 1902 }, "average_number_of_employees" : 41171.5 }
{ "_id" : { "founded_year" : 1887 }, "average_number_of_employees" : 35000 }
...
```

The output includes documents that have a document as their "_id" value, and then a report on the average number of employees. This is the type of analysis we might do as a first step in assessing the correlation between the year in which a company was founded and its growth, possibly normalizing for how old the company is.

As you can see, the pipeline we built has two stages: a group stage and a sort stage. Fundamental to the group stage is the "_id" field that we specify as part of the document. This is the value of the $group operator itself, using a very strict interpretation.

We use this field to define what the group stage uses to organize the documents that it sees. Since the group stage is first, the aggregate command will pass all documents in the *companies* collection through this stage. The group stage will take every document that has the same value for "founded_year" and treat them as a single group. In constructing the value for this field, this stage will use the $avg accumulator to calculate an average number of employees for all companies with the same "founded_year".

You can think of it this way. Each time the group stage encounters a document with a specific founding year, it adds the value for "number_of_employees" from that document to a running sum of the number of employees and adds one to a count of the number of documents seen so far for that year. Once all documents have passed through the group stage, it can then calculate the average using that running sum and count for every grouping of documents it identified based on the year of founding.

At the end of this pipeline, we sort the documents into descending order by average_number_of_employees.

Let's look at another example. One field we've not yet considered in the *companies* dataset is the relationships. The relationships field appears in documents in the following form:

```
{
  "_id" : "52cdef7c4bab8bd675297d8e",
  "name" : "Facebook",
  "permalink" : "facebook",
  "category_code" : "social",
  "founded_year" : 2004,
  ...
  "relationships" : [
    {
      "is_past" : false,
      "title" : "Founder and CEO, Board Of Directors",
      "person" : {
        "first_name" : "Mark",
        "last_name" : "Zuckerberg",
        "permalink" : "mark-zuckerberg"
      }
    },
    {
      "is_past" : true,
      "title" : "CFO",
      "person" : {
        "first_name" : "David",
        "last_name" : "Ebersman",
```

```
        "permalink" : "david-ebersman"
      }
    },
    ...
  ],
  "funding_rounds" : [
    ...
    {
      "id" : 4,
      "round_code" : "b",
      "source_url" : "http://www.facebook.com/press/info.php?factsheet",
      "source_description" : "Facebook Funding",
      "raised_amount" : 27500000,
      "raised_currency_code" : "USD",
      "funded_year" : 2006,
      "funded_month" : 4,
      "funded_day" : 1,
      "investments" : [
        {
          "company" : null,
          "financial_org" : {
            "name" : "Greylock Partners",
            "permalink" : "greylock"
          },
          "person" : null
        },
        {
          "company" : null,
          "financial_org" : {
            "name" : "Meritech Capital Partners",
            "permalink" : "meritech-capital-partners"
          },
          "person" : null
        },
        {
          "company" : null,
          "financial_org" : {
            "name" : "Founders Fund",
            "permalink" : "founders-fund"
          },
          "person" : null
        },
        {
          "company" : null,
          "financial_org" : {
            "name" : "SV Angel",
            "permalink" : "sv-angel"
          },
          "person" : null
        }
      ]
    },
```

```
    ...
  "ipo" : {
    "valuation_amount" : NumberLong("104000000000"),
    "valuation_currency_code" : "USD",
    "pub_year" : 2012,
    "pub_month" : 5,
    "pub_day" : 18,
    "stock_symbol" : "NASDAQ:FB"
  },
  ...
}
```

The "relationships" field gives us the ability to dive in and look for people who have, in one way or another, been associated with a relatively large number of companies. Let's take a look at this aggregation:

```
db.companies.aggregate( [
  { $match: { "relationships.person": { $ne: null } } },
  { $project: { relationships: 1, _id: 0 } },
  { $unwind: "$relationships" },
  { $group: {
    _id: "$relationships.person",
    count: { $sum: 1 }
  } },
  { $sort: { count: -1 } }
]).pretty()
```

We're matching on relationships.person. If we look at our Facebook example document, we can see how relationships are structured and get a sense for what it means to do this. We are filtering for all relationships for which "person" is not null. Then we project out all relationships for documents that match. We will pass only relationships to the next stage in the pipeline, which is unwind. We unwind the relationships so that every relationship in the array comes through to the group stage that follows. In the group stage, we use a field path to identify the person within each "relationship" document. All documents with the same "person" value will be grouped together. As we saw previously, it's perfectly fine for a document to be the value around which we group. So, every match to a document for a first name, last name, and permalink for a person will be aggregated together. We use the $sum accumulator to count the number of relationships in which each person has participated. Finally, we sort into descending order. The output for this pipeline resembles the following:

```
{
  "_id" : {
    "first_name" : "Tim",
    "last_name" : "Hanlon",
    "permalink" : "tim-hanlon"
  },
  "count" : 28
}
```

```
{
  "_id" : {
    "first_name" : "Pejman",
    "last_name" : "Nozad",
    "permalink" : "pejman-nozad"
  },
  "count" : 24
}
{
  "_id" : {
    "first_name" : "David S.",
    "last_name" : "Rose",
    "permalink" : "david-s-rose"
  },
  "count" : 24
}
{
  "_id" : {
    "first_name" : "Saul",
    "last_name" : "Klein",
    "permalink" : "saul-klein"
  },
  "count" : 24
}
...
```

Tim Hanlon is the individual who has participated in the most relationships with companies in this collection. It could be that Mr. Hanlon has actually had a relationship with 28 companies, but we can't know that for sure, because it's also possible that he has had multiple relationships with one or more companies, each with a different title. This example illustrates a very important point about aggregation pipelines: make sure you fully understand what it is you're working with as you do calculations, particularly when you're calculating aggregate values using accumulator expressions of some kind.

In this case, we can say that Tim Hanlon appears 28 times in "relationships" documents throughout the companies in our collection. We would have to dig a little deeper to see exactly how many unique companies he was associated with, but we'll leave the construction of that pipeline to you as an exercise.

The _id Field in Group Stages

Before we go any further with our discussion of the group stage, let's talk a little more about the _id field and look at some best practices for constructing values for this field in group aggregation stages. We'll walk through a few examples that illustrate several different ways in which we commonly group documents. As our first example, consider this pipeline:

```
db.companies.aggregate([
  { $match: { founded_year: { $gte: 2013 } } },
  { $group: {
    _id: { founded_year: "$founded_year"},
    companies: { $push: "$name" }
  } },
  { $sort: { "_id.founded_year": 1 } }
]).pretty()
```

The output for this pipeline resembles the following:

```
{
  "_id" : {
    "founded_year" : 2013
  },
  "companies" : [
    "Fixya",
    "Wamba",
    "Advaliant",
    "Fluc",
    "iBazar",
    "Gimigo",
    "SEOGroup",
    "Clowdy",
    "WhosCall",
    "Pikk",
    "Tongxue",
    "Shopseen",
    "VistaGen Therapeutics"
  ]
}
...
```

In our output we have documents with two fields: "_id" and "companies". Each of these documents contains a list of the companies founded in whatever the "founded_year" is, "companies" being an array of company names.

Notice here how we've constructed the "_id" field in the group stage. Why not just provide the founding year rather than putting it inside a document with a field labeled "founded_year". The reason we don't do it that way is that if we don't label the group value, it's not explicit that we are grouping on the year in which the company was founded. In order to avoid confusion, it is a best practice to explicitly label values on which we group.

In some circumstances it might be necessary to use another approach in which our _id value is a document composed of multiple fields. In this case, we're actually grouping documents on the basis of their founding year and category code:

```
db.companies.aggregate([
  { $match: { founded_year: { $gte: 2010 } } },
  { $group: {
```

```
    _id: { founded_year: "$founded_year", category_code: "$category_code" },
    companies: { $push: "$name" }
  } },
  { $sort: { "_id.founded_year": 1 } }
]).pretty()
```

It is perfectly fine to use documents with multiple fields as our _id value in group stages. In other cases, it might also be necessary to do something like this:

```
db.companies.aggregate([
  { $group: {
    _id: { ipo_year: "$ipo.pub_year" },
    companies: { $push: "$name" }
  } },
  { $sort: { "_id.ipo_year": 1 } }
]).pretty()
```

In this case, we're grouping documents based on the year in which the companies had their IPO, and that year is actually a field of an embedded document. It is common practice to use field paths that reach into embedded documents as the value on which to group in a group stage. In this case, the output will resemble the following:

```
{
  "_id" : {
    "ipo_year" : 1999
  },
  "companies" : [
    "Akamai Technologies",
    "TiVo",
    "XO Group",
    "Nvidia",
    "Blackberry",
    "Blue Coat Systems",
    "Red Hat",
    "Brocade Communications Systems",
    "Juniper Networks",
    "F5 Networks",
    "Informatica",
    "Iron Mountain",
    "Perficient",
    "Sitestar",
    "Oxford Instruments"
  ]
}
```

Note that the examples in this section use an accumulator we haven't seen before: $push. As the group stage processes documents in its input stream, a $push expression will add the resulting value to an array that it builds throughout its run. In the case of the preceding pipeline, the group stage is building an array composed of company names.

Our final example is one we've already seen, but it's included here for the sake of completeness:

```
db.companies.aggregate( [
  { $match: { "relationships.person": { $ne: null } } },
  { $project: { relationships: 1, _id: 0 } },
  { $unwind: "$relationships" },
  { $group: {
    _id: "$relationships.person",
    count: { $sum: 1 }
  } },
  { $sort: { count: -1 } }
] )
```

In the preceding example where we were grouping on IPO year, we used a field path that resolved to a scalar value—the IPO year. In this case, our field path resolves to a document containing three fields: "first_name", "last_name", and "permalink". This demonstrates that the group stage supports grouping on document values.

You've now seen several ways in which we can construct _id values in group stages. In general, bear in mind that what we want to do here is make sure that in our output, the semantics of our _id value are clear.

Group Versus Project

To round out our discussion of the group aggregation stage, we'll take a look at a couple of additional accumulators that are not available in the project stage. This is to encourage you to think a little more deeply about what we can do in a project stage with respect to accumulators, and what we can do in group. As an example, consider this aggregation query:

```
db.companies.aggregate([
  { $match: { funding_rounds: { $ne: [ ] } } },
  { $unwind: "$funding_rounds" },
  { $sort: { "funding_rounds.funded_year": 1,
    "funding_rounds.funded_month": 1,
    "funding_rounds.funded_day": 1 } },
  { $group: {
    _id: { company: "$name" },
    funding: {
      $push: {
        amount: "$funding_rounds.raised_amount",
        year: "$funding_rounds.funded_year"
      } }
  } },
] ).pretty()
```

Here, we begin by filtering for documents for which the array funding_rounds is not empty. Then we unwind funding_rounds. Therefore, the sort and group stages will see one document for each element of the funding_rounds array for every company.

Our sort stage in this pipeline sorts on first year, then month, then day, all in ascending order. This means that this stage will output the oldest funding rounds first. And as you are aware from Chapter 5, we can support this type of sort with a compound index.

In the group stage that follows the sort, we group by company name and use the $push accumulator to construct a sorted array of funding rounds. The fund ing_rounds array will be sorted for each company because we sorted all funding rounds, globally, in the sort stage.

Documents output from this pipeline will resemble the following:

```
{
  "_id" : {
    "company" : "Green Apple Media"
  },
  "funding" : [
    {
      "amount" : 30000000,
      "year" : 2013
    },
    {
      "amount" : 100000000,
      "year" : 2013
    },
    {
      "amount" : 2000000,
      "year" : 2013
    }
  ]
}
```

In this pipeline, with $push, we are accumulating an array. In this case, we have specified our $push expression so that it adds documents to the end of the accumulation array. Since the funding rounds are in chronological order, pushing onto the end of the array guarantees that the the funding amounts for each company are sorted in chronological order.

$push expressions only work in group stages. This is because group stages are designed to take an input stream of documents and accumulate values by processing each document in turn. Project stages, on the other hand, work with each document in their input stream individually.

Let's take a look at one other example. This is a little longer, but it builds on the previous one:

```
db.companies.aggregate([
  { $match: { funding_rounds: { $exists: true, $ne: [ ] } } },
  { $unwind: "$funding_rounds" },
  { $sort: { "funding_rounds.funded_year": 1,
```

```
        "funding_rounds.funded_month": 1,
        "funding_rounds.funded_day": 1 } },
  { $group: {
    _id: { company: "$name" },
    first_round: { $first: "$funding_rounds" },
    last_round: { $last: "$funding_rounds" },
    num_rounds: { $sum: 1 },
    total_raised: { $sum: "$funding_rounds.raised_amount" }
  } },
  { $project: {
    _id: 0,
    company: "$_id.company",
    first_round: {
      amount: "$first_round.raised_amount",
      article: "$first_round.source_url",
      year: "$first_round.funded_year"
    },
    last_round: {
      amount: "$last_round.raised_amount",
      article: "$last_round.source_url",
      year: "$last_round.funded_year"
    },
    num_rounds: 1,
    total_raised: 1,
  } },
  { $sort: { total_raised: -1 } }
] ).pretty()
```

Again, we are unwinding funding_rounds and sorting chronologically. However, in this case, instead of accumulating an array of entries, each entry representing a single funding_rounds, we are using two accumulators we've not yet seen in action: $first and $last. A $first expression simply saves the first value that passes through the input stream for the stage. A $last expression simply tracks the values that pass through the group stage and hangs onto the last one.

As with $push, we can't use $first and $last in project stages because, again, project stages are not designed to accumulate values based on multiple documents streaming through them. Rather, they are designed to reshape documents individually.

In addition to $first and $last, we also use $sum in this example to calculate the total number of funding rounds. For this expression we can just specify the value, 1. A $sum expression like this simply serves to count the number of documents that it sees in each grouping.

Finally, this pipeline includes a fairly complex project stage. However, all it is really doing is making the output prettier. Rather than show the first_round values, or entire documents for the first and last funding rounds, this project stage creates a summary. Note that this maintains good semantics, because each value is clearly labeled. For first_round we'll produce a simple embedded document that contains just the essential details of amount, article, and year, pulling those values from the original funding round document that will be the value of $first_round. The project stage does something similar for $last_round. Finally, this project stage just passes through to output documents the num_rounds and total_raised values for documents it receives in its input stream.

Documents output from this pipeline resemble the following:

```
{
  "first_round" : {
    "amount" : 7500000,
    "article" : "http://www.teslamotors.com/display_data/pressguild.swf",
    "year" : 2004
  },
  "last_round" : {
    "amount" : 10000000,
    "article" : "http://www.bizjournals.com/sanfrancisco/news/2012/10/10/
                tesla-motors-to-get-10-million-from.html",
    "year" : 2012
  },
  "num_rounds" : 11,
  "total_raised" : 823000000,
  "company" : "Tesla Motors"
}
```

And with that, we've concluded an overview of the group stage.

Writing Aggregation Pipeline Results to a Collection

There are two specific stages, $out and $merge, that can write documents resulting from the aggregation pipeline to a collection. You can use only one of these two stages, and it must be the last stage of an aggregation pipeline. $merge was introduced in MongoDB version 4.2 and is the preferred stage for writing to a collection, if available. $out has some limitations: it can only write to the same database, it overwrites any existing collection if present, and it cannot write to a sharded collection. $merge can write to any database and collection, sharded or not. $merge can also incorporate results (insert new documents, merge with existing documents, fail the operation, keep existing documents, or process all documents with a custom update) when working with an existing collection. But the real advantage of using $merge is that it can create on-demand materialized views, where the content of the output collection is incrementally updated when the pipeline is run.

In this chapter, we have covered a number of different accumulators, some that are available in the project stage, and we've also covered how to think about when to use group versus project when considering various accumulators. Next, we'll take a look at transactions in MongoDB.

## CHAPTER 8

Transactions

Transactions are logical groups of processing in a database, and each group or trans-action can contain one or more operations such as reads and/or writes across multiple documents. MongoDB supports ACID-compliant transactions across multiple operations, collections, databases, documents, and shards. In this chapter, we introduce transactions, define what ACID means for a database, highlight how you use these in your applications, and provide tips for tuning transactions in MongoDB. We will cover:

- What a transaction is
- How to use transactions
- Tuning transaction limits for your application

Introduction to Transactions

As we mentioned above, a transaction is a logical unit of processing in a database that includes one or more database operations, which can be read or write operations. There are situations where your application may require reads and writes to multiple documents (in one or more collections) as part of this logical unit of processing. An important aspect of a transaction is that it is never partially completed—it either succeeds or fails.

In order to use transactions, your MongoDB deployment must be on MongoDB version 4.2 or later and your MongoDB drivers must be updated for MongoDB 4.2 or later. MongoDB provides a Driver Compatibility Reference page (*https://oreil.ly/Oe9NE*) that you can use to ensure your MongoDB Driver version is compatible.

A Definition of ACID

ACID is the accepted set of properties a transaction must meet to be a "true" transaction. ACID is an acronym for Atomicity, Consistency, Isolation, and Durability. ACID transactions guarantee the validity of your data and of your database's state even where power failures or other errors occur.

Atomicity ensures that all operations inside a transaction will either be applied or nothing will be applied. A transaction can never be partially applied; either it is committed or it aborts.

Consistency ensures that if a transaction succeeds, the database will move from one consistent state to the next consistent state.

Isolation is the property that permits multiple transactions to run at the same time in your database. It guarantees that a transaction will not view the partial results of any other transaction, which means multiple parallel transactions will have the same results as running each of the transactions sequentially.

Durability ensures that when a transaction is committed all data will persist even in the case of a system failure.

A database is said to be ACID-compliant when it ensures that all these properties are met and that only successful transactions can be processed. In situations where a failure occurs before a transaction is completed, ACID compliance ensures that no data will be changed.

MongoDB is a distributed database with ACID compliant transactions across replica sets and/or across shards. The network layer adds an additional level of complexity. The engineering team at MongoDB provided several chalk and talk videos (*https://www.mongodb.com/transactions*) that describe how they implemented the necessary features to support ACID transactions.

How to Use Transactions

MongoDB provides two APIs to use transactions. The first is a similar syntax to relational databases (e.g., `start_transaction` and `commit_transaction`) called the core API and the second is called the callback API, which is the recommended approach to using transactions.

The core API does not provide retry logic for the majority of errors and requires the developer to code the logic for the operations, the transaction commit function, and any retry and error logic required.

The callback API provides a single function that wraps a large degree of functionality when compared to the core API, including starting a transaction associated with a specified logical session, executing a function supplied as the callback function, and then committing the transaction (or aborting on error). This function also includes retry logic that handle commit errors. The callback API was added in MongoDB 4.2 to simplify application development with transactions as well as make it easier to add application retry logic to handle any transaction errors.

In both APIs, the developer is responsible for starting the logical session that will be used by the transaction. Both APIs require operations in a transaction to be associated with a specific logical session (i.e., pass in the session to each operation). A logical session in MongoDB tracks the time and sequencing of the operations in the context of the entire MongoDB deployment. A logical session or server session is part of the underlying framework used by client sessions to support retryable writes and causal consistency in MongoDB—both of these features were added in MongoDB version 3.6 as part of the foundation required to support transactions. A specific sequence of read and write operations that have a causal relationship reflected by their ordering is defined as a causally consistent client session in MongoDB. A client session is started by an application and used to interact with a server session.

In 2019, six senior engineers from MongoDB published a paper at the SIGMOD 2019 conference entitled "Implementation of Cluster-wide Logical Clock and Causal Consistency in MongoDB" (*https://oreil.ly/IFLvm*).[1] This paper provides a deeper technical explanation of the mechanics behind logical sessions and causal consistency in MongoDB. The paper documents the efforts from a multiteam, multiyear engineering project. The work involved changing aspects of the storage layer, adding a new replication consensus protocol, modifying the sharding architecture, refactoring sharding cluster metadata, and adding a global logical clock. These changes provide the foundation required by the database before ACID-compliant transactions can be added.

The complexity and additional coding required in applications are the main reasons to recommend the callback API over the core API. These differences between the APIs are summarized in Table 8-1.

---

[1] The authors are Misha Tyulenev, staff software engineer for sharding; Andy Schwerin, vice president for Distributed Systems; Asya Kamsky, principal product manager for Distributed Systems; Randolph Tan, senior software engineer for sharding; Alyson Cabral, product manager for Distributed Systems; and Jack Mulrow, software engineer for sharding.

Table 8-1. Comparison of Core API versus Callback API

Core API	Callback API
Requires explicit call to start the transaction and commit the transaction.	Starts a transaction, executes the specified operations, and commits (or aborts on error).
Does not incorporate error-handling logic for TransientTransactionError and UnknownTransactionCommitResult, and instead provides the flexibility to incorporate custom error handling for these errors.	Automatically incorporates error-handling logic for TransientTransactionError and UnknownTransactionCommitResult.
Requires explicit logical session to be passed to API for the specific transaction.	Requires explicit logical session to be passed to API for the specific transaction.

To understand the differences between these two APIs, we can compare the APIs using a simple transaction example for an ecommerce site where an order is placed and the corresponding items are removed from the available stock as they are sold. This involves two documents in different collections in a single transaction. The two operations, which will be the core of our transaction example, are:

```
orders.insert_one({"sku": "abc123", "qty": 100}, session=session)
inventory.update_one({"sku": "abc123", "qty": {"$gte": 100}},
                     {"$inc": {"qty": -100}}, session=session)
```

First, let's see how the core API can be used in Python for our transaction example. The two operations of our transaction are highlighted in Step 1 of the program listing below:

```
# Define the uriString using the DNS Seedlist Connection Format
# for the connection
uri = 'mongodb+srv://server.example.com/'
client = MongoClient(uriString)

my_wc_majority = WriteConcern('majority', wtimeout=1000)

# Prerequisite / Step 0: Create collections, if they don't already exist.
# CRUD operations in transactions must be on existing collections.

client.get_database( "webshop",
                    write_concern=my_wc_majority).orders.insert_one({"sku":
                    "abc123", "qty":0})
client.get_database( "webshop",
                    write_concern=my_wc_majority).inventory.insert_one(
                    {"sku": "abc123", "qty": 1000})

# Step 1: Define the operations and their sequence within the transaction
def update_orders_and_inventory(my_session):
    orders = session.client.webshop.orders
    inventory = session.client.webshop.inventory
```

```
    with session.start_transaction(
            read_concern=ReadConcern("snapshot"),
            write_concern=WriteConcern(w="majority"),
            read_preference=ReadPreference.PRIMARY):

        orders.insert_one({"sku": "abc123", "qty": 100}, session=my_session)
        inventory.update_one({"sku": "abc123", "qty": {"$gte": 100}},
                             {"$inc": {"qty": -100}}, session=my_session)
        commit_with_retry(my_session)

# Step 2: Attempt to run and commit transaction with retry logic
def commit_with_retry(session):
    while True:
        try:
            # Commit uses write concern set at transaction start.
            session.commit_transaction()
            print("Transaction committed.")
            break
        except (ConnectionFailure, OperationFailure) as exc:
            # Can retry commit
            if exc.has_error_label("UnknownTransactionCommitResult"):
                print("UnknownTransactionCommitResult, retrying "
                        "commit operation ...")
                continue
            else:
                print("Error during commit ...")
                raise

# Step 3: Attempt with retry logic to run the transaction function txn_func
def run_transaction_with_retry(txn_func, session):
    while True:
        try:
            txn_func(session)  # performs transaction
            break
        except (ConnectionFailure, OperationFailure) as exc:
            # If transient error, retry the whole transaction
            if exc.has_error_label("TransientTransactionError"):
                print("TransientTransactionError, retrying transaction ...")
                continue
            else:
                raise

# Step 4: Start a session.
with client.start_session() as my_session:

# Step 5: Call the function 'run_transaction_with_retry' passing it the function
# to call 'update_orders_and_inventory' and the session 'my_session' to associate
# with this transaction.

    try:
        run_transaction_with_retry(update_orders_and_inventory, my_session)
    except Exception as exc:
```

```
        # Do something with error. The error handling code is not
        # implemented for you with the Core API.
        raise
```

Now, let's look at how the the callback API can be used in Python for this same transaction example. The two operations of our transaction are highlighted in Step 1 of the
program listing below:

```
# Define the uriString using the DNS Seedlist Connection Format
# for the connection
uriString = 'mongodb+srv://server.example.com/'
client = MongoClient(uriString)

my_wc_majority = WriteConcern('majority', wtimeout=1000)

# Prerequisite / Step 0: Create collections, if they don't already exist.
# CRUD operations in transactions must be on existing collections.

client.get_database( "webshop",
                     write_concern=my_wc_majority).orders.insert_one({"sku":
                     "abc123", "qty":0})
client.get_database( "webshop",
                     write_concern=my_wc_majority).inventory.insert_one(
                     {"sku": "abc123", "qty": 1000})

# Step 1: Define the callback that specifies the sequence of operations to
# perform inside the transactions.

def callback(my_session):
    orders = my_session.client.webshop.orders
    inventory = my_session.client.webshop.inventory

    # Important:: You must pass the session variable 'my_session' to
    # the operations.

    orders.insert_one({"sku": "abc123", "qty": 100}, session=my_session)
    inventory.update_one({"sku": "abc123", "qty": {"$gte": 100}},
                         {"$inc": {"qty": -100}}, session=my_session)

#. Step 2: Start a client session.

with client.start_session() as session:

# Step 3: Use with_transaction to start a transaction, execute the callback,
# and commit (or abort on error).

    session.with_transaction(callback,
                             read_concern=ReadConcern('local'),
                             write_concern=my_write_concern_majority,
                             read_preference=ReadPreference.PRIMARY)
}
```

In MongoDB multidocument transactions, you may only perform read/write (CRUD) operations on existing collections or databases. As shown in our example, you must first create a collection outside of a transaction if you wish to insert it into a transaction. Create, drop, or index operations are not permitted in a transaction.

Tuning Transaction Limits for Your Application

There are a few parameters that are important to be aware of when using transactions. They can be adjusted to ensure your application can make the optimal use of transactions.

Timing and Oplog Size Limits

There are two main categories of limits in MongoDB transactions. The first relates to timing limits of the transaction, controlling how long a specific transaction can run, the time a transaction will wait to acquire locks, and the maximum length that all transactions will run. The second category specifically relates to the MongoDB oplog entry and size limits for an individual entry.

Time limits

The default maximum runtime of a transaction is one minute or less. This can be increased by modifying the limit controlled by transactionLifetimeLimitSec onds at a mongod instance level. In the case of sharded clusters, the parameter must be set on all shard replica set members. After this time has elapsed, a transaction will be considered expired and will be aborted by a cleanup process, which runs periodically. The cleanup process will run once every 60 seconds or every transactionLifetimeLimitSeconds/2, whichever is lower.

To explicitly set a time limit on a transaction, it is recommended that you specify a maxTimeMS on commitTransaction. If maxTimeMS is not set then transaction LifetimeLimitSeconds will be used or if it is set but would exceed transaction LifetimeLimitSeconds then transactionLifetimeLimitSeconds will be used instead.

The default maximum time a transaction will wait to acquire the locks it needs for the operations in the transaction is 5 ms. This can be increased by modifying the limit controlled by maxTransactionLockRequestTimeoutMillis. If the transaction is unable to acquire the locks within this time, it will abort. maxTran sactionLockRequestTimeoutMillis can be set to 0, -1, or a number greater than 0. Setting it to 0 means a transaction will abort if it is unable to immediately acquire all the locks it requires. A setting of -1 will use the operation-specific timeout as specified by maxTimeMS. Any number greater than 0 configures the wait time to that time in seconds as the specified period that a transaction will attempt to acquire the required locks.

Oplog size limits

MongoDB will create as many oplog entries as required for the write operations in a transaction. However, each oplog entry must be within the BSON document size limit of 16MB.

Transactions provide a useful feature in MongoDB to ensure consistency, but they should be used with the rich document model. The flexibility of this model and using best practices such as schema design patterns will help avoid the use of transactions for most situations. Transactions are a powerful feature, best used sparingly in your applications.

## CHAPTER 9

Application Design

This chapter covers designing applications to work effectively with MongoDB. It discusses:

- Schema design considerations
- Trade-offs when deciding whether to embed data or to reference it
- Tips for optimization
- Consistency considerations
- How to migrate schemas
- How to manage schemas
- When MongoDB isn't a good choice of data store

Schema Design Considerations

A key aspect of data representation is the design of the schema, which is the way your data is represented in your documents. The best approach to this design is to represent the data the way your application wants to see it. Thus, unlike in relational databases, you first need to understand your queries and data access patterns before modeling your schema.

Here are the key aspects you need to consider when designing a schema:

Constraints
> You need to understand any database or hardware limitations. You also need to consider a number of MongoDB's specific aspects, such as the maximum document size of 16 MB, that full documents get read and written from disk, that an

update rewrites the whole document, and that atomic updates are at the document level.

Access patterns of your queries and of your writes

You will need to identify and quantify the workload of your application and of the wider system. The workload encompasses both the reads and the writes in your application. Once you know when queries are running and how frequently, you can identify the most common queries. These are the queries you need to design your schema to support. Once you have identified these queries, you should try to minimize the number of queries and ensure in your design that data that gets queried together is stored in the same document.

Data not used in these queries should be put into a different collection. Data that is infrequently used should also be moved to a different collection. It is worth considering if you can separate your dynamic (read/write) data and your static (mostly read) data. The best performance results occur when you prioritize your schema design for your most common queries.

Relation types

You should consider which data is related in terms of your application's needs, as well as the relationships between documents. You can then determine the best approaches to embed or reference the data or documents. You will need to work out how you can reference documents without having to perform additional queries, and how many documents are updated when there is a relationship change. You must also consider if the data structure is easy to query, such as with nested arrays (arrays in arrays), which support modeling certain relationships.

Cardinality

Once you have determined how your documents and your data are related, you should consider the cardinality of these relationships. Specifically, is it one-to-one, one-to-many, many-to-many, one-to-millions, or many-to-billions? It is very important to establish the cardinality of the relationships to ensure you use the best format to model them in your MongoDB schema. You should also consider whether the object on the many/millions side is accessed separately or only in the context of the parent object, as well as the ratio of updates to reads for the data field in question. The answers to these questions will help you to determine whether you should embed documents or reference documents and if you should be denormalizing data across documents.

Schema Design Patterns

Schema design is important in MongoDB, as it impacts directly on application performance. There are many common issues in schema design that can be addressed through the use of known patterns, or "building blocks." It is best practice in schema design to use one or more of these patterns together.

Scheme design patterns that might apply include:

Polymorphic pattern

This is suitable where all documents in a collection have a similar, but not identical, structure. It involves identifying the common fields across the documents that support the common queries that will be run by the application. Tracking specific fields in the documents or subdocuments will help identify the differences between the data and different code paths or classes/subclasses that can be coded in your application to manage these differences. This allows for the use of simple queries in a single collection of not-quite-identical documents to improve query performance.

Attribute pattern

This is suitable when there are a subset of fields in a document that share common features on which you want to sort or query, or when the fields you need to sort on only exist in a subset of the documents, or when both of these conditions are true. It involves reshaping the data into an array of key/value pairs and creating an index on the elements in this array. Qualifiers can be added as additional fields to these key/value pairs. This pattern assists in targeting many similar fields per document so that fewer indexes are required and queries become simpler to write.

Bucket pattern

This is suitable for time series data where the data is captured as a stream over a period of time. It is much more efficient in MongoDB to "bucket" this data into a set of documents each holding the data for a particular time range than it is to create a document per point in time/data point. For example, you might use a one-hour bucket and place all readings for that hour in an array in a single document. The document itself will have start and end times indicating the period this "bucket" covers.

Outlier pattern

This addresses the rare instances where a few queries of documents fall outside the normal pattern for the application. It is an advanced schema pattern designed for situations where popularity is a factor. This can be seen in social networks with major influencers, book sales, movie reviews, etc. It uses a flag to indicate the document is an outlier and stores the additional overflow into one or more documents that refer back to the first document via the "_id". The flag will be used by your application code to make the additional queries to retrieve the overflow document(s).

Computed pattern

This is used when data needs to be computed frequently, and it can also be used when the data access pattern is read-intensive. This pattern recommends that the calculations be done in the background, with the main document being updated periodically. This provides a valid approximation of the computed fields or documents without having to continuously generate these for individual queries. This can significantly reduce the strain on the CPU by avoiding repetition of the same calculations, particularly in use cases where reads trigger the calculation and you have a high read-to-write ratio.

Subset pattern

This is used when you have a working set that exceeds the available RAM of the machine. This can be caused by large documents that contain a lot of information that isn't being used by your application. This pattern suggests that you split frequently used data and infrequently used data into two separate collections. A typical example might be an ecommerce application keeping the 10 most recent reviews of a product in the "main" (frequently accessed) collection and moving all the older reviews into a second collection queried only if the application needs more than the last 10 reviews.

Extended Reference pattern

This is used for scenarios where you have many different logical entities or "things," each with their own collection, but you may want to gather these entities together for a specific function. A typical ecommerce schema might have separate collections for orders, customers, and inventory. This can have a negative performance impact when we want to collect together all the information for a single order from these separate collections. The solution is to identify the frequently accessed fields and duplicate these within the order document. In the case of an ecommerce order, this would be the name and address of the customer we are shipping the item to. This pattern trades off the duplication of data for a reduction in the number of queries necessary to collate the information together.

Approximation pattern

This is useful for situations where resource-expensive (time, memory, CPU cycles) calculations are needed but where exact precision is not absolutely required. An example of this is an image or post like/love counter or a page view counter, where knowing the exact count (e.g., whether it's 999,535 or 1,000,0000) isn't necessary. In these situations, applying this pattern can greatly reduce the number of writes—for example, by only updating the counter after every 100 or more views instead of after every view.

Tree pattern

This can be applied when you have a lot of queries and have data that is primarily hierarchical in structure. It follows the earlier concept of storing data together that is typically queried together. In MongoDB, you can easily store a hierarchy in an array within the same document. In the example of the ecommerce site, specifically its product catalog, there are often products that belong to multiple categories or to categories that are part of other categories. An example might be "Hard Drive," which is itself a category but comes under the "Storage" category, which itself is under the "Computer Parts" category, which is part of the "Electronics" category. In this kind of scenario, we would have a field that would track the entire hierarchy and another field that would hold the immediate category ("Hard Drive"). The entire hierarchy field, kept in an array, provides the ability to use a multikey index on those values. This ensures all items related to categories in the hierarchy will be easily found. The immediate category field allows all items directly related to this category to be found.

Preallocation pattern

This was primarily used with the MMAP storage engine, but there are still uses for this pattern. The pattern recommends creating an initial empty structure that will be populated later. An example use could be for a reservation system that manages a resource on a day-by-day basis, keeping track of whether it is free or already booked/unavailable. A two-dimensional structure of resources (x) and days (y) makes it trivially easy to check availability and perform calculations.

Document Versioning pattern

This provides a mechanism to enable retention of older revisions of documents. It requires an extra field to be added to each document to track the document version in the "main" collection, and an additional collection that contains all the revisions of the documents. This pattern makes a few assumptions: specifically, that each document has a limited number of revisions, that there are not large numbers of documents that need to be versioned, and that the queries are primarily done on the current version of each document. In situations where these assumptions are not valid, you may need to modify the pattern or consider a different schema design pattern.

MongoDB provides several useful resources online on patterns and schema design. MongoDB University offers a free course, M320 Data Modeling (*https://oreil.ly/BYtSr*), as well as a "Building with Patterns" blog series (*https://oreil.ly/MjSld*).

Normalization Versus Denormalization

There are many ways to represent data, and one of the most important issues to consider is how much you should normalize your data. *Normalization* refers to dividing up data into multiple collections with references between collections. Each piece of data lives in one collection, although multiple documents may reference it. Thus, to change the data, only one document must be updated. The MongoDB Aggregation Framework offers joins with the $lookup stage, which performs a left outer join by adding documents to the "joined" collection where there is a matching document in the source collection—it adds a new array field to each matched document in the "joined" collection with the details of the document from the source collection. These reshaped documents are then available in the next stage for further processing.

Denormalization is the opposite of normalization: embedding all of the data in a single document. Instead of documents containing references to one definitive copy of the data, many documents may have copies of the data. This means that multiple documents need to be updated if the information changes, but enables all related data to be fetched with a single query.

Deciding when to normalize and when to denormalize can be difficult: typically, normalizing makes writes faster and denormalizing makes reads faster. Thus, you need to decide what trade-offs make sense for your application.

Examples of Data Representations

Suppose we are storing information about students and the classes that they are taking. One way to represent this would be to have a *students* collection (each student is one document) and a *classes* collection (each class is one document). Then we could have a third collection (*studentClasses*) that contains references to the students and the classes they are taking:

```
> db.studentClasses.findOne({"studentId" : id})
{
    "_id" : ObjectId("512512c1d86041c7dca81915"),
    "studentId" : ObjectId("512512a5d86041c7dca81914"),
    "classes" : [
        ObjectId("512512ced86041c7dca81916"),
        ObjectId("512512dcd86041c7dca81917"),
        ObjectId("512512e6d86041c7dca81918"),
        ObjectId("512512f0d86041c7dca81919")
    ]
}
```

If you are familiar with relational databases, you may have seen this type of join table before (although typically you'd have one student and one class per document, instead of a list of class "_id"s). It's a bit more MongoDB-ish to put the classes in an array, but you usually wouldn't want to store the data this way because it requires a lot of querying to get to the actual information.

Suppose we wanted to find the classes a student was taking. We'd query for the student in the *students* collection, query *studentClasses* for the course "_id"s, and then query the *classes* collection for the class information. Thus, finding this information would take three trips to the server. This is generally *not* the way you want to structure data in MongoDB, unless the classes and students are changing constantly and reading the data does not need to be done quickly.

We can remove one of the dereferencing queries by embedding class references in the student's document:

```
{
    "_id" : ObjectId("512512a5d86041c7dca81914"),
    "name" : "John Doe",
    "classes" : [
        ObjectId("512512ced86041c7dca81916"),
        ObjectId("512512dcd86041c7dca81917"),
        ObjectId("512512e6d86041c7dca81918"),
        ObjectId("512512f0d86041c7dca81919")
    ]
}
```

The "classes" field keeps an array of "_id"s of classes that John Doe is taking. When we want to find out information about those classes, we can query the *classes* collection with those "_id"s. This only takes two queries. This is a fairly popular way to structure data that does not need to be instantly accessible and changes, but not constantly.

If we need to optimize reads further, we can get all of the information in a single query by fully denormalizing the data and storing each class as an embedded document in the "classes" field:

```
{
    "_id" : ObjectId("512512a5d86041c7dca81914"),
    "name" : "John Doe",
    "classes" : [
        {
            "class" : "Trigonometry",
            "credits" : 3,
            "room" : "204"
        },
        {
            "class" : "Physics",
            "credits" : 3,
            "room" : "159"
        },
        {
            "class" : "Women in Literature",
            "credits" : 3,
            "room" : "14b"
        },
        {
            "class" : "AP European History",
            "credits" : 4,
            "room" : "321"
        }
    ]
}
```

The upside of this is that it only takes one query to get the information. The downsides are that it takes up more space and is more difficult to keep in sync. For example, if it turns out that physics was supposed to be worth four credits (not three), every student in the physics class would need to have their document updated (instead of just updating a central "Physics" document).

Finally, you can use the Extended Reference pattern mentioned earlier, which is a hybrid of embedding and referencing—you create an array of subdocuments with the frequently used information, but with a reference to the actual document for more information:

```
{
    "_id" : ObjectId("512512a5d86041c7dca81914"),
    "name" : "John Doe",
    "classes" : [
        {
            "_id" : ObjectId("512512ced86041c7dca81916"),
            "class" : "Trigonometry"
        },
        {
            "_id" : ObjectId("512512dcd86041c7dca81917"),
            "class" : "Physics"
        },
        {
            "_id" : ObjectId("512512e6d86041c7dca81918"),
            "class" : "Women in Literature"
        },
        {
            "_id" : ObjectId("512512f0d86041c7dca81919"),
            "class" : "AP European History"
        }
    ]
}
```

This approach is also a nice option because the amount of information embedded can change over time as your requirements change: if you want to include more or less information on a page, you can embed more or less of it in the document.

Another important consideration is how often this information will change, versus how often it's read. If it will be updated regularly, then normalizing it is a good idea. However, if it changes infrequently, then there is little benefit to optimizing the update process at the expense of every read your application performs.

For example, a textbook normalization use case is to store a user and their address in separate collections. However, people's addresses rarely change, so you generally shouldn't penalize every read on the off chance that someone's moved. Your application should embed the address in the user document.

If you decide to use embedded documents and you need to update them, you should set up a cron job to ensure that any updates you do are successfully propagated to every document. For example, suppose you attempt to do a multi-update but the server crashes before all of the documents have been updated. You need a way to detect this and retry the update.

In terms of update operators, `"$set"` is idempotent but `"$inc"` is not. Idempotent operations will have the same outcome whether tried once or several times; in the case of a network error, retrying the operation will be sufficient for the update to occur. In the case of operators that are not idempotent, the operation should be broken into two operations that are individually idempotent and safe to retry. This can be achieved by including a unique pending token in the first operation and having the second operation use both a unique key and the unique pending token. This approach allows `"$inc"` to be idempotent because each individual `updateOne` operation is idempotent.

To some extent, the more information you are generating, the less of it you should embed. If the content of the embedded fields or number of embedded fields is supposed to grow without bound then they should generally be referenced, not embedded. Things like comment trees or activity lists should be stored as their own documents, not embedded. It is also worth considering using the Subset pattern (described in "Schema Design Patterns" on page 208) to store the most recent items (or some other subset) in the document.

Finally, the fields that are included should be integral to the data in the document. If a field is almost always excluded from your results when you query for a document, it's a good sign that it may belong in another collection. These guidelines are summarized in Table 9-1.

Table 9-1. Comparison of embedding versus references

Embedding is better for...	References are better for...
Small subdocuments	Large subdocuments
Data that does not change regularly	Volatile data
When eventual consistency is acceptable	When immediate consistency is necessary
Documents that grow by a small amount	Documents that grow by a large amount
Data that you'll often need to perform a second query to fetch	Data that you'll often exclude from the results
Fast reads	Fast writes

Suppose we had a *users* collection. Here are some example fields we might have in the user documents and an indication of whether or not they should be embedded:

Account preferences
  These are only relevant to this user document, and will probably be exposed with other user information in the document. Account preferences should generally be embedded.

Recent activity
  This depends on how much recent activity grows and changes. If it is a fixed-size field (say, the last 10 things), it might be useful to embed this information or to implement the Subset pattern.

Friends
> Generally this information should not be embedded, or at least not fully. See "Friends, Followers, and Other Inconveniences" on page 216.

All of the content this user has produced
> This should not be embedded.

Cardinality

Cardinality is an indication of how many references a collection has to another collection. Common relationships are one-to-one, one-to-many, or many-to-many. For example, suppose we had a blog application. Each *post* has a *title*, so that's a one-to-one relationship. Each *author* has many *posts*, so that's a one-to-many relationship. And *posts* have many *tags* and *tags* refer to many *posts*, so that's a many-to-many relationship.

When using MongoDB, it can be conceptually useful to split "many" into subcategories: "many" and "few." For example, you might have a one-to-few relationship between authors and posts: each author only writes a few posts. You might have many-to-few relation between blog posts and tags: you probably have many more blog posts than you have tags. However, you'd have a one-to-many relationship between blog posts and comments: each post has many comments.

Determining few versus many relations can help you decide what to embed versus what to reference. Generally, "few" relationships will work better with embedding, and "many" relationships will work better as references.

Friends, Followers, and Other Inconveniences

> *Keep your friends close and your enemies embedded.*

This section covers considerations for social graph data. Many social applications need to link people, content, followers, friends, and so on. Figuring out how to balance embedding and referencing this highly connected information can be tricky, but generally following, friending, or favoriting can be simplified to a publication/subscription system: one user is subscribing to notifications from another. Thus, there are two basic operations that need to be efficient: storing subscribers and notifying all interested parties of an event.

There are three ways people typically implement subscribing. The first option is to put the producer in the subscriber's document, which looks something like this:

```
{
    "_id" : ObjectId("51250a5cd86041c7dca8190f"),
    "username" : "batman",
    "email" : "batman@waynetech.com"
    "following" : [
        ObjectId("51250a72d86041c7dca81910"),
```

```
            ObjectId("51250a7ed86041c7dca81936")
    ]
}
```

Now, given a user's document, you can issue a query like the following to find all of the activities that have been published that they might be interested in:

```
db.activities.find({"user" : {"$in" :
    user["following"]}})
```

However, if you need to find everyone who is interested in a newly published activity, you'd have to query the "following" field across all users.

Alternatively, you could append the followers to the producer's document, like so:

```
{
    "_id" : ObjectId("51250a7ed86041c7dca81936"),
    "username" : "joker",
    "email" : "joker@mailinator.com"
    "followers" : [
        ObjectId("512510e8d86041c7dca81912"),
        ObjectId("51250a5cd86041c7dca8190f"),
        ObjectId("512510ffd86041c7dca81910")
    ]
}
```

Whenever this user does something, all the users you need to notify are right there. The downside is that now you need to query the whole *users* collection to find everyone a user follows (the opposite limitation as in the previous case).

Either of these options comes with an additional downside: they make your user documents larger and more volatile. The "following" (or "followers") field often won't even need to be returned: how often do you want to list every follower? Thus, the final option neutralizes these downsides by normalizing even further and storing subscriptions in another collection. Normalizing this far is often overkill, but it can be useful for an extremely volatile field that often isn't returned with the rest of the document. "followers" may be a sensible field to normalize this way.

In this case you keep a collection that matches publishers to subscribers, with documents that look something like this:

```
{
    "_id" : ObjectId("51250a7ed86041c7dca81936"), // followee's "_id"
    "followers" : [
        ObjectId("512510e8d86041c7dca81912"),
        ObjectId("51250a5cd86041c7dca8190f"),
        ObjectId("512510ffd86041c7dca81910")
    ]
}
```

This keeps your user documents svelte but means an extra query is needed to get the followers.

Dealing with the Wil Wheaton effect

Regardless of which strategy you use, embedding only works with a limited number of subdocuments or references. If you have celebrity users, they may overflow any document that you're storing followers in. The typical way of compensating for this is to use the Outlier pattern discussed in "Schema Design Patterns" on page 208 and have a "continuation" document, if necessary. For example, you might have:

```
> db.users.find({"username" : "wil"})
{
    "_id" : ObjectId("51252871d86041c7dca8191a"),
    "username" : "wil",
    "email" : "wil@example.com",
    "tbc" : [
        ObjectId("512528ced86041c7dca8191e"),
        ObjectId("5126510dd86041c7dca81924")
    ]
    "followers" : [
        ObjectId("512528a0d86041c7dca8191b"),
        ObjectId("512528a2d86041c7dca8191c"),
        ObjectId("512528a3d86041c7dca8191d"),
        ...
    ]
}
{
    "_id" : ObjectId("512528ced86041c7dca8191e"),
    "followers" : [
        ObjectId("512528f1d86041c7dca8191f"),
        ObjectId("512528f6d86041c7dca81920"),
        ObjectId("512528f8d86041c7dca81921"),
        ...
    ]
}
{
    "_id" : ObjectId("5126510dd86041c7dca81924"),
    "followers" : [
        ObjectId("512673e1d86041c7dca81925"),
        ObjectId("512650efd86041c7dca81922"),
        ObjectId("512650fdd86041c7dca81923"),
        ...
    ]
}
```

Then add application logic to support fetching the documents in the "to be continued" ("tbc") array.

Optimizations for Data Manipulation

To optimize your application, you must first determine what its bottleneck is by evaluating its read and write performance. Optimizing reads generally involves having the correct indexes and returning as much of the information as possible in a single document. Optimizing writes usually involves minimizing the number of indexes you have and making updates as efficient as possible.

There is often a trade-off between schemas that are optimized for writing quickly and those that are optimized for reading quickly, so you may have to decide which is more important for your application. Factor in not only the importance of reads versus writes, but also their proportions: if writes are more important but you're doing a thousand reads to every write, you may still want to optimize reads first.

Removing Old Data

Some data is only important for a brief time: after a few weeks or months it is just wasting storage space. There are three popular options for removing old data: using capped collections, using TTL collections, and dropping collections per time period.

The easiest option is to use a capped collection: set it to a large size and let old data "fall off" the end. However, capped collections pose certain limitations on the operations you can do and are vulnerable to spikes in traffic, temporarily lowering the length of time that they can hold. See "Capped Collections" on page 151 for more information.

The second option is to use a TTL collections. This gives you finer-grain control over when documents are removed, but it may not be fast enough for collections with a very high write volume: it removes documents by traversing the TTL index the same way a user-requested remove would. If a TTL collection can keep up, though, this is probably the easiest solution to implement. See "Time-To-Live Indexes" on page 155 for more information about TTL indexes.

The final option is to use multiple collections: for example, one collection per month. Every time the month changes, your application starts using this month's (empty) collection and searching for data in both the current and previous months' collections. Once a collection is older than, say, six months, you can drop it. This strategy can keep up with nearly any volume of traffic, but it's more complex to build an application around because you have to use dynamic collection (or database) names and possibly query multiple databases.

Planning Out Databases and Collections

Once you have sketched out what your documents look like, you must decide what collections or databases to put them in. This is often a fairly intuitive process, but there are some guidelines to keep in mind.

In general, documents with a similar schema should be kept in the same collection. MongoDB generally disallows combining data from multiple collections, so if there are documents that need to be queried or aggregated together, those are good candidates for putting in one big collection. For example, you might have documents that are fairly different "shapes," but if you're going to be aggregating them, they should all live in the same collection (or you can use the $merge stage if they are in separate collections or databases).

For collections, the big issues to consider are locking (you get a read/write lock per document) and storage. Generally, if you have a high-write workload you may need to consider using multiple physical volumes to reduce I/O bottlenecks. Each database can reside in its own directory when you use the --directoryperdb option, allowing you to mount different databases to different volumes. Thus, you may want all items within a database to be of similar "quality," with a similar access pattern or similar traffic levels.

For example, suppose you have an application with several components: a logging component that creates a huge amount of not-very-valuable data, a user collection, and a couple of collections for user-generated data. These collections are high-value: it is important that user data is safe. There is also a high-traffic collection for social activities, which is of lower importance but not quite as unimportant as the logs. This collection is mainly used for user notifications, so it is almost an append-only collection.

Splitting these up by importance, you might end up with three databases: *logs*, *activities*, and *users*. The nice thing about this strategy is that you may find that your highest-value data is also what you have the least of (e.g., users probably don't generate as much data as logging does). You might not be able to afford an SSD for your entire dataset, but you might be able to get one for your users, or you might use RAID10 for users and RAID0 for logs and activities.

Be aware that there are some limitations when using multiple databases prior to MongoDB 4.2 and the introduction of the $merge operator in the Aggregation Framework, which allows you to store results from an aggregation from one database to a different database and a different collection within that database. An additional point to note is that the renameCollection command is slower when copying an existing collection from one database to a different database, as it must copy all the documents to the new database.

Managing Consistency

You must figure out how consistent your application's reads need to be. MongoDB supports a huge variety of consistency levels, from always being able to read your own writes to reading data of unknown oldness. If you're reporting on the last year of activity, you might only need data that's correct to the last couple of days. Conversely, if you're doing real-time trading, you might need to immediately read the latest writes.

To understand how to achieve these varying levels of consistency, it is important to understand what MongoDB is doing under the hood. The server keeps a queue of requests for each connection. When the client sends a request, it will be placed at the end of its connection's queue. Any subsequent requests on the connection will occur after the previously enqueued operation is processed. Thus, a single connection has a consistent view of the database and can always read its own writes.

Note that this is a per-connection queue: if we open two shells, we will have two connections to the database. If we perform an insert in one shell, a subsequent query in the other shell might not return the inserted document. However, within a single shell, if we query for a document after inserting it, the document will be returned. This behavior can be difficult to duplicate by hand, but on a busy server interleaved inserts and queries are likely to occur. Often developers run into this when they insert data in one thread and then check that it was successfully inserted in another. For a moment or two, it looks like the data was not inserted, and then it suddenly appears.

This behavior is especially worth keeping in mind when using the Ruby, Python, and Java drivers, because all three use connection pooling. For efficiency, these drivers open multiple connections (a *pool*) to the server and distribute requests across them. They all, however, have mechanisms to guarantee that a series of requests is processed by a single connection. There is detailed documentation on connection pooling for the various languages in the MongoDB Drivers Connection Monitoring and Pooling specification (*https://oreil.ly/nAt9i*).

When you send reads to a replica set secondary (see Chapter 12), this becomes an even larger issue. Secondaries may lag behind the primary, leading to reading data from seconds, minutes, or even hours ago. There are several ways to deal with this, the easiest being to simply send all reads to the primary if you care about staleness.

MongoDB offers the `readConcern` option to control the consistency and isolation properties of the data being read. It can be combined with `writeConcern` to control the consistency and availability guarantees made to your application. There are five levels: `"local"`, `"available"`, `"majority"`, `"linearizable"`, and `"snapshot"`. Depending on the application, in cases where you want to avoid read staleness you could consider using `"majority"`, which returns only durable data that has been acknowledged by the majority of the replica set members and will not be rolled back.

"linearizable" may also be an option: it returns data that reflects all successful majority-acknowledged writes that have completed prior to the start of the read operation. MongoDB may wait for concurrently executing writes to finish before returning the results with the "linearizable" readConcern.

Three senior engineers from MongoDB published a paper called "Tunable Consistency in MongoDB" (*https://oreil.ly/PfcBx*) at the PVLDB conference in 2019.[1] This paper outlines the different MongoDB consistency models used for replication and how application developers can utilize the various models.

Migrating Schemas

As your application grows and your needs change, your schema may have to grow and change as well. There are a couple of ways of accomplishing this, but regardless of the method you choose, you should carefully document each schema that your application has used. Ideally, you should consider if the Document Versioning pattern (see "Schema Design Patterns" on page 208) is applicable.

The simplest method is to simply have your schema evolve as your application requires, making sure that your application supports all old versions of the schema (e.g., accepting the existence or nonexistence of fields or dealing with multiple possible field types gracefully). But this technique can become messy, particularly if you have conflicting schema versions. For instance, one version might require a "mobile" field, another version might require *not* having a "mobile" field but instead require a different field, and yet another version might treat the "mobile" field as optional. Keeping track of these shifting requirements can gradually turn your code into spaghetti.

To handle changing requirements in a slightly more structured way, you can include a "version" field (or just "v") in each document and use that to determine what your application will accept for document structure. This enforces your schema more rigorously: a document has to be valid for some version of the schema, if not the current one. However, it still requires supporting old versions.

The final option is to migrate all of your data when the schema changes. Generally this is not a good idea: MongoDB allows you to have a dynamic schema in order to avoid migrates because they put a lot of pressure on your system. However, if you do decide to change every document, you will need to ensure that all the documents were successfully updated. MongoDB supports *transactions*, which support this type

---

1 The authors are William Schultz, senior software engineer for replication; Tess Avitabile, team lead of the replication team; and Alyson Cabral, product manager for Distributed Systems.

of migration. If MongoDB crashes in the middle of a transaction, the older schema will be retained.

Managing Schemas

MongoDB introduced schema validation in version 3.2, which allows for validation during updates and insertions. In version 3.6 it added JSON Schema validation via the `$jsonSchema` operator, which is now the recommended method for all schema validation in MongoDB. At the time of writing MongoDB supports draft 4 of JSON Schema, but please check the documentation for the most up-to-date information on this feature.

Validation does not check existing documents until they are modified, and it is configured per collection. To add validation to an existing collection, you use the `coll Mod` command with the `validator` option. You can add validation to a new collection by specifying the `validator` option when using `db.createCollection()`. MongoDB also provides two additional options, `validationLevel` and `validationAction`. `validationLevel` determines how strictly validation rules are applied to existing documents during an update, and `validationAction` decides whether an error plus rejection or a warning with allowance for illegal documents should occur.

When Not to Use MongoDB

While MongoDB is a general-purpose database that works well for most applications, it isn't good at everything. There are a few reasons you might need to avoid it:

- Joining many different types of data across many different dimensions is something relational databases are fantastic at. MongoDB isn't supposed to do this well and most likely never will.

- One of the big (if, hopefully, temporary) reasons to use a relational database over MongoDB is if you're using tools that don't support it. From SQLAlchemy to WordPress, there are thousands of tools that just weren't built to support MongoDB. The pool of tools that do support it is growing, but its ecosystem is hardly the size of relational databases' yet.

## PART III

Replication

## CHAPTER 10

Setting Up a Replica Set

This chapter introduces MongoDB's high-availability system: replica sets. It covers:

- What replica sets are
- How to set up a replica set
- What configuration options are available for replica set members

Introduction to Replication

Since the first chapter, we've been using a standalone server, a single *mongod* server. It's an easy way to get started but a dangerous way to run in production. What if your server crashes or becomes unavailable? Your database will be unavailable for at least a little while. If there are problems with the hardware, you might have to move your data to another machine. In the worst case, disk or network issues could leave you with corrupt or inaccessible data.

Replication is a way of keeping identical copies of your data on multiple servers and is recommended for all production deployments. Replication keeps your application running and your data safe, even if something happens to one or more of your servers.

With MongoDB, you set up replication by creating a *replica set*. A replica set is a group of servers with one *primary*, the server taking writes, and multiple *secondaries*, servers that keep copies of the primary's data. If the primary crashes, the secondaries can elect a new primary from amongst themselves.

If you are using replication and a server goes down, you can still access your data from the other servers in the set. If the data on a server is damaged or inaccessible, you can make a new copy of the data from one of the other members of the set.

This chapter introduces replica sets and covers how to set up replication on your system. If you are less interested in replication mechanics and simply want to create a replica set for testing/development or production, use MongoDB's cloud solution, MongoDB Atlas (*https://atlas.mongodb.com*). It's easy to use and provides a free-tier option for experimentation. Alternatively, to manage MongoDB clusters in your own infrastructure, you can use Ops Manager (*https://oreil.ly/-X6yp*).

Setting Up a Replica Set, Part 1

In this chapter, we'll show you how to set up a three-node replica set on a single machine so you can start experimenting with replica set mechanics. This is the type of setup that you might script just to get a replica set up and running and then poke at it with administrative commands in the *mongo* shell or simulate network partitions or server failures to better understand how MongoDB handles high availability and disaster recovery. In production, you should always use a replica set and allocate a dedicated host to each member to avoid resource contention and provide isolation against server failure. To provide further resilience, you should also use the DNS Seedlist Connection format (*https://oreil.ly/cCORE*) to specify how your applications connect to your replica set. The advantage to using DNS is that servers hosting your MongoDB replica set members can be changed in rotation without needing to reconfigure the clients (specifically, their connection strings).

Given the variety of virtualization and cloud options available, it is nearly as easy to bring up a test replica set with each member on a dedicated host. We've provided a Vagrant script to allow you to experiment with this option.[1]

To get started with our test replica set, let's first create separate data directories for each node. On Linux or macOS, run the following command in the terminal to create the three directories:

```
$ mkdir -p ~/data/rs{1,2,3}
```

This will create the directories *~/data/rs1*, *~/data/rs2*, and *~/data/rs3* (~ identifies your home directory).

On Windows, to create these directories, run the following in the Command Prompt (cmd) or PowerShell:

```
> md c:\data\rs1 c:\data\rs2 c:\data\rs3
```

Then, on Linux or macOS, run each of the following commands in a separate terminal:

---

1 See *https://github.com/mongodb-the-definitive-guide-3e/mongodb-the-definitive-guide-3e*.

```
$ mongod --replSet mdbDefGuide --dbpath ~/data/rs1 --port 27017 \
    --smallfiles --oplogSize 200
$ mongod --replSet mdbDefGuide --dbpath ~/data/rs2 --port 27018 \
    --smallfiles --oplogSize 200
$ mongod --replSet mdbDefGuide --dbpath ~/data/rs3 --port 27019 \
    --smallfiles --oplogSize 200
```

On Windows, run each of the following commands in its own Command Prompt or PowerShell window:

```
> mongod --replSet mdbDefGuide --dbpath c:\data\rs1 --port 27017 \
    --smallfiles --oplogSize 200
> mongod --replSet mdbDefGuide --dbpath c:\data\rs2 --port 27018 \
    --smallfiles --oplogSize 200
> mongod --replSet mdbDefGuide --dbpath c:\data\rs3 --port 27019 \
    --smallfiles --oplogSize 200
```

Once you've started them, you should have three separate *mongod* processes running.

 In general, the principles we will walk through in the rest of this chapter apply to replica sets used in production deployments where each *mongod* has a dedicated host. However, there are additional details pertaining to securing replica sets that we address in Chapter 19; we'll touch on those just briefly here as a preview.

Networking Considerations

Every member of a set must be able to make connections to every other member of the set (including itself). If you get errors about members not being able to reach other members that you know are running, you may have to change your network configuration to allow connections between them.

The processes you've launched can just as easily be running on separate servers. However, with the release of MongoDB 3.6, *mongod* binds to *localhost* (127.0.0.1) only by default. In order for each member of replica set to communicate with the others, you must also bind to an IP address that is reachable by other members. If we were running a *mongod* instance on a server with a network interface having an IP address of 198.51.100.1 and we wanted to run it as a member of replica set with each member on different servers, we could specify the command-line parameter --bind_ip or use bind_ip in the configuration file for this instance:

```
$ mongod --bind_ip localhost,192.51.100.1 --replSet mdbDefGuide \
    --dbpath ~/data/rs1 --port 27017 --smallfiles --oplogSize 200
```

We would make similar modifications to launch the other *mongod*s as well in this case, regardless of whether we're running on Linux, macOS, or Windows.

Security Considerations

Before you bind to IP addresses other than *localhost*, when configuring a replica set, you should enable authorization controls and specify an authentication mechanism. In addition, it is a good idea to encrypt data on disk and communication among replica set members and between the set and clients. We'll go into more detail on securing replica sets in Chapter 19.

Setting Up a Replica Set, Part 2

Returning to our example, with the work we've done so far, each *mongod* does not yet know that the others exist. To tell them about one another, we need to create a configuration that lists each of the members and send this configuration to one of our *mongod* processes. It will take care of propagating the configuration to the other members.

In a fourth terminal, Windows Command Prompt, or PowerShell window, launch a *mongo* shell that connects to one of the running *mongod* instances. You can do this by typing the following command. With this command, we'll connect to the *mongod* running on port 27017:

```
$ mongo --port 27017
```

Then, in the *mongo* shell, create a configuration document and pass this to the rs.initiate() helper to initiate a replica set. This will initiate a replica set containing three members and propagate the configuration to the rest of the *mongods* so that a replica set is formed:

```
> rsconf = {
    _id: "mdbDefGuide",
    members: [
        {_id: 0, host: "localhost:27017"},
        {_id: 1, host: "localhost:27018"},
        {_id: 2, host: "localhost:27019"}
    ]
}
> rs.initiate(rsconf)
{ "ok" : 1, "operationTime" : Timestamp(1501186502, 1) }
```

There are several important parts of a replica set configuration document. The config's "_id" is the name of the replica set that you passed in on the command line (in this example, "mdbDefGuide"). Make sure that this name matches exactly.

The next part of the document is an array of members of the set. Each of these needs two fields: an "_id" that is an integer and unique among the replica set members, and a hostname.

Note that we are using *localhost* as a hostname for the members in this set. This is for example purposes only. In later chapters where we discuss securing replica sets, we'll look at configurations that are more appropriate for production deployments. MongoDB allows all-*localhost* replica sets for testing locally but will protest if you try to mix *localhost* and non-*localhost* servers in a config.

This config document is your replica set configuration. The member running on *localhost:27017* will parse the configuration and send messages to the other members, alerting them of the new configuration. Once they have all loaded the configuration, they will elect a primary and start handling reads and writes.

 Unfortunately, you cannot convert a standalone server to a replica set without some downtime for restarting it and initializing the set. Thus, even if you only have one server to start out with, you may want to configure it as a one-member replica set. That way, if you want to add more members later, you can do so without downtime.

If you are starting a brand-new set, you can send the configuration to any member in the set. If you are starting with data on one of the members, you must send the configuration to the member with data. You cannot initiate a replica set with data on more than one member.

Once initiated, you should have a fully functional replica set. The replica set should elect a primary. You can view the status of a replica set using `rs.status()`. The output from `rs.status()` tells you quite a bit about the replica set, including a number of things we've not yet covered, but don't worry, we'll get there! For now, take a look at the `members` array. Note that all three of our *mongod* instances are listed in this array and that one of them, in this case the *mongod* running on port 27017, has been elected primary. The other two are secondaries. If you try this for yourself you will certainly have different values for `"date"` and the several `Timestamp` values in this output, but you might also find that a different *mongod* was elected primary (that's totally fine):

```
> rs.status()
{
    "set" : "mdbDefGuide",
    "date" : ISODate("2017-07-27T20:23:31.457Z"),
    "myState" : 1,
    "term" : NumberLong(1),
    "heartbeatIntervalMillis" : NumberLong(2000),
    "optimes" : {
        "lastCommittedOpTime" : {
            "ts" : Timestamp(1501187006, 1),
            "t" : NumberLong(1)
        },
        "appliedOpTime" : {
```

```
                    "ts" : Timestamp(1501187006, 1),
                    "t" : NumberLong(1)
            },
            "durableOpTime" : {
                    "ts" : Timestamp(1501187006, 1),
                    "t" : NumberLong(1)
            }
    },
    "members" : [
            {
                    "_id" : 0,
                    "name" : "localhost:27017",
                    "health" : 1,
                    "state" : 1,
                    "stateStr" : "PRIMARY",
                    "uptime" : 688,
                    "optime" : {
                        "ts" : Timestamp(1501187006, 1),
                        "t" : NumberLong(1)
                    },
                    "optimeDate" : ISODate("2017-07-27T20:23:26Z"),
                    "electionTime" : Timestamp(1501186514, 1),
                    "electionDate" : ISODate("2017-07-27T20:15:14Z"),
                    "configVersion" : 1,
                    "self" : true
            },
            {
                    "_id" : 1,
                    "name" : "localhost:27018",
                    "health" : 1,
                    "state" : 2,
                    "stateStr" : "SECONDARY",
                    "uptime" : 508,
                    "optime" : {
                        "ts" : Timestamp(1501187006, 1),
                        "t" : NumberLong(1)
                    },
                    "optimeDurable" : {
                        "ts" : Timestamp(1501187006, 1),
                        "t" : NumberLong(1)
                    },
                    "optimeDate" : ISODate("2017-07-27T20:23:26Z"),
                    "optimeDurableDate" : ISODate("2017-07-27T20:23:26Z"),
                    "lastHeartbeat" : ISODate("2017-07-27T20:23:30.818Z"),
                    "lastHeartbeatRecv" : ISODate("2017-07-27T20:23:30.113Z"),
                    "pingMs" : NumberLong(0),
                    "syncingTo" : "localhost:27017",
                    "configVersion" : 1
            },
            {
                    "_id" : 2,
                    "name" : "localhost:27019",
```

```
            "health" : 1,
            "state" : 2,
            "stateStr" : "SECONDARY",
            "uptime" : 508,
            "optime" : {
                "ts" : Timestamp(1501187006, 1),
                "t" : NumberLong(1)
            },
            "optimeDurable" : {
                "ts" : Timestamp(1501187006, 1),
                "t" : NumberLong(1)
            },
            "optimeDate" : ISODate("2017-07-27T20:23:26Z"),
            "optimeDurableDate" : ISODate("2017-07-27T20:23:26Z"),
            "lastHeartbeat" : ISODate("2017-07-27T20:23:30.818Z"),
            "lastHeartbeatRecv" : ISODate("2017-07-27T20:23:30.113Z"),
            "pingMs" : NumberLong(0),
            "syncingTo" : "localhost:27017",
            "configVersion" : 1
        }
    ],
    "ok" : 1,
    "operationTime" : Timestamp(1501187006, 1)
}
```

---

rs Helper Functions

rs is a global variable that contains replication helper functions (run rs.help() to see the helpers it exposes). These functions are almost always just wrappers around database commands. For example, the following database command is equivalent to rs.initiate(config):

```
> db.adminCommand({"replSetInitiate" : config})
```

It is good to have familiarity with both the helpers and the underlying commands, because it might be easier to use the command form instead of the helper.

Observing Replication

If your replica set elected the *mongod* on port 27017 as primary, then the *mongo* shell used to initiate the replica set is currently connected to the primary. You should see the prompt change to something like the following:

```
mdbDefGuide:PRIMARY>
```

This indicates that we are connected to the primary of the replica set having the "_id" "mdbDefGuide". To simplify and for the sake of clarity, we'll abbreviate the *mongo* shell prompt to just > throughout the replication examples.

If your replica set elected a different node primary, quit the shell and connect to the primary by specifying the correct port number in the command line, as we did when launching the *mongo* shell earlier. For example, if your set's primary is on port 27018, connect using the following command:

```
$ mongo --port 27018
```

Now that you're connected to the primary, try doing some writes and see what happens. First, insert 1,000 documents:

```
> use test
> for (i=0; i<1000; i++) {db.coll.insert({count: i})}
>
> // make sure the docs are there
> db.coll.count()
1000
```

Now check one of the secondaries and verify that it has a copy of all of these documents. You could do this by quitting the shell and connecting using the port number of one of the secondaries, but it's easy to acquire a connection to one of the secondaries by instantiating a connection object using the `Mongo` constructor within the shell you're already running.

First, use your connection to the *test* database on the primary to run the `isMaster` command. This will show you the status of the replica set, in a much more concise form than `rs.status()`. It is also a convenient means of determining which member is primary when writing application code or scripting:

```
> db.isMaster()
{
    "hosts" : [
        "localhost:27017",
        "localhost:27018",
        "localhost:27019"
    ],
    "setName" : "mdbDefGuide",
    "setVersion" : 1,
    "ismaster" : true,
    "secondary" : false,
    "primary" : "localhost:27017",
    "me" : "localhost:27017",
    "electionId" : ObjectId("7fffffff0000000000000004"),
    "lastWrite" : {
        "opTime" : {
            "ts" : Timestamp(1501198208, 1),
            "t" : NumberLong(4)
        },
        "lastWriteDate" : ISODate("2017-07-27T23:30:08Z")
    },
    "maxBsonObjectSize" : 16777216,
    "maxMessageSizeBytes" : 48000000,
```

```
            "maxWriteBatchSize" : 1000,
            "localTime" : ISODate("2017-07-27T23:30:08.722Z"),
            "maxWireVersion" : 6,
            "minWireVersion" : 0,
            "readOnly" : false,
            "compression" : [
                "snappy"
            ],
            "ok" : 1,
            "operationTime" : Timestamp(1501198208, 1)
        }
```

If at any point an election is called and the *mongod* you're connected to becomes a secondary, you can use the isMaster command to determine which member has become primary. The output here tells us that *localhost:27018* and *localhost:27019* are both secondaries, so we can use either for our purposes. Let's instantiate a connection to *localhost:27019*:

```
> secondaryConn = new Mongo("localhost:27019")
connection to localhost:27019
>
> secondaryDB = secondaryConn.getDB("test")
test
```

Now, if we attempt to do a read on the collection that has been replicated to the secondary, we'll get an error. Let's attempt to do a find on this collection and then review the error and why we get it:

```
> secondaryDB.coll.find()
Error: error: {
    "operationTime" : Timestamp(1501200089, 1),
    "ok" : 0,
    "errmsg" : "not master and slaveOk=false",
    "code" : 13435,
    "codeName" : "NotMasterNoSlaveOk"
}
```

Secondaries may fall behind the primary (or *lag*) and not have the most current writes, so secondaries will refuse read requests by default to prevent applications from accidentally reading stale data. Thus, if you attempt to query a secondary, you'll get an error stating that it's not the primary. This is to protect your application from accidentally connecting to a secondary and reading stale data. To allow queries on the secondary, we can set an "I'm okay with reading from secondaries" flag, like so:

```
> secondaryConn.setSlaveOk()
```

Note that slaveOk is set on the *connection* (secondaryConn), not the database (secondaryDB).

Now you're all set to read from this member. Query it normally:

```
> secondaryDB.coll.find()
{ "_id" : ObjectId("597a750696fd35621b4b85db"), "count" : 0 }
{ "_id" : ObjectId("597a750696fd35621b4b85dc"), "count" : 1 }
{ "_id" : ObjectId("597a750696fd35621b4b85dd"), "count" : 2 }
{ "_id" : ObjectId("597a750696fd35621b4b85de"), "count" : 3 }
{ "_id" : ObjectId("597a750696fd35621b4b85df"), "count" : 4 }
{ "_id" : ObjectId("597a750696fd35621b4b85e0"), "count" : 5 }
{ "_id" : ObjectId("597a750696fd35621b4b85e1"), "count" : 6 }
{ "_id" : ObjectId("597a750696fd35621b4b85e2"), "count" : 7 }
{ "_id" : ObjectId("597a750696fd35621b4b85e3"), "count" : 8 }
{ "_id" : ObjectId("597a750696fd35621b4b85e4"), "count" : 9 }
{ "_id" : ObjectId("597a750696fd35621b4b85e5"), "count" : 10 }
{ "_id" : ObjectId("597a750696fd35621b4b85e6"), "count" : 11 }
{ "_id" : ObjectId("597a750696fd35621b4b85e7"), "count" : 12 }
{ "_id" : ObjectId("597a750696fd35621b4b85e8"), "count" : 13 }
{ "_id" : ObjectId("597a750696fd35621b4b85e9"), "count" : 14 }
{ "_id" : ObjectId("597a750696fd35621b4b85ea"), "count" : 15 }
{ "_id" : ObjectId("597a750696fd35621b4b85eb"), "count" : 16 }
{ "_id" : ObjectId("597a750696fd35621b4b85ec"), "count" : 17 }
{ "_id" : ObjectId("597a750696fd35621b4b85ed"), "count" : 18 }
{ "_id" : ObjectId("597a750696fd35621b4b85ee"), "count" : 19 }
Type "it" for more
```

You can see that all of our documents are there.

Now, try to write to a secondary:

```
> secondaryDB.coll.insert({"count" : 1001})
WriteResult({ "writeError" : { "code" : 10107, "errmsg" : "not master" } })
> secondaryDB.coll.count()
1000
```

You can see that the secondary does not accept the write. A secondary will only perform writes that it gets through replication, not from clients.

There is one other interesting feature that you should try out: automatic failover. If the primary goes down, one of the secondaries will automatically be elected primary. To test this, stop the primary:

```
> db.adminCommand({"shutdown" : 1})
```

You'll see some error messages generated when you run this command because the *mongod* running on port 27017 (the member we're connected to) will terminate and the shell we're using will lose its connection:

```
2017-07-27T20:10:50.612-0400 E QUERY    [thread1] Error: error doing query:
 failed: network error while attempting to run command 'shutdown' on host
 '127.0.0.1:27017'  :
DB.prototype.runCommand@src/mongo/shell/db.js:163:1
DB.prototype.adminCommand@src/mongo/shell/db.js:179:16
@(shell):1:1
2017-07-27T20:10:50.614-0400 I NETWORK  [thread1] trying reconnect to
 127.0.0.1:27017 (127.0.0.1) failed
```

```
2017-07-27T20:10:50.615-0400 I NETWORK  [thread1] reconnect
  127.0.0.1:27017 (127.0.0.1) ok
MongoDB Enterprise mdbDefGuide:SECONDARY>
2017-07-27T20:10:56.051-0400 I NETWORK  [thread1] trying reconnect to
  127.0.0.1:27017 (127.0.0.1) failed
2017-07-27T20:10:56.051-0400 W NETWORK  [thread1] Failed to connect to
  127.0.0.1:27017, in(checking socket for error after poll), reason:
  Connection refused
2017-07-27T20:10:56.051-0400 I NETWORK  [thread1] reconnect
  127.0.0.1:27017 (127.0.0.1) failed failed
MongoDB Enterprise >
MongoDB Enterprise > secondaryConn.isMaster()
2017-07-27T20:11:15.422-0400 E QUERY    [thread1] TypeError:
  secondaryConn.isMaster is not a function :
@(shell):1:1
```

This isn't a problem. It won't cause the shell to crash. Go ahead and run `isMaster` on the secondary to see who has become the new primary:

```
> secondaryDB.isMaster()
```

The output from `isMaster` should look something like this:

```
{
    "hosts" : [
        "localhost:27017",
        "localhost:27018",
        "localhost:27019"
    ],
    "setName" : "mdbDefGuide",
    "setVersion" : 1,
    "ismaster" : true,
    "secondary" : false,
    "primary" : "localhost:27018",
    "me" : "localhost:27019",
    "electionId" : ObjectId("7fffffff0000000000000005"),
    "lastWrite" : {
        "opTime" : {
            "ts" : Timestamp(1501200681, 1),
            "t" : NumberLong(5)
        },
        "lastWriteDate" : ISODate("2017-07-28T00:11:21Z")
    },
    "maxBsonObjectSize" : 16777216,
    "maxMessageSizeBytes" : 48000000,
    "maxWriteBatchSize" : 1000,
    "localTime" : ISODate("2017-07-28T00:11:28.115Z"),
    "maxWireVersion" : 6,
    "minWireVersion" : 0,
    "readOnly" : false,
    "compression" : [
        "snappy"
    ],
```

```
        "ok" : 1,
        "operationTime" : Timestamp(1501200681, 1)
    }
```

Note that the primary has switched to 27018. Your primary may be the other server; whichever secondary noticed that the primary was down first will be elected. Now you can send writes to the new primary.

 isMaster is a very old command, predating replica sets to when MongoDB only supported master/slave replication. Thus, it does not use the replica set terminology consistently: it still calls the primary a "master." You can generally think of "master" as equivalent to "primary" and "slave" as equivalent to "secondary."

Go ahead and bring back up the server we had running at *localhost:27017*. You simply need to find the command-line interface from which you launched it. You'll see some messages indicating that it terminated. Just run it again using the same command you used to launch it originally.

Congratulations! You just set up, used, and even poked a little at a replica set to force a shutdown and an election for a new primary.

There are a few key concepts to remember:

- Clients can send a primary all the same operations they could send a standalone server (reads, writes, commands, index builds, etc.).
- Clients cannot write to secondaries.
- Clients, by default, cannot read from secondaries. You can enable this by explicitly setting an "I know I'm reading from a secondary" setting on the connection.

Changing Your Replica Set Configuration

Replica set configurations can be changed at any time: members can be added, removed, or modified. There are shell helpers for some common operations. For example, to add a new member to the set, you can use rs.add:

```
> rs.add("localhost:27020")
```

Similarly, you can remove members:

```
> rs.remove("localhost:27017")
{ "ok" : 1, "operationTime" : Timestamp(1501202441, 2) }
```

You can check that a reconfiguration succeeded by running rs.config() in the shell. It will print the current configuration:

```
> rs.config()
{
    "_id" : "mdbDefGuide",
    "version" : 3,
    "protocolVersion" : NumberLong(1),
    "members" : [
        {
            "_id" : 1,
            "host" : "localhost:27018",
            "arbiterOnly" : false,
            "buildIndexes" : true,
            "hidden" : false,
            "priority" : 1,
            "tags" : {

            },
            "slaveDelay" : NumberLong(0),
            "votes" : 1
        },
        {
            "_id" : 2,
            "host" : "localhost:27019",
            "arbiterOnly" : false,
            "buildIndexes" : true,
            "hidden" : false,
            "priority" : 1,
            "tags" : {

            },
            "slaveDelay" : NumberLong(0),
            "votes" : 1
        },
        {
            "_id" : 3,
            "host" : "localhost:27020",
            "arbiterOnly" : false,
            "buildIndexes" : true,
            "hidden" : false,
            "priority" : 1,
            "tags" : {

            },
            "slaveDelay" : NumberLong(0),
            "votes" : 1
        }
    ],
    "settings" : {
        "chainingAllowed" : true,
        "heartbeatIntervalMillis" : 2000,
        "heartbeatTimeoutSecs" : 10,
        "electionTimeoutMillis" : 10000,
        "catchUpTimeoutMillis" : -1,
```

```
        "getLastErrorModes" : {
        },
        "getLastErrorDefaults" : {
            "w" : 1,
            "wtimeout" : 0
        },
        "replicaSetId" : ObjectId("597a49c67e297327b1e5b116")
    }
}
```

Each time you change the configuration, the "version" field will increase. It starts at version 1.

You can also modify existing members, not just add and remove them. To make modifications, create the configuration document that you want in the shell and call rs.reconfig(). For example, suppose we have a configuration such as the one shown here:

```
> rs.config()
{
    "_id" : "testReplSet",
    "version" : 2,
    "members" : [
        {
            "_id" : 0,
            "host" : "198.51.100.1:27017"
        },
        {
            "_id" : 1,
            "host" : "localhost:27018"
        },
        {
            "_id" : 2,
            "host" : "localhost:27019"
        }
    ]
}
```

Someone accidentally added member 0 by IP address, instead of its hostname. To change that, first we load the current configuration in the shell and then we change the relevant fields:

```
> var config = rs.config()
> config.members[0].host = "localhost:27017"
```

Now that the config document is correct, we need to send it to the database using the rs.reconfig() helper:

```
> rs.reconfig(config)
```

`rs.reconfig()` is often more useful than `rs.add()` and `rs.remove()` for complex operations, such as modifying members' configurations or adding/removing multiple members at once. You can use it to make any legal configuration change you need: simply create the config document that represents your desired configuration and pass it to `rs.reconfig()`.

How to Design a Set

To plan out your set, there are certain concepts that you must be familiar with. The next chapter goes into more detail about these, but the most important is that replica sets are all about majorities: you need a majority of members to elect a primary, a primary can only stay primary as long as it can reach a majority, and a write is safe when it's been replicated to a majority. This majority is defined to be "more than half of all members in the set," as shown in Table 10-1.

Table 10-1. What is a majority?

Number of members in the set	Majority of the set
1	1
2	2
3	2
4	3
5	3
6	4
7	4

Note that it doesn't matter how many members are down or unavailable; majority is based on the set's configuration.

For example, suppose that we have a five-member set and three members go down, as shown in Figure 10-1. There are still two members up. These two members cannot reach a majority of the set (at least three members), so they cannot elect a primary. If one of them were primary, it would step down as soon as it noticed that it could not reach a majority. After a few seconds, your set would consist of two secondaries and three unreachable members.

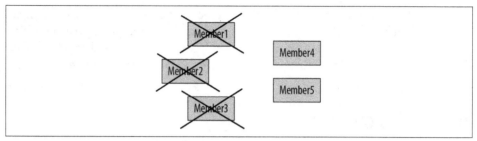

Figure 10-1. With a minority of the set available, all members will be secondaries

Many users find this frustrating: why can't the two remaining members elect a primary? The problem is that it's possible that the other three members didn't actually go down, and that it was instead the network that went down, as shown in Figure 10-2. In this case, the three members on the left will elect a primary, since they can reach a majority of the set (three members out of five). In the case of a network partition, we do not want both sides of the partition to elect a primary, because then the set would have two primaries. Both primaries would be writing to the database, and the datasets would diverge. Requiring a majority to elect or stay a primary is a neat way of avoiding ending up with more than one primary.

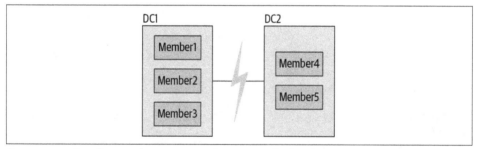

Figure 10-2. For the members, a network partition looks identical to servers on the other side of the partition going down

It is important to configure your set in such a way that you'll usually be able to have one primary. For example, in the five-member set described here, if members 1, 2, and 3 are in one data center and members 4 and 5 are in another, there should almost always be a majority available in the first data center (it's more likely to have a network break between data centers than within them).

There are a couple of common configurations that are recommended:

- A majority of the set in one data center, as in Figure 10-2. This is a good design if you have a primary data center where you always want your replica set's primary to be located. So long as your primary data center is healthy, you will have a primary. However, if that data center becomes unavailable, your secondary data center will not be able to elect a new primary.

- An equal number of servers in each data center, plus a tie-breaking server in a third location. This is a good design if your data centers are "equal" in preference, since generally servers from either data center will be able to see a majority of the set. However, it involves having three separate locations for servers.

More complex requirements might require different configurations, but you should keep in mind how your set will acquire a majority under adverse conditions.

All of these complexities would disappear if MongoDB supported having more than one primary. However, this would bring its own host of complexities. With two primaries, you would have to handle conflicting writes (e.g., if someone updates a document on one primary and someone deletes it on another primary). There are two popular ways of handling conflicts in systems that support multiple writers: manual reconciliation or having the system arbitrarily pick a "winner." Neither of these options is a very easy model for developers to code against, seeing as you can't be sure that the data you've written won't change out from under you. Thus, MongoDB chose to only support having a single primary. This makes development easier but can result in periods when the replica set is read-only.

How Elections Work

When a secondary cannot reach a primary, it will contact all the other members and request that it be elected primary. These other members do several sanity checks: Can they reach a primary that the member seeking election cannot? Is the member seeking election up to date with replication? Is there any member with a higher priority available that should be elected instead?

In version 3.2, MongoDB introduced version 1 of the replication protocol. Protocol version 1 is based on the RAFT consensus protocol developed by Diego Ongaro and John Ousterhout at Stanford University. It is best described as RAFT-like and is tailored to include a number of replication concepts that are specific to MongoDB, such as arbiters, priority, nonvoting members, write concern, etc. Protocol version 1 provided the foundation for new features such as a shorter failover time and greatly reduces the time to detect false primary situations. It also prevents double voting through the use of term IDs.

 RAFT is a consensus algorithm that is broken into relatively independent subproblems. Consensus is the process through which multiple servers or processes agree on values. RAFT ensures consensus such that the same series of commands produces the same series of results and arrives at the same series of states across the members of a deployment.

Replica set members send heartbeats (pings) to each other every two seconds. If a heartbeat does not return from a member within 10 seconds, the other members mark the delinquent member as inaccessible. The election algorithm will make a "best-effort" attempt to have the secondary with the highest priority available call an election. Member priority affects both the timing and the outcome of elections; secondaries with higher priority call elections relatively sooner than secondaries with lower priority, and are also more likely to win. However, a lower-priority instance can be elected as primary for brief periods, even if a higher-priority secondary is available. Replica set members continue to call elections until the highest-priority member available becomes primary.

To be elected primary, a member must be up to date with replication, as far as the members it can reach know. All replicated operations are strictly ordered by an ascending identifier, so the candidate must have operations later than or equal to those of any member it can reach.

Member Configuration Options

The replica sets we have set up so far have been fairly uniform in that every member has the same configuration as every other member. However, there are many situations when you don't want members to be identical: you might want one member to preferentially be primary or make a member invisible to clients so that no read requests can be routed to it. These and many other configuration options can be specified in the member subdocuments of the replica set configuration. This section outlines the member options that you can set.

Priority

Priority is an indication of how strongly this member "wants" to become primary. Its value can range from 0 to 100, and the default is 1. Setting "priority" to 0 has a special meaning: members with a priority of 0 can never become primary. These are called *passive* members.

The highest-priority member will always be elected primary (so long as it can reach a majority of the set and has the most up-to-date data). For example, suppose you add a member with a priority of 1.5 to the set, like so:

```
> rs.add({"host" : "server-4:27017", "priority" : 1.5})
```

Assuming the other members of the set have priority 1, once *server-4* caught up with the rest of the set, the current primary would automatically step down and *server-4* would elect itself. If *server-4* was, for some reason, unable to catch up, the current primary would stay primary. Setting priorities will never cause your set to go primaryless. It will also never cause a member that is behind to become primary (until it has caught up).

The absolute value of "priority" only matters in relation to whether it is greater or less than the other priorities in the set: members with priorities of 100, 1, and 1 will behave the same way as members of another set with priorities 2, 1, and 1.

Hidden Members

Clients do not route requests to hidden members, and hidden members are not preferred as replication sources (although they will be used if more desirable sources are not available). Thus, many people will hide less powerful or backup servers.

For example, suppose you had a set that looked like this:

```
> rs.isMaster()
{
    ...
    "hosts" : [
        "server-1:27107",
        "server-2:27017",
        "server-3:27017"
    ],
    ...
}
```

To hide *server-3*, you could add the hidden: true field to its configuration. A member must have a priority of 0 to be hidden (you can't have a hidden primary):

```
> var config = rs.config()
> config.members[2].hidden = true
0
> config.members[2].priority = 0
0
> rs.reconfig(config)
```

Now running isMaster will show:

```
> rs.isMaster()
{
    ...
    "hosts" : [
        "server-1:27107",
        "server-2:27017"
    ],
    ...
}
```

rs.status() and rs.config() will still show the member; it only disappears from isMaster. When clients connect to a replica set, they call isMaster to determine the members of the set. Thus, hidden members will never be used for read requests.

To unhide a member, change the hidden option to false or remove the option entirely.

Election Arbiters

A two-member set has clear disadvantages for majority requirements. However, many people with small deployments do not want to keep three copies of their data, feeling that two is enough and that keeping a third copy is not worth the administrative, operational, and financial costs.

For these deployments, MongoDB supports a special type of member called an *arbiter*, whose only purpose is to participate in elections. Arbiters hold no data and aren't used by clients: they just provide a majority for two-member sets. In general, deployments without arbiters are preferable.

As arbiters don't have any of the traditional responsibilities of a *mongod* server, you can run an arbiter as a lightweight process on a wimpier server than you'd generally use for MongoDB. It's often a good idea, if possible, to run an arbiter in a separate failure domain from the other members, so that it has an "outside perspective" on the set, as described in the deployment recommendations in "How to Design a Set" on page 241.

You start up an arbiter in the same way that you start a normal *mongod*, using the `--replSet` *name* option and an empty data directory. You can add it to the set using the `rs.addArb()` helper:

```
> rs.addArb("server-5:27017")
```

Equivalently, you can specify the `"arbiterOnly"` option in the member configuration:

```
> rs.add({"_id" : 4, "host" : "server-5:27017", "arbiterOnly" : true})
```

An arbiter, once added to the set, is an arbiter forever: you cannot reconfigure an arbiter to become a nonarbiter, or vice versa.

One other thing that arbiters are good for is breaking ties in larger clusters. If you have an even number of nodes, you may have half the nodes vote for one member and half for another. An arbiter can cast the deciding vote. There are a few things to keep in mind when using arbiters, though; we'll look at these next.

Use at most one arbiter

Note that, in both of the use cases just described, you need *at most* one arbiter. You do not need an arbiter if you have an odd number of nodes. A common misconception seems to be that you should add extra arbiters "just in case." However, it doesn't help elections go any faster or provide any additional data safety to add extra arbiters.

Suppose you have a three-member set. Two members are required to elect a primary. If you add an arbiter, you'll have a four-member set, so three members will be required to choose a primary. Thus, your set is potentially less stable: instead of requiring 67% of your set to be up, you're now requiring 75%.

Having extra members can also make elections take longer. If you have an even number of nodes because you added an arbiter, your arbiters can cause ties, not prevent them.

The downside to using an arbiter

If you have a choice between a data node and an arbiter, choose a data node. Using an arbiter instead of a data node in a small set can make some operational tasks more difficult. For example, suppose you are running a replica set with two "normal" members and one arbiter, and one of the data-holding members goes down. If that member is well and truly dead (the data is unrecoverable), you will have to get a copy of the data from the current primary to the new server you'll be using as a secondary. Copying data can put a lot of stress on a server, and thus slow down your application. (Generally, copying a few gigabytes to a new server is trivial but more than a hundred starts becoming impractical.)

Conversely, if you have three data-holding members, there's more "breathing room" if a server completely dies. You can use the remaining secondary to bootstrap a new server instead of depending on your primary.

In the two-member-plus-arbiter scenario, the primary is the last remaining good copy of your data *and* the one trying to handle load from your application while you're trying to get another copy of your data online.

Thus, if possible, use an odd number of "normal" members instead of an arbiter.

 In three-member replica sets with a primary-secondary-arbiter (PSA) architecture or sharded clusters with a three-member PSA shard, there is a known issue with cache pressure increasing if either of the two data-bearing nodes are down and the "majority" read concern is enabled. Ideally, you should replace the arbiter with a data-bearing member for these deployments. Alternatively, to prevent storage cache pressure the "majority" read concern can be disabled (*https://oreil.ly/p6nUm*) on each of the *mongod* instances in the deployment or shards.

Building Indexes

Sometimes a secondary does not need to have the same (or any) indexes that exist on the primary. If you are using a secondary only for backup data or offline batch jobs, you might want to specify "buildIndexes" : false in the member's configuration. This option prevents the secondary from building any indexes.

This is a permanent setting: members that have `"buildIndexes"` : `false` specified can never be reconfigured to be "normal" index-building members again. If you want to change a non-index-building member to an index-building one, you must remove it from the set, delete all of its data, add it to the set again, and allow it to resync from scratch.

As with hidden members, this option requires the member's priority to be `0`.

## CHAPTER 11

Components of a Replica Set

This chapter covers how the pieces of a replica set fit together, including:

- How replica set members replicate new data
- How bringing up new members works
- How elections work
- Possible server and network failure scenarios

Syncing

Replication is concerned with keeping an identical copy of data on multiple servers. The way MongoDB accomplishes this is by keeping a log of operations, or *oplog*, containing every write that a primary performs. This is a capped collection that lives in the *local* database on the primary. The secondaries query this collection for operations to replicate.

Each secondary maintains its own oplog, recording each operation it replicates from the primary. This allows any member to be used as a sync source for any other member, as shown in Figure 11-1. Secondaries fetch operations from the member they are syncing from, apply the operations to their dataset, and then write the operations to their oplog. If applying an operation fails (which should only happen if the underlying data has been corrupted or in some way differs from the primary's), the secondary will exit.

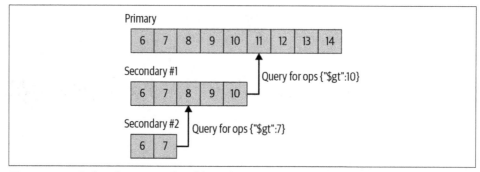

Figure 11-1. Oplogs keep an ordered list of write operations that have occurred; each member has its own copy of the oplog, which should be identical to the primary's (modulo some lag)

If a secondary goes down for any reason, when it restarts it will start syncing from the last operation in its oplog. As operations are applied to data and then written to the oplog, the secondary may replay operations that it has already applied to its data. MongoDB is designed to handle this correctly: replaying oplog ops multiple times yields the same result as replaying them once. Each operation in the oplog is idempotent. That is, oplog operations produce the same results whether applied once or multiple times to the target dataset.

Because the oplog is a fixed size, it can only hold a certain number of operations. In general, the oplog will use space at approximately the same rate as writes come into the system: if you're writing 1 KB/minute on the primary, your oplog is probably going to fill up at about 1 KB/minute. However, there are a few exceptions: operations that affect multiple documents, such as removes or a multi-updates, will be exploded into many oplog entries. The single operation on the primary will be split into one oplog op per document affected. Thus, if you remove 1,000,000 documents from a collection with `db.coll.remove()`, it will become 1,000,000 oplog entries removing one document at a time. If you are doing lots of bulk operations, this can fill up your oplog more quickly than you might expect.

In most cases, the default oplog size is sufficient. If you can predict your replica set's workload to resemble one of the following patterns, then you might want to create an oplog that is larger than the default. Conversely, if your application predominantly performs reads with a minimal amount of write operations, a smaller oplog may be sufficient. These are the kinds of workloads that might require a larger oplog size:

Updates to multiple documents at once
> The oplog must translate multi-updates into individual operations in order to maintain idempotency. This can use a great deal of oplog space without a corresponding increase in data size or disk use.

Deletions equal the same amount of data as inserts

If you delete roughly the same amount of data as you insert, the database will not grow significantly in terms of disk use, but the size of the operation log can be quite large.

Significant number of in-place updates

If a significant portion of the workload is updates that do not increase the size of the documents, the database records a large number of operations but the quantity of data on disk does not change.

Before *mongod* creates an oplog, you can specify its size with the `oplogSizeMB` option. However, after you have started a replica set member for the first time, you can only change the size of the oplog using the "Change the Size of the Oplog" procedure (*https://oreil.ly/mh5SX*).

MongoDB uses two forms of data synchronization: an initial sync to populate new members with the full dataset, and replication to apply ongoing changes to the entire dataset. Let's take a closer look at each of these.

Initial Sync

MongoDB performs an initial sync to copy all the data from one member of the replica set to another member. When a member of the set starts up, it will check if it is in a valid state to begin syncing from someone. If it is in a valid state, it will attempt to make a full copy of the data from another member of the set. There are several steps to the process, which you can follow in the *mongod*'s log.

First, MongoDB clones all databases except the *local* database. The *mongod* scans every collection in each source database and inserts all the data into its own copies of these collections on the target member. Prior to beginning the clone operations, any existing data on the target member will be dropped.

> Only do an initial sync for a member if you do not want the data in your data directory or have moved it elsewhere, as *mongod*'s first action is to delete it all.

In MongoDB 3.4 and later, the initial sync builds all the collection indexes as the documents are copied for each collection (in earlier versions, only the "_id" indexes are built during this stage). It also pulls newly added oplog records during the data copy, so you should ensure that the target member has enough disk space in the *local* database to store these records during this data copy stage.

Once all the databases are cloned, the *mongod* uses the oplog from the source to update its dataset to reflect the current state of the replica set, applying all changes to the dataset that occurred while the copy was in progress. These changes might include any type of write (inserts, updates, and deletes), and this process might mean that *mongod* has to reclone certain documents that were moved and therefore missed by the cloner.

This is roughly what the logs will look like if some documents had to be recloned. Depending on the level of traffic and the types of operations that where happening on the sync source, you may or may not have missing objects:

```
Mon Jan 30 15:38:36 [rsSync] oplog sync 1 of 3
Mon Jan 30 15:38:36 [rsBackgroundSync] replSet syncing to: server-1:27017
Mon Jan 30 15:38:37 [rsSyncNotifier] replset setting oplog notifier to
    server-1:27017
Mon Jan 30 15:38:37 [repl writer worker 2] replication update of non-mod
    failed:
    { ts: Timestamp 1352215827000|17, h: -5618036261007523082, v: 2, op: "u",
      ns: "db1.someColl", o2: { _id: ObjectId('50992a2a7852201e750012b7') },
      o: { $set: { count.0: 2, count.1: 0 } } }
Mon Jan 30 15:38:37 [repl writer worker 2] replication info
    adding missing object
Mon Jan 30 15:38:37 [repl writer worker 2] replication missing object
    not found on source. presumably deleted later in oplog
```

At this point, the data should exactly match the dataset as it existed at some point on the primary. The member finishes the initial sync process and transitions to normal syncing, which allows it to become a secondary.

Doing an initial sync is very easy from an operator's perspective: just start up a *mongod* with a clean data directory. However, it is often preferable to restore from a backup instead, as covered in Chapter 23. Restoring from a backup is often faster than copying all of your data through *mongod*.

Also, cloning can ruin the sync source's working set. Many deployments end up with a subset of their data that's frequently accessed and always in memory (because the OS is accessing it often). Performing an initial sync forces the member to page all of its data into memory, evicting the frequently used data. This can slow down a member dramatically as requests that were being handled by data in RAM are suddenly forced to go to disk. However, for small datasets and servers with some breathing room, initial syncing is a good, easy option.

One of the most common issues people run into with initial sync is it taking too long. In these cases, the new member can "fall off" the end of sync source's oplog: it gets so far behind the sync source that it can no longer catch up because the sync source's oplog has overwritten the data the member would need to use to continue replicating.

There is no way to fix this other than attempting the initial sync at a less busy time or restoring from a backup. The initial sync cannot proceed if the member has fallen off

---

of the sync source's oplog. "Handling Staleness" on page 253 covers this in more depth.

Replication

The second type of synchronization MongoDB performs is replication. Secondary members replicate data continuously after the initial sync. They copy the oplog from their sync source and apply these operations in an asynchronous process. Secondaries may automatically change their sync-from source as needed, in response to changes in the ping time and the state of other members' replication. There are several rules that govern which members a given node can sync from. For example, replica set members with one vote cannot sync from members with zero votes, and secondaries avoid syncing from delayed members and hidden members. Elections and different classes of replica set members are discussed in later sections.

Handling Staleness

If a secondary falls too far behind the actual operations being performed on the sync source, the secondary will go *stale*. A stale secondary is unable to catch up because every operation in the sync source's oplog is too far ahead: it would be skipping operations if it continued to sync. This could happen if the secondary has had downtime, has more writes than it can handle, or is too busy handling reads.

When a secondary goes stale, it will attempt to replicate from each member of the set in turn to see if there's anyone with a longer oplog that it can bootstrap from. If there is no one with a long-enough oplog, replication on that member will halt and it will need to be fully resynced (or restored from a more recent backup).

To avoid out-of-sync secondaries, it's important to have a large oplog so that the primary can store a long history of operations. A larger oplog will obviously use more disk space, but in general this is a good tradeoff to make because disk space tends to be cheap and little of the oplog is typically in use, so it doesn't take up much RAM. A general rule of thumb is that the oplog should provide coverage (replication window) for two to three days' worth of normal operations. For more information on sizing the oplog, see "Resizing the Oplog" on page 282.

Heartbeats

Members need to know about the other members' states: who's primary, who they can sync from, and who's down. To keep an up-to-date view of the set, a member sends out a *heartbeat request* to every other member of the set every two seconds. A heartbeat request is a short message that checks everyone's state.

One of the most important functions of heartbeats is to let the primary know if it can reach a majority of the set. If a primary can no longer reach a majority of the servers, it will demote itself and become a secondary (see "How to Design a Set" on page 241).

Member States

Members also communicate what state they are in via heartbeats. We've already discussed two states: primary and secondary. There are several other normal states that you'll often see members be in:

STARTUP

This is the state a member is in when it's first started, while MongoDB is attempting to load its replica set configuration. Once the configuration has been loaded, it transitions to STARTUP2.

STARTUP2

This state lasts throughout the initial sync process, which typically takes just a few seconds. The member forks off a couple of threads to handle replication and elections and then transitions into the next state: RECOVERING.

RECOVERING

This state indicates that the member is operating correctly but is not available for reads. You may see it in a variety of situations.

On startup, a member has to make a few checks to make sure it's in a valid state before accepting reads; therefore, all members go through the RECOVERING state briefly on startup before becoming secondaries. A member can also go into this state during long-running operations such as compacting or in response to the `replSetMaintenance` command (*https://oreil.ly/6mJu-*).

A member will also go into the RECOVERING state if it has fallen too far behind the other members to catch up. This is, generally, a failure state that requires resyncing the member. The member does not go into an error state at this point because it lives in hope that someone will come online with a long-enough oplog that it can bootstrap itself back to non-staleness.

ARBITER

Arbiters (see "Election Arbiters" on page 246) have a special state and should always be in this state during normal operation.

There are also a few states that indicate a problem with the system. These include:

DOWN

If a member was up but then becomes unreachable, it will enter this state. Note that a member reported as "down" might, in fact, still be up, just unreachable due to network issues.

UNKNOWN

If a member has never been able to reach another member, it will not know what state it's in, so it will report it as UNKNOWN. This generally indicates that the unknown member is down or that there are network problems between the two members.

REMOVED

This is the state of a member that has been removed from the set. If a removed member is added back into the set, it will transition back into its "normal" state.

ROLLBACK

This state is used when a member is rolling back data, as described in "Rollbacks" on page 255. At the end of the rollback process, a server will transition back into the RECOVERING state and then become a secondary.

Elections

A member will seek election if it cannot reach a primary (and is itself eligible to become primary). A member seeking election will send out a notice to all of the members it can reach. These members may know why this member is an unsuitable primary: it may be behind in replication or there may already be a primary that the member seeking election cannot reach. In these cases, the other members will vote against the candidate.

Assuming that there is no reason to object, the other members will vote for the member seeking election. If the member seeking election receives votes from a majority of the set, the election was successful and the member will transition into PRIMARY state. If it did not receive a majority if votes, it will remain a secondary and may try to become a primary again later. A primary will remain primary until it cannot reach a majority of members, goes down, or is stepped down, or the set is reconfigured.

Assuming that the network is healthy and a majority of the servers are up, elections should be fast. It will take a member up to two seconds to notice that a primary has gone down (due to the heartbeats mentioned earlier) and it will immediately start an election, which should only take a few milliseconds. However, the situation is often nonoptimal: an election may be triggered due to networking issues or overloaded servers responding too slowly. In these cases, an election might take more time—even up to a few minutes.

Rollbacks

The election process described in the previous section means that if a primary does a write and goes down before the secondaries have a chance to replicate it, the next primary elected may not have the write. For example, suppose we have two data centers, one with the primary and a secondary, and the other with three secondaries, as shown in Figure 11-2.

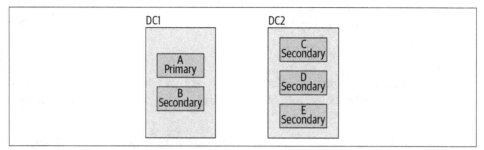

Figure 11-2. A possible two-data-center configuration

Suppose that there is a network partition between the two data centers, as shown in Figure 11-3. The servers in the first data center are up to operation 126, but that data center hasn't yet replicated to the servers in the other data center.

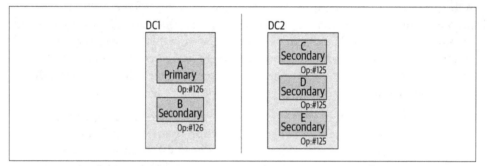

Figure 11-3. Replication across data centers can be slower than within a single data center

The servers in the other data center can still reach a majority of the set (three out of five servers). Thus, one of them may be elected primary. This new primary begins taking its own writes, as shown in Figure 11-4.

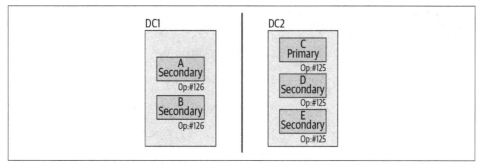

Figure 11-4. Unreplicated writes won't match writes on the other side of a network partition

When the network is repaired, the servers in the first data center will look for operation 126 to start syncing from the other servers, but will not be able to find it. When this happens, *A* and *B* will begin a process called *rollback*. Rollback is used to undo ops that were not replicated before failover. The servers with 126 in their oplogs will look back through the oplogs of the servers in the other data center for a common point. They'll find that operation 125 is the latest operation that matches. Figure 11-5 shows what the oplogs would look like. A apparently crashed before replicating ops 126–128, so these operations are not present on B, which has more recent operations. A will have to roll back these three operations before resuming syncing.

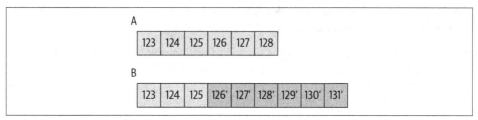

Figure 11-5. Two members with conflicting oplogs—the last common op was 125, so as B has more recent operations A will need to roll back ops 126-128

At this point, the server will go through the ops it has and write its version of each document affected by those ops to a *.bson* file in a *rollback* directory of your data directory. Thus, if (for example) operation 126 was an update, it will write the document updated by 126 to *<collectionName>.bson*. Then it will copy the version of that document from the current primary.

The following is a paste of the log entries generated from a typical rollback:

```
Fri Oct  7 06:30:35 [rsSync] replSet syncing to: server-1
Fri Oct  7 06:30:35 [rsSync] replSet our last op time written: Oct  7
    06:30:05:3
Fri Oct  7 06:30:35 [rsSync] replset source's GTE: Oct  7 06:30:31:1
Fri Oct  7 06:30:35 [rsSync] replSet rollback 0
```

```
Fri Oct  7 06:30:35 [rsSync] replSet ROLLBACK
Fri Oct  7 06:30:35 [rsSync] replSet rollback 1
Fri Oct  7 06:30:35 [rsSync] replSet rollback 2 FindCommonPoint
Fri Oct  7 06:30:35 [rsSync] replSet info rollback our last optime:   Oct  7
    06:30:05:3
Fri Oct  7 06:30:35 [rsSync] replSet info rollback their last optime: Oct  7
    06:30:31:2
Fri Oct  7 06:30:35 [rsSync] replSet info rollback diff in end of log times:
    -26 seconds
Fri Oct  7 06:30:35 [rsSync] replSet rollback found matching events at Oct  7
    06:30:03:4118
Fri Oct  7 06:30:35 [rsSync] replSet rollback findcommonpoint scanned : 6
Fri Oct  7 06:30:35 [rsSync] replSet replSet rollback 3 fixup
Fri Oct  7 06:30:35 [rsSync] replSet rollback 3.5
Fri Oct  7 06:30:35 [rsSync] replSet rollback 4 n:3
Fri Oct  7 06:30:35 [rsSync] replSet minvalid=Oct  7 06:30:31 4e8ed4c7:2
Fri Oct  7 06:30:35 [rsSync] replSet rollback 4.6
Fri Oct  7 06:30:35 [rsSync] replSet rollback 4.7
Fri Oct  7 06:30:35 [rsSync] replSet rollback 5 d:6 u:0
Fri Oct  7 06:30:35 [rsSync] replSet rollback 6
Fri Oct  7 06:30:35 [rsSync] replSet rollback 7
Fri Oct  7 06:30:35 [rsSync] replSet rollback done
Fri Oct  7 06:30:35 [rsSync] replSet RECOVERING
Fri Oct  7 06:30:36 [rsSync] replSet syncing to: server-1
Fri Oct  7 06:30:36 [rsSync] replSet SECONDARY
```

The server begins syncing from another member (*server-1*, in this case) and realizes
that it cannot find its latest operation on the sync source. At that point, it starts the
rollback process by going into the ROLLBACK state (replSet ROLLBACK).

At step 2, it finds the common point between the two oplogs, which was 26 seconds
ago. It then begins undoing the operations from the last 26 seconds from its oplog.
Once the rollback is complete, it transitions into the RECOVERING state and begins
syncing normally again.

To apply operations that have been rolled back to the current primary, first use *mongorestore* to load them into a temporary collection:

```
$ mongorestore --db stage --collection stuff \
    /data/db/rollback/important.stuff.2018-12-19T18-27-14.0.bson
```

Then examine the documents (using the shell) and compare them to the current contents of the collection from whence they came. For example, if someone had created a
"normal" index on the rollback member and a unique index on the current primary,
you'd want to make sure that there weren't any duplicates in the rolled-back data and
resolve them if there were.

Once you have a version of the documents that you like in your staging collection,
load it into your main collection:

```
> staging.stuff.find().forEach(function(doc) {
...     prod.stuff.insert(doc);
... })
```

If you have any insert-only collections, you can directly load the rollback documents into the collection. However, if you are doing updates on the collection you will need to be more careful about how you merge rollback data.

One often-misused member configuration option is the number of votes each member has. Manipulating the number of votes is almost always not what you want to do and causes a lot of rollbacks (which is why it was not included in the list of member configuration options in the last chapter). Do not change the number of votes unless you are prepared to deal with regular rollbacks.

For more information on preventing rollbacks, see Chapter 12.

When Rollbacks Fail

In older versions of MongoDB, it could decide that the rollback was too large to undertake. Since MongoDB version 4.0, there is no limit on the amount of data that can be rolled back. A rollback in versions before 4.0 can fail if there are more than 300 MB of data or about 30 minutes of operations to roll back. In these cases, you must resync the node that is stuck in rollback.

The most common cause of this is when secondaries are lagging and the primary goes down. If one of the secondaries becomes primary, it will be missing a lot of operations from the old primary. The best way to make sure you don't get a member stuck in rollback is to keep your secondaries as up to date as possible.

Connecting to a Replica Set from Your Application

This chapter covers how applications interact with replica sets, including:

- How connections and failovers work
- Waiting for replication on writes
- Routing reads to the correct member

Client–to–Replica Set Connection Behavior

MongoDB client libraries ("drivers" in MongoDB parlance) are designed to manage communication with MongoDB servers, regardless of whether the server is a stand-alone MongoDB instance or a replica set. For replica sets, by default, drivers will connect to the primary and route all traffic to it. Your application can perform reads and writes as though it were talking to a standalone server while your replica set quietly keeps hot standbys ready in the background.

Connections to a replica set are similar to connections to a single server. Use the `MongoClient` class (or equivalent) in your driver and provide a seed list for the driver to connect to. A seed list is simply a list of server addresses. *Seeds* are members of the replica set your application will read from and write data to. You do not need to list all members in the seed list (although you can). When the driver connects to the seeds, it will discover the other members from them. A connection string usually looks something like this:

```
"mongodb://server-1:27017,server-2:27017,server-3:27017"
```

See your driver's documentation for details.

To provide further resilience, you should also use the DNS Seedlist Connection format (*https://oreil.ly/Uq4za*) to specify how your applications connect to your replica set. The advantage to using DNS is that servers hosting your MongoDB replica set members can be changed in rotation without needing to reconfigure the clients (specifically, their connection strings).

All MongoDB drivers adhere to the server discovery and monitoring (SDAM) spec (*https://oreil.ly/ZsS8p*). They persistently monitor the topology of your replica set to detect any changes in your application's ability to reach all members of the set. In addition, the drivers monitor the set to maintain information on which member is the primary.

The purpose of replica sets is to make your data highly available in the face of network partitions or servers going down. In ordinary circumstances, replica sets respond gracefully to such problems by electing a new primary so that applications can continue to read and write data. If a primary goes down, the driver will automatically find the new primary (once one is elected) and will route requests to it as soon as possible. However, while there is no reachable primary, your application will be unable to perform writes.

There may be no primary available for a brief time (during an election) or for an extended period of time (if no reachable member can become primary). By default, the driver will not service any requests—read or write—during this period. If necessary to your application, you can configure the driver to use secondaries for read requests.

A common desire is to have the driver hide the entire election process (the primary going away and a new primary being elected) from the user. However, no driver handles failover this way, for a few reasons. First, a driver can only hide a lack of primary for so long. Second, a driver often finds out that the primary went down because an operation failed, which means that the driver doesn't know whether or not the primary processed the operation before going down. This is a fundamental distributed systems problem that is impossible to avoid, so we need a strategy for dealing with it when it emerges. Should we retry the operation on the new primary, if one is elected quickly? Assume it got through on the old primary? Check and see if the new primary has the operation?

The correct strategy, it turns out, is to retry at most one time. Huh? To explain, let's consider our options. These boil down to the following: don't retry, give up after retrying some fixed number of times, or retry at most once. We also need to consider the type of error that could be the source of our problem. There are three types of errors we might see in attempting to write to a replica set: a transient network error, a persistent outage (either network or server), or an error caused by a command the server rejects as incorrect (e.g., not authorized). For each type of error, let's consider our retry options.

For the sake of this discussion, let's look at the example of a write to simply increment a counter. If our application attempts to increment our counter but gets no response from the server, we don't know whether the server received the message and performed the update. So, if we follow a strategy of not retrying this write, for a transient network error, we might undercount. For a persistent outage or a command error not retrying is the correct strategy, because no amount of retrying the write operation will have the desired effect.

If we follow a strategy of retrying some fixed number of times, for transient network errors, we might overcount (in the case where our first attempt succeeded). For a persistent outage or command error, retrying multiple times will simply waste cycles.

Let's look now at the strategy of retrying just once. For a transient network error, we might overcount. For a persistent outage or command error, this is the correct strategy. However, what if we could ensure that our operations are idempotent? Idempotent operations are those that have the same outcome whether we do them once or multiple times. With idempotent operations, retrying network errors once has the best chance of correctly dealing with all three types of errors.

As of MongoDB 3.6, the server and all MongoDB drivers support a retryable writes option. See your driver's documentation for details on how to use this option. With retryable writes, the driver will automatically follow the retry-at-most-once strategy. Command errors will be returned to the application for client-side handling. Network errors will be retried once after an appropriate delay that should accommodate a primary election under ordinary circumstances. With retryable writes turned on, the server maintains a unique identifier for each write operation and can therefore determine when the driver is attempting to retry a command that already succeeded. Rather than apply the write again, it will simply return a message indicating the write succeeded and thereby overcome the problem caused by the transient network issue.

Waiting for Replication on Writes

Depending on the needs of your application, you might want to require that all writes are replicated to a majority of the replica set before they are acknowledged by the server. In the rare circumstance where the primary of a set goes down and the newly elected primary (formerly a secondary) did not replicate the very last writes to the former primary, those writes will be rolled back when the former primary comes back up. They can be recovered, but it requires manual intervention. For many applications, having a small number of writes rolled back is not a problem. In a blog application, for example, there is little real danger in rolling back one or two comments from one reader.

However, for other applications, rollback of any writes should be avoided. Suppose your application sends a write to the primary. It receives confirmation that the write was written, but the primary crashes before any secondaries have had a chance to replicate that write. Your application thinks that it'll be able to access that write, but the current members of the replica set don't have a copy of it.

At some point, a secondary may be elected primary and start taking new writes. When the former primary comes back up, it will discover that it has writes that the current primary does not. To correct this, it will undo any writes that do not match the sequence of operations on the current primary. These operations are not lost, but they are written to special rollback files that have to be manually applied to the current primary. MongoDB cannot automatically apply these writes, since they may conflict with other writes that have happened since the crash. Thus, the writes essentially disappear until an admin gets a chance to apply the rollback files to the current primary (see Chapter 11 for more details on rollbacks).

The requirement of writing to a majority prevents this situation: if the application gets a confirmation that a write succeeded, then the new primary will have to have a copy of the write to be elected (a member must be up to date to be elected primary). If the application does not receive acknowledgment from the server or receives an error, then it will know to try again, because the write was not propagated to a majority of the set before the primary crashed.

Thus, to ensure that writes will be persisted no matter what happens to the set, we must ensure that each write propagates to a majority of the members of the set. We can achieve this using `writeConcern`.

As of MongoDB 2.6, `writeConcern` is integrated with write operations. For example, in JavaScript, we can use `writeConcern` as follows:

```
try {
   db.products.insertOne(
       { "_id": 10, "item": "envelopes", "qty": 100, type: "Self-Sealing" },
       { writeConcern: { "w" : "majority", "wtimeout" : 100 } }
   );
} catch (e) {
   print (e);
}
```

The specific syntax in your driver will vary depending on the programming language, but the semantics remain the same. In the example here, we specify a write concern of `"majority"`. Upon success, the server will respond with a message such as the following:

```
{ "acknowledged" : true, "insertedId" : 10 }
```

But the server will not respond until this write operation has replicated to a majority of the members of the replica set. Only then will our application receive acknowledgment that this write succeeded. If the write does not succeed within the timeout we've specified, the server will respond with an error message:

```
WriteConcernError({
    "code" : 64,
    "errInfo" : {
        "wtimeout" : true
    },
    "errmsg" : "waiting for replication timed out"
})
```

Write concern majority and the replica set election protocol ensure that in the event of a primary election, only secondaries that are up to date with acknowledged writes can be elected primary. In this way, we guarantee that rollback will not happen. With the timeout option, we also have a tunable setting that enables us to detect and flag any long-running writes at the application layer.

Other Options for "w"

"majority" is not the only writeConcern option. MongoDB also lets you specify an arbitrary number of servers to replicate to by passing "w" a number, as shown here:

```
db.products.insertOne(
    { "_id": 10, "item": "envelopes", "qty": 100, type: "Self-Sealing" },
    { writeConcern: { "w" : 2, "wtimeout" : 100 } }
);
```

This will wait until two members (the primary and one secondary) have the write.

Note that the "w" value includes the primary. If you want the write propagated to n secondaries, you should set "w" to n+1 (to include the primary). Setting "w" : 1 is the same as not passing the "w" option at all because it just checks that the write was successful on the primary.

The downside to using a literal number is that you have to change your application if your replica set configuration changes.

Custom Replication Guarantees

Writing to a majority of a set is considered "safe." However, some sets may have more complex requirements: you may want to make sure that a write makes it to at least one server in each data center or a majority of the nonhidden nodes. Replica sets allow you to create custom rules that you can pass to "getLastError" to guarantee replication to whatever combination of servers you need.

Guaranteeing One Server per Data Center

Network issues between data centers are much more common than within data centers, and it is more likely for an entire data center to go dark than an equivalent smattering of servers across multiple data centers. Thus, you might want some data center –specific logic for writes. Guaranteeing a write to every data center before confirming success means that, in the case of a write followed by the data center going offline, every other data center will have at least one local copy.

To set this up, we first classify the members by data center. We do this by adding a "tags" field to their replica set configuration:

```
> var config = rs.config()
> config.members[0].tags = {"dc" : "us-east"}
> config.members[1].tags = {"dc" : "us-east"}
> config.members[2].tags = {"dc" : "us-east"}
> config.members[3].tags = {"dc" : "us-east"}
> config.members[4].tags = {"dc" : "us-west"}
> config.members[5].tags = {"dc" : "us-west"}
> config.members[6].tags = {"dc" : "us-west"}
```

The "tags" field is an object, and each member can have multiple tags. It might be a "high quality" server in the "us-east" data center, for example, in which case we'd want a "tags" field such as {"dc": "us-east", "quality" : "high"}.

The second step is to add a rule by creating a "getLastErrorModes" field in our replica set config. The name "getLastErrorModes" is vestigial in the sense that prior to MongoDB 2.6, applications used a method called "getLastError" to specify write concern. In replica configs, for "getLastErrorModes" each rule is of the form "*name*" : {"*key*" : *number*}}. "*name*" is the name for the rule, which should describe what the rule does in a way that clients can understand, as they'll be using this name when they call getLastError. In this example, we might call this rule "eachDC" or something more abstract such as "user-level safe".

The "*key*" field is the key field from the tags, so in this example it will be "dc". The *number* is the number of groups that are needed to fulfill this rule. In this case, *number* is 2 (because we want at least one server from "us-east" and one from "us-west"). *number* always means "at least one server from each of *number* groups."

We add "getLastErrorModes" to the replica set config as follows and reconfigure to create the rule:

```
> config.settings = {}
> config.settings.getLastErrorModes = [{"eachDC" : {"dc" : 2}}]
> rs.reconfig(config)
```

"getLastErrorModes" lives in the "settings" subobject of a replica set config, which contains a few set-level optional settings.

Now we can use this rule for writes:

```
db.products.insertOne(
    { "_id": 10, "item": "envelopes", "qty": 100, type: "Self-Sealing" },
    { writeConcern: { "w" : "eachDC", wtimeout : 1000 } }
);
```

Note that rules are somewhat abstracted away from the application developer: they don't have to know which servers are in `"eachDC"` to use the rule, and the rule can change without their application having to change. We could add a data center or change set members and the application would not have to know.

Guaranteeing a Majority of Nonhidden Members

Often, hidden members are somewhat second-class citizens: you're never going to fail over to them and they certainly aren't taking any reads. Thus, you may only care that nonhidden members received a write and let the hidden members sort it out for themselves.

Suppose we have five members, *host0* through *host4*, *host4* being a hidden member. We want to make sure that a majority of the nonhidden members have a write—that is, at least three of *host0*, *host1*, *host2*, and *host3*. To create a rule for this, first we tag each of the nonhidden members with its own tag:

```
> var config = rs.config()
> config.members[0].tags = [{"normal" : "A"}]
> config.members[1].tags = [{"normal" : "B"}]
> config.members[2].tags = [{"normal" : "C"}]
> config.members[3].tags = [{"normal" : "D"}]
```

The hidden member, *host4*, is not given a tag.

Now we add a rule for the majority of these servers:

```
> config.settings.getLastErrorModes = [{"visibleMajority" : {"normal" : 3}}]
> rs.reconfig(config)
```

Finally, we can use this rule in our application:

```
db.products.insertOne(
    { "_id": 10, "item": "envelopes", "qty": 100, type: "Self-Sealing" },
    { writeConcern: { "w" : "visibleMajority", wtimeout : 1000 } }
);
```

This will wait until at least three of the nonhidden members have the write.

Creating Other Guarantees

The rules you can create are limitless. Remember that there are two steps to creating a custom replication rule:

1. Tag members by assigning them key/value pairs. The keys describe classifications; for example, you might have keys such as `"data_center"` or `"region"` or `"serverQuality"`. Values determine which group a server belongs to within a classification. For example, for the key `"data_center"`, you might have some servers tagged `"us-east"`, some `"us-west"`, and others `"aust"`.

2. Create a rule based on the classifications you create. Rules are always of the form `{"name" : {"key" : number}}`, where at least one server from *number* groups must have a write before it has succeeded. For example, you could create a rule `{"twoDCs" : {"data_center" : 2}}`, which would mean that at least one server in two of the data centers tagged must confirm a write before it is successful.

Then you can use this rule in `getLastErrorModes`.

Rules are immensely powerful ways to configure replication, although they are complex to understand and set up. Unless you have fairly involved replication requirements, you should be perfectly safe sticking with `"w" : "majority"`.

Sending Reads to Secondaries

By default, drivers will route all requests to the primary. This is generally what you want, but you can configure other options by setting read preferences in your driver. Read preferences let you specify the types of servers queries should be sent to.

Sending read requests to secondaries is generally a bad idea. There are some specific situations in which it makes sense, but you should generally send all traffic to the primary. If you are considering sending reads to secondaries, make sure to weigh the pros and cons very carefully before allowing it. This section covers why it's a bad idea and the specific conditions when it makes sense to do so.

Consistency Considerations

Applications that require strongly consistent reads should not read from secondaries.

Secondaries should usually be within a few milliseconds of the primary. However, there is no guarantee of this. Sometimes secondaries can fall behind by minutes, hours, or even days due to load, misconfiguration, network errors, or other issues. Client libraries cannot tell how up to date a secondary is, so clients will cheerfully send queries to secondaries that are far behind. Hiding a secondary from client reads can be done but is a manual process. Thus, if your application needs data that is predictably up to date, it should not read from secondaries.

If your application needs to read its own writes (e.g., insert a document and then query for it and find it) you should not send the read to a secondary (unless the write waits for replication to all secondaries using `"w"` as shown earlier). Otherwise, an application may perform a successful write, attempt to read the value, and not be able to find it (because it sent the read to a secondary that hasn't replicated yet). Clients can issue requests faster than replication can copy operations.

To always send read requests to the primary, set your read preference to `primary` (or leave it alone, since `primary` is the default). If there is no primary, queries will error out. This means that your application cannot perform queries if the primary goes down. However, it is certainly an acceptable option if your application can deal with downtime during failovers or network partitions or if getting stale data is unacceptable.

Load Considerations

Many users send reads to secondaries to distribute load. For example, if your servers can only handle 10,000 queries a second and you need to handle 30,000, you might set up a couple of secondaries and have them take some of the load. However, this is a dangerous way to scale because it's easy to accidentally overload your system and difficult to recover from once you do.

For example, suppose that you have the situation just described: 30,000 reads per second. You decide to create a replica set with four members (one of these would be configured as nonvoting, to prevent ties in elections) to handle this: each secondary is well below its maximum load and the system works perfectly.

Until one of the secondaries crashes.

Now each of the remaining members are handling 100% of their possible load. If you need to rebuild the member that crashed, it may need to copy data from one of the other servers, overwhelming the remaining servers. Overloading a server often makes it perform slower, lowering the set's capacity even further and forcing other members to take on more load, causing them to slow down in a death spiral.

Overloading can also cause replication to slow down, making the remaining secondaries fall behind. Suddenly you have a member down and a member lagging, and everything is too overloaded to have any wiggle room.

If you have a good idea of how much load a server can take, you might feel like you can plan this out better: use five servers instead of four and the set won't be overloaded if one goes down. However, even if you plan it out perfectly (and only lose the number of servers you expected), you still have to fix the situation with the other servers under more stress than they would be otherwise.

A better choice is to use sharding to distribute load. We'll cover how to set sharding up in Chapter 14.

Reasons to Read from Secondaries

There are a few cases in which it's reasonable to send application reads to secondaries. For instance, you may want your application to still be able to perform reads if the primary goes down (and you do not care if those reads are somewhat stale). This is the most common case for distributing reads to secondaries: you'd like a temporary read-only mode when your set loses a primary. This read preference is called `primary Preferred`.

One common argument for reading from secondaries is to get low-latency reads. You can specify `nearest` as your read preference to route requests to the lowest-latency member based on average ping time from the driver to the replica set member. If your application needs to access the same document with low latency in multiple data centers, this is the only way to do it. If, however, your documents are more location-based (application servers in this data center need low-latency access to some of your data, or application servers in another data center need low-latency access to other data), this should be done with sharding. Note that you must use sharding if your application requires low-latency reads *and* low-latency writes: replica sets only allow writes to one location (wherever the primary is).

You must be willing to sacrifice consistency if you are reading from members that may not have replicated all the writes yet. Alternatively, you could sacrifice write speed if you wanted to wait until writes had been replicated to all members.

If your application can truly function acceptably with arbitrarily stale data, you can use the `secondary` or `secondaryPreferred` read preferences. `secondary` will always send read requests to a secondary. If there are no secondaries available, this will error out rather than send reads to the primary. It can be used for applications that do not care about stale data and want to use the primary for writes only. If you have any concerns about staleness of data, this is not recommended.

`secondaryPreferred` will send read requests to a secondary if one is available. If no secondaries are available, requests will be sent to the primary.

Sometimes, read load is drastically different than write load—i.e., you're reading entirely different data than you're writing. You might want dozens of indexes for off-line processing that you don't want to have on the primary. In this case, you might want to set up a secondary with different indexes than the primary. If you'd like to use a secondary for this purpose, you'd probably create a connection directly to it from the driver, instead of using a replica set connection.

Consider which of the options makes sense for your application. You can also combine options: if some read requests must be from the primary, use `primary` for those. If you are OK with other reads not having the most up-to-date data, use `primaryPreferred` for those. And if certain requests require low latency over consistency, use `nearest` for those.

## CHAPTER 13

Administration

This chapter covers replica set administration, including:

- Performing maintenance on individual members
- Configuring sets under a variety of circumstances
- Getting information about and resizing your oplog
- Doing some more exotic set configurations
- Converting from master/slave to a replica set

Starting Members in Standalone Mode

A lot of maintenance tasks cannot be performed on secondaries (because they involve writes) and shouldn't be performed on primaries because of the impact this could have on application performance. Thus, the following sections frequently mention starting up a server in standalone mode. This means restarting the member so that it is a standalone server, not a member of a replica set (temporarily).

To start up a member in standalone mode, first look at the command-line options used to start it. Suppose they look something like this:

```
> db.serverCmdLineOpts()
{
    "argv" : [ "mongod", "-f", "/var/lib/mongod.conf" ],
    "parsed" : {
        "replSet": "mySet",
        "port": "27017",
        "dbpath": "/var/lib/db"
    },
```

```
      "ok" : 1
}
```

To perform maintenance on this server we can restart it without the `replSet` option. This will allow us to read and write to it as a normal standalone *mongod*. We don't want the other servers in the set to be able to contact it, so we'll make it listen on a different port (so that the other members won't be able to find it). Finally, we want to keep the `dbpath` the same, as we are presumably starting it up this way to manipulate the server's data somehow.

First, we shut down the server from the *mongo* shell:

```
> db.shutdownServer()
```

Then, in an operating system shell (e.g., bash), we restart *mongod* on another port and without the `replSet` parameter:

```
$ mongod --port 30000 --dbpath /var/lib/db
```

It will now be running as a standalone server, listening on port 30000 for connections. The other members of the set will attempt to connect to it on port 27017 and assume that it is down.

When we have finished performing maintenance on the server, we can shut it down and restart it with its original options. It will automatically sync up with the rest of the set, replicating any operations that it missed while it was "away."

Replica Set Configuration

Replica set configuration is always kept in a document in the *local.system.replset* collection. This document is the same on all members of the set. Never update this document using `update`. Always use an `rs` helper or the `replSetReconfig` command.

Creating a Replica Set

You create a replica set by starting up the *mongods* that you want to be members and then passing one of them a configuration through `rs.initiate()`:

```
> var config = {
... "_id" : <setName>,
... "members" : [
...     {"_id" : 0, "host" : <host1>},
...     {"_id" : 1, "host" : <host2>},
...     {"_id" : 2, "host" : <host3>}
... ]}
> rs.initiate(config)
```

You should always pass a config object to rs.initiate(). If you do not, MongoDB will attempt to automatically generate a config for a one-member replica set; it might not use the hostname that you want or correctly configure the set.

You only call rs.initiate() on one member of the set. The member that receives the configuration will pass it on to the other members.

Changing Set Members

When you add a new set member, it should either have nothing in its data directory —in which case it will perform an initial sync—or have a copy of the data from another member (see Chapter 23 for more information about backing up and restoring replica set members).

Connect to the primary and add a new member as follows:

```
> rs.add("spock:27017")
```

Alternatively, you can specify a more complex member config as a document:

```
> rs.add({"host" : "spock:27017", "priority" : 0, "hidden" : true})
```

You can also remove members by their "host" field:

```
> rs.remove("spock:27017")
```

You can change a member's settings by reconfiguring. There are a few restrictions in changing a member's settings:

- You cannot change a member's "_id".
- You cannot make the member you're sending the reconfig to (generally the primary) priority 0.
- You cannot turn an arbiter into a nonarbiter, or vice versa.
- You cannot change a member's "buildIndexes" field from false to true.

Notably, you *can* change a member's "host" field. Thus, if you incorrectly specify a host (say, if you use a public IP instead of a private one) you can later go back and simply change the config to use the correct IP.

To change a hostname, you could do something like this:

```
> var config = rs.config()
> config.members[0].host = "spock:27017"
spock:27017
> rs.reconfig(config)
```

This same strategy applies to changing any other option: fetch the config with `rs.con fig()`, modify any parts of it that you wish, and reconfigure the set by passing `rs.reconfig()` the new configuration.

Creating Larger Sets

Replica sets are limited to 50 members in total and only 7 voting members. This is to reduce the amount of network traffic required for everyone to heartbeat everyone else and to limit the amount of time elections take.

If you are creating a replica set that has more than seven members, every additional member must be given zero votes. You can do this by specifying it in the member's config:

```
> rs.add({"_id" : 7, "host" : "server-7:27017", "votes" : 0})
```

This prevents these members from casting positive votes in elections.

Forcing Reconfiguration

When you permanently lose a majority of a set, you may want to reconfigure the set while it doesn't have a primary. This is a little tricky, as usually you'd send the reconfig to the primary. In this case, you can force-reconfigure the set by sending a reconfig command to a secondary. Connect to a secondary in the shell and pass it a reconfig with the `"force"` option:

```
> rs.reconfig(config, {"force" : true})
```

Forced reconfigurations follow the same rules as a normal reconfiguration: you must send a valid, well-formed configuration with the correct options. The `"force"` option doesn't allow invalid configs; it just allows a secondary to accept a reconfig.

Forced reconfigurations bump the replica set `"version"` number by a large amount. You may see it jump by tens or hundreds of thousands. This is normal: it is to prevent version number collisions (just in case there's a reconfig on either side of a network partition).

When the secondary receives the reconfig, it will update its configuration and pass the new config along to the other members. The other members of the set will only pick up on a change of config if they recognize the sending server as a member of their current config. Thus, if some of your members have changed hostnames, you should force reconfig from a member that kept its old hostname. If every member has a new hostname, you should shut down each member of the set, start a new one up in standalone mode, change its *local.system.replset* document manually, and then restart the member.

Manipulating Member State

There are several ways to manually change a member's state for maintenance or in response to load. Note that there is no way to force a member to become primary, however, other than configuring the set appropriately—in this case, by giving the replica set member a priority higher than any other member of the set.

Turning Primaries into Secondaries

You can demote a primary to a secondary using the `stepDown` function:

```
> rs.stepDown()
```

This makes the primary step down into SECONDARY state for 60 seconds. If no other primary is elected in that time period, it will be able to attempt a reelection. If you would like it to remain a secondary for a longer or shorter amount of time, you can specify your own number of seconds for it to stay in SECONDARY state:

```
> rs.stepDown(600) // 10 minutes
```

Preventing Elections

If you need to do some maintenance on the primary but don't want any of the other eligible members to become primary in the interim, you can force them to stay secondaries by running `freeze` on each of them:

```
> rs.freeze(10000)
```

Again, this takes a number of seconds for the member to remain a secondary.

If you finish whatever maintenance you're doing on the primary before this time elapses and want to unfreeze the other members, simply run the command again on each of them, giving a timeout of 0 seconds:

```
> rs.freeze(0)
```

An unfrozen member will be able to hold an election, if it chooses.

You can also unfreeze primaries that have been stepped down by running `rs.freeze(0)`.

Monitoring Replication

It is important to be able to monitor the status of a set: not only that all members are up, but what states they are in and how up to date the replication is. There are several commands you can use to see replica set information. MongoDB hosting services and management tools including Atlas, Cloud Manager, and Ops Manager (see Chapter 22) also provide mechanisms to monitor replication and dashboards on the key replication metrics.

Often issues with replication are transient: a server could not reach another server, but now it can. The easiest way to see issues like this is to look at the logs. Make sure you know where the logs are being stored (and that they *are* being stored) and that you can access them.

Getting the Status

One of the most useful commands you can run is `replSetGetStatus`, which gets the current information about every member of the set (from the view of the member you're running it on). There is a helper for this command in the shell:

```
> rs.status()
    "set" : "replset",
    "date" : ISODate("2019-11-02T20:02:16.543Z"),
    "myState" : 1,
    "term" : NumberLong(1),
    "heartbeatIntervalMillis" : NumberLong(2000),
    "optimes" : {
        "lastCommittedOpTime" : {
            "ts" : Timestamp(1478116934, 1),
            "t" : NumberLong(1)
        },
        "readConcernMajorityOpTime" : {
            "ts" : Timestamp(1478116934, 1),
            "t" : NumberLong(1)
        },
        "appliedOpTime" : {
            "ts" : Timestamp(1478116934, 1),
            "t" : NumberLong(1)
        },
        "durableOpTime" : {
            "ts" : Timestamp(1478116934, 1),
            "t" : NumberLong(1)
        }
    },

    "members" : [
        {
            "_id" : 0,
            "name" : "m1.example.net:27017",
            "health" : 1,
            "state" : 1,
            "stateStr" : "PRIMARY",
            "uptime" : 269,
            "optime" : {
                    "ts" : Timestamp(1478116934, 1),
                    "t" : NumberLong(1)
```

```
        },
        "optimeDate" : ISODate("2019-11-02T20:02:14Z"),
        "infoMessage" : "could not find member to sync from",
        "electionTime" : Timestamp(1478116933, 1),
        "electionDate" : ISODate("2019-11-02T20:02:13Z"),
        "configVersion" : 1,
        "self" : true
    },
    {

        "_id" : 1,
        "name" : "m2.example.net:27017",
        "health" : 1,
        "state" : 2,
        "stateStr" : "SECONDARY",
        "uptime" : 14,
        "optime" : {
            "ts" : Timestamp(1478116934, 1),
            "t" : NumberLong(1)
        },
        "optimeDurable" : {
            "ts" : Timestamp(1478116934, 1),
            "t" : NumberLong(1)
        },
        "optimeDate" : ISODate("2019-11-02T20:02:14Z"),
        "optimeDurableDate" : ISODate("2019-11-02T20:02:14Z"),
        "lastHeartbeat" : ISODate("2019-11-02T20:02:15.618Z"),
        "lastHeartbeatRecv" : ISODate("2019-11-02T20:02:14.866Z"),
        "pingMs" : NumberLong(0),
        "syncingTo" : "m3.example.net:27017",
        "configVersion" : 1
    },
    {

        "_id" : 2,
        "name" : "m3.example.net:27017",
        "health" : 1,
        "state" : 2,
        "stateStr" : "SECONDARY",
        "uptime" : 14,
        "optime" : {
            "ts" : Timestamp(1478116934, 1),
            "t" : NumberLong(1)
        },
        "optimeDurable" : {
            "ts" : Timestamp(1478116934, 1),
            "t" : NumberLong(1)
        },
        "optimeDate" : ISODate("2019-11-02T20:02:14Z"),
        "optimeDurableDate" : ISODate("2019-11-02T20:02:14Z"),
        "lastHeartbeat" : ISODate("2019-11-02T20:02:15.619Z"),
        "lastHeartbeatRecv" : ISODate("2019-11-02T20:02:14.787Z"),
        "pingMs" : NumberLong(0),
        "syncingTo" : "m1.example.net:27018",
```

```
              "configVersion" : 1
         }
      ],
      "ok" : 1
   }
```

These are some of the most useful fields:

`"self"`

This field is only present in the member `rs.status()` was run on—in this case, *server-2 (m1.example.net:27017)*.

`"stateStr"`

A string describing the state of the server. See "Member States" on page 254 for descriptions of the various states.

`"uptime"`

The number of seconds a member has been reachable, or the time since this server was started for the `"self"` member. Thus, *server-1* has been up for 269 seconds, and *server-2* and *server-3* for 14 seconds.

`"optimeDate"`

The last optime in each member's oplog (where that member is synced to). Note that this is the state of each member as reported by the heartbeat, so the optime reported here may be off by a couple of seconds.

`"lastHeartbeat"`

The time this server last received a heartbeat from the `"self"` member. If there have been network issues or the server has been busy, this may be longer than two seconds ago.

`"pingMs"`

The running average of how long heartbeats to this server have taken. This is used in determining which member to sync from.

`"errmsg"`

Any status message that the member chose to return in the heartbeat request. These are often merely informational, not error messages. For example, the `"errmsg"` field in *server-3* indicates that this server is in the process of initial syncing. The hexadecimal number 507e9a30:851 is the timestamp of the operation this member needs to get to to complete the initial sync.

There are several fields that give overlapping information. `"state"` is the same as `"stateStr"`; it's simply the internal ID for the state. `"health"` merely reflects whether a given server is reachable (1) or unreachable (0), which is also shown by `"state"` and `"stateStr"` (they'll be UNKNOWN or DOWN if the server is unreachable). Similarly, `"optime"` and `"optimeDate"` are the same value represented in two ways: one represents milliseconds since the epoch ("t" : 135...) and the other is a more human-readable date.

 Note that this report is from the point of view of whichever member of the set you run it on: the information it contains may be incorrect or out of date due to network issues.

Visualizing the Replication Graph

If you run rs.status() on a secondary, there will be a top-level field called "syncingTo". This gives the host that this member is replicating from. By running the replSetGetStatus command on each member of the set, you can figure out the replication graph. For example, assuming server1 was a connection to *server1*, server2 was a connection to *server2*, and so on, you might have something like:

```
> server1.adminCommand({replSetGetStatus: 1})['syncingTo']
server0:27017
> server2.adminCommand({replSetGetStatus: 1})['syncingTo']
server1:27017
> server3.adminCommand({replSetGetStatus: 1})['syncingTo']
server1:27017
> server4.adminCommand({replSetGetStatus: 1})['syncingTo']
server2:27017
```

Thus, *server0* is the replication source for *server1*, *server1* is the replication source for *server2* and *server3*, and *server2* is the replication source for *server4*.

MongoDB determines who to sync to based on ping time. When one member heartbeats another, it times how long that request takes. MongoDB keeps a running average of these times. When a member has to choose another member to sync from, it looks for the one that is closest to it and ahead of it in replication (thus, you cannot end up with a replication cycle: members will only replicate from the primary or secondaries that are further ahead).

This means that if you bring up a new member in a secondary data center, it is more likely to sync from another member in that data center than a member in your primary data center (thus minimizing WAN traffic), as shown in Figure 13-1.

However, there is a downside to automatic replication chaining: more replication hops means that it takes a bit longer to replicate writes to all servers. For example, let's say that everything is in one data center but, due to the vagaries of network speeds when you added members, MongoDB ends up replicating in a line, as shown in Figure 13-2.

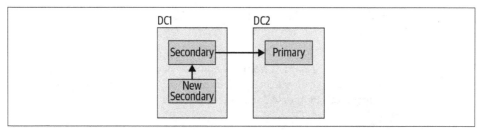

Figure 13-1. New secondaries will generally choose to sync from a member in the same data center

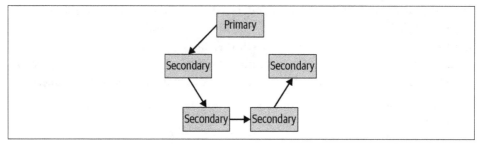

Figure 13-2. As replication chains get longer, it takes longer for all members to get a copy of the data

This is highly unlikely, but not impossible. It is, however, probably undesirable: each secondary in the chain will have to be a bit further behind than the secondary "in front" of it. You can fix this by modifying the replication source for a member using the replSetSyncFrom command (or the rs.syncFrom() helper).

Connect to the secondary whose replication source you want to change and run this command, passing it the server you'd prefer this member to sync from:

```
> secondary.adminCommand({"replSetSyncFrom" : "server0:27017"})
```

It may take a few seconds to switch sync sources, but if you run rs.status() on that member again, you should see that the "syncingTo" field now says "server0:27017".

This member (*server4*) will now continue replicating from *server0* until *server0* becomes unavailable or, if it happened to be a secondary, falls significantly behind the other members.

Replication Loops

A *replication loop* is when members end up replicating from one another—for example, *A* is syncing from *B* who is syncing from *C* who is syncing from *A*. As none of the members in a replication loop can be a primary, the members will not receive any new operations to replicate and will fall behind.

Replication loops should be impossible when members choose who to sync from automatically. However, you can force replication loops using the `replSetSyncFrom` command. Inspect the `rs.status()` output carefully before manually changing sync targets, and be careful not to create loops. The `replSetSyncFrom` command will warn you if you do not choose to sync from a member that is strictly ahead, but it will allow it.

Disabling Chaining

Chaining is when a secondary syncs from another secondary (instead of the primary). As mentioned earlier, members may decide to sync from other members automatically. You can disable chaining, forcing everyone to sync from the primary, by changing the `"chainingAllowed"` setting to `false` (if not specified, it defaults to `true`):

```
> var config = rs.config()
> // create the settings subobject, if it does not already exist
> config.settings = config.settings || {}
> config.settings.chainingAllowed = false
> rs.reconfig(config)
```

With `"chainingAllowed"` set to `false`, all members will sync from the primary. If the primary becomes unavailable, they will fall back to syncing from secondaries.

Calculating Lag

One of the most important metrics to track for replication is how well the secondaries are keeping up with the primary. *Lag* is how far behind a secondary is, which means the difference between the timestamp of the last operation the primary has performed and the timestamp of the last operation the secondary has applied.

You can use `rs.status()` to see a member's replication state, but you can also get a quick summary by running `rs.printReplicationInfo()` or `rs.printSlaveReplica tionInfo()`.

`rs.printReplicationInfo()` gives a summary of the primary's oplog, including its size and the date range of its operations:

```
> rs.printReplicationInfo();
   configured oplog size:   10.48576MB
   log length start to end: 3590 secs (1.00hrs)
   oplog first event time:  Tue Apr 10 2018 09:27:57 GMT-0400 (EDT)
   oplog last event time:   Tue Apr 10 2018 10:27:47 GMT-0400 (EDT)
   now:                     Tue Apr 10 2018 10:27:47 GMT-0400 (EDT)
```

In this example, the oplog is about 10 MB (10 MiB) and is only able to fit about an hour of operations.

If this were a real deployment, the oplog should probably be larger (see the next section for instructions on changing oplog size). We want the log length to be *at least* as long as the time it takes to do a full resync. That way, we don't run into a case where a secondary falls off the end of the oplog before finishing its initial sync.

 The log length is computed by taking the time difference between the first and last operation in the oplog once the oplog has filled up. If the server has just started with nothing in the oplog, then the earliest operation will be relatively recent. In that case, the log length will be small, even though the oplog probably still has free space available. The length is a more useful metric for servers that have been operating long enough to write through their entire oplog at least once.

You can also use the `rs.printSlaveReplicationInfo()` function to get the `syncedTo` value for each member and the time when the last oplog entry was written to each secondary, as shown in the following example:

```
> rs.printSlaveReplicationInfo();
source: m1.example.net:27017
    syncedTo: Tue Apr 10 2018 10:27:47 GMT-0400 (EDT)
    0 secs (0 hrs) behind the primary
source: m2.example.net:27017
    syncedTo: Tue Apr 10 2018 10:27:43 GMT-0400 (EDT)
    0 secs (0 hrs) behind the primary
source: m3.example.net:27017
    syncedTo: Tue Apr 10 2018 10:27:39 GMT-0400 (EDT)
    0 secs (0 hrs) behind the primary
```

Remember that a replica set member's lag is calculated relative to the primary, not against "wall time." This usually is irrelevant, but on very low-write systems, this can cause phantom replication lag "spikes." For example, suppose you do a write once an hour. Right after that write, before it's replicated, the secondary will look like it's an hour behind the primary. However, it'll be able to catch up with that "hour" of operations in a few milliseconds. This can sometimes cause confusion when monitoring a low-throughput system.

Resizing the Oplog

Your primary's oplog should be thought of as your maintenance window. If your primary has an oplog that is an hour long, then you only have one hour to fix anything that goes wrong before your secondaries fall too far behind and must be resynced from scratch. Thus, you generally want to have an oplog that can hold a couple days' to a week's worth of data, to give yourself some breathing room if something goes wrong.

Unfortunately, there's no easy way to tell how long your oplog is going to be before it fills up. The WiredTiger storage engine allows online resizing of your oplog while your server is running. You should perform these steps on each secondary replica set member first; once these have been changed, then and only then should you make the changes to your primary. Remember that each server that could become a primary should have a large enough oplog to give you a sane maintenance window.

To increase the size of your oplog, perform the following steps:

1. Connect to the replica set member. If authentication is enabled, be sure to use a user with privileges that can modify the local database.

2. Verify the current size of the oplog:

```
> use local
> db.oplog.rs.stats(1024*1024).maxSize
```

This will display the collection size in megabytes.

3. Change the oplog size of the replica set member:

```
> db.adminCommand({replSetResizeOplog: 1, size: 16000})
```

The following operation changes the oplog size of the replica set member to 16 gigabytes, or 16000 megabytes.

4. Finally, if you have reduced the size of the oplog, you may need to run the com pact to reclaim the disk space allocated. This should not be run against a member while it is a primary. Please see the "Change the Size of the Oplog" tutorial in the MongoDB documentation (*https://oreil.ly/krv0R*) for more details on this case and on the entire procedure.

You generally should not decrease the size of your oplog: although it may be months long, there is usually ample disk space for it and it does not use up any valuable resources like RAM or CPU.

Building Indexes

If you send an index build to the primary, the primary will build the index normally and then the secondaries will build the index when they replicate the "build index" operation. Although this is the easiest way to build an index, index builds are resource-intensive operations that can make members unavailable. If all of your secondaries start building an index at the same time, almost every member of your set will be offline until the index build completes. This process is only for replica sets; for a sharded cluster, please see the MongoDB documentation tutorial about building indexes on a sharded cluster (*https://oreil.ly/wJNeE*).

 You must stop all writes to a collection when you are creating a "unique" index. If the writes are not stopped, you can end up with inconsistent data across the replica set members.

Therefore, you may want to build an index on one member at a time to minimize the impact on your application. To accomplish this, do the following:

1. Shut down a secondary.
2. Restart it as a standalone server.
3. Build the index on the standalone server.
4. When the index build is complete, restart the server as a member of the replica set. When restarting this member, you need to remove the `disableLogicalSes sionCacheRefresh` parameter if it is present in your command-line options or configuration file.
5. Repeat steps 1 through 4 for each secondary in the replica set.

You should now have a set where every member other than the primary has the index built. Now there are two options, and you should choose the one that will impact your production system the least:

1. Build the index on the primary. If you have an "off" time when you have less traffic, that would probably be a good time to build it. You also might want to modify read preferences to temporarily shunt more load onto secondaries while the build is in progress.

   The primary will replicate the index build to the secondaries, but they will already have the index so it will be a no-op for them.
2. Step down the primary, then follow steps 2 through 4 of the procedure outlined previously. This requires a failover, but you will have a normally functioning primary while the old primary is building its index. After its index build is complete, you can reintroduce it to the set.

Note that you could also use this technique to build different indexes on a secondary than you have on the rest of the set. This could be useful for offline processing, but make sure a member with different indexes can never become primary: its priority should always be 0.

If you are building a unique index, make sure that the primary is not inserting duplicates or that you build the index on the primary first. Otherwise, the primary could be inserting duplicates that would then cause replication errors on secondaries. If this occurs, the secondary will shut itself down. You will have to restart it as a standalone server, remove the unique index, and restart it.

Replication on a Budget

If it is difficult to get more than one high-quality server, consider getting a secondary server that is strictly for disaster recovery, with less RAM and CPU, slower disk I/O, etc. The good server will always be your primary and the cheaper server will never handle any client traffic (configure your clients to send all reads to the primary). Here are the options to set for the cheaper box:

`"priority" : 0`
> You do not want this server to ever become primary.

`"hidden" : true`
> You do not want clients ever sending reads to this secondary.

`"buildIndexes" : false`
> This is optional, but it can decrease the load this server has to handle considerably. If you ever need to restore from this server, you'll need to rebuild the indexes.

`"votes" : 0`
> If you only have two machines, set `"votes"` on this secondary to 0 so that the primary can stay primary if this machine goes down. If you have a third server (even just your application server), run an arbiter on that instead of setting `"votes"` to 0.

This will give you the safety and security of having a secondary without having to invest in two high-performance servers.

## PART IV

Sharding

## CHAPTER 14

Introduction to Sharding

This chapter covers how to scale with MongoDB. We'll look at:

- What sharding is and the components of a cluster
- How to configure sharding
- The basics of how sharding interacts with your application

What Is Sharding?

Sharding refers to the process of splitting data up across machines; the term *partitioning* is also sometimes used to describe this concept. By putting a subset of data on each machine, it becomes possible to store more data and handle more load without requiring larger or more powerful machines—just a larger quantity of less-powerful machines. Sharding may be used for other purposes as well, including placing more frequently accessed data on more performant hardware or splitting a dataset based on geography to locate a subset of documents in a collection (e.g., for users based in a particular locale) close to the application servers from which they are most commonly accessed.

Manual sharding can be done with almost any database software. With this approach, an application maintains connections to several different database servers, each of which are completely independent. The application manages storing different data on different servers and querying against the appropriate server to get data back. This setup can work well but becomes difficult to maintain when adding or removing nodes from the cluster or in the face of changing data distributions or load patterns.

MongoDB supports autosharding, which tries to both abstract the architecture away from the application and simplify the administration of such a system. MongoDB allows your application to ignore the fact that it isn't talking to a standalone MongoDB server, to some extent. On the operations side, MongoDB automates balancing data across shards and makes it easier to add and remove capacity.

Sharding is the most complex way of configuring MongoDB, both from a development and an operational point of view. There are many components to configure and monitor, and data moves around the cluster automatically. You should be comfortable with standalone servers and replica sets before attempting to deploy or use a sharded cluster. Also, as with replica sets, the recommended means of configuring and deploying sharded clusters is through either MongoDB Ops Manager or MongoDB Atlas. Ops Manager is recommended if you need to maintain control of your computing infrastructure. MongoDB Atlas is recommended if you can leave the infrastructure management to MongoDB (you have the option of running in Amazon AWS, Microsoft Azure, or Google Compute Cloud).

Understanding the Components of a Cluster

MongoDB's sharding allows you to create a cluster of many machines (shards) and break up a collection across them, putting a subset of data on each shard. This allows your application to grow beyond the resource limits of a standalone server or replica set.

 Many people are confused about the difference between replication and sharding. Remember that replication creates an exact copy of your data on multiple servers, so every server is a mirror image of every other server. Conversely, every shard contains a different subset of data.

One of the goals of sharding is to make a cluster of 2, 3, 10, or even hundreds of shards look like a single machine to your application. To hide these details from the application, we run one or more routing processes called a *mongos* in front of the shards. A *mongos* keeps a "table of contents" that tells it which shard contains which data. Applications can connect to this router and issue requests normally, as shown in Figure 14-1. The router, knowing what data is on which shard, is able to forward the requests to the appropriate shard(s). If there are responses to a request the router collects them and, if necessary, merges them, and sends them back to the application. As far as the application knows, it's connected to a standalone *mongod*, as illustrated in Figure 14-2.

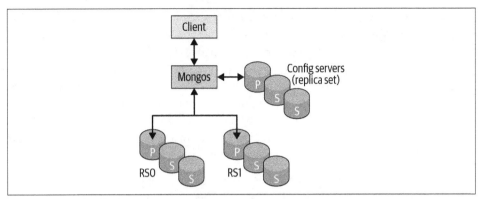

Figure 14-1. Sharded client connection

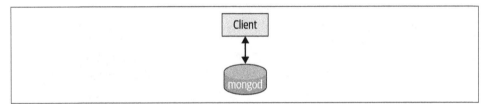

Figure 14-2. Nonsharded client connection

Sharding on a Single-Machine Cluster

We'll start by setting up a quick cluster on a single machine. First, start a *mongo* shell with the `--nodb` and `--norc` options:

```
$ mongo --nodb --norc
```

To create a cluster, use the `ShardingTest` class. Run the following in the *mongo* shell you just launched:

```
st = ShardingTest({
  name:"one-min-shards",
  chunkSize:1,
  shards:2,
  rs:{
    nodes:3,
    oplogSize:10
  },
  other:{
    enableBalancer:true
  }
});
```

The `chunksize` option is covered in Chapter 17. For now, simply set it to 1. As for the other options passed to `ShardingTest` here, `name` simply provides a label for our sharded cluster, shards specifies that our cluster will be composed of two shards (we do this to keep the resource requirements low for this example), and rs defines each shard as a three-node replica set with an oplogSize of 10 MiB (again, to keep resource shard as a three-node replica set with an oplogSize of 10 MiB (again, to keep resource utilization low). Though it is possible to run one standalone *mongod* for each shard, it paints a clearer picture of the typical architecture of a sharded cluster if we create each shard as a replica set. In the last option specified, we are instructing ShardingTest to enable the balancer once the cluster is spun up. This will ensure that data is evenly distributed across both shards.

ShardingTest is a class designed for internal use by MongoDB Engineering and is therefore undocumented externally. However, because it ships with the MongoDB server, it provides the most straightforward means of experimenting with a sharded cluster. ShardingTest was originally designed to support server test suites and is still used for this purpose. By default it provides a number of conveniences that help in keeping resource utilization as small as possible and in setting up the relatively complex architecture of a sharded cluster. It makes an assumption about the presence of a /data /db directory on your machine; if ShardingTest fails to run then create this directory and rerun the command again.

When you run this command, ShardingTest will do a lot for you automatically. It will create a new cluster with two shards, each of which is a replica set. It will configure the replica sets and launch each node with the necessary options to establish replication protocols. It will launch a *mongos* to manage requests across the shards so that clients can interact with the cluster as if communicating with a standalone *mongod*, to some extent. Finally, it will launch an additional replica set for the config servers that maintain the routing table information necessary to ensure queries are directed to the correct shard. Remember that the primary use cases for sharding are to split a dataset to address hardware and cost constraints or to provide better performance to applications (e.g., geographical partitioning). MongoDB sharding provides these capabilities in a way that is seamless to the application in many respects.

Once ShardingTest has finished setting up your cluster, you will have 10 processes up and running to which you can connect: two replica sets of three nodes each, one config server replica set of three nodes, and one *mongos*. By default, these processes should begin at port 20000. The *mongos* should be running at port 20009. Other processes you have running on your local machine and previous calls to ShardingTest can have an effect on which ports ShardingTest uses, but you should not have too much difficulty determining the ports on which your cluster processes are running.

Next, you'll connect to the *mongos* to play around with the cluster. Your entire cluster will be dumping its logs to your current shell, so open up a second terminal window and launch another *mongo* shell:

```
$ mongo --nodb
```

Use this shell to connect to your cluster's *mongos*. Again, your *mongos* should be running on port 20009:

```
> db = (new Mongo("localhost:20009")).getDB("accounts")
```

Note that the prompt in your *mongo* shell should change to reflect that you are connected to a *mongos*. Now you are in the situation shown earlier, in Figure 14-1: the shell is the client and is connected to a *mongos*. You can start passing requests to the *mongos* and it'll route them to the shards. You don't really have to know anything about the shards, like how many there are or what their addresses are. So long as there are some shards out there, you can pass the requests to the *mongos* and allow it to forward them appropriately.

Start by inserting some data:

```
> for (var i=0; i<100000; i++) {
...     db.users.insert({"username" : "user"+i, "created_at" : new Date()});
... }
> db.users.count()
100000
```

As you can see, interacting with *mongos* works the same way as interacting with a standalone server does.

You can get an overall view of your cluster by running sh.status(). It will give you a summary of your shards, databases, and collections:

```
> sh.status()
--- Sharding Status ---
sharding version: {
  "_id": 1,
  "minCompatibleVersion": 5,
  "currentVersion": 6,
  "clusterId": ObjectId("5a4f93d6bcde690005986071")
}
shards:
{
  "_id" : "one-min-shards-rs0",
  "host" :
    "one-min-shards-rs0/MBP:20000,MBP:20001,MBP:20002",
  "state" : 1 }
{ "_id" : "one-min-shards-rs1",
  "host" :
    "one-min-shards-rs1/MBP:20003,MBP:20004,MBP:20005",
  "state" : 1 }
active mongoses:
  "3.6.1" : 1
autosplit:
  Currently enabled: no
balancer:
  Currently enabled:  no
  Currently running:  no
```

```
    Failed balancer rounds in last 5 attempts:  0
    Migration Results for the last 24 hours:
      No recent migrations
  databases:
    {  "_id" : "accounts",  "primary" : "one-min-shards-rs1",
       "partitioned" : false }
    {  "_id" : "config",  "primary" : "config",
       "partitioned" : true }
    config.system.sessions
  shard key: { "_id" : 1 }
  unique: false
  balancing: true
  chunks:
    one-min-shards-rs0    1
    { "_id" : { "$minKey" : 1 } } -->> { "_id" : { "$maxKey" : 1 } }
    on : one-min-shards-rs0 Timestamp(1, 0)
```

 sh is similar to rs, but for sharding: it is a global variable that
defines a number of sharding helper functions, which you can see
by running sh.help(). As you can see from the sh.status() output, you have two shards and two databases (*config* is created
automatically).

Your *accounts* database may have a different primary shard than the one shown here.
A primary shard is a "home base" shard that is randomly chosen for each database.
All of your data will be on this primary shard. MongoDB cannot automatically dis-
tribute your data yet because it doesn't know how (or if) you want it to be distributed.
You have to tell it, per collection, how you want it to distribute data.

 A primary shard is different from a replica set primary. A primary
shard refers to the entire replica set composing a shard. A primary
in a replica set is the single server in the set that can take writes.

To shard a particular collection, first enable sharding on the collection's database. To
do so, run the enableSharding command:

```
> sh.enableSharding("accounts")
```

Now sharding is enabled on the *accounts* database, which allows you to shard collections within the database.

When you shard a collection, you choose a shard key. This is a field or two that MongoDB uses to break up data. For example, if you chose to shard on "username", MongoDB would break up the data into ranges of usernames: "a1-steak-sauce" through
"defcon", "defcon1" through "howie1998", and so on. Choosing a shard key can be

---

thought of as choosing an ordering for the data in the collection. This is a similar concept to indexing, and for good reason: the shard key becomes the most important index on your collection as it gets bigger. To even create a shard key, the field(s) must be indexed.

So, before enabling sharding, you have to create an index on the key you want to shard by:

```
> db.users.createIndex({"username" : 1})
```

Now you can shard the collection by `"username"`:

```
> sh.shardCollection("accounts.users", {"username" : 1})
```

Although we are choosing a shard key without much thought here, it is an important decision that should be carefully considered in a real system. See Chapter 16 for more advice on choosing a shard key.

If you wait a few minutes and run `sh.status()` again, you'll see that there's a lot more information displayed than there was before:

```
> sh.status()
--- Sharding Status ---
sharding version: {
  "_id" : 1,
  "minCompatibleVersion" : 5,
  "currentVersion" : 6,
  "clusterId" : ObjectId("5a4f93d6bcde690005986071")
}
shards:
  {  "_id" : "one-min-shards-rs0",
     "host" :
       "one-min-shards-rs0/MBP:20000,MBP:20001,MBP:20002",
     "state" : 1 }
  {  "_id" : "one-min-shards-rs1",
     "host" :
       "one-min-shards-rs1/MBP:20003,MBP:20004,MBP:20005",
     "state" : 1 }
active mongoses:
  "3.6.1" : 1
autosplit:
  Currently enabled: no
balancer:
  Currently enabled:  yes
  Currently running:  no
  Failed balancer rounds in last 5 attempts:  0
  Migration Results for the last 24 hours:
    6 : Success
databases:
  {  "_id" : "accounts",  "primary" : "one-min-shards-rs1",
     "partitioned" : true }
accounts.users
```

```
shard key: { "username" : 1 }
unique: false
balancing: true
chunks:
  one-min-shards-rs0  6
  one-min-shards-rs1  7
  { "username" : { "$minKey" : 1 } } -->>
    { "username" : "user17256" } on : one-min-shards-rs0 Timestamp(2, 0)
  { "username" : "user17256" } -->>
    { "username" : "user24515" } on : one-min-shards-rs0 Timestamp(3, 0)
  { "username" : "user24515" } -->>
    { "username" : "user31775" } on : one-min-shards-rs0 Timestamp(4, 0)
  { "username" : "user31775" } -->>
    { "username" : "user39034" } on : one-min-shards-rs0 Timestamp(5, 0)
  { "username" : "user39034" } -->>
    { "username" : "user46294" } on : one-min-shards-rs0 Timestamp(6, 0)
  { "username" : "user46294" } -->>
    { "username" : "user53553" } on : one-min-shards-rs0 Timestamp(7, 0)
  { "username" : "user53553" } -->>
    { "username" : "user60812" } on : one-min-shards-rs1 Timestamp(7, 1)
  { "username" : "user60812" } -->>
    { "username" : "user68072" } on : one-min-shards-rs1 Timestamp(1, 7)
  { "username" : "user68072" } -->>
    { "username" : "user75331" } on : one-min-shards-rs1 Timestamp(1, 8)
  { "username" : "user75331" } -->>
    { "username" : "user82591" } on : one-min-shards-rs1 Timestamp(1, 9)
  { "username" : "user82591" } -->>
    { "username" : "user89851" } on : one-min-shards-rs1 Timestamp(1, 10)
  { "username" : "user89851" } -->>
    { "username" : "user9711" } on : one-min-shards-rs1 Timestamp(1, 11)
  { "username" : "user9711" } -->>
    { "username" : { "$maxKey" : 1 } } on : one-min-shards-rs1 Timestamp(1, 12)
    { "_id" : "config",  "primary" : "config",  "partitioned" : true }
config.system.sessions
  shard key: { "_id" : 1 }
  unique: false
  balancing: true
  chunks:
    one-min-shards-rs0  1
    { "_id" : { "$minKey" : 1 } } -->>
      { "_id" : { "$maxKey" : 1 } } on : one-min-shards-rs0 Timestamp(1, 0)
```

The collection has been split up into 13 chunks, where each chunk is a subset of your data. These are listed by shard key range (the {"username" : *minValue*} -->> {"username" : *maxValue*} denotes the range of each chunk). Looking at the "on" : *shard* part of the output, you can see that these chunks have been evenly distributed between the shards.

This process of a collection being split into chunks is shown graphically in Figures 14-3 through 14-5. Before sharding, the collection is essentially a single chunk. Sharding splits it into smaller chunks based on the shard key, as shown in

---

Figure 14-4. These chunks can then be distributed across the cluster, as Figure 14-5 shows.

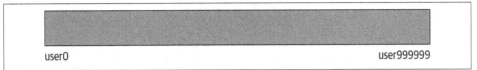

Figure 14-3. *Before a collection is sharded, it can be thought of as a single chunk from the smallest value of the shard key to the largest*

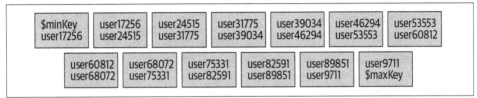

Figure 14-4. *Sharding splits the collection into many chunks based on shard key ranges*

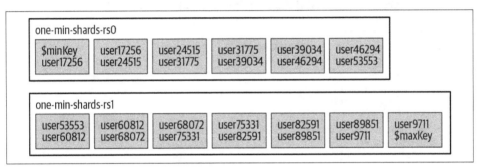

Figure 14-5. *Chunks are evenly distributed across the available shards*

Notice the keys at the beginning and end of the chunk list: $minKey and $maxKey. $minKey can be thought of as "negative infinity." It is smaller than any other value in MongoDB. Similarly, $maxKey is like "positive infinity." It is greater than any other value. Thus, you'll always see these as the "caps" on your chunk ranges. The values for your shard key will always be between $minKey and $maxKey. These values are actually BSON types and should not be used in your application; they are mainly for internal use. If you wish to refer to them in the shell, use the MinKey and MaxKey constants.

Now that the data is distributed across multiple shards, let's try doing some queries. First, try a query on a specific username:

```
> db.users.find({username: "user12345"})
{
    "_id" : ObjectId("5a4fb11dbb9ce6070f377880"),
```

```
        "username" : "user12345",
        "created_at" : ISODate("2018-01-05T17:08:45.657Z")
    }
```

As you can see, querying works normally. However, let's run an `explain` to see what MongoDB is doing under the covers:

```
> db.users.find({username: "user12345"}}).explain()
{
  "queryPlanner" : {
    "mongosPlannerVersion" : 1,
    "winningPlan" : {
      "stage" : "SINGLE_SHARD",
      "shards" : [{
    "shardName" : "one-min-shards-rs0",
    "connectionString" :
      "one-min-shards-rs0/MBP:20000,MBP:20001,MBP:20002",
    "serverInfo" : {
        "host" : "MBP",
        "port" : 20000,
        "version" : "3.6.1",
        "gitVersion" : "025d4f4fe61efd1fb6f0005be20cb45a004093d1"
    },
    "plannerVersion" : 1,
    "namespace" : "accounts.users",
    "indexFilterSet" : false,
    "parsedQuery" : {
        "username" : {
          "$eq" : "user12345"
        }
    },
    "winningPlan" : {
      "stage" : "FETCH",
      "inputStage" : {
        "stage" : "SHARDING_FILTER",
          "inputStage" : {
              "stage" : "IXSCAN",
          "keyPattern" : {
            "username" : 1
          },
          "indexName" : "username_1",
          "isMultiKey" : false,
          "multiKeyPaths" : {
                "username" : [ ]
          },
          "isUnique" : false,
              "isSparse" : false,
            "isPartial" : false,
          "indexVersion" : 2,
          "direction" : "forward",
          "indexBounds" : {
            "username" : [
                    "[\"user12345\", \"user12345\"]"
```

```
            ]
          }
        }
      }
    },
    "rejectedPlans" : [ ]
      }]
    }
  },
  "ok" : 1,
  "$clusterTime" : {
    "clusterTime" : Timestamp(1515174248, 1),
    "signature" : {
      "hash" : BinData(0,"AAAAAAAAAAAAAAAAAAAAAAAAAAA="),
      "keyId" : NumberLong(0)
    }
  },
  "operationTime" : Timestamp(1515173700, 201)
}
```

From the `"winningPlan"` field in the explain output, we can see that our cluster sat-
isfied this query using a single shard, *one-min-shards-rs0*. Based on the output of
sh.status() shown earlier, we can see that *user12345* does fall within the key range
for the first chunk listed for that shard in our cluster.

Because `"username"` is the shard key, *mongos* was able to route the query directly to
the correct shard. Contrast that with the results for querying for all of the users:

```
> db.users.find().explain()
{
  "queryPlanner":{
    "mongosPlannerVersion":1,
    "winningPlan":{
      "stage":"SHARD_MERGE",
      "shards":[
        {
          "shardName":"one-min-shards-rs0",
          "connectionString":
            "one-min-shards-rs0/MBP:20000,MBP:20001,MBP:20002",
          "serverInfo":{
            "host":"MBP.fios-router.home",
            "port":20000,
            "version":"3.6.1",
            "gitVersion":"025d4f4fe61efd1fb6f0005be20cb45a004093d1"
          },
          "plannerVersion":1,
          "namespace":"accounts.users",
          "indexFilterSet":false,
          "parsedQuery":{

          },
          "winningPlan":{
```

```
              "stage":"SHARDING_FILTER",
              "inputStage":{
                "stage":"COLLSCAN",
                "direction":"forward"
              }
            },
            "rejectedPlans":[

            ]
          },
          {
            "shardName":"one-min-shards-rs1",
            "connectionString":
              "one-min-shards-rs1/MBP:20003,MBP:20004,MBP:20005",
            "serverInfo":{
              "host":"MBP.fios-router.home",
              "port":20003,
              "version":"3.6.1",
              "gitVersion":"025d4f4fe61efd1fb6f0005be20cb45a004093d1"
            },
            "plannerVersion":1,
            "namespace":"accounts.users",
            "indexFilterSet":false,
            "parsedQuery":{

            },
            "winningPlan":{
              "stage":"SHARDING_FILTER",
              "inputStage":{
                "stage":"COLLSCAN",
                "direction":"forward"
              }
            },
            "rejectedPlans":[

            ]
          }
        ]
      }
    },
    "ok":1,
    "$clusterTime":{
      "clusterTime":Timestamp(1515174893, 1),
      "signature":{
        "hash":BinData(0, "AAAAAAAAAAAAAAAAAAAAAAAAAAA="),
        "keyId":NumberLong(0)
      }
    },
    "operationTime":Timestamp(1515173709, 514)
}
```

As you can see from this `explain`, this query has to visit both shards to find all the data. In general, if we are not using the shard key in the query, *mongos* will have to send the query to every shard.

Queries that contain the shard key and can be sent to a single shard or a subset of shards are called *targeted queries*. Queries that must be sent to all shards are called *scatter-gather* (broadcast) queries: *mongos* scatters the query to all the shards and then gathers up the results.

Once you are finished experimenting, shut down the set. Switch back to your original shell and hit Enter a few times to get back to the command line, then run `st.stop()` to cleanly shut down all of the servers:

```
> st.stop()
```

If you are ever unsure of what an operation will do, it can be helpful to use `ShardingTest` to spin up a quick local cluster and try it out.

## CHAPTER 15

Configuring Sharding

In the previous chapter, you set up a "cluster" on one machine. This chapter covers how to set up a more realistic cluster and how each piece fits. In particular, you'll learn:

- How to set up config servers, shards, and *mongos* processes
- How to add capacity to a cluster
- How data is stored and distributed

When to Shard

Deciding when to shard is a balancing act. You generally do not want to shard too early because it adds operational complexity to your deployment and forces you to make design decisions that are difficult to change later. On the other hand, you do not want to wait too long to shard because it is difficult to shard an overloaded system without downtime.

In general, sharding is used to:

- Increase available RAM
- Increase available disk space
- Reduce load on a server
- Read or write data with greater throughput than a single *mongod* can handle

Thus, good monitoring is important to decide when sharding will be necessary. Carefully measure each of these metrics. Generally people speed toward one of these bottlenecks much faster than the others, so figure out which one your deployment will need to provision for first and make plans well in advance about when and how you plan to convert your replica set.

Starting the Servers

The first step in creating a cluster is to start up all of the processes required. As mentioned in the previous chapter, you need to set up the *mongos* and the shards. There's also a third component, the config servers, which are an important piece. Config servers are normal *mongod* servers that store the cluster configuration: which replica sets host the shards, what collections are sharded by, and on which shard each chunk is located. MongoDB 3.2 introduced the use of replica sets as config servers. Replica sets replace the original syncing mechanism used by config servers; the ability to use that mechanism was removed in MongoDB 3.4.

Config Servers

Config servers are the brains of your cluster: they hold all of the metadata about which servers hold what data. Thus, they must be set up first, and the data they hold is *extremely* important: make sure that they are running with journaling enabled and that their data is stored on nonephemeral drives. In production deployments, your config server replica set should consist of at least three members. Each config server should be on a separate physical machine, preferable geographically distributed.

The config servers must be started before any of the *mongos* processes, as *mongos* pulls its configuration from them. To begin, run the following commands on three separate machines to start your config servers:

```
$ mongod --configsvr --replSet configRS --bind_ip localhost,198.51.100.51 mongod
  --dbpath /var/lib/mongodb

$ mongod --configsvr --replSet configRS --bind_ip localhost,198.51.100.52 mongod
  --dbpath /var/lib/mongodb

$ mongod --configsvr --replSet configRS --bind_ip localhost,198.51.100.53 mongod
  --dbpath /var/lib/mongodb
```

Then initiate the config servers as a replica set. To do this, connect a *mongo* shell to one of the replica set members:

```
$ mongo --host <hostname> --port <port>
```

and use the rs.initiate() helper:

```
> rs.initiate(
  {
    _id: "configRS",
    configsvr: true,
    members: [
      { _id : 0, host : "cfg1.example.net:27019" },
```

```
        { _id : 1, host : "cfg2.example.net:27019" },
        { _id : 2, host : "cfg3.example.net:27019" }
      ]
    }
  )
```

Here we're using *configRS* as the replica set name. Note that this name appears both on the command line when instantiating each config server and in the call to `rs.initiate()`.

The `--configsvr` option indicates to the *mongod* that you are planning to use it as a config server. On a server running with this option, clients (i.e., other cluster components) cannot write data to any database other than *config* or *admin*.

The *admin* database contains the collections related to authentication and authorization, as well as the other *system.** collections for internal use. The *config* database contains the collections that hold the sharded cluster metadata. MongoDB writes data to the *config* database when the metadata changes, such as after a chunk migration or a chunk split.

When writing to config servers, MongoDB uses a `writeConcern` level of `"majority"`. Similarly, when reading from config servers, MongoDB uses a `readConcern` level of `"majority"`. This ensures that sharded cluster metadata will not be committed to the config server replica set until it can't be rolled back. It also ensures that only metadata that will survive a failure of the config servers will be read. This is necessary to ensure all *mongos* routers have a consistent view of how data is organized in a sharded cluster.

In terms of provisioning, config servers should be provisioned adequately in terms of networking and CPU resources. They only hold a table of contents of the data in the cluster so the storage resources required are minimal. They should be deployed on separate hardware to avoid contention for the machine's resources.

 If all of your config servers are lost, you must dig through the data on your shards to figure out which data is where. This is possible, but slow and unpleasant. Take frequent backups of config server data. Always take a backup of your config servers before performing any cluster maintenance.

The mongos Processes

Once you have three config servers running, start a *mongos* process for your application to connect to. *mongos* processes need to know where the config servers are, so you must always start *mongos* with the `--configdb` option:

```
$ mongos --configdb \
    configRS/cfg1.example.net:27019, \
```

```
        cfg2.example.net:27019,cfg3.example.net:27019 \
    --bind_ip localhost,198.51.100.100 --logpath /var/log/mongos.log
```

By default, *mongos* runs on port 27017. Note that it does not need a data directory (*mongos* holds no data itself; it loads the cluster configuration from the config servers on startup). Make sure that you set `--logpath` to save the *mongos* log somewhere safe.

You should start a small number of *mongos* processes and locate them as close to all the shards as possible. This improves performance of queries that need to access multiple shards or which perform scatter/gather operations. The minimal setup is at least two *mongos* processes to ensure high availability. It is possible to run tens or hundreds of *mongos* processes but this causes resource contention on the *config servers*. The recommended approach is to provide a small pool of routers.

Adding a Shard from a Replica Set

Finally, you're ready to add a shard. There are two possibilities: you may have an existing replica set or you may be starting from scratch. We will cover starting from an existing set. If you are starting from scratch, initialize an empty set and follow the steps outlined here.

If you already have a replica set serving your application, that will become your first shard. To convert it into a shard, you need to make some small configuration modifications to the members and then tell the *mongos* how to find the replica set that will comprise the shard.

For example, if you have a replica set named *rs0* on *svr1.example.net*, *svr2.example.net*, and *svr3.example.net*, you would first connect to one of the members using the *mongo* shell:

```
$ mongo srv1.example.net
```

Then use `rs.status()` to determine which member is the primary and which are secondaries:

```
> rs.status()
    "set" : "rs0",
    "date" : ISODate("2018-11-02T20:02:16.543Z"),
    "myState" : 1,
    "term" : NumberLong(1),
    "heartbeatIntervalMillis" : NumberLong(2000),
    "optimes" : {


        "lastCommittedOpTime" : {
            "ts" : Timestamp(1478116934, 1),
            "t" : NumberLong(1)
        },
```

```
        "readConcernMajorityOpTime" : {
            "ts" : Timestamp(1478116934, 1),
            "t" : NumberLong(1)
        },
        "appliedOpTime" : {
            "ts" : Timestamp(1478116934, 1),
            "t" : NumberLong(1)
        },
        "durableOpTime" : {
            "ts" : Timestamp(1478116934, 1),
            "t" : NumberLong(1)
        }
    },

    "members" : [
        {
            "_id" : 0,
            "name" : "svr1.example.net:27017",
            "health" : 1,
            "state" : 1,
            "stateStr" : "PRIMARY",
            "uptime" : 269,
            "optime" : {
                    "ts" : Timestamp(1478116934, 1),
                    "t" : NumberLong(1)
            },
            "optimeDate" : ISODate("2018-11-02T20:02:14Z"),
            "infoMessage" : "could not find member to sync from",
            "electionTime" : Timestamp(1478116933, 1),
            "electionDate" : ISODate("2018-11-02T20:02:13Z"),
            "configVersion" : 1,
            "self" : true
        },
        {
            "_id" : 1,
            "name" : "svr2.example.net:27017",
            "health" : 1,
            "state" : 2,
            "stateStr" : "SECONDARY",
            "uptime" : 14,
            "optime" : {
                "ts" : Timestamp(1478116934, 1),
                "t" : NumberLong(1)
            },
            "optimeDurable" : {
                "ts" : Timestamp(1478116934, 1),
                "t" : NumberLong(1)
            },
            "optimeDate" : ISODate("2018-11-02T20:02:14Z"),
            "optimeDurableDate" : ISODate("2018-11-02T20:02:14Z"),
            "lastHeartbeat" : ISODate("2018-11-02T20:02:15.618Z"),
            "lastHeartbeatRecv" : ISODate("2018-11-02T20:02:14.866Z"),
```

```
                "pingMs" : NumberLong(0),
                "syncingTo" : "m1.example.net:27017",
                "configVersion" : 1
        },
        {
                "_id" : 2,
                "name" : "svr3.example.net:27017",
                "health" : 1,
                "state" : 2,
                "stateStr" : "SECONDARY",
                "uptime" : 14,
                "optime" : {
                    "ts" : Timestamp(1478116934, 1),
                    "t" : NumberLong(1)
                },
                "optimeDurable" : {
                    "ts" : Timestamp(1478116934, 1),
                    "t" : NumberLong(1)
                },
                "optimeDate" : ISODate("2018-11-02T20:02:14Z"),
                "optimeDurableDate" : ISODate("2018-11-02T20:02:14Z"),
                "lastHeartbeat" : ISODate("2018-11-02T20:02:15.619Z"),
                "lastHeartbeatRecv" : ISODate("2018-11-02T20:02:14.787Z"),
                "pingMs" : NumberLong(0),
                "syncingTo" : "m1.example.net:27017",
                "configVersion" : 1
        }
    ],
    "ok" : 1
}
```

Beginning with MongoDB 3.4, for sharded clusters, *mongod* instances for shards *must* be configured with the --shardsvr option, either via the configuration file setting sharding.clusterRole or via the command-line option --shardsvr.

You will need to do this for each of the members of the replica set you are in the process of converting to a shard. You'll do this by first restarting each secondary in turn with the --shardsvr option, then stepping down the primary and restarting it with the --shardsvr option.

After shutting down a secondary, restart it as follows:

```
$ mongod --replSet "rs0" --shardsvr --port 27017
     --bind_ip localhost,<ip address of member>
```

Note that you'll need to use the correct IP address for each secondary for the --bind_ip parameter.

Now connect a *mongo* shell to the primary:

```
$ mongo m1.example.net
```

and step it down:

```
> rs.stepDown()
```

Then restart the former primary with the `--shardsvr` option:

```
$ mongod --replSet "rs0" --shardsvr --port 27017
    --bind_ip localhost,<ip address of the former primary>
```

Now you're ready to add your replica set as a shard. Connect a *mongo* shell to the *admin* database of the *mongos*:

```
$ mongo mongos1.example.net:27017/admin
```

And add a shard to the cluster using the `sh.addShard()` method:

```
> sh.addShard(
    "rs0/svr1.example.net:27017,svr2.example.net:27017,svr3.example.net:27017" )
```

You can specify all the members of the set, but you do not have to. *mongos* will automatically detect any members that were not included in the seed list. If you run `sh.status()`, you'll see that MongoDB soon lists the shard as

```
rs0/svr1.example.net:27017,svr2.example.net:27017,svr3.example.net:27017
```

The set name, *rs0*, is taken on as an identifier for this shard. If you ever want to remove this shard or migrate data to it, you can use *rs0* to describe it. This works better than using a specific server (e.g., *svr1.example.net*), as replica set membership and status can change over time.

Once you've added the replica set as a shard you can convert your application from connecting to the replica set to connecting to the *mongos*. When you add the shard, *mongos* registers that all the databases in the replica set are "owned" by that shard, so it will pass through all queries to your new shard. *mongos* will also automatically handle failover for your application as your client library would: it will pass the errors through to you.

Test failing over a shard's primary in a development environment to ensure that your application handles the errors received from *mongos* correctly (they should be identical to the errors that you receive from talking to the primary directly).

Once you have added a shard, you *must* set up all clients to send requests to the *mongos* instead of contacting the replica set. Sharding will not function correctly if some clients are still making requests to the replica set directly (not through the *mongos*). Switch all clients to contacting the *mongos* immediately after adding the shard and set up a firewall rule to ensure that they are unable to connect directly to the shard.

Prior to MongoDB 3.6 it was possible to create a standalone *mongod* as a shard. This is no longer an option in versions of MongoDB later than 3.6. All shards must be replica sets.

Adding Capacity

When you want to add more capacity, you'll need to add more shards. To add a new, empty shard, create a replica set. Make sure it has a distinct name from any of your other shards. Once it is initialized and has a primary, add it to your cluster by running the addShard command through *mongos*, specifying the new replica set's name and its hosts as seeds.

If you have several existing replica sets that are not shards, you can add all of them as new shards in your cluster so long as they do not have any database names in common. For example, if you had one replica set with a *blog* database, one with a *calendar* database, and one with *mail*, *tel*, and *music* databases, you could add each replica set as a shard and end up with a cluster with three shards and five databases. However, if you had a fourth replica set that also had a database named *tel*, *mongos* would refuse to add it to the cluster.

Sharding Data

MongoDB won't distribute your data automatically until you tell it how to do so. You must explicitly tell both the database and the collection that you want them to be distributed. For example, suppose you wanted to shard the *artists* collection in the *music* database on the "name" key. First, you'd enable sharding for the database:

```
> db.enableSharding("music")
```

Sharding a database is always a prerequisite to sharding one of its collections.

Once you've enabled sharding on the database level, you can shard a collection by running sh.shardCollection():

```
> sh.shardCollection("music.artists", {"name" : 1})
```

Now the *artists* collection will be sharded by the "name" key. If you are sharding an existing collection there must be an index on the "name" field; otherwise, the shard Collection call will return an error. If you get an error, create the index (*mongos* will return the index it suggests as part of the error message) and retry the shardCollec tion command.

If the collection you are sharding does not yet exist, *mongos* will automatically create the shard key index for you.

The shardCollection command splits the collection into chunks, which are the units MongoDB uses to move data around. Once the command returns successfully,

MongoDB will begin balancing the collection across the shards in your cluster. This process is not instantaneous. For large collections it may take hours to finish this initial balancing. This time can be reduced with presplitting where chunks are created on the shards prior to loading the data. Data loaded after this point will be inserted directly to the current shard without requiring additional balancing.

How MongoDB Tracks Cluster Data

Each *mongos* must always know where to find a document, given its shard key. Theoretically, MongoDB could track where each and every document lived, but this becomes unwieldy for collections with millions or billions of documents. Thus, MongoDB groups documents into chunks, which are documents in a given range of the shard key. A chunk always lives on a single shard, so MongoDB can keep a small table of chunks mapped to shards.

For example, if a user collection's shard key is {"age" : 1}, one chunk might be all documents with an "age" field between 3 and 17. If *mongos* gets a query for {"age" : 5}, it can route the query to the shard where this chunk lives.

As writes occur, the number and size of the documents in a chunk might change. Inserts can make a chunk contain more documents, and removes fewer. For example, if we were making a game for children and preteens, our chunk for ages 3–17 might get larger and larger (one would hope). Almost all of our users would be in that chunk and so would be on a single shard, somewhat defeating the point of distributing our data. Thus, once a chunk grows to a certain size, MongoDB automatically splits it into two smaller chunks. In this example, the original chunk might be split into one chunk containing documents with ages 3 through 11 and another with ages 12 through 17. Note that these two chunks still cover the entire age range that the original chunk covered: 3–17. As these new chunks grow, they can be split into still smaller chunks until there is a chunk for each age.

You cannot have chunks with overlapping ranges, like 3–15 and 12–17. If you could, MongoDB would need to check both chunks when attempting to find an age in the overlap, like 14. It is more efficient to only have to look in one place, particularly once chunks begin moving around the cluster.

A document always belongs to one and only one chunk. One consequence of this rule is that you cannot use an array field as your shard key, since MongoDB creates multiple index entries for arrays. For example, if a document had [5, 26, 83] in its "age" field, it would belong in up to three chunks.

A common misconception is that the data in a chunk is physically grouped on disk. This is incorrect: chunks have no effect on how *mongod* stores collection data.

Chunk Ranges

Each chunk is described by the range it contains. A newly sharded collection starts off with a single chunk, and every document lives in this chunk. This chunk's bounds are negative infinity to infinity, shown as $minKey and $maxKey in the shell.

As this chunk grows, MongoDB will automatically split it into two chunks, with the range negative infinity to *<some value>* and *<some value>* to infinity. *<some value>* is the same for both chunks: the lower chunk contains everything up to (but not including) *<some value>*, and the upper chunk contains *<some value>* and everything higher.

This may be more intuitive with an example. Suppose we were sharding by "age" as described earlier. All documents with "age" between 3 and 17 are contained in one chunk: 3 ≤ "age" < 17. When this is split, we end up with two ranges: 3 ≤ "age" < 12 in one chunk and 12 ≤ "age" < 17 in the other. 12 is called the *split point*.

Chunk information is stored in the *config.chunks* collection. If you looked at the contents of that collection, you'd see documents that looked something like this (some fields have been omitted for clarity):

```
> db.chunks.find(criteria, {"min" : 1, "max" : 1})
{
    "_id" : "test.users-age_-100.0",
    "min" : {"age" : -100},
    "max" : {"age" : 23}
}
{
    "_id" : "test.users-age_23.0",
    "min" : {"age" : 23},
    "max" : {"age" : 100}
}
{
    "_id" : "test.users-age_100.0",
    "min" : {"age" : 100},
    "max" : {"age" : 1000}
}
```

Based on the *config.chunks* documents shown, here are a few examples of where various documents would live:

```
{"_id" : 123, "age" : 50}
```
This document would live in the second chunk, as that chunk contains all docu-ments with `"age"` between 23 and 100.

```
{"_id" : 456, "age" : 100}
```
This document would live in the third chunk, as lower bounds are inclusive. The second chunk contains all documents up to `"age"` : 100, but not any documents where `"age"` equals 100.

```
{"_id" : 789, "age" : -101}
```
This document would not be in any of these chunks. It would be in some chunk with a range lower than the first chunk's.

With a compound shard key, shard ranges work the same way that sorting by the two keys would work. For example, suppose that we had a shard key on `{"username"` : 1, `"age"` : 1}`. Then we might have chunk ranges such as:

```
{
    "_id" : "test.users-username_MinKeyage_MinKey",
    "min" : {
        "username" : { "$minKey" : 1 },
        "age" : { "$minKey" : 1 }
    },
    "max" : {
        "username" : "user107487",
        "age" : 73
    }
}
{
    "_id" : "test.users-username_\"user107487\"age_73.0",
    "min" : {
        "username" : "user107487",
        "age" : 73
    },
    "max" : {
        "username" : "user114978",
        "age" : 119
    }
}
{
    "_id" : "test.users-username_\"user114978\"age_119.0",
    "min" : {
        "username" : "user114978",
        "age" : 119
    },
    "max" : {
        "username" : "user122468",
        "age" : 68
    }
}
```

Thus, *mongos* can easily find which chunk someone with a given username (or a given username and age) lives in. However, given just an age, *mongos* would have to check all, or almost all, of the chunks. If we wanted to be able to target queries on age to the right chunk, we'd have to use the "opposite" shard key: {"age" : 1, "user name" : 1}. This is often a point of confusion: a range over the second half of a shard key will cut across multiple chunks.

Splitting Chunks

Each shard primary *mongod* tracks their current chunks and, once they reach a certain threshold, checks if the chunk needs to be split, as shown in Figures 15-1 and 15-2. If the chunk does need to be split, the *mongod* will request the global chunk size configuration value from the config servers. It will then perform the chunk split and update the metadata on the config servers. New chunk documents are created on the config servers and the old chunk's range ("max") is modified. If the chunk is the top chunk of the shard, then the *mongod* will request the balancer move this chunk to a different shard. The idea is to prevent a shard from becoming "hot" where the shard key uses a monotonically increasing key.

A shard may not be able to find any split points, though, even for a large chunk, as there are a limited number of ways to legally split a chunk. Any two documents with the same shard key must live in the same chunk, so chunks can only be split between documents where the shard key's value changes. For example, if the shard key was "age", the following chunk could be split at the points where the shard key changed, as indicated:

```
{"age" : 13, "username" : "ian"}
{"age" : 13, "username" : "randolph"}
------------ // split point
{"age" : 14, "username" : "randolph"}
{"age" : 14, "username" : "eric"}
{"age" : 14, "username" : "hari"}
{"age" : 14, "username" : "mathias"}
------------ // split point
{"age" : 15, "username" : "greg"}
{"age" : 15, "username" : "andrew"}
```

The primary *mongod* for the shard only requests that the top chunk for a shard when split be moved to the balancer. The other chunks will remain on the shard unless manually moved.

If, however, the chunk contained the following documents, it could not be split (unless the application started inserting fractional ages):

```
{"age" : 12, "username" : "kevin"}
{"age" : 12, "username" : "spencer"}
{"age" : 12, "username" : "alberto"}
{"age" : 12, "username" : "tad"}
```

Thus, having a variety of values for your shard key is important. Other important properties will be covered in the next chapter.

If one of the config servers is down when a *mongod* tries to do a split, the *mongod* won't be able to update the metadata (as shown in Figure 15-3). All config servers must be up and reachable for splits to happen. If the *mongod* continues to receive write requests for the chunk, it will keep trying to split the chunk and fail. As long as the config servers are not healthy, splits will continue not to work, and all the split attempts can slow down the *mongod* and the shard involved (which repeats the process shown in Figures 15-1 through 15-3 for each incoming write). This process of *mongod* repeatedly attempting to split a chunk and being unable to is called a *split storm*. The only way to prevent split storms is to ensure that your config servers are up and healthy as much of the time as possible.

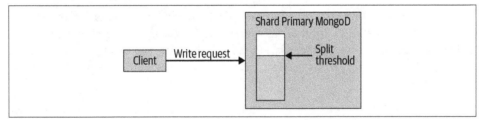

Figure 15-1. When a client writes to a chunk, the mongod will check its split threshold for the chunk

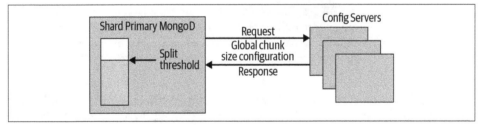

Figure 15-2. If the split threshold has been reached, the mongod will send a request to the balancer to migrate the top chunk; otherwise the chunk remains on the shard

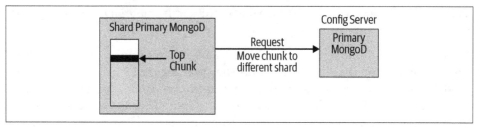

Figure 15-3. The mongod chooses a split point and attempts to inform the config server, but cannot reach it; thus, it is still over its split threshold for the chunk and any subsequent writes will trigger this process again

The Balancer

The *balancer* is responsible for migrating data. It regularly checks for imbalances between shards and, if it finds an imbalance, will begin migrating chunks. In MongoDB version 3.4+, the balancer is located on the primary member of the config server replica set; prior to this version, each *mongos* used to play the part of "the balancer" occasionally.

The balancer is a background process on the primary of the config server replica set, which monitors the number of chunks on each shard. It becomes active only when a shard's number of chunks reaches a specific migration threshold.

In MongoDB 3.4+, the number of concurrent migrations increased to one migration per shard with a maximum number of concurrent migrations being half the total number of shards. In earlier versions only one concurrent migration in total was supported.

Assuming that some collections have hit the threshold, the balancer will begin migrating chunks. It chooses a chunk from the overloaded shard and asks the shard if it should split the chunk before migrating. Once it does any necessary splits, it migrates the chunk(s) to a machine with fewer chunks.

An application using the cluster does not need be aware that the data is moving: all reads and writes are routed to the old chunk until the move is complete. Once the metadata is updated, any *mongos* process attempting to access the data in the old location will get an error. These errors should not be visible to the client: the *mongos* will silently handle the error and retry the operation on the new shard.

This is a common cause of errors you might see in *mongos* logs that relate to being "unable to setShardVersion." When a *mongos* gets this type of error, it looks up the new location of the data from the config servers, updates its chunk table, and attempts the request again. If it successfully retrieves the data from the new location, it will return it to the client as though nothing went wrong (but it will print a message in the log that the error occurred).

If the *mongos* is unable to retrieve the new chunk location because the config servers are unavailable, it will return an error to the client. This is another reason why it is important to always have config servers up and healthy.

Collations

Collations in MongoDB allow for the specification of language-specific rules for string comparison. Examples of these rules include how lettercase and accent marks are compared. It is possible to shard a collection that is a default collation. There are two requirements: the collection must have an index whose prefix is the shard key, and the index must also have the collation { `locale: "simple"` }.

Change Streams

Change Streams allow applications to track real-time changes to the data in the database. Prior to MongoDB 3.6, this was only possible by tailing the oplog and was a complex error-prone operation. Change streams provide a subscription mechanism for all data changes on a collection, a set of collections, a database, or across a full deployment. The aggregation framework is used by this feature. It allows applications to filter for specific changes or to transform the change notifications received. In a sharded cluster, all change stream operations must be issued against a *mongos*.

The changes across a sharded cluster are kept ordered through the use of a global logical clock. This guarantees the order of changes, and stream notifications can be safely interpreted by the order of their receipt. The *mongos* needs to check with each shard upon receipt of a change notification, to ensure that no shard has seen more recent changes. The activity level of the cluster and the geographical distribution of the shards can both impact the response time for this checking. The use of notification filters can improve the response time in these situations.

There are a few notes and caveats when using change streams with a sharded cluster. You open a change stream by issuing an open change stream operation. In sharded deployments, this *must* be issued against a *mongos*. If an update operation with multi: true is run against a sharded collection with an open change stream, then it is possible for notifications to be sent for orphaned documents. If a shard is removed, it may cause an open change stream cursor to close—furthermore, that cursor may not be fully resumable.

## CHAPTER 16

Choosing a Shard Key

The most important task when using sharding is choosing how your data will be distributed. To make intelligent choices about this, you have to understand how MongoDB distributes data. This chapter helps you make a good choice of shard key by covering:

- How to decide among multiple possible shard keys
- Shard keys for several use cases
- What you can't use as a shard key
- Some alternative strategies if you want to customize how data is distributed
- How to manually shard your data

It assumes that you understand the basic components of sharding as covered in the previous two chapters.

Taking Stock of Your Usage

When you shard a collection you choose a field or two to use to split up the data. This key (or keys) is called a *shard key*. Once you shard a collection you cannot change your shard key, so it is important to choose correctly.

To choose a good shard key, you need to understand your workload and how your shard key is going to distribute your application's requests. This can be difficult to picture, so try to work out some examples—or, even better, try it out on a backup dataset with sample traffic. This section has lots of diagrams and explanations, but there is no substitute for trying it on your own data.

For each collection that you're planning to shard, start by answering the following questions:

- How many shards are you planning to grow to? A three-shard cluster has a great deal more flexibility than a thousand-shard cluster. As a cluster gets larger, you should not plan to fire off queries that can hit all shards, so almost all queries must include the shard key.

- Are you sharding to decrease read or write latency? (Latency refers to how long something takes; e.g., a write takes 20 ms, but you need it to take 10 ms.) Decreasing write latency usually involves sending requests to geographically closer or more powerful machines.

- Are you sharding to increase read or write throughput? (Throughput refers to how many requests the cluster can handle at the same time; e.g., the cluster can do 1,000 writes in 20 ms, but you need it to do 5,000 writes in 20 ms.) Increasing throughput usually involves adding more parallelization and making sure that requests are distributed evenly across the cluster.

- Are you sharding to increase system resources (e.g., give MongoDB more RAM per GB of data)? If so, you want to keep the working set size as small as possible.

Use these answers to evaluate the following shard key descriptions and decide whether the shard key you're considering would work well in your situation. Does it give you the targeted queries that you need? Does it change the throughput or latency of your system in the ways you need? If you need a compact working set, does it provide that?

Picturing Distributions

The most common ways people choose to split their data are via ascending, random, and location-based keys. There are other types of keys that could be used, but most use cases fall into one of these categories. The different types of distributions are discussed in the following sections.

Ascending Shard Keys

Ascending shard keys are generally something like a `"date"` field or `ObjectId`—anything that steadily increases over time. An autoincrementing primary key is another example of an ascending field, albeit one that doesn't show up in MongoDB much (unless you're importing from another database).

Suppose that we shard on an ascending field, like `"_id"` on a collection using `ObjectId`s. If we shard on `"_id"`, then the data will be split into chunks of `"_id"` ranges, as in Figure 16-1. These chunks will be distributed across our sharded cluster of, let's say, three shards, as shown in Figure 16-2.

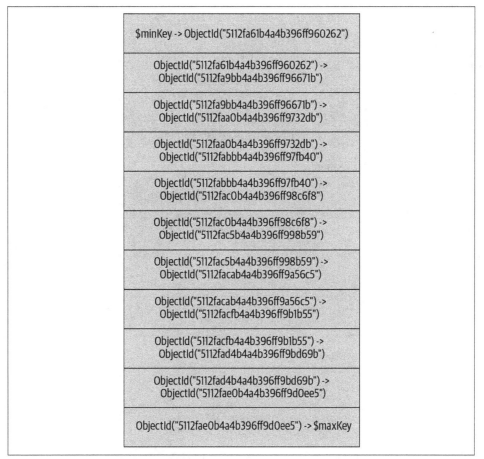

Figure 16-1. The collection is split into ranges of ObjectIds; each range is a chunk

Suppose we create a new document. Which chunk will it be in? The answer is the chunk with the range `ObjectId("5112fae0b4a4b396ff9d0ee5")` through `$maxKey`. This is called the *max chunk*, as it is the chunk containing `$maxKey`.

If we insert another document, it will also be in the max chunk. In fact, every subsequent insert will be into the max chunk! Every insert's `"_id"` field will be closer to infinity than the previous one (because `ObjectId`s are always ascending), so they will all go into the max chunk.

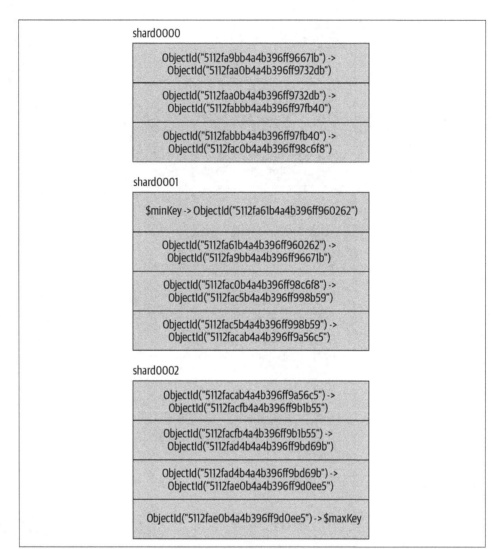

Figure 16-2. Chunks are distributed across shards in a random order

This has a couple of interesting (and often undesirable) properties. First, all of your writes will be routed to one shard (*shard0002*, in this case). This chunk will be the only one growing and splitting, as it is the only one that receives inserts. As you insert data, new chunks will "fall off" of this chunk, as shown in Figure 16-3.

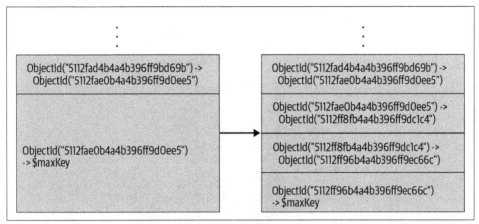

Figure 16-3. The max chunk continues growing and being split into multiple chunks

This pattern often makes it more difficult for MongoDB to keep chunks evenly balanced because all the chunks are being created by one shard. Therefore, MongoDB must constantly move chunks to other shards instead of correcting the small imbalances that might occur in more evenly distributed systems.

> In MongoDB 4.2, the move of the autosplit functionality to the shard primary *mongod* added top chunk optimization to address the ascending shard key pattern. The balancer will decide in which other shard to place the top chunk. This helps avoid a situation in which all new chunks are created on just one shard.

Randomly Distributed Shard Keys

At the other end of the spectrum are randomly distributed shard keys. Randomly distributed keys could be usernames, email addresses, UUIDs, MD5 hashes, or any other key that has no identifiable pattern in your dataset.

Suppose the shard key is a random number between 0 and 1. We'll end up with a random distribution of chunks on the various shards, as shown in Figure 16-4.

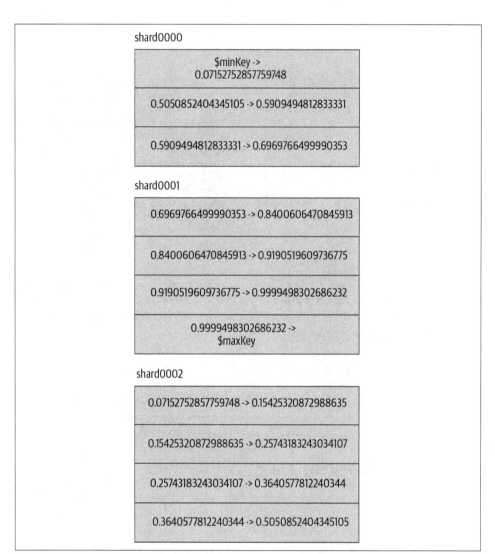

Figure 16-4. As in the previous section, chunks are distributed randomly around the cluster

As more data is inserted, the data's random nature means that inserts should hit every chunk fairly evenly. You can prove this to yourself by inserting 10,000 documents and seeing where they end up:

```
> var servers = {}
> var findShard = function (id) {
...      var explain = db.random.find({_id:id}).explain();
...      for (var i in explain.shards) {
...          var server = explain.shards[i][0];
```

```
...            if (server.n == 1) {
...                if (server.server in servers) {
...                    servers[server.server]++;
...                } else {
...                    servers[server.server] = 1;
...                }
...            }
...        }
... }
> for (var i = 0; i < 10000; i++) {
...        var id = ObjectId();
...        db.random.insert({"_id" : id, "x" : Math.random()});
...        findShard(id);
... }
> servers
{
    "spock:30001" : 2942,
    "spock:30002" : 4332,
    "spock:30000" : 2726
}
```

As writes are randomly distributed, the shards should grow at roughly the same rate, limiting the number of migrates that need to occur.

The only downside to randomly distributed shard keys is that MongoDB isn't efficient at randomly accessing data beyond the size of RAM. However, if you have the capacity or don't mind the performance hit, random keys nicely distribute load across your cluster.

Location-Based Shard Keys

Location-based shard keys may be things like a user's IP, latitude and longitude, or address. They're not necessarily related to a physical location field: the "location" might be a more abstract way that data should be grouped together. In any case, a location-based key is a key where documents with some similarity fall into a range based on this field. This can be handy for both putting data close to its users and keeping related data together on disk. It may also be a legal requirement to remain compliant with GDPR or other similar data privacy legislation. MongoDB uses Zoned Sharding to manage this.

 In MongoDB 4.0.3+, you can define the zones and the zone ranges prior to sharding a collection, which populates chunks for both the zone ranges and for the shard key values as well as performing an initial chunk distribution of these. This greatly reduces the complexity for sharded zone setup.

For example, suppose we have a collection of documents that are sharded on IP address. Documents will be organized into chunks based on their IPs and randomly spread across the cluster, as shown in Figure 16-5.

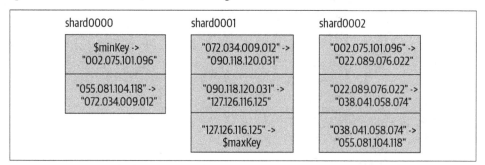

Figure 16-5. A sample distribution of chunks in the IP address collection

If we wanted certain chunk ranges to be attached to certain shards, we could zone these shards and then assign chunk ranges to each zone. In this example, suppose that we wanted to keep certain IP blocks on certain shards: say, 56.*.*.* (the United States Postal Service's IP block) on *shard0000* and 17.*.*.* (Apple's IP block) on either *shard0000* or *shard0002*. We do not care where the other IPs live. We could request that the balancer do this by setting up zones:

```
> sh.addShardToZone("shard0000", "USPS")
> sh.addShardToZone("shard0000", "Apple")
> sh.addShardToZone("shard0002", "Apple")
```

Next, we create the rules:

```
> sh.updateZoneKeyRange("test.ips", {"ip" : "056.000.000.000"},
... {"ip" : "057.000.000.000"}, "USPS")
```

This attaches all IPs greater than or equal to 56.0.0.0 and less than 57.0.0.0 to the shard zoned as "USPS". Next, we add a rule for Apple:

```
> sh.updateZoneKeyRange("test.ips", {"ip" : "017.000.000.000"},
... {"ip" : "018.000.000.000"}, "Apple")
```

When the balancer moves chunks, it will attempt to move chunks with those ranges to those shards. Note that this process is not immediate. Chunks that were not covered by a zone key range will be moved around normally. The balancer will continue attempting to distribute chunks evenly among shards.

Shard Key Strategies

This section presents a number of shard key options for various types of applications.

Hashed Shard Key

For loading data as fast as possible, hashed shard keys are the best option. A hashed shard key can make any field randomly distributed, so it is a good choice if you're going to be using an ascending key in a lot of queries but want writes to be randomly distributed.

The trade-off is that you can never do a targeted range query with a hashed shard key. If you will not be doing range queries, though, hashed shard keys are a good option.

To create a hashed shard key, first create a hashed index:

```
> db.users.createIndex({"username" : "hashed"})
```

Next, shard the collection with:

```
> sh.shardCollection("app.users", {"username" : "hashed"})
{ "collectionsharded" : "app.users", "ok" : 1 }
```

If you create a hashed shard key on a nonexistent collection, shardCollection behaves interestingly: it assumes that you want evenly distributed chunks, so it immediately creates a bunch of empty chunks and distributes them around your cluster. For example, suppose our cluster looked like this before creating the hashed shard key:

```
> sh.status()
--- Sharding Status ---
  sharding version: { "_id" : 1, "version" : 3 }
  shards:
        { "_id" : "shard0000",  "host" : "localhost:30000" }
        { "_id" : "shard0001",  "host" : "localhost:30001" }
        { "_id" : "shard0002",  "host" : "localhost:30002" }
  databases:
        { "_id" : "admin",  "partitioned" : false,  "primary" : "config" }
        { "_id" : "test",  "partitioned" : true,   "primary" : "shard0001" }
```

Immediately after shardCollection returns there are two chunks on each shard, evenly distributing the key space across the cluster:

```
> sh.status()
--- Sharding Status ---
  sharding version: { "_id" : 1, "version" : 3 }
  shards:
    { "_id" : "shard0000",  "host" : "localhost:30000" }
    { "_id" : "shard0001",  "host" : "localhost:30001" }
    { "_id" : "shard0002",  "host" : "localhost:30002" }
```

```
databases:
    { "_id" : "admin", "partitioned" : false, "primary" : "config" }
    { "_id" : "test", "partitioned" : true, "primary" : "shard0001" }
        test.foo
            shard key: { "username" : "hashed" }
            chunks:
                shard0000        2
                shard0001        2
                shard0002        2
            { "username" : { "$MinKey" : true } }
                -->> { "username" : NumberLong("-6148914691236517204") }
                on : shard0000 { "t" : 3000, "i" : 2 }
            { "username" : NumberLong("-6148914691236517204") }
                -->> { "username" : NumberLong("-3074457345618258602") }
                on : shard0000 { "t" : 3000, "i" : 3 }
            { "username" : NumberLong("-3074457345618258602") }
                -->> { "username" : NumberLong(0) }
                on : shard0001 { "t" : 3000, "i" : 4 }
            { "username" : NumberLong(0) }
                -->> { "username" : NumberLong("3074457345618258602") }
                on : shard0001 { "t" : 3000, "i" : 5 }
            { "username" : NumberLong("3074457345618258602") }
                -->> { "username" : NumberLong("6148914691236517204") }
                on : shard0002 { "t" : 3000, "i" : 6 }
            { "username" : NumberLong("6148914691236517204") }
                -->> { "username" : { "$MaxKey" : true } }
                on : shard0002 { "t" : 3000, "i" : 7 }
```

Note that there are no documents in the collection yet, but when you start inserting them, writes should be evenly distributed across the shards from the get-go. Ordinarily, you would have to wait for chunks to grow, split, and move to start writing to other shards. With this automatic priming, you'll immediately have chunk ranges on all shards.

There are some limitations on what your shard key can be if you're using a hashed shard key. First, you cannot use the unique option. As with other shard keys, you cannot use array fields. Finally, be aware that floating-point values will be rounded to whole numbers before hashing, so 1 and 1.999999 will both be hashed to the same value.

Hashed Shard Keys for GridFS

Before attempting to shard GridFS collections, make sure that you understand how GridFS stores data (see Chapter 6 for an explanation).

In the following explanation, the term "chunks" is overloaded since GridFS splits files into chunks and sharding splits collections into chunks. Thus, the two types of chunks are referred to as "GridFS chunks" and "sharding chunks."

GridFS collections are generally excellent candidates for sharding, as they contain massive amounts of file data. However, neither of the indexes that are automatically created on *fs.chunks* are particularly good shard keys: {"_id" : 1} is an ascending key and {"files_id" : 1, "n" : 1} picks up *fs.files*'s "_id" field, so it is also an ascending key.

However, if you create a hashed index on the "files_id" field, each file will be randomly distributed across the cluster, and a file will always be contained in a single chunk. This is the best of both worlds: writes will go to all shards evenly and reading a file's data will only ever have to hit a single shard.

To set this up, you must create a new index on {"files_id" : "hashed"} (as of this writing, *mongos* cannot use a subset of the compound index as a shard key). Then shard the collection on this field:

```
> db.fs.chunks.ensureIndex({"files_id" : "hashed"})
> sh.shardCollection("test.fs.chunks", {"files_id" : "hashed"})
{ "collectionsharded" : "test.fs.chunks", "ok" : 1 }
```

As a side note, the *fs.files* collection may or may not need to be sharded, as it will be much smaller than *fs.chunks*. You can shard it if you would like, but it is not likely to be necessary.

The Firehose Strategy

If you have some servers that are more powerful than others, you might want to let them handle proportionally more load than your less-powerful servers. For example, suppose you have one shard that can handle 10 times the load of your other machines. Luckily, you have 10 other shards. You could force all inserts to go to the more powerful shard, and then allow the balancer to move older chunks to the other shards. This would give lower-latency writes.

To use this strategy, we have to pin the highest chunk to the more powerful shard. First, we zone this shard:

```
> sh.addShardToZone("<shard-name>", "10x")
```

Then we pin the current value of the ascending key through infinity to that shard, so all new writes go to it:

```
> sh.updateZoneKeyRange("<dbName.collName>", {"_id" : ObjectId()},
... {"_id" : MaxKey}, "10x")
```

Now all inserts will be routed to this last chunk, which will always live on the shard zoned "10x".

However, ranges from now through infinity will be trapped on this shard unless we modify the zone key range. To get around this, we could set up a cron job to update the key range once a day, like this:

```
> use config
> var zone = db.tags.findOne({"ns" : "<dbName.collName>",
... "max" : {"<shardKey>" : MaxKey}})
> zone.min.<shardKey> = ObjectId()
> db.tags.save(zone)
```

Then all of the previous day's chunks would be able to move to other shards.

Another downside of this strategy is that it requires some changes to scale. If your most powerful server can no longer handle the number of writes coming in, there is no trivial way to split the load between this server and another.

If you do not have a high-performance server to firehose into or you are not using zone sharding, do not use an ascending key as the shard key. If you do, all writes will go to a single shard.

Multi-Hotspot

Standalone *mongod* servers are most efficient when doing ascending writes. This conflicts with sharding, in that sharding is most efficient when writes are spread over the cluster. The technique described here basically creates multiple hotspots—optimally several on each shard—so that writes are evenly balanced across the cluster but, within a shard, ascending.

To accomplish this, we use a compound shard key. The first value in the compound key is a rough, random value with low-ish cardinality. You can picture each value in the first part of the shard key as a chunk, as shown in Figure 16-6. This will eventually work itself out as you insert more data, although it will probably never be divided up this neatly (right on the $minKey lines). However, if you insert enough data, you should eventually have approximately one chunk per random value. As you continue to insert data, you'll end up with multiple chunks with the same random value, which brings us to the second part of the shard key.

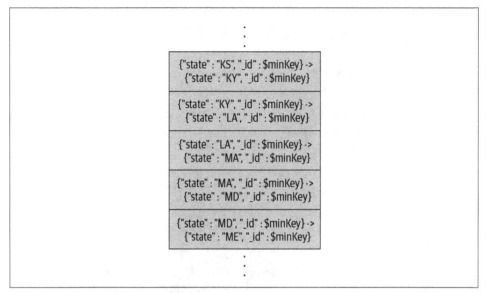

Figure 16-6. A subset of the chunks: each chunk contains a single state and a range of "_id" values

The second part of the shard key is an ascending key. This means that within a chunk, values are always increasing, as shown in the sample documents in Figure 16-7. Thus, if you had one chunk per shard, you'd have the perfect setup: ascending writes on every shard, as shown in Figure 16-8. Of course, having *n* chunks with *n* hotspots spread across *n* shards isn't very extensible: add a new shard and it won't get any writes because there's no hotspot chunk to put on it. Thus, you want a few hotspot chunks per shard (to give you room to grow), but not too many. Having a few hotspot chunks will keep the effectiveness of ascending writes, but having, say, a thousand hotspots on a shard will end up being equivalent to random writes.

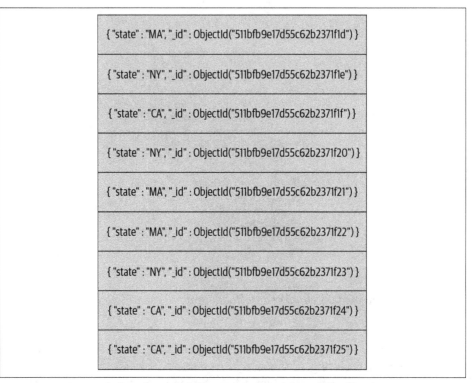

{ "state" : "MA", "_id" : ObjectId("511bfb9e17d55c62b2371f1d") }

{ "state" : "NY", "_id" : ObjectId("511bfb9e17d55c62b2371f1e") }

{ "state" : "CA", "_id" : ObjectId("511bfb9e17d55c62b2371f1f") }

{ "state" : "NY", "_id" : ObjectId("511bfb9e17d55c62b2371f20") }

{ "state" : "MA", "_id" : ObjectId("511bfb9e17d55c62b2371f21") }

{ "state" : "MA", "_id" : ObjectId("511bfb9e17d55c62b2371f22") }

{ "state" : "NY", "_id" : ObjectId("511bfb9e17d55c62b2371f23") }

{ "state" : "CA", "_id" : ObjectId("511bfb9e17d55c62b2371f24") }

{ "state" : "CA", "_id" : ObjectId("511bfb9e17d55c62b2371f25") }

Figure 16-7. A sample list of inserted documents (note that all "_id" values are increasing)

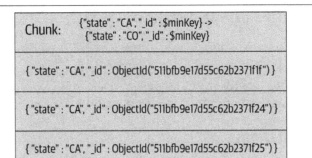

Figure 16-8. The inserted documents, split into chunks (note that, within each chunk, the "_id" values are increasing)

You can picture this setup as each chunk being a stack of ascending documents. There are multiple stacks on each shard, each ascending until the chunk is split. Once a chunk is split, only one of the new chunks will be a hotspot chunk: the other chunk will essentially be "dead" and never grow again. If the stacks are evenly distributed across the shards, writes will be evenly distributed.

Shard Key Rules and Guidelines

There are several practical restrictions to be aware of before choosing a shard key.

Determining which key to shard on and creating shard keys should be reminiscent of indexing because the two concepts are similar. In fact, often your shard key may just be the index you use most often (or some variation on it).

Shard Key Limitations

Shard keys cannot be arrays. `sh.shardCollection()` will fail if any key has an array value, and inserting an array into that field is not allowed.

Once inserted, a document's shard key value may be modified unless the shard key field is an immutable `_id` field. In older versions of MongoDB prior to 4.2, it was not possible to modify a document's shard key value.

Most special types of indexes cannot be used for shard keys. In particular, you cannot shard on a geospatial index. Using a hashed index for a shard key is allowed, as covered previously.

Shard Key Cardinality

Whether your shard key jumps around or increases steadily, it is important to choose a key with values that will vary. As with indexes, sharding performs better on high-cardinality fields. If, for example, you had a `"logLevel"` key that had only values `"DEBUG"`, `"WARN"`, or `"ERROR"`, MongoDB wouldn't be able to break up your data into more than three chunks (because there would be only three different values for the shard key). If you have a key with little variation and want to use it as a shard key anyway, you can do so by creating a compound shard key on that key and a key that varies more, like `"logLevel"` and `"timestamp"`. It is important that the combination of keys has high cardinality.

Controlling Data Distribution

Sometimes, automatic data distribution will not fit your requirements. This section gives you some options beyond choosing a shard key and allowing MongoDB to do everything automatically.

As your cluster gets larger or busier, these solutions become less practical. However, for small clusters, you may want more control.

Using a Cluster for Multiple Databases and Collections

MongoDB evenly distributes collections across every shard in your cluster, which works well if you're storing homogeneous data. However, if you have a log collection that is "lower value" than your other data, you might not want it taking up space on your more expensive servers. Or, if you have one powerful shard, you might want to use it for only a real-time collection and not allow other collections to use it. You can create separate clusters, but you can also give MongoDB specific directions about where you want it to put certain data.

To set this up, use the `sh.addShardToZone()` helper in the shell:

```
> sh.addShardToZone("shard0000", "high")
> // shard0001 - no zone
> // shard0002 - no zone
> // shard0003 - no zone
> sh.addShardToZone("shard0004", "low")
> sh.addShardToZone("shard0005", "low")
```

Then you can assign different collections to different shards. For instance, for your super-important real-time collection:

```
> sh.updateZoneKeyRange("super.important", {"<shardKey>" : MinKey},
... {"<shardKey>" : MaxKey}, "high")
```

This says, "for negative infinity to infinity for this collection, store it on shards tagged "high"." This means that no data from the *super.important* collection will be stored on any other server. Note that this does not affect how other collections are distributed: they will still be evenly distributed between this shard and the others.

You can perform a similar operation to keep the log collection on a low-quality server:

```
> sh.updateZoneKeyRange("some.logs", {"<shardKey>" : MinKey},
... {"<shardKey>" : MaxKey}, "low")
```

The log collection will now be split evenly between *shard0004* and *shard0005*.

Assigning a zone key range to a collection does not affect it instantly. It is an instruction to the balancer stating that, when it runs, these are the viable targets to move the collection to. Thus, if the entire log collection is on *shard0002* or evenly distributed among the shards, it will take a little while for all of the chunks to be migrated to *shard0004* and *shard0005*.

As another example, perhaps you have a collection that you don't want on the shard zoned "high", but you don't care which other shard it goes on. You can zone all of the non-high-performance shards to create a new grouping. Shards can have as many zones as you need:

```
> sh.addShardToZone("shard0001", "whatever")
> sh.addShardToZone("shard0002", "whatever")
> sh.addShardToZone("shard0003", "whatever")
> sh.addShardToZone("shard0004", "whatever")
> sh.addShardToZone("shard0005", "whatever")
```

Now you can specify that you want this collection (call it *normal.coll*) distributed across these five shards:

```
> sh.updateZoneKeyRange("normal.coll", {"<shardKey>" : MinKey},
... {"<shardKey>" : MaxKey}, "whatever")
```

 You cannot assign collections dynamically—i.e., you can't say, "when a collection is created, randomly home it to a shard." However, you could have a cron job that went through and did this for you.

If you make a mistake or change your mind, you can remove a shard from a zone with `sh.removeShardFromZone()`:

```
> sh.removeShardFromZone("shard0005", "whatever")
```

If you remove all shards from zones described by a zone key range (e.g., if you remove *shard0000* from the zone `"high"`), the balancer won't distribute the data anywhere because there aren't any valid locations listed. All the data will still be readable and writable; it just won't be able to migrate until you modify your tags or tag ranges.

To remove a key range from a zone, use `sh.removeRangeFromZone()`. The following is an example. The range specified must be an exact match to a range previously defined for the namespace *some.logs* and a given zone:

```
> sh.removeRangeFromZone("some.logs", {"<shardKey>" : MinKey},
... {"<shardKey>" : MaxKey})
```

Manual Sharding

Sometimes, for complex requirements or special situations, you may prefer to have complete control over which data is distributed where. You can turn off the balancer if you don't want data to be automatically distributed and use the `moveChunk` command to manually distribute data.

To turn off the balancer, connect to a *mongos* (any *mongos* is fine) using the *mongo* shell and disable the balancer using the shell helper `sh.stopBalancer()`:

```
> sh.stopBalancer()
```

If there is currently a migrate in progress, this setting will not take effect until the migrate has completed. However, once any in-flight migrations have finished, the balancer will stop moving data around. To verify no migrations are in progress after disabling, issue the following in the *mongo* shell:

```
> use config
> while(sh.isBalancerRunning()) {
...   print("waiting...");
...   sleep(1000);
... }
```

Once the balancer is off, you can move data around manually (if necessary). First, find out which chunks are where by looking at *config.chunks*:

```
> db.chunks.find()
```

Now, use the moveChunk command to migrate chunks to other shards. Specify the lower bound of the chunk to be migrated and give the name of the shard that you want to move the chunk to:

```
> sh.moveChunk(
... "test.manual.stuff",
... {user_id: NumberLong("-1844674407370955160")},
... "test-rs1")
```

However, unless you are in an exceptional situation, you should use MongoDB's automatic sharding instead of doing it manually. If you end up with a hotspot on a shard that you weren't expecting, you might end up with most of your data on that shard.

In particular, do not combine setting up unusual distributions manually with running the balancer. If the balancer detects an uneven number of chunks it will simply reshuffle all of your work to get the collection evenly balanced again. If you want uneven distribution of chunks, use the zone sharding technique discussed in "Using a Cluster for Multiple Databases and Collections" on page 335.

## CHAPTER 17

Sharding Administration

As with replica sets, you have a number of options for administering sharded clusters. Manual administration is one option. These days it is becoming increasingly common to use tools such as Ops Manager and Cloud Manager and the Atlas Database-as-a-Service (DBaaS) offering for all cluster administration. In this chapter, we will demonstrate how to administer a sharded cluster manually, including:

- Inspecting the cluster's state: who its members are, where data is held, and what connections are open
- Adding, removing, and changing members of a cluster
- Administering data movement and manually moving data

Seeing the Current State

There are several helpers available to find out what data is where, what the shards are, and what the cluster is doing.

Getting a Summary with sh.status()

`sh.status()` gives you an overview of your shards, databases, and sharded collections. If you have a small number of chunks, it will print a breakdown of which chunks are where as well. Otherwise it will simply give the collection's shard key and report how many chunks each shard has:

```
> sh.status()
--- Sharding Status ---
sharding version: {
  "_id" : 1,
  "minCompatibleVersion" : 5,
```

```
    "currentVersion" : 6,
    "clusterId" : ObjectId("5bdf51ecf8c192ed922f3160")
}
shards:
  {  "_id" : "shard01",
     "host" : "shard01/localhost:27018,localhost:27019,localhost:27020",
     "state" : 1 }
  {  "_id" : "shard02",
     "host" : "shard02/localhost:27021,localhost:27022,localhost:27023",
     "state" : 1 }
  {  "_id" : "shard03",
     "host" : "shard03/localhost:27024,localhost:27025,localhost:27026",
     "state" : 1 }
active mongoses:
  "4.0.3" : 1
autosplit:
  Currently enabled: yes
balancer:
  Currently enabled:  yes
  Currently running:  no
  Failed balancer rounds in last 5 attempts:  0
  Migration Results for the last 24 hours:
    6 : Success
  databases:
    {  "_id" : "config",  "primary" : "config",  "partitioned" : true }
      config.system.sessions
        shard key: { "_id" : 1 }
        unique: false
        balancing: true
        chunks:
          shard01     1
          { "_id" : { "$minKey" : 1 } } -->>
          { "_id" : { "$maxKey" : 1 } } on : shard01 Timestamp(1, 0)
    {  "_id" : "video",  "primary" : "shard02",  "partitioned" : true,
       "version" :
          {  "uuid" : UUID("3d83d8b8-9260-4a6f-8d28-c3732d40d961"),
             "lastMod" : 1 } }
      video.movies
        shard key: { "imdbId" : "hashed" }
        unique: false
        balancing: true
        chunks:
          shard01 3
          shard02 4
          shard03 3
          { "imdbId" : { "$minKey" : 1 } } -->>
              { "imdbId" : NumberLong("-7262221363006655132") } on :
              shard01 Timestamp(2, 0)
          { "imdbId" : NumberLong("-7262221363006655132") } -->>
              { "imdbId" : NumberLong("-5315530662268120007") } on :
              shard03 Timestamp(3, 0)
          { "imdbId" : NumberLong("-5315530662268120007") } -->>
```

```
          { "imdbId" : NumberLong("-3362204802044524341") } on :
            shard03 Timestamp(4, 0)
      { "imdbId" : NumberLong("-3362204802044524341") } -->>
          { "imdbId" : NumberLong("-1412311662519947087") }
          on : shard01 Timestamp(5, 0)
      { "imdbId" : NumberLong("-1412311662519947087") } -->>
          { "imdbId" : NumberLong("524277486033652998") } on :
            shard01 Timestamp(6, 0)
      { "imdbId" : NumberLong("524277486033652998") } -->>
          { "imdbId" : NumberLong("2484315172280977547") } on :
            shard03 Timestamp(7, 0)
      { "imdbId" : NumberLong("2484315172280977547") } -->>
          { "imdbId" : NumberLong("4436141279217488250") } on :
            shard02 Timestamp(7, 1)
      { "imdbId" : NumberLong("4436141279217488250") } -->>
          { "imdbId" : NumberLong("6386258634539951337") } on :
            shard02 Timestamp(1, 7)
      { "imdbId" : NumberLong("6386258634539951337") } -->>
          { "imdbId" : NumberLong("8345072417171006784") } on :
            shard02 Timestamp(1, 8)
      { "imdbId" : NumberLong("8345072417171006784") } -->>
          { "imdbId" : { "$maxKey" : 1 } } on :
            shard02 Timestamp(1, 9)
```

Once there are more than a few chunks, `sh.status()` will summarize the chunk stats instead of printing each chunk. To see all chunks, run `sh.status(true)` (the `true` tells `sh.status()` to be verbose).

All the information `sh.status()` shows is gathered from your *config* database.

Seeing Configuration Information

All of the configuration information about your cluster is kept in collections in the *config* database on the config servers. The shell has several helpers for exposing this information in a more readable way. However, you can always directly query the *config* database for metadata about your cluster.

 Never connect directly to your config servers, as you do not want to take the chance of accidentally changing or removing config server data. Instead, connect to the *mongos* process and use the *config* database to see its data, as you would for any other database:

```
> use config
```

If you manipulate config data through *mongos* (instead of connecting directly to the config servers), *mongos* will ensure that all of your config servers stay in sync and prevent various dangerous actions like accidentally dropping the *config* database.

In general, you should not directly change any data in the *config* database (exceptions are noted in the following sections). If you change anything, you will generally have to restart all of your *mongos* servers to see its effect.

There are several collections in the *config* database. This section covers what each one contains and how it can be used.

config.shards

The *shards* collection keeps track of all the shards in the cluster. A typical document in the *shards* collection might look something like this:

```
> db.shards.find()
{ "_id" : "shard01",
  "host" : "shard01/localhost:27018,localhost:27019,localhost:27020",
  "state" : 1 }
{ "_id" : "shard02",
  "host" : "shard02/localhost:27021,localhost:27022,localhost:27023",
  "state" : 1 }
{ "_id" : "shard03",
  "host" : "shard03/localhost:27024,localhost:27025,localhost:27026",
  "state" : 1 }
```

The shard's "_id" is picked up from the replica set name, so each replica set in your cluster must have a unique name.

When you update your replica set configuration (e.g., adding or removing members), the "host" field will be updated automatically.

config.databases

The *databases* collection keeps track of all of the databases, sharded and not, that the cluster knows about:

```
> db.databases.find()
{ "_id" : "video", "primary" : "shard02", "partitioned" : true,
  "version" : { "uuid" : UUID("3d83d8b8-9260-4a6f-8d28-c3732d40d961"),
  "lastMod" : 1 } }
```

If enableSharding has been run on a database, "partitioned" will be true. The "primary" is the database's "home base." By default, all new collections in that database will be created on the database's primary shard.

config.collections

The *collections* collection keeps track of all sharded collections (nonsharded collections are not shown). A typical document looks something like this:

```
> db.collections.find().pretty()
{
    "_id" : "config.system.sessions",
```

```
    "lastmodEpoch" : ObjectId("5bdf53122ad9c6907510c22d"),
    "lastmod" : ISODate("1970-02-19T17:02:47.296Z"),
    "dropped" : false,
    "key" : {
        "_id" : 1
    },
    "unique" : false,
    "uuid" : UUID("7584e4cd-fac4-4305-a9d4-bd73e93621bf")
}
{
    "_id" : "video.movies",
    "lastmodEpoch" : ObjectId("5bdf72c021b6e3be02fabe0c"),
    "lastmod" : ISODate("1970-02-19T17:02:47.305Z"),
    "dropped" : false,
    "key" : {
        "imdbId" : "hashed"
    },
    "unique" : false,
    "uuid" : UUID("e6580ffa-fcd3-418f-aa1a-0dfb71bc1c41")
}
```

The important fields are:

`"_id"`

The namespace of the collection.

`"key"`

The shard key. In this case, it is a hashed shard key on `"imdbId"`.

`"unique"`

Indicates that the shard key is not a unique index. By default, the shard key is not unique.

config.chunks

The *chunks* collection keeps a record of each chunk in all the collections. A typical document in the *chunks* collection looks something like this:

```
> db.chunks.find().skip(1).limit(1).pretty()
{
    "_id" : "video.movies-imdbId_MinKey",
    "lastmod" : Timestamp(2, 0),
    "lastmodEpoch" : ObjectId("5bdf72c021b6e3be02fabe0c"),
    "ns" : "video.movies",
    "min" : {
        "imdbId" : { "$minKey" : 1 }
    },
    "max" : {
        "imdbId" : NumberLong("-7262221363006655132")
    },
    "shard" : "shard01",
    "history" : [
```

```
        {
            "validAfter" : Timestamp(1541370579, 3096),
            "shard" : "shard01"
        }
    ]
}
```

The most useful fields are:

`"_id"`

> The unique identifier for the chunk. Generally this is the namespace, shard key, and lower chunk boundary.

`"ns"`

> The collection that this chunk is from.

`"min"`

> The smallest value in the chunk's range (inclusive).

`"max"`

> All values in the chunk are smaller than this value.

`"shard"`

> Which shard the chunk resides on.

The `"lastmod"` field tracks chunk versioning. For example, if the chunk `"video.movies-imdbId_MinKey"` were split into two chunks, we'd want a way of distinguishing the new, smaller `"video.movies-imdbId_MinKey"` chunks from their previous incarnation as a single chunk. Thus, the first component of the `Timestamp` value reflects the number of times a chunk has been migrated to a new shard. The second component of this value reflects the number of splits. The `"lastmodEpoch"` field specifies the collection's creation epoch. It is used to differentiate requests for the same collection name in the cases where the collection was dropped and immediately recreated.

`sh.status()` uses the *config.chunks* collection to gather most of its information.

config.changelog

The *changelog* collection is useful for keeping track of what a cluster is doing, since it records all of the splits and migrations that have occurred.

Splits are recorded in a document that looks like this:

```
> db.changelog.find({what: "split"}).pretty()
{
    "_id" : "router1-2018-11-05T09:58:58.915-0500-5be05ab2f8c192ed922ffbe7",
    "server" : "bob",
    "clientAddr" : "127.0.0.1:64621",
    "time" : ISODate("2018-11-05T14:58:58.915Z"),
```

```
    "what" : "split",
    "ns" : "video.movies",
    "details" : {
        "before" : {
            "min" : {
                "imdbId" : NumberLong("2484315172280977547")
            },
            "max" : {
                "imdbId" : NumberLong("4436141279217488250")
            },
            "lastmod" : Timestamp(9, 1),
            "lastmodEpoch" : ObjectId("5bdf72c021b6e3be02fabe0c")
        },
        "left" : {
            "min" : {
                "imdbId" : NumberLong("2484315172280977547")
            },
            "max" : {
                "imdbId" : NumberLong("3459137475094092005")
            },
            "lastmod" : Timestamp(9, 2),
            "lastmodEpoch" : ObjectId("5bdf72c021b6e3be02fabe0c")
        },
        "right" : {
            "min" : {
                "imdbId" : NumberLong("3459137475094092005")
            },
            "max" : {
                "imdbId" : NumberLong("4436141279217488250")
            },
            "lastmod" : Timestamp(9, 3),
            "lastmodEpoch" : ObjectId("5bdf72c021b6e3be02fabe0c")
        }
    }
}
```

The "details" field gives information about what the original document looked like and what it was split into.

This output shows what the first chunk split of a collection looks like. Note that the second component of "lastmod" for each new chunk was updated so that the values are Timestamp(9, 2) and Timestamp(9, 3), respectively.

Migrations are a bit more complicated and actually create four separate changelog documents: one noting the start of the migrate, one for the "from" shard, one for the "to" shard, and one for the commit that occurs when the migration is finalized. The middle two documents are of interest because these give a breakdown of how long each step in the process took. This can give you an idea of whether it's the disk, network, or something else that is causing a bottleneck on migrates.

For example, the document created by the "from" shard looks like this:

```
> db.changelog.findOne({what: "moveChunk.to"})
{
    "_id" : "router1-2018-11-04T17:29:39.702-0500-5bdf72d32ad9c69075112f08",
    "server" : "bob",
    "clientAddr" : "",
    "time" : ISODate("2018-11-04T22:29:39.702Z"),
    "what" : "moveChunk.to",
    "ns" : "video.movies",
    "details" : {
        "min" : {
            "imdbId" : { "$minKey" : 1 }
        },
        "max" : {
            "imdbId" : NumberLong("-7262221363006655132")
        },
        "step 1 of 6" : 965,
        "step 2 of 6" : 608,
        "step 3 of 6" : 15424,
        "step 4 of 6" : 0,
        "step 5 of 6" : 72,
        "step 6 of 6" : 258,
        "note" : "success"
    }
}
```

Each of the steps listed in `"details"` is timed and the `"stepN of N"` messages show how long each step took, in milliseconds.

When the "from" shard receives a `moveChunk` command from the *mongos*, it:

1. Checks the command parameters.
2. Confirms with the config servers that it can acquire a distributed lock for the migrate.
3. Tries to contact the "to" shard.
4. Copies the data. This is referred to and logged as "the critical section."
5. Coordinates with the "to" shard and config servers to confirm the migration.

Note that the "to" and "from" shards must be in close communication starting at `"step4 of 6"`: the shards directly talk to one another and the config server to perform the migration. If the "from" server has flaky network connectivity during the final steps, it may end up in a state where it cannot undo the migration and cannot move forward with it. In this case, the *mongod* will shut down.

The "to" shard's changelog document is similar to the "from" shard's, but the steps are a bit different. It looks like this:

```
> db.changelog.find({what: "moveChunk.from", "details.max.imdbId":
  NumberLong("-7262221363006655132")}).pretty()
{
```

```
    "_id" : "router1-2018-11-04T17:29:39.753-0500-5bdf72d321b6e3be02fabf0b",
    "server" : "bob",
    "clientAddr" : "127.0.0.1:64743",
    "time" : ISODate("2018-11-04T22:29:39.753Z"),
    "what" : "moveChunk.from",
    "ns" : "video.movies",
    "details" : {
        "min" : {
            "imdbId" : { "$minKey" : 1 }
        },
        "max" : {
            "imdbId" : NumberLong("-7262221363006655132")
        },
        "step 1 of 6" : 0,
        "step 2 of 6" : 4,
        "step 3 of 6" : 191,
        "step 4 of 6" : 17000,
        "step 5 of 6" : 341,
        "step 6 of 6" : 39,
        "to" : "shard01",
        "from" : "shard02",
        "note" : "success"
    }
}
```

When the "to" shard receives a command from the "from" shard, it:

1. Migrates indexes. If this shard has never held chunks from the migrated collection before, it needs to know what fields are indexed. If this isn't the first time a chunk from this collection is being moved to this shard, then this should be a no-op.

2. Deletes any existing data in the chunk range. There might be data left over from a failed migration or restore procedure that we wouldn't want to interfere with the current data.

3. Copies all documents in the chunk to the "to" shard.

4. Replays any operations that happened to these documents during the copy (on the "to" shard).

5. Waits for the "to" shard to have replicated the newly migrated data to a majority of servers.

6. Commits the migrate by changing the chunk's metadata to say that it lives on the "to" shard.

config.settings

This collection contains documents representing the current balancer settings and chunk size. By changing the documents in this collection, you can turn the balancer on or off or change the chunk size. Note that you should always connect to *mongos*, not the config servers directly, to change values in this collection.

Tracking Network Connections

There are a lot of connections between the components of a cluster. This section covers some sharding-specific information (see Chapter 24 for more information on networking).

Getting Connection Statistics

The command connPoolStats returns information regarding the open outgoing connections from the current database instance to other members of the sharded cluster or replica set.

To avoid interference with any running operations, connPoolStats does not take any locks. As such, the counts may change slightly as connPoolStats gathers information, resulting in slight differences between the hosts and pools connection counts:

```
> db.adminCommand({"connPoolStats": 1})
{
    "numClientConnections" : 10,
    "numAScopedConnections" : 0,
    "totalInUse" : 0,
    "totalAvailable" : 13,
    "totalCreated" : 86,
    "totalRefreshing" : 0,
    "pools" : {
        "NetworkInterfaceTL-TaskExecutorPool-0" : {
            "poolInUse" : 0,
            "poolAvailable" : 2,
            "poolCreated" : 2,
            "poolRefreshing" : 0,
            "localhost:27027" : {
                "inUse" : 0,
                "available" : 1,
                "created" : 1,
                "refreshing" : 0
            },
            "localhost:27019" : {
                "inUse" : 0,
                "available" : 1,
                "created" : 1,
                "refreshing" : 0
            }
        },
        "NetworkInterfaceTL-ShardRegistry" : {
            "poolInUse" : 0,
            "poolAvailable" : 1,
            "poolCreated" : 13,
```

```
            "poolRefreshing" : 0,
            "localhost:27027" : {
                "inUse" : 0,
                "available" : 1,
                "created" : 13,
                "refreshing" : 0
            }
    },
    "global" : {
        "poolInUse" : 0,
        "poolAvailable" : 10,
        "poolCreated" : 71,
        "poolRefreshing" : 0,
        "localhost:27026" : {
            "inUse" : 0,
            "available" : 1,
            "created" : 8,
            "refreshing" : 0
        },
        "localhost:27027" : {
            "inUse" : 0,
            "available" : 1,
            "created" : 1,
            "refreshing" : 0
        },
        "localhost:27023" : {
            "inUse" : 0,
            "available" : 1,
            "created" : 7,
            "refreshing" : 0
        },
        "localhost:27024" : {
            "inUse" : 0,
            "available" : 1,
            "created" : 6,
            "refreshing" : 0
        },
        "localhost:27022" : {
            "inUse" : 0,
            "available" : 1,
            "created" : 9,
            "refreshing" : 0
        },
        "localhost:27019" : {
            "inUse" : 0,
            "available" : 1,
            "created" : 8,
            "refreshing" : 0
        },
        "localhost:27021" : {
            "inUse" : 0,
            "available" : 1,
```

```
                    "created" : 8,
                    "refreshing" : 0
                },
                "localhost:27025" : {
                    "inUse" : 0,
                    "available" : 1,
                    "created" : 9,
                    "refreshing" : 0
                },
                "localhost:27020" : {
                    "inUse" : 0,
                    "available" : 1,
                    "created" : 8,
                    "refreshing" : 0
                },
                "localhost:27018" : {
                    "inUse" : 0,
                    "available" : 1,
                    "created" : 7,
                    "refreshing" : 0
                }
            }
        }
    },
    "hosts" : {
        "localhost:27026" : {
            "inUse" : 0,
            "available" : 1,
            "created" : 8,
            "refreshing" : 0
        },
        "localhost:27027" : {
            "inUse" : 0,
            "available" : 3,
            "created" : 15,
            "refreshing" : 0
        },
        "localhost:27023" : {
            "inUse" : 0,
            "available" : 1,
            "created" : 7,
            "refreshing" : 0
        },
        "localhost:27024" : {
            "inUse" : 0,
            "available" : 1,
            "created" : 6,
            "refreshing" : 0
        },
        "localhost:27022" : {
            "inUse" : 0,
            "available" : 1,
            "created" : 9,
```

```
                "refreshing" : 0
            },
            "localhost:27019" : {
                "inUse" : 0,
                "available" : 2,
                "created" : 9,
                "refreshing" : 0
            },
            "localhost:27021" : {
                "inUse" : 0,
                "available" : 1,
                "created" : 8,
                "refreshing" : 0
            },
            "localhost:27025" : {
                "inUse" : 0,
                "available" : 1,
                "created" : 9,
                "refreshing" : 0
            },
            "localhost:27020" : {
                "inUse" : 0,
                "available" : 1,
                "created" : 8,
                "refreshing" : 0
            },
            "localhost:27018" : {
                "inUse" : 0,
                "available" : 1,
                "created" : 7,
                "refreshing" : 0
            }
        },
        "replicaSets" : {
            "shard02" : {
                "hosts" : [
                    {
                        "addr" : "localhost:27021",
                        "ok" : true,
                        "ismaster" : true,
                        "hidden" : false,
                        "secondary" : false,
                        "pingTimeMillis" : 0
                    },
                    {
                        "addr" : "localhost:27022",
                        "ok" : true,
                        "ismaster" : false,
                        "hidden" : false,
                        "secondary" : true,
                        "pingTimeMillis" : 0
                    },
```

```
                      {
                          "addr" : "localhost:27023",
                          "ok" : true,
                          "ismaster" : false,
                          "hidden" : false,
                          "secondary" : true,
                          "pingTimeMillis" : 0
                      }
                  ]
              },
              "shard03" : {
                  "hosts" : [
                      {
                          "addr" : "localhost:27024",
                          "ok" : true,
                          "ismaster" : false,
                          "hidden" : false,
                          "secondary" : true,
                          "pingTimeMillis" : 0
                      },
                      {
                          "addr" : "localhost:27025",
                          "ok" : true,
                          "ismaster" : true,
                          "hidden" : false,
                          "secondary" : false,
                          "pingTimeMillis" : 0
                      },
                      {
                          "addr" : "localhost:27026",
                          "ok" : true,
                          "ismaster" : false,
                          "hidden" : false,
                          "secondary" : true,
                          "pingTimeMillis" : 0
                      }
                  ]
              },
              "configRepl" : {
                  "hosts" : [
                      {
                          "addr" : "localhost:27027",
                          "ok" : true,
                          "ismaster" : true,
                          "hidden" : false,
                          "secondary" : false,
                          "pingTimeMillis" : 0
                      }
                  ]
              },
              "shard01" : {
                  "hosts" : [
```

```
          {
              "addr" : "localhost:27018",
              "ok" : true,
              "ismaster" : false,
              "hidden" : false,
              "secondary" : true,
              "pingTimeMillis" : 0
          },
          {
              "addr" : "localhost:27019",
              "ok" : true,
              "ismaster" : true,
              "hidden" : false,
              "secondary" : false,
              "pingTimeMillis" : 0
          },
          {
              "addr" : "localhost:27020",
              "ok" : true,
              "ismaster" : false,
              "hidden" : false,
              "secondary" : true,
              "pingTimeMillis" : 0
          }
        ]
      }
  },
  "ok" : 1,
  "operationTime" : Timestamp(1541440424, 1),
  "$clusterTime" : {
      "clusterTime" : Timestamp(1541440424, 1),
      "signature" : {
          "hash" : BinData(0,"AAAAAAAAAAAAAAAAAAAAAAAAAAA="),
          "keyId" : NumberLong(0)
      }
  }
}
```

In this output:

- `"totalAvailable"` shows the total number of available outgoing connections from the current *mongod*/*mongos* instance to other members of the sharded cluster or replica set.

- `"totalCreated"` reports the total number of outgoing connections ever created by the current *mongod*/*mongos* instance to other members of the sharded cluster or replica set.

- `"totalInUse"` provides the total number of outgoing connections from the current *mongod*/*mongos* instance to other members of the sharded cluster or replica set that are currently in use.

- `"totalRefreshing"` displays the total number of outgoing connections from the current *mongod/mongos* instance to other members of the sharded cluster or replica set that are currently being refreshed.

- `"numClientConnections"` identifies the number of active and stored outgoing synchronous connections from the current *mongod/mongos* instance to other members of the sharded cluster or replica set. These represent a subset of the connections reported by `"totalAvailable"`, `"totalCreated"`, and `"totalInUse"`.

- `"numAScopedConnection"` reports the number of active and stored outgoing scoped synchronous connections from the current *mongod/mongos* instance to other members of the sharded cluster or replica set. These represent a subset of the connections reported by `"totalAvailable"`, `"totalCreated"`, and `"totalInUse"`.

- `"pools"` shows connection statistics (in use/available/created/refreshing) grouped by the connection pools. A *mongod* or *mongos* has two distinct families of outgoing connection pools:

  — DBClient-based pools (the "write path," identified by the field name `"global"` in the `"pools"` document)

  — NetworkInterfaceTL-based pools (the "read path")

- `"hosts"` shows connection statistics (in use/available/created/refreshing) grouped by the hosts. It reports on connections between the current *mongod/mongos* instance and each member of the sharded cluster or replica set.

You might see connections to other shards in the output of connPoolStats. These indicate that shards are connecting to other shards to migrate data. The primary of one shard will connect directly to the primary of another shard and "suck" its data.

When a migrate occurs, a shard sets up a ReplicaSetMonitor (a process that monitors replica set health) to track the health of the shard on the other side of the migrate. *mongod* never destroys this monitor, so you may see messages in one replica set's log about the members of another replica set. This is totally normal and should have no effect on your application.

Limiting the Number of Connections

When a client connects to a *mongos*, the *mongos* creates a connection to at least one shard to pass along the client's request. Thus, every client connection into a *mongos* yields at least one outgoing connection from *mongos* to the shards.

If you have many *mongos* processes, they may create more connections than your shards can handle: by default a *mongos* will accept up to 65,536 connections (the same as *mongod*), so if you have 5 *mongos* processes with 10,000 client connections each, they may be attempting to create 50,000 connections to a shard!

To prevent this, you can use the `--maxConns` option to your command-line configuration for *mongos* to limit the number of connections it can create. The following formula can be used to calculate the maximum number of connections a shard can handle from a single *mongos*:

$$maxConns = maxConnsPrimary - (numMembersPerReplicaSet \times 3) - (other \times 3) / numMongosProcesses$$

Breaking down the pieces of this formula:

maxConnsPrimary
> The maximum number of connections on the Primary, typically set to 20,000 to avoid overwhelming the shard with connections from the *mongos*.

(numMembersPerReplicaSet × 3)
> The primary creates a connection to each secondary and each secondary creates two connections to the primary, for a total of three connections.

(other × 3)
> Other is the number of miscellaneous processes that may connect to your *mongo*ds, such as monitoring or backup agents, direct shell connections (for administration), or connections to other shards for migrations.

numMongosProcesses
> The total number of *mongos* in the sharded cluster.

Note that `--maxConns` only prevents *mongos* from creating more than this many connections. It doesn't do anything particularly helpful when this limit is reached: it will simply block requests, waiting for connections to be "freed." Thus, you must prevent your application from using this many connections, especially as your number of *mongos* processes grows.

When a MongoDB instance exits cleanly it closes all connections before stopping. The members that were connected to it will immediately get socket errors on those connections and be able to refresh them. However, if a MongoDB instance suddenly goes offline due to a power loss, crash, or network problems, it probably won't cleanly close all of its sockets. In this case, other servers in the cluster may be under the impression that their connection is healthy until they try to perform an operation on it. At that point, they will get an error and refresh the connection (if the member is up again at that point).

This is a quick process when there are only a few connections. However, when there are thousands of connections that must be refreshed one by one you can get a lot of errors because each connection to the downed member must be tried, determined to be bad, and reestablished. There isn't a particularly good way of preventing this, aside from restarting processes that get bogged down in a reconnection storm.

Server Administration

As your cluster grows, you'll need to add capacity or change configurations. This section covers how to add and remove servers in your cluster.

Adding Servers

You can add new *mongos* processes at any time. Make sure their `--configdb` option specifies the correct set of config servers and they should be immediately available for clients to connect to.

To add new shards, use the `addShard` command as shown in Chapter 15.

Changing Servers in a Shard

As you use your sharded cluster, you may want to change the servers in individual shards. To change a shard's membership, connect directly to the shard's primary (not through the *mongos*) and issue a replica set reconfig. The cluster configuration will pick up the change and update *config.shards* automatically. Do not modify *config.shards* by hand.

The only exception to this is if you started your cluster with standalone servers as shards, not replica sets.

Changing a shard from a standalone server to a replica set

The easiest way to do this is to add a new, empty replica set shard and then remove the standalone server shard (as discussed in the next section). Migrations will take care of moving your data to the new shard.

Removing a Shard

In general, shards should not be removed from a cluster. If you are regularly adding and removing shards, you are putting a lot more stress on the system than necessary. If you add too many shards it is better to let your system grow into them, not remove them and add them back later. However, if necessary, you can remove shards.

First make sure that the balancer is on. The balancer will be tasked with moving all the data on the shard you want to remove to other shards in a process called *draining*. To start draining, run the `removeShard` command. `removeShard` takes the shard's name and drains all the chunks on that shard to the other shards:

```
> db.adminCommand({"removeShard" : "shard03"})
{
    "msg" : "draining started successfully",
    "state" : "started",
    "shard" : "shard03",
    "note" : "you need to drop or movePrimary these databases",
    "dbsToMove" : [ ],
    "ok" : 1,
    "operationTime" : Timestamp(1541450091, 2),
    "$clusterTime" : {
        "clusterTime" : Timestamp(1541450091, 2),
        "signature" : {
            "hash" : BinData(0,"AAAAAAAAAAAAAAAAAAAAAAAAAAA="),
            "keyId" : NumberLong(0)
        }
    }
}
```

Draining can take a long time if there are a lot of chunks or large chunks to move. If you have jumbo chunks (see "Jumbo Chunks" on page 364), you may have to temporarily increase the chunk size to allow draining to move them.

If you want to keep tabs on how much has been moved, run removeShard again to give you the current status:

```
> db.adminCommand({"removeShard" : "shard02"})
{
    "msg" : "draining ongoing",
    "state" : "ongoing",
    "remaining" : {
        "chunks" : NumberLong(3),
        "dbs" : NumberLong(0)
    },
    "note" : "you need to drop or movePrimary these databases",
    "dbsToMove" : [
            "video"
      ],
    "ok" : 1,
    "operationTime" : Timestamp(1541450139, 1),
    "$clusterTime" : {
        "clusterTime" : Timestamp(1541450139, 1),
        "signature" : {
            "hash" : BinData(0,"AAAAAAAAAAAAAAAAAAAAAAAAAAA="),
            "keyId" : NumberLong(0)
        }
    }
}
```

You can run removeShard as many times as you want.

Chunks may have to be split to be moved, so you may see the number of chunks increase in the system during the drain. For example, suppose we have a five-shard cluster with the following chunk distributions:

```
test-rs0    10
test-rs1    10
test-rs2    10
test-rs3    11
test-rs4    11
```

This cluster has a total of 52 chunks. If we remove *test-rs3*, we might end up with:

```
test-rs0    15
test-rs1    15
test-rs2    15
test-rs4    15
```

The cluster now has 60 chunks, 18 of which came from shard *test-rs3* (11 were there to start and 7 were created from draining splits).

Once all the chunks have been moved, if there are still databases that have the removed shard as their primary, you'll need to remove them before the shard can be removed. Each database in a sharded cluster has a primary shard. If the shard you want to remove is also the primary of one of the cluster's databases, removeShard lists the database in the "dbsToMove" field. To finish removing the shard, you must either move the database to a new shard after migrating all data from the shard or drop the database, deleting the associated data files. The output of removeShard will be something like:

```
> db.adminCommand({"removeShard" : "shard02"})
{
    "msg" : "draining ongoing",
    "state" : "ongoing",
    "remaining" : {
        "chunks" : NumberLong(3),
        "dbs" : NumberLong(0)
    },
    "note" : "you need to drop or movePrimary these databases",
    "dbsToMove" : [
            "video"
        ],
    "ok" : 1,
    "operationTime" : Timestamp(1541450139, 1),
    "$clusterTime" : {
        "clusterTime" : Timestamp(1541450139, 1),
        "signature" : {
            "hash" : BinData(0,"AAAAAAAAAAAAAAAAAAAAAAAAAAA="),
            "keyId" : NumberLong(0)
        }
    }
}
```

To finish the remove, move the listed databases with the movePrimary command:

```
> db.adminCommand({"movePrimary" : "video", "to" : "shard01"})
{
    "ok" : 1,
    "operationTime" : Timestamp(1541450554, 12),
    "$clusterTime" : {
        "clusterTime" : Timestamp(1541450554, 12),
        "signature" : {
            "hash" : BinData(0,"AAAAAAAAAAAAAAAAAAAAAAAAAAA="),
            "keyId" : NumberLong(0)
        }
    }
}
```

Once you have done this, run removeShard one more time:

```
> db.adminCommand({"removeShard" : "shard02"})
{
    "msg" : "removeshard completed successfully",
    "state" : "completed",
    "shard" : "shard03",
    "ok" : 1,
    "operationTime" : Timestamp(1541450619, 2),
    "$clusterTime" : {
        "clusterTime" : Timestamp(1541450619, 2),
        "signature" : {
            "hash" : BinData(0,"AAAAAAAAAAAAAAAAAAAAAAAAAAA="),
            "keyId" : NumberLong(0)
        }
    }
}
```

This is not strictly necessary, but it confirms that you have completed the process. If there are no databases that have this shard as their primary, you will get this response as soon as all chunks have been migrated off the shard.

 Once you have started a shard draining, there is no built-in way to stop it.

Balancing Data

In general, MongoDB automatically takes care of balancing data. This section covers how to enable and disable this automatic balancing as well as how to intervene in the balancing process.

The Balancer

Turning off the balancer is a prerequisite to nearly any administrative activity. There is a shell helper to make this easier:

```
> sh.setBalancerState(false)
{
    "ok" : 1,
    "operationTime" : Timestamp(1541450923, 2),
    "$clusterTime" : {
        "clusterTime" : Timestamp(1541450923, 2),
        "signature" : {
            "hash" : BinData(0,"AAAAAAAAAAAAAAAAAAAAAAAAAAA="),
            "keyId" : NumberLong(0)
        }
    }
}
```

With the balancer off a new balancing round will not begin, but turning it off will not force an ongoing balancing round to stop immediately—migrations generally cannot stop on a dime. Thus, you should check the *config.locks* collection to see whether or not a balancing round is still in progress:

```
> db.locks.find({"_id" : "balancer"})["state"]
0
```

0 means the balancer is off.

Balancing puts load on your system: the destination shard must query the source shard for all the documents in a chunk and insert them, and then the source shard must delete them. There are two circumstances in particular where migrations can cause performance problems:

1. Using a hotspot shard key will force constant migrations (as all new chunks will be created on the hotspot). Your system must have the capacity to handle the flow of data coming off of your hotspot shard.

2. Adding a new shard will trigger a stream of migrations as the balancer attempts to populate it.

If you find that migrations are affecting your application's performance, you can schedule a window for balancing in the *config.settings* collection. Run the following update to only allow balancing between 1 p.m. and 4 p.m. First make sure the balancer is on, then schedule the window:

```
> sh.setBalancerState( true )
{
    "ok" : 1,
    "operationTime" : Timestamp(1541451846, 4),
    "$clusterTime" : {
        "clusterTime" : Timestamp(1541451846, 4),
```

```
        "signature" : {
            "hash" : BinData(0,"AAAAAAAAAAAAAAAAAAAAAAAAAAAA="),
            "keyId" : NumberLong(0)
        }
    }
}
> db.settings.update(
    { _id: "balancer" },
    { $set: { activeWindow : { start : "13:00", stop : "16:00" } } },
    { upsert: true }
)
WriteResult({ "nMatched" : 1, "nUpserted" : 0, "nModified" : 1 })
```

If you set a balancing window, monitor it closely to ensure that *mongos* can actually keep your cluster balanced in the time that you have allotted it.

You must be careful if you plan to combine manual balancing with the automatic balancer, since the automatic balancer always determines what to move based on the current state of the set and does not take into account the set's history. For example, suppose you have *shardA* and *shardB*, each holding 500 chunks. *shardA* is getting a lot of writes, so you turn off the balancer and move 30 of the most active chunks to *shardB*. If you turn the balancer back on at this point, it will immediately swoop in and move 30 chunks (possibly a different 30) back from *shardB* to *shardA* to balance the chunk counts.

To prevent this, move 30 quiescent chunks from *shardB* to *shardA* before starting the balancer. That way there will be no imbalance between the shards and the balancer will be happy to leave things as they are. Alternatively, you could perform 30 splits on *shardA*'s chunks to even out the chunk counts.

Note that the balancer only uses number of chunks as a metric, not size of data. Moving a chunk is called a migration and is how MongoDB balances data across your cluster. Thus, a shard with a few large chunks may end up as the target of a migration from a shard with many small chunks (but a smaller data size).

Changing Chunk Size

There can be anywhere from zero to millions of documents in a chunk. Generally, the larger a chunk is, the longer it takes to migrate to another shard. In Chapter 14, we used a chunk size of 1 MB, so that we could see chunk movement easily and quickly. This is generally impractical in a live system; MongoDB would be doing a lot of unnecessary work to keep shards within a few megabytes of each other in size. By default chunks are 64 MB, which generally provides a good balance between ease of migration and migratory churn.

Sometimes you may find that migrations are taking too long with 64 MB chunks. To speed them up, you can decrease your chunk size. To do this, connect to *mongos* through the shell and update the *config.settings* collection:

```
> db.settings.findOne()
{
    "_id" : "chunksize",
    "value" : 64
}
> db.settings.save({"_id" : "chunksize", "value" : 32})
WriteResult({ "nMatched" : 1, "nUpserted" : 0, "nModified" : 1 })
```

The previous update would change your chunk size to 32 MB. Existing chunks would not be changed immediately, however; automatic splitting only occurs on insert or update. Thus, if you lower the chunk size, it may take time for all chunks to split to the new size.

Splits cannot be undone. If you increase the chunk size, existing chunks grow only through insertion or updates until they reach the new size. The allowed range of the chunk size is between 1 and 1,024 MB, inclusive.

Note that this is a cluster-wide setting: it affects all collections and databases. Thus, if you need a small chunk size for one collection and a large chunk size for another, you may have to compromise with a chunk size in between the two ideals (or put the collections in different clusters).

> If MongoDB is doing too many migrations or your documents are large, you may want to increase your chunk size.

Moving Chunks

As mentioned earlier, all the data in a chunk lives on a certain shard. If that shard ends up with more chunks than the other shards, MongoDB will move some chunks off it.

You can manually move chunks using the moveChunk shell helper:

```
> sh.moveChunk("video.movies", {imdbId: 500000}, "shard02")
{ "millis" : 4079, "ok" : 1 }
```

This would move the chunk containing the document with an "imdbId" of 500000 to the shard named *shard02*. You must use the shard key ("imdbId", in this case) to find which chunk to move. Generally, the easiest way to specify a chunk is by its lower bound, although any value in the chunk will work (the upper bound will not, as it is not actually in the chunk). This command will move the chunk before returning, so it may take a while to run. The logs are the best place to see what it is doing if it takes a long time.

If a chunk is larger than the max chunk size, *mongos* will refuse to move it:

```
> sh.moveChunk("video.movies", {imdbId: NumberLong("8345072417171006784")},
  "shard02")
{
    "cause" : {
        "chunkTooBig" : true,
        "estimatedChunkSize" : 2214960,
        "ok" : 0,
        "errmsg" : "chunk too big to move"
    },
    "ok" : 0,
    "errmsg" : "move failed"
}
```

In this case, you must manually split the chunk before moving it, using the `splitAt` command:

```
> db.chunks.find({ns: "video.movies", "min.imdbId":
  NumberLong("6386258634539951337")}).pretty()
{
    "_id" : "video.movies-imdbId_6386258634539951337",
    "ns" : "video.movies",
    "min" : {
        "imdbId" : NumberLong("6386258634539951337")
    },
    "max" : {
        "imdbId" : NumberLong("8345072417171006784")
    },
    "shard" : "shard02",
    "lastmod" : Timestamp(1, 9),
    "lastmodEpoch" : ObjectId("5bdf72c021b6e3be02fabe0c"),
    "history" : [
        {
            "validAfter" : Timestamp(1541370559, 4),
            "shard" : "shard02"
        }
    ]
}
> sh.splitAt("video.movies", {"imdbId":
  NumberLong("7000000000000000000")})
{
    "ok" : 1,
    "operationTime" : Timestamp(1541453304, 1),
    "$clusterTime" : {
        "clusterTime" : Timestamp(1541453306, 5),
        "signature" : {
            "hash" : BinData(0,"AAAAAAAAAAAAAAAAAAAAAAAAAAA="),
            "keyId" : NumberLong(0)
        }
    }
}
> db.chunks.find({ns: "video.movies", "min.imdbId":
  NumberLong("6386258634539951337")}).pretty()
{
```

```
    "_id" : "video.movies-imdbId_6386258634539951337",
    "lastmod" : Timestamp(15, 2),
    "lastmodEpoch" : ObjectId("5bdf72c021b6e3be02fabe0c"),
    "ns" : "video.movies",
    "min" : {
        "imdbId" : NumberLong("6386258634539951337")
    },
    "max" : {
        "imdbId" : NumberLong("7000000000000000000")
    },
    "shard" : "shard02",
    "history" : [
        {
            "validAfter" : Timestamp(1541370559, 4),
            "shard" : "shard02"
        }
    ]
}
```

Once the chunk has been split into smaller pieces, it should be movable. Alternatively, you can raise the max chunk size and then move it, but you should break up large chunks whenever possible. Sometimes, though, chunks cannot be broken up—we'll look at this situation next.[1]

Jumbo Chunks

Suppose you choose the `"date"` field as your shard key. The `"date"` field in this collection is a string that looks like `"year/month/day"`, which means that *mongos* can create at most one chunk per day. This works fine for a while, until your application suddenly goes viral and gets a thousand times its typical traffic for one day.

This day's chunk is going to be much larger than any other day's, but it is also completely unsplittable because every document has the same value for the shard key.

Once a chunk is larger than the max chunk size set in *config.settings*, the balancer will not be allowed to move the chunk. These unsplittable, unmovable chunks are called *jumbo chunks* and they are inconvenient to deal with.

Let's take an example. Suppose you have three shards, *shard1*, *shard2*, and *shard3*. If you use the hotspot shard key pattern described in "Ascending Shard Keys" on page 320, all your writes will be going to one shard—say, *shard1*. The shard primary *mongod* will request that the *balancer* move each new top chunk evenly between the other

---

1 MongoDB 4.4 is planning to add a new parameter (forceJumbo) in the moveChunk function, as well as a new balancer configuration setting attemptToBalanceJumboChunks to address jumbo chunks. The details are in this JIRA ticket describing the work (*https://jira.mongodb.org/browse/SERVER-42273*).

---

shards, but the only chunks that the balancer can move are the nonjumbo chunks, so it will migrate all the small chunks off the hot shard.

Now all the shards will have roughly the same number of chunks, but all of *shard2* and *shard3*'s chunks will be less than 64 MB in size. And if jumbo chunks are being created, more and more of *shard1*'s chunks will be more than 64 MB in size. Thus, *shard1* will fill up a lot faster than the other two shards, even though the number of chunks is perfectly balanced between the three.

Thus, one of the indicators that you have jumbo chunk problems is that one shard's size is growing much faster than the others. You can also look at the output of sh.sta tus() to see if you have jumbo chunks—they will be marked with the jumbo attribute:

```
> sh.status()
...
    { "x" : -7 } -->> { "x" : 5 } on : shard0001
    { "x" : 5 } -->> { "x" : 6 } on : shard0001 jumbo
    { "x" : 6 } -->> { "x" : 7 } on : shard0001 jumbo
    { "x" : 7 } -->> { "x" : 339 } on : shard0001
...
```

You can use the dataSize command to check chunk sizes. First, use the *config.chunks* collection to find the chunk ranges:

```
> use config
> var chunks = db.chunks.find({"ns" : "acme.analytics"}).toArray()
```

Then use these chunk ranges to find possible jumbo chunks:

```
> use <dbName>
> db.runCommand({"dataSize" : "<dbName.collName>",
... "keyPattern" : {"date" : 1}, // shard key
... "min" : chunks[0].min,
... "max" : chunks[0].max})
{
    "size" : 33567917,
    "numObjects" : 108942,
    "millis" : 634,
    "ok" : 1,
    "operationTime" : Timestamp(1541455552, 10),
    "$clusterTime" : {
        "clusterTime" : Timestamp(1541455552, 10),
        "signature" : {
            "hash" : BinData(0,"AAAAAAAAAAAAAAAAAAAAAAAAAAA="),
            "keyId" : NumberLong(0)
        }
    }
}
```

Be careful, though—the dataSize command does have to scan the chunk's data to figure out how big it is. If you can, narrow down your search by using your knowledge of your data: were jumbo chunks created on a certain date? For example, if July 1 was a really busy day, look for chunks with that day in their shard key range.

 If you're using GridFS and sharding by "files_id", you can look at the *fs.files* collection to find a file's size.

Distributing jumbo chunks

To fix a cluster thrown off-balance by jumbo chunks, you must evenly distribute them among the shards.

This is a complex manual process, but should not cause any downtime (it may cause slowness, as you'll be migrating a lot of data). In the following description, the shard with the jumbo chunks is referred to as the "from" shard. The shards that the jumbo chunks are migrated to are called the "to" shards. Note that you may have multiple "from" shards that you wish to move chunks off of. Repeat these steps for each:

1. Turn off the balancer. You don't want the balancer trying to "help" during this process:

    ```
    > sh.setBalancerState(false)
    ```

2. MongoDB will not allow you to move chunks larger than the max chunk size, so temporarily increase the chunk size. Make a note of what your original chunk size is and then change it to something large, like 10000. Chunk size is specified in megabytes:

    ```
    > use config
    > db.settings.findOne({"_id" : "chunksize"})
    {
        "_id" : "chunksize",
        "value" : 64
    }
    > db.settings.save({"_id" : "chunksize", "value" : 10000})
    ```

3. Use the moveChunk command to move jumbo chunks off the "from" shard.

4. Run splitChunk on the remaining chunks on the "from" shard until it has roughly the same number of chunks as the "to" shards.

5. Set the chunk size back to its original value:

    ```
    > db.settings.save({"_id" : "chunksize", "value" : 64})
    ```

6. Turn on the balancer:

    ```
    > sh.setBalancerState(true)
    ```

When the balancer is turned on again, it will once again be unable to move the jumbo chunks; they are essentially held in place by their size.

Preventing jumbo chunks

As the amount of data you are storing grows, the manual process described in the previous section becomes unsustainable. Thus, if you're having problems with jumbo chunks, you should make it a priority to prevent them from forming.

To prevent jumbo chunks, modify your shard key to have more granularity. You want almost every document to have a unique value for the shard key, or at least to never have more than the chunk size's worth of data with a single shard key value.

For example, if you were using the year/month/day key described earlier, it could quickly be made more fine-grained by adding hours, minutes, and seconds. Similarly, if you're sharding on something coarse-grained like log level, you can add to your shard key a second field with a lot of granularity, such as an MD5 hash or UUID. Then you can always split a chunk, even if the first field is the same for many documents.

Refreshing Configurations

As a final tip, sometimes *mongos* will not update its configuration correctly from the config servers. If you ever get a configuration that you don't expect or a *mongos* seems to be out of date or cannot find data that you know is there, use the `flushRouterConfig` command to manually clear all caches:

```
> db.adminCommand({"flushRouterConfig" : 1})
```

If `flushRouterConfig` does not work, restarting all your *mongos* or *mongod* processes clears any cached data.

PART V

Application Administration

## CHAPTER 18

Seeing What Your Application Is Doing

Once you have an application up and running, how do you know what it's doing? This chapter covers how to figure out what kinds of queries MongoDB is running, how much data is being written, and other details about what it's actually doing. You'll learn about:

- Finding slow operations and killing them
- Getting and interpreting statistics about your collections and databases
- Using command-line tools to give you a picture of what MongoDB is doing

Seeing the Current Operations

An easy way to find slow operations is to see what is running. Anything slow is more likely to show up and have been running for longer. It's not guaranteed, but it's a good first step to see what might be slowing down an application.

To see the operations that are running, use the `db.currentOp()` function:

```
> db.currentOp()
{
  "inprog": [{
    "type" : "op",
    "host" : "eoinbrazil-laptop-osx:27017",
    "desc" : "conn3",
    "connectionId" : 3,
    "client" : "127.0.0.1:57181",
    "appName" : "MongoDB Shell",
    "clientMetadata" : {
        "application" : {
            "name" : "MongoDB Shell"
        },
```

```
            "driver" : {
                "name" : "MongoDB Internal Client",
                "version" : "4.2.0"
            },
            "os" : {
                "type" : "Darwin",
                "name" : "Mac OS X",
                "architecture" : "x86_64",
                "version" : "18.7.0"
            }
        },
        "active" : true,
        "currentOpTime" : "2019-09-03T23:25:46.380+0100",
        "opid" : 13594,
        "lsid" : {
            "id" : UUID("63b7df66-ca97-41f4-a245-eba825485147"),
            "uid" : BinData(0,"47DEQpj8HBSa+/TImW+5JCeuQeRkm5NMpJWZG3hSuFU=")
        },
        "secs_running" : NumberLong(0),
        "microsecs_running" : NumberLong(969),
        "op" : "insert",
        "ns" : "sample_mflix.items",
        "command" : {
            "insert" : "items",
            "ordered" : false,
            "lsid" : {
                "id" : UUID("63b7df66-ca97-41f4-a245-eba825485147")
            },
            "$readPreference" : {
                "mode" : "secondaryPreferred"
            },
            "$db" : "sample_mflix"
        },
        "numYields" : 0,
        "locks" : {
            "ParallelBatchWriterMode" : "r",
            "ReplicationStateTransition" : "w",
            "Global" : "w",
            "Database" : "w",
            "Collection" : "w"
        },
        "waitingForLock" : false,
        "lockStats" : {
            "ParallelBatchWriterMode" : {
                "acquireCount" : {
                    "r" : NumberLong(4)
                }
            },
            "ReplicationStateTransition" : {
                "acquireCount" : {
                    "w" : NumberLong(4)
                }
            }
```

```
            },
            "Global" : {
                "acquireCount" : {
                    "w" : NumberLong(4)
                }
            },
            "Database" : {
                "acquireCount" : {
                    "w" : NumberLong(4)
                }
            },
            "Collection" : {
                "acquireCount" : {
                    "w" : NumberLong(4)
                }
            },
            "Mutex" : {
                "acquireCount" : {
                    "r" : NumberLong(196)
                }
            }
        },
        "waitingForFlowControl" : false,
        "flowControlStats" : {
            "acquireCount" : NumberLong(4)
        }
    }],
    "ok": 1
}
```

This displays a list of operations that the database is performing. Here are some of the more important fields in the output:

`"opid"`

The operation's unique identifier. You can use this number to kill an operation (see "Killing Operations" on page 375).

`"active"`

Whether this operation is running. If this field is `false`, it means the operation has yielded or is waiting for a lock.

`"secs_running"`

The duration of this operation in seconds. You can use this to find queries that are taking too long.

`"microsecs_running"`

The duration of this operation in microseconds. You can use this to find queries that are taking too long.

"op"

The type of operation. This is generally "query", "insert", "update", or "remove". Note that database commands are processed as queries.

"desc"

An identifier for the client. This can be correlated with messages in the logs. Every log message related to the connection in our example will be prefixed with [conn3], so you can use this to grep the logs for relevant information.

"locks"

A description of the types of locks taken by this operation.

"waitingForLock"

Whether this operation is currently blocking, waiting to acquire a lock.

"numYields"

The number of times this operation has yielded, releasing its lock to allow other operations to go. Generally, any operation that searches for documents (queries, updates, and removes) can yield. An operation will only yield if there are other operations enqueued and waiting to take its lock. Basically, if there are no operations in the "waitingForLock" state, the current operations will not yield.

"lockstats.timeAcquiringMicros"

How long it took this operation to acquire the locks it needed.

You can filter currentOp to only look for operations fulfilling certain criteria, such as operations on a certain namespace or ones that have been running for a certain length of time. You filter the results by passing in a query argument:

```
> db.currentOp(
  {
    "active" : true,
    "secs_running" : { "$gt" : 3 },
    "ns" : /^db1\./
  }
)
```

You can query on any field in currentOp, using all the normal query operators.

Finding Problematic Operations

The most common use for db.currentOp() is looking for slow operations. You can use the filtering technique described in the previous section to find all queries that take longer than a certain amount of time, which may suggest a missing index or improper field filtering.

Sometimes people will find that unexpected queries are running, generally because there's an app server running an old or buggy version of the software. The "client" field can help you track down where unexpected operations are coming from.

Killing Operations

If you find an operation that you want to stop, you can kill it by passing db.killOp() its "opid":

```
> db.killOp(123)
```

Not all operations can be killed. In general, operations can only be killed when they yield—so updates, finds, and removes can all be killed, but operations holding or waiting for a lock usually cannot be killed.

Once you have sent a "kill" message to an operation, it will have a "killed" field in the db.currentOp() output. However, it won't actually be dead until it disappears from the list of current operations.

In MongoDB 4.0, the killOP method was extended to allow it to run on a *mongos*. It can now kill queries (read operations) that are running across more than one shard in a cluster. In previous versions, this involved manually issuing the kill command across each shard on the respective primary *mongod*.

False Positives

If you look for slow operations, you may see some long-running internal operations listed. There are several long-running requests MongoDB may have running, depending on your setup. The most common are the replication thread (which will continue fetching more operations from the sync source for as long as possible) and the writeback listener for sharding. Any long-running query on *local.oplog.rs* can be ignored, as well as any *writebacklistener* commands (*https://oreil.ly/95e3x*).

If you kill either of these operations, MongoDB will just restart them. However, you generally should not do that. Killing the replication thread will briefly halt replication, and killing the writeback listener may cause *mongos* to miss legitimate write errors.

Preventing Phantom Operations

There is an odd, MongoDB-specific issue that you may run into, particularly if you're bulk-loading data into a collection. Suppose you have a job that is firing thousands of update operations at MongoDB and MongoDB is grinding to a halt. You quickly stop the job and kill off all the updates that are currently occurring. However, you continue to see new updates appearing as soon as you kill the old ones, even though the job is no longer running!

If you are loading data using unacknowledged writes, your application will fire writes at MongoDB, potentially faster than MongoDB can process them. If MongoDB gets backed up, these writes will pile up in the operating system's socket buffer. When you kill the writes MongoDB is working on, this allows MongoDB to start processing the writes in the buffer. Even if you stop the client from sending writes, any writes that made it into the buffer will get processed by MongoDB, since they've already been "received" (just not processed).

The best way to prevent these phantom writes is to do *acknowledged* writes: make each write wait until the previous write is complete, not just until the previous write is sitting in a buffer on the database server.

Using the System Profiler

To find slow operations you can use the system profiler, which records operations in a special *system.profile* collection. The profiler can give you tons of information about operations that are taking a long time, but at a cost: it slows down *mongod*'s overall performance. Thus, you may only want to turn on the profiler periodically to capture a slice of traffic. If your system is already heavily loaded, you may wish to use another technique described in this chapter to diagnose issues.

By default, the profiler is off and does not record anything. You can turn it on by running `db.setProfilingLevel()` in the shell:

```
> db.setProfilingLevel(2)
{ "was" : 0, "slowms" : 100, "ok" : 1 }
```

Level 2 means "profile everything." Every read and write request received by the database will be recorded in the *system.profile* collection of the current database. Profiling is enabled per-database and incurs a heavy performance penalty: every write has to be written an extra time and every read has to take a write lock (because it must write an entry to the *system.profile* collection). However, it will give you an exhaustive listing of what your system is doing:

```
> db.foo.insert({x:1})
> db.foo.update({},{$set:{x:2}})
> db.foo.remove()
> db.system.profile.find().pretty()
{
    "op" : "insert",
    "ns" : "sample_mflix.foo",
    "command" : {
        "insert" : "foo",
        "ordered" : true,
        "lsid" : {
            "id" : UUID("63b7df66-ca97-41f4-a245-eba825485147")
        },
        "$readPreference" : {
```

```
                "mode" : "secondaryPreferred"
            },
            "$db" : "sample_mflix"
        },
        "ninserted" : 1,
        "keysInserted" : 1,
        "numYield" : 0,
        "locks" : { ... },
        "flowControl" : {
            "acquireCount" : NumberLong(3)
        },
        "responseLength" : 45,
        "protocol" : "op_msg",
        "millis" : 33,
        "client" : "127.0.0.1",
        "appName" : "MongoDB Shell",
        "allUsers" : [ ],
        "user" : ""
}
{
        "op" : "update",
        "ns" : "sample_mflix.foo",
        "command" : {
            "q" : {

            },
            "u" : {
                "$set" : {
                    "x" : 2
                }
            },
            "multi" : false,
            "upsert" : false
        },
        "keysExamined" : 0,
        "docsExamined" : 1,
        "nMatched" : 1,
        "nModified" : 1,
        "numYield" : 0,
        "locks" : { ... },
        "flowControl" : {
            "acquireCount" : NumberLong(1)
        },
        "millis" : 0,
        "planSummary" : "COLLSCAN",
        "execStats" : { ...
            "inputStage" : {

                ...
            }
        },
        "ts" : ISODate("2019-09-03T22:39:33.856Z"),
        "client" : "127.0.0.1",
```

```
        "appName" : "MongoDB Shell",
        "allUsers" : [ ],
        "user" : ""
}
{
    "op" : "remove",
    "ns" : "sample_mflix.foo",
    "command" : {
        "q" : {

        },
        "limit" : 0
    },
    "keysExamined" : 0,
    "docsExamined" : 1,
    "ndeleted" : 1,
    "keysDeleted" : 1,
    "numYield" : 0,
    "locks" : { ... },
    "flowControl" : {
        "acquireCount" : NumberLong(1)
    },
    "millis" : 0,
    "planSummary" : "COLLSCAN",
    "execStats" : { ...
        "inputStage" : { ... }
    },
    "ts" : ISODate("2019-09-03T22:39:33.858Z"),
    "client" : "127.0.0.1",
    "appName" : "MongoDB Shell",
    "allUsers" : [ ],
    "user" : ""
}
```

You can use the `"client"` field to see which users are sending which operations to the database. If you're using authentication, you can see which user is doing each operation, too.

Often, you do not care about most of the operations that your database is doing, just the slow ones. For this, you can set the profiling level to 1. By default, level 1 profiles operations that take longer than 100 ms. You can also specify a second argument, which defines what "slow" means to you. This would record all operations that took longer than 500 ms:

```
> db.setProfilingLevel(1, 500)
{ "was" : 2, "slowms" : 100, "ok" : 1 }
```

To turn profiling off, set the profiling level to 0:

```
> db.setProfilingLevel(0)
{ "was" : 1, "slowms" : 500, "ok" : 1 }
```

It's generally not a good idea to set `slowms` to a low value. Even with profiling off, `slowms` has an effect on *mongod*: it sets the threshold for printing slow operations in the log. Thus, if you set `slowms` to 2, every operation that takes longer than 2 ms will show up in the log, even with profiling off. So, if you lower `slowms` to profile something, you might want to raise it again before turning off profiling.

You can see the current profiling level with `db.getProfilingLevel()`. The profiling level is not persistent: restarting the database clears the level.

There are command-line options for configuring the profiling level, namely `--profile` *level* and `--slowms` *time*, but bumping up the profiling level is generally a temporary debugging measure, not something you want to add to your configuration long-term.

In MongoDB 4.2, profiler entries and diagnostic log messages were extended for read/write operations to help improve the identification of slow queries, with the addition of the `queryHash` and `planCacheKey` fields. The `queryHash` string represents a hash of the query shape and is dependent only on the query shape. Each query shape is associated with a `queryHash`, making it easier to highlight those queries using the same shape. The `planCacheKey` is the hash of the key for the plan cache entry associated with the query. It includes the details of both the query shape and the currently available indexes for the shape. These help you correlate the available information from the profiler to assist with query performance diagnosis.

If you turn on profiling and the *system.profile* collection does not already exist, MongoDB creates a small capped collection for it (a few megabytes in size). If you want to run the profiler for an extended period of time, this may not be enough space for the number of operations you need to record. You can make a larger *system.profile* collection by turning off profiling, dropping the *system.profile* collection, and creating a new *system.profile* capped collection that is the size you desire. Then enable profiling on the database.

Calculating Sizes

In order to provision the correct amount of disk and RAM, it is useful to know how much space documents, indexes, collections, and databases are taking up. See "Calculating the Working Set" on page 429 for information on calculating your working set.

Documents

The easiest way to get the size of a document is to use the shell's `Object.bsonsize()` function. Pass in any document to get the size it would be when stored in MongoDB.

For example, you can see that storing `_ids` as `ObjectIds` is more efficient than storing them as strings:

```
> Object.bsonsize({_id:ObjectId()})
22
> // ""+ObjectId() converts the ObjectId to a string
> Object.bsonsize({_id:""+ObjectId()})
39
```

More practically, you can pass in documents directly from your collections:

```
> Object.bsonsize(db.users.findOne())
```

This shows you exactly how many bytes a document is taking up on disk. However, this does not count padding or indexes, which can often be significant factors in the size of a collection.

Collections

For seeing information about a whole collection, there is a `stats` function:

```
>db.movies.stats()
{
    "ns" : "sample_mflix.movies",
    "size" : 65782298,
    "count" : 45993,
    "avgObjSize" : 1430,
    "storageSize" : 45445120,
    "capped" : false,
    "wiredTiger" : {
        "metadata" : {
            "formatVersion" : 1
        },
        "creationString" : "access_pattern_hint=none,allocation_size=4KB,\
            app_metadata=(formatVersion=1),assert=(commit_timestamp=none,\
            read_timestamp=none),block_allocation=best,block_compressor=\
            snappy,cache_resident=false,checksum=on,colgroups=,collator=,\
            columns=,dictionary=0,encryption=(keyid=,name=),exclusive=\
            false,extractor=,format=btree,huffman_key=,huffman_value=,\
            ignore_in_memory_cache_size=false,immutable=false,internal_item_\
            max=0,internal_key_max=0,internal_key_truncate=true,internal_\
            page_max=4KB,key_format=q,key_gap=10,leaf_item_max=0,leaf_key_\
            max=0,leaf_page_max=32KB,leaf_value_max=64MB,log=(enabled=true),\
            lsm=(auto_throttle=true,bloom=true,bloom_bit_count=16,bloom_\
            config=,bloom_hash_count=8,bloom_oldest=false,chunk_count_limit\
            =0,chunk_max=5GB,chunk_size=10MB,merge_custom=(prefix=,start_\
            generation=0,suffix=),merge_max=15,merge_min=0),memory_page_image\
            _max=0,memory_page_max=10m,os_cache_dirty_max=0,os_cache_max=0,\
            prefix_compression=false,prefix_compression_min=4,source=,split_\
            deepen_min_child=0,split_deepen_per_child=0,split_pct=90,type=file,\
            value_format=u",
        "type" : "file",
        "uri" : "statistics:table:collection-14--2146526997547809066",
        "LSM" : {
            "bloom filter false positives" : 0,
            "bloom filter hits" : 0,
```

```
            "bloom filter misses" : 0,
            "bloom filter pages evicted from cache" : 0,
            "bloom filter pages read into cache" : 0,
            "bloom filters in the LSM tree" : 0,
            "chunks in the LSM tree" : 0,
            "highest merge generation in the LSM tree" : 0,
            "queries that could have benefited from a Bloom filter
                that did not exist" : 0,
            "sleep for LSM checkpoint throttle" : 0,
            "sleep for LSM merge throttle" : 0,
            "total size of bloom filters" : 0
        },
        "block-manager" : {
            "allocations requiring file extension" : 0,
            "blocks allocated" : 1358,
            "blocks freed" : 1322,
            "checkpoint size" : 39219200,
            "file allocation unit size" : 4096,
            "file bytes available for reuse" : 6209536,
            "file magic number" : 120897,
            "file major version number" : 1,
            "file size in bytes" : 45445120,
            "minor version number" : 0
        },
        "btree" : {
            "btree checkpoint generation" : 22,
            "column-store fixed-size leaf pages" : 0,
            "column-store internal pages" : 0,
            "column-store variable-size RLE encoded values" : 0,
            "column-store variable-size deleted values" : 0,
            "column-store variable-size leaf pages" : 0,
            "fixed-record size" : 0,
            "maximum internal page key size" : 368,
            "maximum internal page size" : 4096,
            "maximum leaf page key size" : 2867,
            "maximum leaf page size" : 32768,
            "maximum leaf page value size" : 67108864,
            "maximum tree depth" : 0,
            "number of key/value pairs" : 0,
            "overflow pages" : 0,
            "pages rewritten by compaction" : 1312,
            "row-store empty values" : 0,
            "row-store internal pages" : 0,
            "row-store leaf pages" : 0
        },
        "cache" : {
            "bytes currently in the cache" : 40481692,
            "bytes dirty in the cache cumulative" : 40992192,
            "bytes read into cache" : 37064798,
            "bytes written from cache" : 37019396,
            "checkpoint blocked page eviction" : 0,
            "data source pages selected for eviction unable to be evicted" : 32,
```

```
      "eviction walk passes of a file" : 0,
      "eviction walk target pages histogram - 0-9" : 0,
      "eviction walk target pages histogram - 10-31" : 0,
      "eviction walk target pages histogram - 128 and higher" : 0,
      "eviction walk target pages histogram - 32-63" : 0,
      "eviction walk target pages histogram - 64-128" : 0,
      "eviction walks abandoned" : 0,
      "eviction walks gave up because they restarted their walk twice" : 0,
      "eviction walks gave up because they saw too many pages
      and found no candidates" : 0,
      "eviction walks gave up because they saw too many pages
      and found too few candidates" : 0,
      "eviction walks reached end of tree" : 0,
      "eviction walks started from root of tree" : 0,
      "eviction walks started from saved location in tree" : 0,
      "hazard pointer blocked page eviction" : 0,
      "in-memory page passed criteria to be split" : 0,
      "in-memory page splits" : 0,
      "internal pages evicted" : 8,
      "internal pages split during eviction" : 0,
      "leaf pages split during eviction" : 0,
      "modified pages evicted" : 1312,
      "overflow pages read into cache" : 0,
      "page split during eviction deepened the tree" : 0,
      "page written requiring cache overflow records" : 0,
      "pages read into cache" : 1330,
      "pages read into cache after truncate" : 0,
      "pages read into cache after truncate in prepare state" : 0,
      "pages read into cache requiring cache overflow entries" : 0,
      "pages requested from the cache" : 3383,
      "pages seen by eviction walk" : 0,
      "pages written from cache" : 1334,
      "pages written requiring in-memory restoration" : 0,
      "tracked dirty bytes in the cache" : 0,
      "unmodified pages evicted" : 8
   },
   "cache_walk" : {
      "Average difference between current eviction generation
      when the page was last considered" : 0,
      "Average on-disk page image size seen" : 0,
      "Average time in cache for pages that have been visited
      by the eviction server" : 0,
      "Average time in cache for pages that have not been visited
      by the eviction server" : 0,
      "Clean pages currently in cache" : 0,
      "Current eviction generation" : 0,
      "Dirty pages currently in cache" : 0,
      "Entries in the root page" : 0,
      "Internal pages currently in cache" : 0,
      "Leaf pages currently in cache" : 0,
      "Maximum difference between current eviction generation
      when the page was last considered" : 0,
```

```
        "Maximum page size seen" : 0,
        "Minimum on-disk page image size seen" : 0,
        "Number of pages never visited by eviction server" : 0,
        "On-disk page image sizes smaller than a single allocation unit" : 0,
        "Pages created in memory and never written" : 0,
        "Pages currently queued for eviction" : 0,
        "Pages that could not be queued for eviction" : 0,
        "Refs skipped during cache traversal" : 0,
        "Size of the root page" : 0,
        "Total number of pages currently in cache" : 0
    },
    "compression" : {
        "compressed page maximum internal page size
        prior to compression" : 4096,
        "compressed page maximum leaf page size
        prior to compression " : 131072,
        "compressed pages read" : 1313,
        "compressed pages written" : 1311,
        "page written failed to compress" : 1,
        "page written was too small to compress" : 22
    },
    "cursor" : {
        "bulk loaded cursor insert calls" : 0,
        "cache cursors reuse count" : 0,
        "close calls that result in cache" : 0,
        "create calls" : 1,
        "insert calls" : 0,
        "insert key and value bytes" : 0,
        "modify" : 0,
        "modify key and value bytes affected" : 0,
        "modify value bytes modified" : 0,
        "next calls" : 0,
        "open cursor count" : 0,
        "operation restarted" : 0,
        "prev calls" : 1,
        "remove calls" : 0,
        "remove key bytes removed" : 0,
        "reserve calls" : 0,
        "reset calls" : 2,
        "search calls" : 0,
        "search near calls" : 0,
        "truncate calls" : 0,
        "update calls" : 0,
        "update key and value bytes" : 0,
        "update value size change" : 0
    },
    "reconciliation" : {
        "dictionary matches" : 0,
        "fast-path pages deleted" : 0,
        "internal page key bytes discarded using suffix compression" : 0,
        "internal page multi-block writes" : 0,
        "internal-page overflow keys" : 0,
```

```
                    "leaf page key bytes discarded using prefix compression" : 0,
                    "leaf page multi-block writes" : 0,
                    "leaf-page overflow keys" : 0,
                    "maximum blocks required for a page" : 1,
                    "overflow values written" : 0,
                    "page checksum matches" : 0,
                    "page reconciliation calls" : 1334,
                    "page reconciliation calls for eviction" : 1312,
                    "pages deleted" : 0
                },
                "session" : {
                    "object compaction" : 4
                },
                "transaction" : {
                    "update conflicts" : 0
                }
            },
            "nindexes" : 5,
            "indexBuilds" : [ ],
            "totalIndexSize" : 46292992,
            "indexSizes" : {
                "_id_" : 446464,
                "$**_text" : 44474368,
                "genres_1_imdb.rating_1_metacritic_1" : 724992,
                "tomatoes_rating" : 307200,
                "getMovies" : 339968
            },
            "scaleFactor" : 1,
            "ok" : 1
    }
```

stats starts with the namespace ("sample_mflix.movies") and then the count of all
documents in the collection. The next couple of fields have to do with the size of the
collection. "size" is what you'd get if you called Object.bsonsize() on each element
in the collection and added up all the sizes: it's the actual number of bytes in memory
the documents in the collection are taking up when uncompressed. Equivalently, if
you take the "avgObjSize" and multiply it by "count", you'll get "size" uncompressed in memory.

As mentioned earlier, a total count of the documents' bytes leaves out the space saved
by compressing a collection. "storageSize" can be a smaller figure than "size",
reflecting the space saved by compression.

"nindexes" is the number of indexes on the collection. An index is not counted in
"nindexes" until it finishes being built and cannot be used until it appears in this list.
In general, indexes will be a lot larger than the amount of data they store. You can
minimize this free space by having right-balanced indexes (as described in "Introduction to Compound Indexes" on page 81). Indexes that are randomly distributed will

generally be approximately 50% free space, whereas ascending-order indexes will be 10% free space.

As your collections get bigger, it may become difficult to read `stats` output with sizes in the billions of bytes or beyond. Thus, you can pass in a scaling factor: `1024` for kilobytes, `1024*1024` for megabytes, and so on. For example, this would get the collection stats in terabytes:

```
> db.big.stats(1024*1024*1024*1024)
```

Databases

Databases have a `stats` function that's similar to collections':

```
> db.stats()
{
    "db" : "sample_mflix",
    "collections" : 5,
    "views" : 0,
    "objects" : 98308,
    "avgObjSize" : 819.8680982219148,
    "dataSize" : 80599593,
    "storageSize" : 53620736,
    "numExtents" : 0,
    "indexes" : 12,
    "indexSize" : 47001600,
    "scaleFactor" : 1,
    "fsUsedSize" : 355637043200,
    "fsTotalSize" : 499963174912,
    "ok" : 1
}
```

First, we have the name of the database, the number of collections it contains, and the number of views for the database. `"objects"` is the total count of documents across all collections in this database.

The bulk of the document contains information about the size of your data. `"fsTotalSize"` should always be the largest: it is the total size of the disk capacity on the filesystem where the MongoDB instance stores data. `"fsUsedSize"` represents the total space used in that filesystem by MongoDB currently. This should correspond to the total space used by all the files in your data directory.

The next-largest field is generally going to be `"dataSize"`, which is the size of the uncompressed data held in this database. This doesn't match `"storageSize"` because data is typically compressed in WiredTiger. `"indexSize"` is the amount of space all of the indexes for this database take up.

`db.stats()` can take a scale argument the same way that the collections' `stats` function can. If you call `db.stats()` on a nonexistent database, the values will all be zero.

Keep in mind that listing databases on a system with a high lock percent can be very slow and block other operations. Avoid doing it, if possible.

Using mongotop and mongostat

MongoDB comes with a few command-line tools that can help you determine what it's doing by printing stats every few seconds.

mongotop is similar to the *top* Unix utility: it gives you an overview of which collections are busiest. You can also run `mongotop --locks` to give you locking statistics for each database.

mongostat gives server-wide information. By default, `mongostat` prints out a list of statistics once per second, although this is configurable by passing a different number of seconds on the command line. Each of the fields gives a count of how many times the activity has happened since the field was last printed:

`insert/query/update/delete/getmore/command`
Simple counts of how many of each of these operations there have been.

`flushes`
How many times *mongod* has flushed data to disk.

`mapped`
The amount of memory *mongod* has mapped. This is generally roughly the size of your data directory.

`vsize`
The amount of virtual memory *mongod* is using. This is generally twice the size of your data directory (once for the mapped files, once again for journaling).

`res`
The amount of memory *mongod* is using. This should generally be as close as possible to all the memory on the machine.

`locked db`
The database that spent the most time locked in the last timeslice. This field reports the percent of time the database was locked combined with how long the global lock was held, meaning that this value might be over 100%.

`idx miss %`
The percentage of index accesses that had to page fault (because the index entry or section of index being searched was not in memory, so *mongod* had to go to disk). This is the most confusingly named field in the output.

`qr|qw`
> The queue size for reads and writes (i.e., how many reads and writes are blocking, waiting to be processed).

`ar|aw`
> How many active clients there are (i.e., clients currently performing reads and writes).

`netIn`
> The number of network bytes in, as counted by MongoDB (not necessarily the same as what the OS would measure).

`netOut`
> The number of network bytes out, as counted by MongoDB.

`conn`
> The number of connections this server has open, both incoming and outgoing.

`time`
> The time at which these statistics were taken.

You can run *mongostat* on a replica set or sharded cluster. If you use the `--discover` option, *mongostat* will try to find all the members of the set or cluster from the member it initially connects to and will print one line per server per second for each. For a large cluster, this can get unmanageable fast, but it can be useful for small clusters and tools that can consume the data and present it in a more readable form.

mongostat is a great way to get a quick snapshot of what your database is doing, but for long-term monitoring a tool like MongoDB Atlas or Ops Manager is preferred (see Chapter 22).

## CHAPTER 19

An Introduction to MongoDB Security

To protect your MongoDB cluster and the data it holds, you will want to employ the following security measures:

- Enable authorization and enforce authentication
- Encrypt communication
- Encrypt data

This chapter demonstrates how to address the first two security measures with a tutorial on using MongoDB's support for x.509 to configure authentication and transport layer encryption to ensure secure communications among clients and servers in a MongoDB replica set. We will touch on encrypting data at the storage layer in a later chapter.

MongoDB Authentication and Authorization

While authentication and authorization are closely connected, it is important to note that authentication is distinct from authorization. The purpose of authentication is to verify the identity of a user, while authorization determines the verified user's access to resources and operations.

Authentication Mechanisms

Enabling authorization on a MongoDB cluster enforces authentication and ensures users can only perform actions they are authorized for, as determined by their roles. The Community version of MongoDB provides support for SCRAM (Salted Challenge Response Authentication Mechanism) and x.509 certificate authentication. In addition to SCRAM and x.509, MongoDB Enterprise supports Kerberos authentication and LDAP proxy authentication. See the documentation (*https://oreil.ly/RQ5Jp*)

for details on the various authentication mechanisms that MongoDB supports. In this chapter, we will focus on x.509 authentication. An x.509 digital certificate uses the widely accepted x.509 public key infrastructure (PKI) standard to verify that a public key belongs to the presenter.

Authorization

When adding a user in MongoDB, you must create the user in a specific database. That database is the authentication database for the user; you can use any database for this purpose. The username and authentication database serves as a unique identifier for a user. However, a user's privileges are not limited to their authentication database. When creating a user, you can specify the operations the user may perform on any resources to which they should have access. Resources include the cluster, databases, and collections.

MongoDB provides a number of built-in roles that grant commonly needed permissions for database users. These include the following:

read
> Read data on all nonsystem collections and on the following system collections: *system.indexes*, *system.js*, and *system.namespaces*.

readWrite
> Provides same privileges as read, plus the ability to modify data on all nonsystem collections and the *system.js* collection.

dbAdmin
> Perform administrative tasks such as schema-related tasks, indexing, and gathering statistics (does not grant privileges for user and role management).

userAdmin
> Create and modify roles and users on the current database.

dbOwner
> Combines the privileges granted by the *readWrite*, *dbAdmin*, and *userAdmin* roles.

clusterManager
> Perform management and monitoring actions on the cluster.

clusterMonitor
> Provides read-only access to monitoring tools such as the MongoDB Cloud Manager and Ops Manager monitoring agent.

hostManager
> Monitor and manage servers.

clusterAdmin

Combines the privileges granted by the *clusterManager*, *clusterMonitor*, and *host-Manager* roles, plus the *dropDatabase* action.

backup

Provides sufficient privileges to use the MongoDB Cloud Manager backup agent or the Ops Manager backup agent, or to use *mongodump* to back up an entire *mongod* instance.

restore

Provides privileges needed to restore data from backups that do not include *system.profile* collection data.

readAnyDatabase

Provides same privileges as *read* on all databases except *local* and *config*, plus the *listDatabases* action on the cluster as a whole.

readWriteAnyDatabase

Provides same privileges as *readWrite* on all databases except *local* and *config*, plus the *listDatabases* action on the cluster as a whole.

userAdminAnyDatabase

Provides same privileges as *userAdmin* on all databases except *local* and *config* (effectively a superuser role).

dbAdminAnyDatabase

Provides same privileges as *dbAdmin* on all databases except *local* and *config*, plus the *listDatabases* action on the cluster as a whole.

root

Provides access to the operations and all the resources of the *readWriteAnyDatabase*, *dbAdminAnyDatabase*, *userAdminAnyDatabase*, *clusterAdmin*, *restore*, and *backup* roles combined.

You may also create what are known as "user-defined roles," which are custom roles that group together authorization to perform specific operations and label them with a name so that you may grant this set of permissions to multiple users easily.

A deep dive on built-in roles or user-defined roles is beyond the scope of this chapter. However, this introduction should give you a pretty good idea of what's possible with MongoDB authorization. For greater detail, please see the authorization section of the MongoDB documentation (*https://docs.mongodb.com/manual/core/authorization/*).

To ensure that you can add new users as needed, you must first create an admin user. MongoDB does not create a default root or admin user when enabling authentication and authorization, regardless of the authentication mode you are using (x.509 is no exception).

In MongoDB, authentication and authorization are not enabled by default. You must explicitly enable them by using the --auth option to the mongod command or specifying a value of "enabled" for the security.authorization setting in a MongoDB config file.

To configure a replica set, first bring it up without authentication and authorization enabled, then create the admin user and the users you'll need for each client.

Using x.509 Certificates to Authenticate Both Members and Clients

Given that all production MongoDB clusters are composed of multiple members, to secure a cluster, it is essential that all services communicating within the cluster authenticate with one another. Each member of a replica set must authenticate with the others in order to exchange data. Likewise, clients must authenticate with the primary and any secondaries that they communicate with.

For x.509, it's necessary that a trusted certification authority (CA) sign all certificates. Signing certifies that the named subject of a certificate owns the public key associated with that certificate. A CA acts as a trusted third party to prevent man-in-the-middle attacks.

Figure 19-1 depicts x.509 authentication used to secure a three-member MongoDB replica set. Note the authentication among the client and members of the replica set and the trust relationships with the CA.

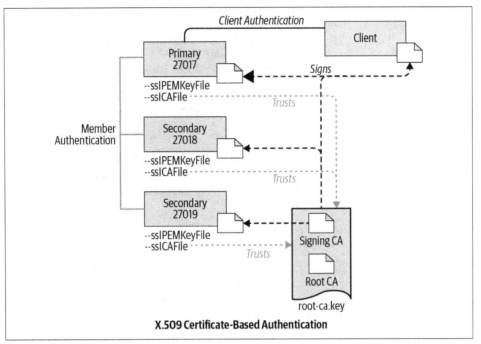

X.509 Certificate-Based Authentication

Figure 19-1. Overview of the trust hierarchy for X.509 authentication for the three-member replica set used in this chapter

The members and the client each have their own certificate signed by the CA. For production use, your MongoDB deployment should use valid certificates generated and signed by a single certificate authority. You or your organization can generate and maintain an independent certificate authority, or you can use certificates generated by a third-party TLS/SSL vendor.

We will refer to certificates used for internal authentication to verify membership in a cluster as member certificates. Both member certificates and client certificates (used to authenticate clients) have a structure resembling the following:

```
Certificate:
    Data:
        Version: 1 (0x0)
        Serial Number: 1 (0x1)
    Signature Algorithm: sha256WithRSAEncryption
        Issuer: C=US, ST=NY, L=New York, O=MongoDB, CN=CA-SIGNER
        Validity
            Not Before: Nov 11 22:00:03 2018 GMT
            Not After : Nov 11 22:00:03 2019 GMT
        Subject: C=US, ST=NY, L=New York, O=MongoDB, OU=MyServers, CN=server1
        Subject Public Key Info:
            Public Key Algorithm: rsaEncryption
                Public-Key: (2048 bit)
```

```
Modulus:
    00:d3:1c:29:ba:3d:29:44:3b:2b:75:60:95:c8:83:
    fc:32:1a:fa:29:5c:56:f3:b3:66:88:7f:f9:f9:89:
    ff:c2:51:b9:ca:1d:4c:d8:b8:5a:fd:76:f5:d3:c9:
    95:9c:74:52:e9:8d:5f:2e:6b:ca:f8:6a:16:17:98:
    dc:aa:bf:34:d0:44:33:33:f3:9d:4b:7e:dd:7a:19:
    1b:eb:3b:9e:21:d9:d9:ba:01:9c:8b:16:86:a3:52:
    a3:e6:e4:5c:f7:0c:ab:7a:1a:be:c6:42:d3:a6:01:
    8e:0a:57:b2:cd:5b:28:ee:9d:f5:76:ca:75:7a:c1:
    7c:42:d1:2a:7f:17:fe:69:17:49:91:4b:ca:2e:39:
    b4:a5:e0:03:bf:64:86:ca:15:c7:b2:f7:54:00:f7:
    02:fe:cf:3e:12:6b:28:58:1c:35:68:86:3f:63:46:
    75:f1:fe:ac:1b:41:91:4f:f2:24:99:54:f2:ed:5b:
    fd:01:98:65:ac:7a:7a:57:2f:a8:a5:5a:85:72:a6:
    9e:fb:44:fb:3b:1c:79:88:3f:60:85:dd:d1:5c:1c:
    db:62:8c:6a:f7:da:ab:2e:76:ac:af:6d:7d:b1:46:
    69:c1:59:db:c6:fb:6f:e1:a3:21:0c:5f:2e:8e:a7:
    d5:73:87:3e:60:26:75:eb:6f:10:c2:64:1d:a6:19:
    f3:0b
Exponent: 65537 (0x10001)
Signature Algorithm: sha256WithRSAEncryption
    5d:dd:b2:35:be:27:c2:41:4a:0d:c7:8c:c9:22:05:cd:eb:88:
    9d:71:4f:28:c1:79:71:3c:6d:30:19:f4:9c:3d:48:3a:84:d0:
    19:00:b1:ec:a9:11:02:c9:a6:9c:74:e7:4e:3c:3a:9f:23:30:
    50:5a:d2:47:53:65:06:a7:22:0b:59:71:b0:47:61:62:89:3d:
    cf:c6:d8:b3:d9:cc:70:20:35:bf:5a:2d:14:51:79:4b:7c:00:
    30:39:2d:1d:af:2c:f3:32:fe:c2:c6:a5:b8:93:44:fa:7f:08:
    85:f0:01:31:29:00:d4:be:75:7e:0d:f9:1a:f5:e9:75:00:9a:
    7b:d0:eb:80:b1:01:00:c0:66:f8:c9:f0:35:6e:13:80:70:08:
    5b:95:53:4b:34:ec:48:e3:02:88:5c:cd:a0:6c:b4:bc:65:15:
    4d:c8:41:9d:00:f5:e7:f2:d7:f5:67:4a:32:82:2a:04:ae:d7:
    25:31:0f:34:e8:63:a5:93:f2:b5:5a:90:71:ed:77:2a:a6:15:
    eb:fc:c3:ac:ef:55:25:d1:a1:31:7a:2c:80:e3:42:c2:b3:7d:
    5e:9a:fc:e4:73:a8:39:50:62:db:b1:85:aa:06:1f:42:27:25:
    4b:24:cf:d0:40:ca:51:13:94:97:7f:65:3e:ed:d9:3a:67:08:
    79:64:a1:ba
-----BEGIN CERTIFICATE-----
MIIDODCCAiACAQEwDQYJKoZIhvcNAQELBQAwWTELMAkGA1UEBhMCQ04xCzAJBgNV
BAgMAkdEMREwDwYDVQQHDAhTaGVuemhlbjEWMBQGA1UECgwNTW9uZ29EQiBDaGlu
YTESMBAGA1UEAwwJQ0EtU0lHTkVSMB4XDTE4MTExMTIyMDAwM1oXDTE5MTExMTIy
MDAwM1owazELMAkGA1UEBhMCQ04xCzAJBgNVBAgMAkdEMREwDwYDVQQHDAhTaGVu
emhlbjEWMBQGA1UECgwNTW9uZ29EQiBDaGluYTESMBAGA1UECwwJTXlTZXJ2ZXJz
MRAwDgYDVQQDDAdzZXJ2ZXIxMIIBIjANBgkqhkiG9w0BAQEFAAOCAQ8AMIIBCgKC
AQEA0xwpuj0pRDsrdWCVyIP8Mhr6KVxW87NmiH/5+Yn/wlG5yh1M2Lha/Xb108mV
nHRS6Y1fLmvK+GoWF5jcqr800EQzM/OdS37dehkb6zueIdnZugGcixaGo1Kj5uRc
9wyrehq+xkLTpgGOCleyzVso7p31dsp1esF8QtEqfxf+aRdJkUvKLjm0peADv2SG
yhXHsvdUAPcC/s8+EmsoWBw1aIY/Y0Z18f6sG0GRT/IkmVTy7Vv9AZhlrHp6Vy+o
pVqFcqae+0T7Oxx5iD9ghd3RXBzbYoxq99qrLnasr219sUZpwVnbxvtv4aMhDF8u
jqfVc4c+YCZ1628QwmQdphnzCwIDAQABMA0GCSqGSIb3DQEBCwUAA4IBAQBd3bI1
vifCQUoNx4zJIgXN64idcU8owXlxPG0wGfScPUg6hNAZALHsqRECyaacdOdOPDqf
IzBQWtJHU2UGpyILWXGwR2FiiT3Pxtiz2cxwIDW/Wi0UUXlLfAAwOS0dryzzMv7C
xqW4k0T6fwiF8AExKQDUvnV+Dfka9el1AJp70OuAsQEAwGb4yfA1bhOAcAhblVNL
```

NOxI4wKIXM2gbLS8ZRVNyEGdAPXn8tf1Z0oygioErtclMQ806GOlk/K1WpBx7Xcq
phXr/MOs71Ul0aExeiyA40LCs31emvzkc6g5UGLbsYWqBh9CJyVLJM/QQMpRE5SX
f2U+7dk6Zwh5ZKG6
-----END CERTIFICATE-----

For use with x.509 authentication in MongoDB, member certificates must have the following properties:

- A single CA must issue all x.509 certificates for the members of the cluster.
- The Distinguished Name (DN), found in the subject of the member certificate, must specify a nonempty value for at least one of the following attributes: Organization (O), Organizational Unit (OU), or Domain Component (DC).
- The O, OU, and DC attributes must match those from the certificates for the other cluster members.
- The Common Name (CN) or a Subject Alternative Name (SAN) must match the hostname of the server used by the other members of the cluster.

A Tutorial on MongoDB Authentication and Transport Layer Encryption

In this tutorial we will set up a root CA and an intermediate CA. Best practice recommends signing the server and client certificates with the intermediate CA.

Establish a CA

Before we can generate signed certificates for the members of our replica set, we must first address the issue of a certificate authority. As mentioned previously, we can either generate and maintain an independent certificate authority or use certificates generated by a third-party TLS/SSL vendor. We will generate our own CA to use for the running example in this chapter. Note that you may access all the code examples in this chapter from the GitHub repository maintained for this book. The examples are drawn from a script you can use to deploy a secure replica set. You'll see comments from this script throughout these examples.

Generate a root CA

To generate our CA, we will use OpenSSL. To follow along, please make sure you have access to OpenSSL on your local machine.

A root CA is at the top of the certificate chain. This is the ultimate source of trust. Ideally, a third-party CA should be used. However, in the case of an isolated network (typical in a large enterprise environment) or for testing purposes, you'll need to use a local CA.

First, we'll initialize some variables:

```
dn_prefix="/C=US/ST=NY/L=New York/O=MongoDB"
ou_member="MyServers"
ou_client="MyClients"
mongodb_server_hosts=( "server1" "server2" "server3" )
mongodb_client_hosts=( "client1" "client2" )
mongodb_port=27017
```

Then, we'll create a key pair and store it in the file *root-ca.key*:

```
# !!! In production you will want to password-protect the keys
# openssl genrsa -aes256 -out root-ca.key 4096
openssl genrsa -out root-ca.key 4096
```

Next, we'll create a configuration file to hold our OpenSSL settings that we will use to generate the certificates:

```
# For the CA policy
[ policy_match ]
countryName = match
stateOrProvinceName = match
organizationName = match
organizationalUnitName = optional
commonName = supplied
emailAddress = optional

[ req ]
default_bits       = 4096
default_keyfile    = server-key.pem
default_md      = sha256
distinguished_name = req_dn
req_extensions = v3_req
x509_extensions = v3_ca # The extensions to add to the self-signed cert

[ v3_req ]
subjectKeyIdentifier  = hash
basicConstraints = CA:FALSE
keyUsage = critical, digitalSignature, keyEncipherment
nsComment = "OpenSSL Generated Certificate"
extendedKeyUsage  = serverAuth, clientAuth

[ req_dn ]
countryName = Country Name (2-letter code)
countryName_default = US
countryName_min = 2
countryName_max = 2

stateOrProvinceName = State or Province Name (full name)
stateOrProvinceName_default = NY
stateOrProvinceName_max = 64

localityName = Locality Name (eg, city)
```

```
localityName_default = New York
localityName_max = 64

organizationName = Organization Name (eg, company)
organizationName_default = MongoDB
organizationName_max = 64

organizationalUnitName = Organizational Unit Name (eg, section)
organizationalUnitName_default = Education
organizationalUnitName_max = 64

commonName = Common Name (eg, YOUR name)
commonName_max = 64

[ v3_ca ]
# Extensions for a typical CA

subjectKeyIdentifier = hash
basicConstraints = critical,CA:true
authorityKeyIdentifier = keyid:always,issuer:always

# Key usage: this is typical for a CA certificate. However, since it will
# prevent it being used as a test self-signed certificate it is best
# left out by default.
keyUsage = critical,keyCertSign,cRLSign
```

Then, using the openssl req command, we will create the root certificate. Since the root is the very top of the authority chain, we'll self-sign this certificate using the private key we created in the previous step (stored in *root-ca.key*). The -x509 option tells the openssl req command we want to self-sign the certificate using the private key supplied to the -key option. The output is a file called *root-ca.crt*:

```
openssl req -new -x509 -days 1826 -key root-ca.key -out root-ca.crt \
  -config openssl.cnf -subj "$dn_prefix/CN=ROOTCA"
```

If you take a look at the *root-ca.crt* file, you'll find that it contains the public certificate for the root CA. You can verify the contents by taking a look at a human-readable version of the certificate produced by this command:

```
openssl x509 -noout -text -in root-ca.crt
```

The output from this command will resemble the following:

```
Certificate:
    Data:
        Version: 3 (0x2)
        Serial Number:
            1e:83:0d:9d:43:75:7c:2b:d6:2a:dc:7e:a2:a2:25:af:5d:3b:89:43
        Signature Algorithm: sha256WithRSAEncryption
        Issuer: C = US, ST = NY, L = New York, O = MongoDB, CN = ROOTCA
        Validity
            Not Before: Sep 11 21:17:24 2019 GMT
```

```
            Not After : Sep 10 21:17:24 2024 GMT
        Subject: C = US, ST = NY, L = New York, O = MongoDB, CN = ROOTCA
        Subject Public Key Info:
            Public Key Algorithm: rsaEncryption
                RSA Public-Key: (4096 bit)
                Modulus:
                    00:e3:de:05:ae:ba:c9:e0:3f:98:37:18:77:02:35:
                    e7:f6:62:bc:c3:ae:38:81:8d:04:88:da:6c:e0:57:
                    c2:90:86:05:56:7b:d2:74:23:54:f8:ca:02:45:0f:
                    38:e7:e2:0b:69:ea:f6:c8:13:8f:6c:2d:d6:c1:72:
                    64:17:83:4e:68:47:cf:de:37:ed:6e:38:b2:ab:3a:
                    e4:45:a8:fa:08:90:a0:f3:0d:3a:14:d8:9a:8d:69:
                    e7:cf:93:1a:71:53:4f:13:29:50:b0:2f:b6:b8:19:
                    2a:40:21:15:90:43:e7:d8:d8:f3:51:e5:95:58:87:
                    6c:45:9f:61:fc:b5:97:cf:5b:4e:4a:1f:72:c9:0c:
                    e9:8c:4c:d1:ca:df:b3:a4:da:b4:10:83:81:01:b1:
                    c8:09:22:76:c7:1e:96:c7:e6:56:27:8d:bc:fb:17:
                    ed:d9:23:3f:df:9c:ef:03:20:cc:c3:c4:55:cc:9f:
                    ad:d4:8d:81:95:c3:f1:87:f8:d4:5a:5e:e0:a8:41:
                    27:c8:0d:52:91:e4:2b:db:25:d6:b7:93:8d:82:33:
                    7a:a7:b8:e8:cd:a8:e2:94:3d:d6:16:e1:4e:13:63:
                    3f:77:08:10:cf:23:f6:15:7c:71:24:97:ef:1c:a2:
                    68:0f:82:e2:f7:24:b3:aa:70:1a:4a:b4:ca:4d:05:
                    92:5e:47:a2:3d:97:82:f6:d8:c8:04:a7:91:6c:a4:
                    7d:15:8e:a8:57:70:5d:50:1c:0b:36:ba:78:28:f2:
                    da:5c:ed:4b:ea:60:8c:39:e6:a1:04:26:60:b3:e2:
                    ee:4f:9b:f9:46:3c:7e:df:82:88:29:c2:76:3e:1a:
                    a4:81:87:1f:ce:9e:41:68:de:6c:f3:89:df:ae:02:
                    e7:12:ee:93:20:f1:d2:d6:3d:36:58:ee:71:bf:b3:
                    c5:e7:5a:4b:a0:12:89:ed:f7:cc:ec:34:c7:b2:28:
                    a8:1a:87:c6:8b:5e:d2:c8:25:71:ba:ff:d0:82:1b:
                    5e:50:a9:8a:c6:0c:ea:4b:17:a6:cc:13:0a:53:36:
                    c6:9d:76:f2:95:cc:ac:b9:64:d5:72:fc:ab:ce:6b:
                    59:b1:3a:f2:49:2f:2c:09:d0:01:06:e4:f2:49:85:
                    79:82:e8:c8:bb:1a:ab:70:e3:49:97:9f:84:e0:96:
                    c2:6d:41:ab:59:0c:2e:70:9a:2e:11:c8:83:69:4b:
                    f1:19:97:87:c3:76:0e:bb:b0:2c:92:4a:07:03:6f:
                    57:bf:a9:ec:19:85:d6:3d:f8:de:03:7f:1b:9a:2f:
                    6c:02:72:28:b0:69:d5:f9:fb:3d:2e:31:8f:61:50:
                    59:a6:dd:43:4b:89:e9:68:4b:a6:0d:9b:00:0f:9a:
                    94:61:71
                Exponent: 65537 (0x10001)
        X509v3 extensions:
            X509v3 Subject Key Identifier:
                8B:D6:F8:BD:B7:82:FC:13:BC:61:3F:8B:FA:84:24:3F:A2:14:C8:27
            X509v3 Basic Constraints: critical
                CA:TRUE
            X509v3 Authority Key Identifier:
                keyid:8B:D6:F8:BD:B7:82:FC:13:BC:61:3F:8B:FA:84:24:3F:A2:14:C8:27
                DirName:/C=US/ST=NY/L=New York/O=MongoDB/CN=ROOTCA
                serial:1E:83:0D:9D:43:75:7C:2B:D6:2A:DC:7E:A2:A2:25:AF:5D:3B:89:43
```

```
              X509v3 Key Usage: critical
                  Certificate Sign, CRL Sign
      Signature Algorithm: sha256WithRSAEncryption
          c2:cc:79:40:8b:7b:a1:87:3a:ec:4a:71:9d:ab:69:00:bb:6f:
          56:0a:25:3b:8f:bd:ca:4d:4b:c5:27:28:3c:7c:e5:cf:84:ec:
          2e:2f:0d:37:35:52:6d:f9:4b:07:fb:9b:da:ea:5b:31:0f:29:
          1f:3c:89:6a:10:8e:ae:20:30:8f:a0:cf:f1:0f:41:99:6a:12:
          5f:5c:ce:15:d5:f1:c9:0e:24:c4:81:70:df:ad:a0:e1:0a:cc:
          52:d4:3e:44:0b:61:48:a9:26:3c:a3:3d:2a:c3:ca:4f:19:60:
          da:f7:7a:4a:09:9e:26:42:50:05:f8:74:13:4b:0c:78:f1:59:
          39:1e:eb:2e:e1:e2:6c:cc:4d:96:95:79:c2:8b:58:41:e8:7a:
          e6:ad:37:e4:87:d7:ed:bb:7d:fa:47:dd:46:dd:e7:62:5f:e9:
          fe:17:4b:e3:7a:0e:a1:c5:80:78:39:b7:6c:a6:85:cf:ba:95:
          d2:8d:09:ab:2d:cb:be:77:9b:3c:22:12:ca:12:86:42:d8:c5:
          3c:31:a0:ed:92:bc:7f:3f:91:2d:ec:db:01:bd:26:65:56:12:
          a3:56:ba:d8:d3:6e:f3:c3:13:84:98:2a:c7:b3:22:05:68:fa:
          8e:48:6f:36:8e:3f:e5:4d:88:ef:15:26:4c:b1:d3:7e:25:84:
          8c:bd:5b:d2:74:55:cb:b3:fa:45:3f:ee:ef:e6:80:e9:f7:7f:
          25:a6:6e:f2:c4:22:f7:b8:40:29:02:f1:5e:ea:8e:df:80:e0:
          60:f1:e5:3a:08:81:25:d5:cc:00:8f:5c:ac:a6:02:da:27:c0:
          cc:4e:d3:f3:14:60:c1:12:3b:21:b4:f7:29:9b:4c:34:39:3c:
          2a:d1:4b:86:cc:c7:de:f3:f7:5e:8f:9d:47:2e:3d:fe:e3:49:
          70:0e:1c:61:1c:45:a0:5b:d6:48:49:be:6d:f9:3c:49:26:d8:
          8b:e6:a1:b2:61:10:fe:0c:e8:44:2c:33:cd:3c:1d:c2:de:c2:
          06:98:7c:92:7b:c4:06:a5:1f:02:8a:03:53:ec:bd:b7:fc:31:
          f3:2a:c1:0e:6a:a5:a8:e4:ea:4d:cc:1d:07:a9:3f:f6:0e:35:
          5d:99:31:35:b3:43:90:f3:1c:92:8e:99:15:13:2b:8f:f6:a6:
          01:c9:18:05:15:2a:e3:d0:cc:45:66:d3:48:11:a2:b9:b1:20:
          59:42:f7:88:15:9f:e0:0c:1d:13:ae:db:09:3d:bf:7a:9d:cf:
          b2:41:1e:7a:fa:6b:35:20:03:58:a1:6c:02:19:21:5f:25:fc:
          ba:2f:fc:79:d7:92:e7:37:77:14:10:d9:33:b6:e5:fb:7a:46:
          ab:d1:86:70:88:92:59:c3
```

Create an intermediate CA for signing

Now that we've created our root CA, we will create an intermediate CA for signing
member and client certificates. An intermediate CA is nothing more than a certificate
signed using our root certificate. It is a best practice to use an intermediate CA to sign
server (i.e., member) and client certificates. Typically, a CA will use different intermediate CAs for signing different categories of certificates. If the intermediate CA is
compromised and the certificate needs to be revoked, only a portion of the trust tree
is affected instead of all certificates signed by the CA, as would be the case if the root
CA were used to sign all certificates.

```
# again, in production you would want to password protect your signing key:
# openssl genrsa -aes256 -out signing-ca.key 4096
openssl genrsa -out signing-ca.key 4096

openssl req -new -key signing-ca.key -out signing-ca.csr \
  -config openssl.cnf -subj "$dn_prefix/CN=CA-SIGNER"
openssl x509 -req -days 730 -in signing-ca.csr -CA root-ca.crt -CAkey \
```

```
root-ca.key -set_serial 01 -out signing-ca.crt -extfile openssl.cnf \
-extensions v3_ca
```

Note that in the statements above we are using the `openssl req` command followed by the `openssl ca` command to sign our signing certificate using our root certificate. The `openssl req` command creates a signing request and the `openssl ca` command uses that request as input to create a signed intermediate (signing) certificate.

As a last step in creating our signing CA, we will concatenate our root certificate (containing our root public key) and signing certificate (containing our signing public key) into a single pem file. This file will be supplied to our mongod or client process later as the value of the `--tlsCAFile` option.

```
cat root-ca.crt > root-ca.pem
cat signing-ca.crt >> root-ca.pem
```

With the root CA and signing CA set up, we are now ready to create the member and client certificates used for authentication in our MongoDB cluster.

Generate and Sign Member Certificates

Member certificates are typically referred to as x.509 server certificates. Use this type of certificate for *mongod* and *mongos* processes. Members of a MongoDB cluster use these certificates to verify membership in the cluster. Stated another way, one *mongod* authenticates itself with other members of a replica set using a server certificate.

To generate certificates for the members of our replica set, we will use a `for` loop to generate multiple certificates.

```
# Pay attention to the OU part of the subject in "openssl req" command
for host in "${mongodb_server_hosts[@]}"; do
    echo "Generating key for $host"
    openssl genrsa -out ${host}.key 4096
        openssl req -new -key ${host}.key -out ${host}.csr -config openssl.cnf \
        -subj "$dn_prefix/OU=$ou_member/CN=${host}"
        openssl x509 -req -days 365 -in ${host}.csr -CA signing-ca.crt -CAkey \
        signing-ca.key -CAcreateserial -out ${host}.crt -extfile openssl.cnf \
        -extensions v3_req
    cat ${host}.crt > ${host}.pem
    cat ${host}.key >> ${host}.pem
done
```

Three steps are involved with each certificate:

- Use the *openssl genrsa* command to create a new key pair.

- Use the *openssl req* command to generate a signing request for the key.

- Use the *openssl x509* command to sign and output a certificate using the signing CA.

Notice the variable $ou_member. This signifies the difference between server certificates and client certificates. Server and client certificates must differ in the organization part of the Distinguished Names. More specifically, they must differ in at least one of the O, OU, or DC values.

Generate and Sign Client Certificates

Client certificates are used by the mongo shell, MongoDB Compass, MongoDB utilities and tools and, of course, by applications using a MongoDB driver. Generating client certificates follows essentially the same process as for member certificates. The one difference is our use of the variable $ou_client. This ensure that the combination of the O, OU, and DC values will be different from those of the server certificates generated above.

```
# Pay attention to the OU part of the subject in "openssl req" command
for host in "${mongodb_client_hosts[@]}"; do
    echo "Generating key for $host"
    openssl genrsa -out ${host}.key 4096
    openssl req -new -key ${host}.key -out ${host}.csr -config openssl.cnf \
-subj "$dn_prefix/OU=$ou_client/CN=${host}"
    openssl x509 -req -days 365 -in ${host}.csr -CA signing-ca.crt -CAkey \
        signing-ca.key -CAcreateserial -out ${host}.crt -extfile openssl.cnf \
        -extensions v3_req
    cat ${host}.crt > ${host}.pem
    cat ${host}.key >> ${host}.pem
done
```

Bring Up the Replica Set Without Authentication and Authorization Enabled

We can start each member of our replica set without auth enabled as follows. Previously, when working with replica sets we've not enabled auth so this should look familiar. Here again we are making use of a few variables we defined in "Generate a root CA" on page 395 (or see the full script for this chapter) and a loop to launch each member (*mongod*) of our replica set.

```
mport=$mongodb_port
for host in "${mongodb_server_hosts[@]}"; do
    echo "Starting server $host in non-auth mode"
    mkdir -p ./db/${host}
    mongod --replSet set509 --port $mport --dbpath ./db/$host \
        --fork --logpath ./db/${host}.log
    let "mport++"
done
```

Once each *mongod* has started, we can then initialize a replica set using these *mongod*s.

```
myhostname=`hostname`
cat > init_set.js <<EOF
rs.initiate();
mport=$mongodb_port;
mport++;
rs.add("localhost:" + mport);
mport++;
rs.add("localhost:" + mport);
EOF
mongo localhost:$mongodb_port init_set.js
```

Note that the code above simply constructs a series of commands, stores these commands in a JavaScript file, and then runs the *mongo* shell to execute the small script that was created. Together, these commands, when executed in the *mongo* shell, will connect to the *mongod* running on port 27017 (value of the $mongodb_port variable set in "Generate a root CA" on page 395), initiate the replica set, and then add each of the other two *mongod*s (on ports 27018 and 27019) to the replica set.

Create the Admin User

Now, we'll create an admin user based on one of the client certificates we created in "Generate and Sign Client Certificates" on page 401. We will authenticate as this user when connecting from the *mongo* shell or another client to perform administrative tasks. To authenticate with a client certificate, you must first add the value of the subject from the client certificate as a MongoDB user. Each unique x.509 client certificate corresponds to a single MongoDB user; i.e., you cannot use a single client certificate to authenticate more than one MongoDB user. We must add the user in the $external database; i.e., the authentication database is the $external database.

First, we'll get the subject from our client certificate using the *openssl x509* command.

```
openssl x509 -in client1.pem -inform PEM -subject -nameopt RFC2253 | grep subject
```

This should result in the following output:

```
subject= CN=client1,OU=MyClients,O=MongoDB,L=New York,ST=NY,C=US
```

To create our admin user, we'll first connect to the primary of our replica set using the *mongo* shell.

```
mongo --norc localhost:27017
```

From within the *mongo* shell, we will issue the following command:

```
db.getSiblingDB("$external").runCommand(
    {
        createUser: "CN=client1,OU=MyClients,O=MongoDB,L=New York,ST=NY,C=US",
        roles: [
            { role: "readWrite", db: 'test' },
            { role: "userAdminAnyDatabase", db: "admin" },
            { role: "clusterAdmin", db:"admin"}
```

```
        ],
        writeConcern: { w: "majority" , wtimeout: 5000 }
    }
);
```

Note the use of the $external database in this command and the fact that we've specified the subject of our client certificate as the user name.

Restart the Replica Set with Authentication and Authorization Enabled

Now that we have an admin user, we can restart the replica set with authentication and authorization enabled and connect as a client. Without a user of any kind, it would be impossible to connect to a replica set with auth enabled.

Let's stop the replica set in it's current form (without auth enabled).

```
kill $(ps -ef | grep mongod | grep set509 | awk '{print $2}')
```

We are now ready to restart the replica set with auth enabled. In a production environment, we would copy each of the certificate and key files to their corresponding hosts. Here we're doing everything on localhost to make things easier. To initiate a secure replica set we will add the following command-line options to each invocation of *mongod*:

- `--tlsMode`
- `--clusterAuthMode`
- `--tlsCAFile`—root CA file (root-ca.key)
- `--tlsCertificateKeyFile`—certificate file for the *mongod*
- `--tlsAllowInvalidHostnames`—only used for testing; allows invalid hostnames

Here the file we provide as the value of the `tlsCAFile` option is used to establish a trust chain. As you recall the *root-ca.key* file contains the certificate of the root CA as well as the signing CA. By providing this file to the *mongod* process, we are stating our desire to trust the certificate contained in this file as well as all other certificates signed by these certificates.

Okay, let's do this.

```
mport=$mongodb_port
for host in "${mongodb_server_hosts[@]}"; do
    echo "Starting server $host"
    mongod --replSet set509 --port $mport --dbpath ./db/$host \
        --tlsMode requireTLS --clusterAuthMode x509 --tlsCAFile root-ca.pem \
        --tlsAllowInvalidHostnames --fork --logpath ./db/${host}.log \
        --tlsCertificateKeyFile ${host}.pem --tlsClusterFile ${host}.pem \
        --bind_ip 127.0.0.1
```

```
        let "mport++"
done
```

And with that, we have a three-member replica set secured using x.509 certificates for authentication and transport-layer encryption. The only thing left to do is to connect with the mongo shell. We'll use the client1 certificate to authenticate, because that is the certificate for which we created an admin user.

```
mongo --norc --tls --tlsCertificateKeyFile client1.pem --tlsCAFile root-ca.pem \
--tlsAllowInvalidHostnames --authenticationDatabase "\$external" \
--authenticationMechanism MONGODB-X509
```

Once connected, we encourage you to experiment by inserting some data to a collection. You should also attempt to connect using any other user (e.g., using the client2.pem). Connections attempts will result in errors like the following.

```
mongo --norc --tls --tlsCertificateKeyFile client2.pem --tlsCAFile root-ca.pem \
--tlsAllowInvalidHostnames --authenticationDatabase "\$external" \
--authenticationMechanism MONGODB-X509
MongoDB shell version v4.2.0
2019-09-11T23:18:31.696+0100 W  NETWORK  [js] The server certificate does not
match the host name. Hostname: 127.0.0.1 does not match
2019-09-11T23:18:31.702+0100 E  QUERY    [js] Error: Could not find user
"CN=client2,OU=MyClients,O=MongoDB,L=New York,ST=NY,C=US" for db "$external" :
connect@src/mongo/shell/mongo.js:341:17
@(connect):3:6
2019-09-11T23:18:31.707+0100 F  -        [main] exception: connect failed
2019-09-11T23:18:31.707+0100 E  -        [main] exiting with code 1
```

In the tutorial in this chapter, we've looked at an example of using x.509 certificates as a basis for authentication and to encrypt communication among clients and members of a replica set. The same procedure works for sharded clusters as well. With respect to securing a MongoDB cluster, please keep the following in mind:

- The directories, root CA and signing CA, as well as the host itself where you generate and sign certificates for the member machines or clients, should be protected from unauthorized access.

- For simplicity, the root CA and signing CA keys are not password protected in this tutorial. In production it is necessary to use passwords to protect the key from unauthorized use.

We encourage you to download and experiment with the demo scripts we have provided for this chapter in the book's GitHub repository.

## CHAPTER 20

Durability

Durability is a property of database systems that guarantees that write operations that have been committed to the database will survive permanently. For example, if a ticket reservation system reports that your concert seats have been booked, then your seats will remain booked even if some part of the reservation system crashes. For MongoDB, we need to consider durability at the cluster (or more specifically, replica set) level.

In this chapter, we will cover:

- How MongoDB guarantees durability at the replica set member level through journaling
- How MongoDB guarantees durability at the cluster level using write concern
- How to configure your application and MongoDB cluster to give you the level of durability you need
- How MongoDB guarantees durability at the cluster level using read concern
- How to set the durability level for transactions in replica sets

Throughout this chapter, we will discuss durability in replica sets. A three-member replica set is the most basic cluster recommended for production applications. The discussion here applies to replica sets with more members and to sharded clusters.

Durability at the Member Level Through Journaling

To provide durability in the event of a server failure, MongoDB uses a write-ahead log (WAL) called the *journal*. A WAL is a commonly used technique for durability in database systems. The idea is that we simply write a representation of the changes to be made to the database to a durable medium (i.e., to disk) before applying those changes to the database itself. In many database systems, a WAL is used to provide the atomicity database property as well. However, MongoDB uses other techniques to ensure atomic writes.

Beginning in MongoDB 4.0, as an application performs writes to a replica set, for the data in all replicated collections MongoDB creates journal entries using the same format as the oplog.[1] As discussed in Chapter 11, MongoDB uses statement-based replication based on an operations log, or *oplog*. The statements in the oplog are a representation of the actual MongoDB changes made to each document affected by a write. Therefore, oplog statements are easy to apply to any member of a replica set regardless of version, hardware, or any other differences between replica set members. In addition, each oplog statement is idempotent, meaning that it can be applied any number of times and the outcome will always be the same change to the database.

Like most databases, MongoDB maintains in-memory views of both the journal and the database data files. By default, it flushes journal entries to disk every 50 milliseconds and flushes database files to disk every 60 seconds. The 60-second interval for flushing data files is called a *checkpoint*. The journal is used to provide durability for data written since the last checkpoint. With respect to durability concerns, if the server suddenly stops, when it's restarted the journal can be used to replay any writes that were not flushed to disk before the shutdown.

For the journal files, MongoDB creates a subdirectory named *journal* under the *dbPath* directory. WiredTiger (MongoDB's default storage engine) journal files have names with the format *WiredTigerLog.<sequence>*, where *<sequence>* is a zero-padded number starting from *0000000001*. Except for very small log records, MongoDB compresses the data written to the journal. Journal files have a maximum size limit of approximately 100 MB. Once a journal file exceeds that limit, MongoDB creates a new journal file and begins writing new records there. Because journal files are only needed to recover data since the last checkpoint, MongoDB automatically removes "old" journal files—i.e., those written prior to the most recent checkpoint—once a new checkpoint is written.

If there is a crash (or `kill -9`), *mongod* will replay its journal files on startup. By default, the greatest extent of lost writes are those made in the last 100 ms plus the time it takes to flush the journal writes to disk.

If your application requires a shorter interval for journal flushes, you have two options. One is to change the interval using the `--journalCommitInterval` option to the *mongod* command. This option accepts values ranging from 1 to 500 ms. The other option, which we'll look at in the next section, is to specify in the write concern

---

1 MongoDB uses a different format for writes to the local database, which stores data used in the replication process and other instance-specific data, but the principles and application are similar.

that all writes should journal to disk. Shortening the interval for journaling to disk will negatively impact performance, so you need to be sure of the implications for your applications before changing the journaling default.

Durability at the Cluster Level Using Write Concern

With write concern, you can specify what level of acknowledgment your application requires in response to write requests. In a replica set, network partitions, server failures, or data center outages may keep writes from being replicated to every member, or even a majority of the members. When a normal state is restored to the replica set, it is possible that writes not replicated to a majority of members will be rolled back. In those situations, clients and the database may have a different view of what data has been committed.

There are applications for which it might be acceptable in some circumstances to have writes rolled back. For example, it might be okay to roll back a small number of comments in a social application of some kind. MongoDB supports a range of durability guarantees at the cluster level to enable application designers to select the durability level that works best for their use case.

The w and wtimeout Options for writeConcern

The MongoDB query language supports specifying a write concern for all insert and update methods. As an example, suppose we have an ecommerce application and want to ensure that all orders are durable. Writing an order to the database might look something like the following:

```
try {
   db.products.insertOne(
       { sku: "H1100335456", item: "Electric Toothbrush Head", quantity: 3 },
       { writeConcern: { w : "majority", wtimeout : 100 } }
   );
} catch (e) {
   print (e);
}
```

All insert and update methods take a second parameter, a document. Within that document you can specify a value for writeConcern. In the preceding example, the write concern we have specified indicates that we want to see an acknowledgment from the server that the write completed successfully only if the write was successfully replicated to a majority of the members of our application's replica set. In addition, the write should return an error if it is not replicated to a majority of replica set members in 100 ms or less. In the case of such an error, MongoDB does not undo successful data modifications performed before the write concern exceeded the time limit—it will be up to the application to choose how to handle timeouts in such situations. In general, you should configure the wtimeout value so that only in unusual circumstances will the application experience timeouts and any actions your application takes in response to a timeout error will ensure the correct state for your data. In most cases, your application should attempt to determine whether the timeout was a result of a transient slowdown in network communications or something more signficant.

As the value for w in the write concern document, you may specify "majority" (as was done in this example). Alternatively, you may specify an integer between zero and the number of members in the replica set. Finally, it is possible to tag replica set members, say to identify those on SSDs versus spinning disks or those used for reporting versus OLTP workloads. You may specify a tag set as the value of w to ensure that writes will only be acknowledged once committed to at least one member of the replica set matching the provided tag set.

The j (Journaling) Option for writeConcern

In addition to providing a value for the w option, you may also request acknowledgment that the write operation has been written to the journal by using the j option in the write concern document. With a value of true for j, MongoDB acknowledges a successful write only after the requested number of members (the value for w) have written the operation to their on-disk journal. Continuing our example, if we want to ensure all writes are journaled on a majority of members, we can update the code as follows:

```
try {
    db.products.insertOne(
        { sku: "H1100335456", item: "Electric Toothbrush Head", quantity: 3 },
        { writeConcern: { w : "majority", wtimeout : 100, j : true } }
    );
} catch (e) {
    print (e);
}
```

Without waiting for journaling, there is a brief window of about 100 ms on each member when, if the server process or hardware goes down, a write could be lost. However, waiting for journaling before acknowledging writes to members of a replica set does have a performance penalty.

It is essential that in addressing durability concerns for your applications, you carefully evaluate the requirements your application has and weigh the performance impacts of the durability settings you select.

Durability at a Cluster Level Using Read Concern

In MongoDB, read concerns allow for the configuration of when results are read. This can allow clients to see write results before those writes are durable. A read concern can be used with a write concern to control the level of consistency and availability guarantees made to an application. They should not be confused with read preferences, which deal with where the data is read from; specifically, read preferences determine the data bearing member(s) in the replica set. The default read preferences is to read from the primary.

Read concern determines the consistency and isolation properties of the data being read. The default readConcern is local, which returns data with no guarantees that the data has been written to the majority of the data bearing replica set members. This can result in the data being rolled back in the future. The majority concern returns only durable data (will not be rolled back) that has been acknowledged by the majority of replica set members. In MongoDB 3.4, the linearizable concern was added. It ensures data returned reflects all successful majority-acknowledged writes that have completed prior to the start of the read operation. It may wait for concurrently executing writes to finish before providing results.

In the same fashion, with write concerns you will need to weight the performance impacts of the read concerns against the durability and isolation guarantees they provide before selecting the appropriate concern for your application.

Durability of Transactions Using a Write Concern

In MongoDB, operations on individual documents are atomic. You can use embedded documents and arrays to express relationships between entities in a single document rather than using a normalized data model splitting entities and relationships across multiple collections. As a result, many applications do not require multi-document transactions.

However, for use cases that require atomicity for updates to multiple documents, MongoDB provides the ability to perform multi-document transactions against replica sets. Multi-document transactions can be used across multiple operations, documents, collections, and databases.

Transactions require that all data changes within the transaction are successful. If any operation fails, the transaction aborts and all data changes are discarded. If all operations are successful, all data changes made in the transaction are saved and the writes become visible to future reads.

As with individual write operations, you may specify a write concern for transactions. You set the write concern at the transaction level, not at the individual operation level. At the time of the commit, transactions use the transaction-level write concern to commit the write operations. Write concerns set for individual operations inside the transaction will be ignored.

You can set the write concern for the transaction commit at the transaction start. A write concern of 0 is not supported for transactions. If you use a write concern of 1

for a transaction, it can be rolled back if there is a failover. You may use a `writeCon`
`cern` of `"majority"` to ensure transactions are durable in the face of network and
server failures that might force a failover in a replica set. The following provides an
example:

```
function updateEmployeeInfo(session) {
    employeesCollection = session.getDatabase("hr").employees;
    eventsCollection = session.getDatabase("reporting").events;

    session.startTransaction( {writeConcern: { w: "majority" } } );

    try{
        employeesCollection.updateOne( { employee: 3 },
                                    { $set: { status: "Inactive" } } );
        eventsCollection.insertOne( { employee: 3, status: { new: "Inactive",
                                    old: "Active" } } );
    } catch (error) {
        print("Caught exception during transaction, aborting.");
        session.abortTransaction();
        throw error;
    }

    commitWithRetry(session);
}
```

What MongoDB Does Not Guarantee

There are a couple of situations where MongoDB cannot guarantee durability, such as
if there are hardware issues or filesystem bugs. In particular, if a hard disk is corrupt,
there is nothing MongoDB can do to protect your data.

Also, different varieties of hardware and software may have different durability guarantees. For example, some cheaper or older hard disks report a write's success while
the write is queued up to be written, not when it has actually been written. MongoDB
cannot defend against misreporting at this level: if the system crashes, data may be
lost.

Basically, MongoDB is only as safe as the underlying system: if the hardware or filesystem destroys the data, MongoDB cannot prevent it. Use replication to defend
against system issues. If one machine fails, hopefully another will still be functioning
correctly.

Checking for Corruption

The `validate` command can be used to check a collection for corruption. To run
`validate` on the *movies* collection, do:

```
db.movies.validate({full: true})
{
        "ns" : "sample_mflix.movies",
        "nInvalidDocuments" : NumberLong(0),
        "nrecords" : 45993,
        "nIndexes" : 5,
        "keysPerIndex" : {
                "_id_" : 45993,
                "$**_text" : 3671341,
                "genres_1_imdb.rating_1_metacritic_1" : 94880,
                "tomatoes_rating" : 45993,
                "getMovies" : 45993
        },
        "indexDetails" : {
                "$**_text" : {
                        "valid" : true
                },
                "_id_" : {
                        "valid" : true
                },
                "genres_1_imdb.rating_1_metacritic_1" : {
                        "valid" : true
                },
                "getMovies" : {
                        "valid" : true
                },
                "tomatoes_rating" : {
                        "valid" : true
                }
        },
        "valid" : true,
        "warnings" : [ ],
        "errors" : [ ],
        "extraIndexEntries" : [ ],
        "missingIndexEntries" : [ ],
        "ok" : 1
}
```

The main field you're looking for is "valid", which will hopefully be true. If it is not, validate will give some details about the corruption it found.

Most of the output from validate describes internal structures of the collection and timestamps used to understand the order of operations across a cluster. These are not particularly useful for debugging. (See Appendix B for more information on collection internals.)

You can only run validate on collections, and it will also check the associated indexes in the field indexDetails. However, this requires a full validate, which is configured with the { full: true } option.

## PART VI

Server Administration

## CHAPTER 21

Setting Up MongoDB in Production

In Chapter 2, we covered the basics of starting MongoDB. This chapter will go into more detail about which options are important for setting up MongoDB in production, including:

- Commonly used options
- Starting up and shutting down MongoDB
- Security-related options
- Logging considerations

Starting from the Command Line

The MongoDB server is started with the `mongod` executable. `mongod` has many configurable startup options; to view all of them, run `mongod --help` from the command line. A couple of the options are widely used and important to be aware of:

`--dbpath`

Specify an alternate directory to use as the data directory; the default is */data/db/* (or, on Windows, *\data\db* on the MongoDB binary's volume). Each `mongod` process on a machine needs its own data directory, so if you are running three instances of `mongod` on one machine, you'll need three separate data directories. When `mongod` starts up, it creates a *mongod.lock* file in its data directory, which prevents any other `mongod` process from using that directory. If you attempt to start another MongoDB server using the same data directory, it will give an error:

```
exception in initAndListen: DBPathInUse: Unable to lock the
    lock file: \ data/db/mongod.lock (Resource temporarily unavailable).
    Another mongod instance is already running on the
```

```
data/db directory,
\ terminating
```

`--port`

Specify the port number for the server to listen on. By default, mongod uses port 27017, which is unlikely to be used by another process (besides other mongod processes). If you would like to run more than one mongod process on a single machine, you'll need to specify different ports for each one. If you try to start mongod on a port that is already being used, it will give an error:

```
Failed to set up listener: SocketException: Address already in use.
```

`--fork`

On Unix-based systems, fork the server process, running MongoDB as a daemon.

If you are starting up *mongod* for the first time (with an empty data directory), it can take the filesystem a few minutes to allocate database files. The parent process will not return from forking until the preallocation is done and *mongod* is ready to start accepting connections. Thus, *fork* may appear to hang. You can tail the log to see what it is doing. You must use `--logpath` if you specify `--fork`.

`--logpath`

Send all output to the specified file rather than outputting on the command line. This will create the file if it does not exist, assuming you have write permissions to the directory. It will also overwrite the log file if it already exists, erasing any older log entries. If you'd like to keep old logs around, use the `--logappend` option in addition to `--logpath` (highly recommended).

`--directoryperdb`

Put each database in its own directory. This allows you to mount different databases on different disks, if necessary or desired. Common uses for this are putting a local database on its own disk (replication) or moving a database to a different disk if the original one fills up. You could also put databases that handle more load on faster disks and databases with a lower load on slower disks. This basically gives you more flexibility to move things around later.

`--config`

Use a configuration file for additional options not specified on the command line. This is typically used to make sure options are the same between restarts. See "File-Based Configuration" on page 419 for details.

For example, to start the server as a daemon listening on port 5586 and sending all output to *mongodb.log*, we could run this:

```
$ ./mongod --dbpath data/db --port 5586 --fork --logpath
    mongodb.log --logappend 2019-09-06T22:52:25.376-0500 I CONTROL [main]
```

```
Automatically disabling TLS 1.0, \ to force-enable TLS 1.0 specify
--sslDisabledProtocols 'none' about to fork child process, waiting until
server is ready for connections. forked process: 27610 child process
started successfully, parent exiting
```

When you first install and start MongoDB, it is a good idea to look at the log. This might be an easy thing to miss, especially if MongoDB is being started from an init script, but the log often contains important warnings that prevent later errors from occurring. If you don't see any warnings in the MongoDB log on startup, then you are all set. (Startup warnings will also appear on shell startup.)

If there are any warnings in the startup banner, take note of them. MongoDB will warn you about a variety of issues: that you're running on a 32-bit machine (which MongoDB is not designed for), that you have NUMA enabled (which can slow your application to a crawl), or that your system does not allow enough open file descriptors (MongoDB uses a lot of file descriptors).

The log preamble won't change when you restart the database, so feel free to run MongoDB from an init script and ignore the logs, once you know what they say. However, it's a good idea to check again each time you do an install, upgrade, or recover from a crash, just to make sure MongoDB and your system are on the same page.

When you start the database, MongoDB will write a document to the *local.startup_log* collection that describes the version of MongoDB, underlying system, and flags used. We can look at this document using the *mongo* shell:

```
> use local
switched to db local
> db.startup_log.find().sort({startTime: -1}).limit(1).pretty()
{
    "_id" : "server1-1544192927184",
    "hostname" : "server1.example.net",
    "startTime" : ISODate("2019-09-06T22:50:47Z"),
    "startTimeLocal" : "Fri Sep  6 22:57:47.184",
    "cmdLine" : {
        "net" : {
            "port" : 5586
        },
        "processManagement" : {
            "fork" : true
        },
        "storage" : {
            "dbPath" : "data/db"
        },
        "systemLog" : {
            "destination" : "file",
            "logAppend" : true,
            "path" : "mongodb.log"
        }
```

```
        },
        "pid" : NumberLong(27278),
        "buildinfo" : {
            "version" : "4.2.0",
            "gitVersion" : "a4b751dcf51dd249c5865812b390cfd1c0129c30",
            "modules" : [
                "enterprise"
            ],
            "allocator" : "system",
            "javascriptEngine" : "mozjs",
            "sysInfo" : "deprecated",
            "versionArray" : [
                4,
                2,
                0,
                0
            ],
            "openssl" : {
                "running" : "Apple Secure Transport"
            },
            "buildEnvironment" : {
                "distmod" : "",
                "distarch" : "x86_64",
                "cc" : "gcc: Apple LLVM version 8.1.0 (clang-802.0.42)",
                "ccflags" : "-mmacosx-version-min=10.10 -fno-omit\
                            -frame-pointer -fno-strict-aliasing \
                            -ggdb -pthread -Wall
                            -Wsign-compare -Wno-unknown-pragmas \
                            -Winvalid-pch -Werror -O2 -Wno-unused\
                            -local-typedefs -Wno-unused-function
                            -Wno-unused-private-field \
                            -Wno-deprecated-declarations \
                            -Wno-tautological-constant-out-of\
                            -range-compare
                            -Wno-unused-const-variable -Wno\
                            -missing-braces -Wno-inconsistent\
                            -missing-override
                            -Wno-potentially-evaluated-expression \
                            -Wno-exceptions -fstack-protector\
                            -strong -fno-builtin-memcmp",
                "cxx" : "g++: Apple LLVM version 8.1.0 (clang-802.0.42)",
                "cxxflags" : "-Woverloaded-virtual -Werror=unused-result \
                            -Wpessimizing-move -Wredundant-move \
                            -Wno-undefined-var-template -stdlib=libc++ \
                            -std=c++14",
                "linkflags" : "-mmacosx-version-min=10.10 -Wl, \
                            -bind_at_load -Wl,-fatal_warnings \
                            -fstack-protector-strong \
                            -stdlib=libc++",
                "target_arch" : "x86_64",
                "target_os" : "macOS"
            },
```

```
        "bits" : 64,
        "debug" : false,
        "maxBsonObjectSize" : 16777216,
        "storageEngines" : [
            "biggie",
            "devnull",
            "ephemeralForTest",
            "inMemory",
            "queryable_wt",
            "wiredTiger"
        ]
    }
}
```

This collection can be useful for tracking upgrades and changes in behavior.

File-Based Configuration

MongoDB supports reading configuration information from a file. This can be useful if you have a large set of options you want to use or are automating the task of starting up MongoDB. To tell the server to get options from a configuration file, use the -f or --config flags. For example, run mongod --config ~/.mongodb.conf to use ~/.mongodb.conf as a configuration file.

The options supported in a configuration file are the same as those accepted at the command line. However, the format is different. As of MongoDB 2.6, MongoDB configuration files use the YAML format. Here's an example configuration file:

```
systemLog:
    destination: file
    path: "mongod.log"
    logAppend: true
storage:
    dbPath: data/db
processManagement:
    fork: true
net:
    port: 5586
...
```

This configuration file specifies the same options we used earlier when starting with regular command-line arguments. Note that these same options are reflected in the *startup_log* collection document we looked at in the previous section. The only real difference is that the options are specified using JSON rather than YAML.

In MongoDB 4.2, expansion directives were added to allow the loading of specific configuration file options or loading of the entire configuration file. The advantage of expansion directives is that confidential information, such as passwords and security certificates, does not have to be stored in the config file directly. The --configExpand command-line option enables this feature and must include the expansion directives you wish to enable. __rest and __exec are the current implementation of the expansion directives in MongoDB. The __rest expansion directive loads specific configuration file values or loads the entire configuration file from a REST endpoint. The __exec expansion directive loads specific configuration file values or loads the entire configuration file from a shell or terminal command.

Stopping MongoDB

Being able to safely stop a running MongoDB server is at least as important as being able to start one. There are a couple of different options for doing this effectively.

The cleanest way to shut down a running server is to use the shutdown command, {"shutdown" : 1}. This is an admin command and must be run on the *admin* database. The shell features a helper function to make this easier:

```
> use admin
switched to db admin
> db.shutdownServer()
server should be down...
```

When run on a primary, the shutdown command steps down the primary and waits for a secondary to catch up before shutting down the server. This minimizes the chance of rollback, but the shutdown isn't guaranteed to succeed. If there is no secondary available that can catch up within a few seconds, the shutdown command will fail and the (former) primary will not shut down:

```
> db.shutdownServer()
{
    "closest" : NumberLong(1349465327),
    "difference" : NumberLong(20),
    "errmsg" : "no secondaries within 10 seconds of my optime",
    "ok" : 0
}
```

You can force the shutdown command to shut down a primary by using the force option:

```
db.adminCommand({"shutdown" : 1, "force" : true})
```

This is equivalent to sending a SIGINT or SIGTERM signal (all three of these options result in a clean shutdown, but there may be unreplicated data). If the server is running as the foreground process in a terminal, a SIGINT can be sent by pressing Ctrl-C. Otherwise, a command like kill can be used to send the signal. If *mongod* had 10014 as its PID, the command would be kill -2 10014 (SIGINT) or kill 10014 (SIGTERM).

When *mongod* receives a SIGINT or SIGTERM, it will do a clean shutdown. This means it will wait for any running operations or file preallocations to finish (this could take a moment), close all open connections, flush all data to disk, and halt.

Security

Do not set up publicly addressable MongoDB servers. You should restrict access as tightly as possible between the outside world and MongoDB. The best way to do this is to set up firewalls and only allow MongoDB to be reachable on internal network addresses. Chapter 24 covers what connections it's necessary to allow between MongoDB servers and clients.

Beyond firewalls, there are a few options you can add to your config file to make it more secure:

--bind_ip
Specify the interfaces that you want MongoDB to listen on. Generally you want this to be an internal IP: something application servers and other members of your cluster can access but that is inaccessible to the outside world. *localhost* is fine for *mongos* processes if you're running the application server on the same machine. For config servers and shards, they'll need to be addressable from other machines, so stick with non-*localhost* addresses.

Starting in MongoDB 3.6, *mongod* and *mongos* processes bind to *localhost* by default. When bound only to *localhost*, *mongod* and *mongos* will only accept connections from clients running on the same machine. This helps limit the exposure of unsecured MongoDB instances. To bind to other addresses, use the net.bindIp configuration file setting or the --bind_ip command-line option to specify a list of hostnames or IP addresses.

--nounixsocket
Disable listening on the UNIX domain socket. If you're not planning to connect via filesystem socket, you might as well disallow it. You would only connect via filesystem socket on a machine that is also running an application server: you must be local to use a filesystem socket.

--noscripting
Disable server-side JavaScript execution. Some security issues that have been reported with MongoDB have been JavaScript-related, so it's generally safer to disallow it, if your application allows.

Several shell helpers assume that JavaScript is available on the server, notably sh.status(). You will see errors if you attempt to run any of these helpers with JavaScript disabled.

Data Encryption

Data encryption is available in MongoDB Enterprise. These options are not supported in the Community version of MongoDB.

The data encryption process includes the following steps:

- Generate a master key.
- Generate keys for each database.
- Encrypt data with the database keys.
- Encrypt the database keys with the master key.

When using data encryption, all data files are encrypted in the filesystem. Data is only unencrypted in memory and during transmission. To encrypt all of MongoDB's network traffic, you can use TLS/SSL. The data encryption options that MongoDB Enterprise users can add to their config files are:

--enableEncryption

Enables encryption in the WiredTiger storage engine. With this option, data stored in memory and on disk will be encrypted. This is sometimes referred to as "encryption at rest." You must set this to true in order to pass in encryption keys and to configure encryption. This option is false by default.

--encryptionCipherMode

Set the cipher mode for encryption at rest in WiredTiger. There are two modes available: AES256-CBC and AES256-GCM. AES256-CBC is an acronym for 256-bit Advanced Encryption Standard in Cipher Block Chaining Mode. AES256-GCM uses Galois/Counter Mode. Both are standard encryption ciphers. As of MongoDB 4.0, MongoDB Enterprise on Windows no longer supports AES256-GCM.

--encryptionKeyFile

Specify the path to the local keyfile if you are managing keys using a process other than the Key Management Interoperability Protocol (KMIP).

MongoDB Enterprise also supports key management using KMIP. A discussion of KMIP is beyond the scope of this book. Please see the MongoDB documentation for details on using KMIP with MongoDB (*https://oreil.ly/TeA4t*).

SSL Connections

As we saw in Chapter 18, MongoDB supports transport encryption using TLS/SSL. This feature is available in all editions of MongoDB. By default, connections to MongoDB transfer data unencrypted. However, TLS/SSL ensures transport encryption. MongoDB uses native TSL/SSL libraries available on your operating system. Use the option `--tlsMode` and related options to configure TLS/SSL. Refer to Chapter 18 for more detail, and consult your driver's documentation on how to create TLS/SSL connections using your language.

Logging

By default, *mongod* sends its logs to stdout. Most init scripts use the `--logpath` option to send logs to a file. If you have multiple MongoDB instances on a single machine (say, a *mongod* and a *mongos*), make sure that their logs are stored in separate files. Be sure that you know where the logs are and have read access to the files.

MongoDB spits out a lot of log messages, but please do not run with the `--quiet` option (which suppresses some of them). Leaving the log level at the default is usually perfect: there is enough information for basic debugging (why is this slow, why isn't this starting up, etc.), but the logs do not take up too much space.

If you are debugging a specific issue with your application, there are a couple of options for getting more information from the logs. You can change the log level by running the `setParameter` command, or by setting the log level at startup time by passing it as a string using the `--setParameter` option.

```
> db.adminCommand({"setParameter" : 1, "logLevel" : 3})
```

You can also change the log level for a particular component. This is helpful if you are debugging a specific aspect of your application and require more information, but only from that component. In this example, we set the default log verbosity to 1 and the query component verbosity to 2:

```
> db.adminCommand({"setParameter" : 1, logComponentVerbosity:
        { verbosity: 1, query: { verbosity: 2 }}})
```

Remember to turn the log level back down to 0 when you're done debugging, or your logs may be needlessly noisy. You can turn the level all the way up to 5, at which point mongod will print out almost every action it takes, including the contents of every request handled. This can cause a lot of I/O as *mongod* writes everything to the log file, which can slow down a busy system. Turning on profiling is a better option if you need to see every operation as it's happening.

By default, MongoDB logs information about queries that take longer than 100 ms to run. If 100 ms is too short or too long for your application, you can change the threshold with `setProfilingLevel`:

```
> // Only log queries that take longer than 500 ms
> db.setProfilingLevel(1, 500)
{ "was" : 0, "slowms" : 100, "ok" : 1 }
> db.setProfilingLevel(0)
{ "was" : 1, "slowms" : 500, "ok" : 1 }
```

The second line will turn off profiling, but the value in milliseconds given in the first line will continue to be used as a threshold for the log (across all databases). You can also set this parameter by restarting MongoDB with the `--slowms` option.

Finally, set up a cron job that rotates your log every day or week. If MongoDB was started with `--logpath`, sending the process a SIGUSR1 signal will make it rotate the log. There is also a `logRotate` command that does the same thing:

```
> db.adminCommand({"logRotate" : 1})
```

You cannot rotate logs if MongoDB was not started with `--logpath`.

## CHAPTER 22

Monitoring MongoDB

Before you deploy, it is important to set up some type of monitoring. Monitoring should allow you to track what your server is doing and alert you if something goes wrong. This chapter will cover:

- How to track MongoDB's memory usage
- How to track application performance metrics
- How to diagnose replication issues

We'll use example graphs from MongoDB Ops Manager to demonstrate what to look for when monitoring (see installation instructions for Ops Manager (*https://oreil.ly/ D4751*)). The monitoring capabilities of MongoDB Atlas (MongoDB's cloud database service) are very similar. MongoDB also offers a free monitoring service that monitors standalones and replica sets. It keeps the monitoring data for 24 hours after it has been uploaded and provides coarse-grained statistics on operation execution times, memory usage, CPU usage, and operation counts.

If you do not want to use Ops Manager, Atlas, or MongoDB's free monitoring service, please use some type of monitoring. It will help you detect potential issues before they cause problems and diagnose issues when they occur.

Monitoring Memory Usage

Accessing data in memory is fast, and accessing data on disk is slow. Unfortunately, memory is expensive (and disk is cheap), and typically MongoDB uses up memory before any other resource. This section covers how to monitor MongoDB's interactions with the CPU, disk, and memory, and what to watch for.

Introduction to Computer Memory

Computers tend to have a small amount of fast-to-access memory and a large amount of slow-to-access disk. When you request a page of data that is stored on disk (and not yet in memory), your system page faults and copies the page from disk into memory. It can then access the page in memory extremely quickly. If your program stops regularly using the page and your memory fills up with other pages, the old page will be evicted from memory and only live on disk again.

Copying a page from disk into memory takes a lot longer than reading a page from memory. Thus, the less MongoDB has to copy data from disk, the better. If MongoDB can operate almost entirely in memory, it will be able to access data much faster. Thus, MongoDB's memory usage is one of the most important stats to track.

Tracking Memory Usage

MongoDB reports on three "types" of memory in Ops Manager: resident memory, virtual memory, and mapped memory. Resident memory is the memory that MongoDB explicitly owns in RAM. For example, if you query for a document and it is paged into memory, that page is added to MongoDB's resident memory.

MongoDB is given an address for that page. This address isn't the literal address of the page in RAM; it's a virtual address. MongoDB can pass it to the kernel and the kernel will look up where the page really lives. This way, if the kernel needs to evict the page from memory, MongoDB can still use the address to access it. MongoDB will request the memory from the kernel, the kernel will look at its page cache, see that the page is not there, page fault to copy the page into memory, and return it to MongoDB.

If your data fits entirely in memory, the resident memory should be approximately the size of your data. When we talk about data being "in memory," we're always talking about the data being in RAM.

MongoDB's mapped memory includes all of the data MongoDB has ever accessed (all the pages of data it has addresses for). It will usually be about the size of your dataset.

Virtual memory is an abstraction provided by the operating system that hides the physical storage details from the software process. Each process sees a contiguous address space of memory that it can use. In Ops Manager, the virtual memory use of MongoDB is typically twice the size of the mapped memory.

Figure 22-1 shows the Ops Manager graph for memory information, which describes how much virtual, resident, and mapped memory MongoDB is using. Mapped memory is relevant only for older (pre-4.0) deployments using the MMAP storage engine. Now that MongoDB uses the WiredTiger storage engine, you should see zero usage for mapped memory. On a machine dedicated to MongoDB, resident memory should be a little less than the total memory size (assuming your working set is as large or larger than memory). Resident memory is the statistic that actually tracks how much data is in physical RAM, but by itself this does not tell you much about how MongoDB is using memory.

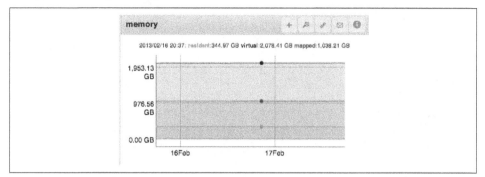

Figure 22-1. From the top line to the bottom: virtual, resident, and mapped memory

If your data fits entirely in memory, resident should be approximately the size of your data. When we talk about data being "in memory," we're always talking about the data being in RAM.

As you can see from Figure 22-1, memory metrics tend to be fairly steady, but as your dataset grows virtual memory (top line) will grow with it. Resident memory (middle line) will grow to the size of your available RAM and then hold steady.

Tracking Page Faults

You can use other statistics to find out how MongoDB is using memory, not just how much of each type it has. One useful stat is the number of page faults, which tells you how often the data MongoDB is looking for is not in RAM. Figures 22-2 and 22-3 are graphs that show page faults over time. Figure 22-3 is page faulting less than Figure 22-2, but by itself this information is not very useful. If the disk in Figure 22-2 can handle that many faults and the application can handle the delay of the disk seeks, there is no particular problem with having so many faults (or more). On the other hand, if your application cannot handle the increased latency of reading data from disk, you have no choice but to store all of your data in memory (or use SSDs).

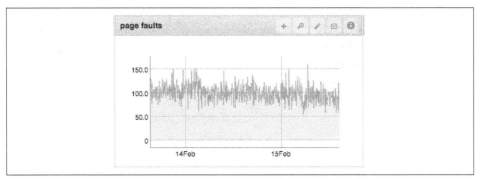

Figure 22-2. A system that is page faulting hundreds of times a minute

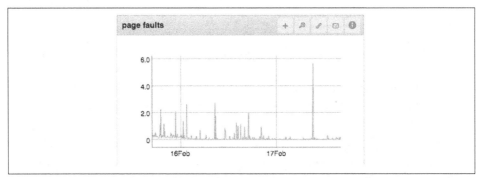

Figure 22-3. A system that is page faulting a few times a minute

Regardless of how forgiving the application is, page faults become a problem when the disk is overloaded. The amount of load a disk can handle isn't linear: once a disk begins getting overloaded, each operation must queue for a longer and longer period of time, creating a chain reaction. There is usually a tipping point where disk performance begins degrading quickly. Thus, it is a good idea to stay away from the maximum load that your disk can handle.

> Track your page fault numbers over time. If your application is behaving well with a certain number of page faults, you have a baseline for how many page faults the system can handle. If page faults begin to creep up and performance deteriorates, you have a threshold to alert on.

You can see page fault stats per database by looking at the `"page_faults"` field of `serverStatus`'s output:

```
> db.adminCommand({"serverStatus": 1})["extra_info"]
{ "note" : "fields vary by platform", "page_faults" : 50 }
```

`"page_faults"` gives you a count of how many times MongoDB has had to go to disk (since startup).

I/O Wait

Page faults in general are closely tied to how long the CPU is idling waiting for the disk, called I/O wait. Some I/O wait is normal; MongoDB has to go to disk sometimes, and although it tries not to block anything when it does, it cannot completely avoid it. The important thing is that I/O wait is not increasing or near 100%, as shown in Figure 22-4. This indicates that the disk is getting overloaded.

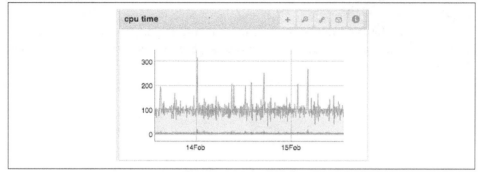

Figure 22-4. I/O wait hovering around 100%

Calculating the Working Set

In general, the more data you have in memory, the faster MongoDB will perform. Thus, in order from fastest to slowest, an application could have:

1. The entire dataset in memory. This is nice to have but is often too expensive or infeasible. It may be necessary for applications that depend on fast response times.

2. The working set in memory. This is the most common choice.

   Your working set is the data and indexes that your application uses. This may be everything, but generally there's a core dataset (e.g., the *users* collection and the last month of activity) that covers 90% of requests. If this working set fits in RAM, MongoDB will generally be fast: it only has to go to disk for a few "unusual" requests.

3. The indexes in memory.

4. The working set of indexes in memory.

5. No useful subset of data in memory. If possible, avoid this. It will be slow.

You must know what your working set is (and how large it is) to know if you can keep it in memory. The best way to calculate the size of the working set is to track common operations to find out how much your application is reading and writing. For example, suppose your application creates 2 GB of new data per week and 800 MB of that data is regularly accessed. Users tend to access data up to a month old, and data that's older than that is mostly unused. Your working set size is probably about 3.2 GB (800 MB/week × 4 weeks), plus a fudge factor for indexes, so call it 5 GB.

One way to think about this is to track data accessed over time, as shown in Figure 22-5. If you choose a cutoff where 90% of your requests fall, like in Figure 22-6, then the data (and indexes) generated in that period of time form your working set. You can measure for that amount of time to figure out how much your dataset grows. Note that this example uses time, but it's possible that there's another access pattern that makes more sense for your application (time being the most common one).

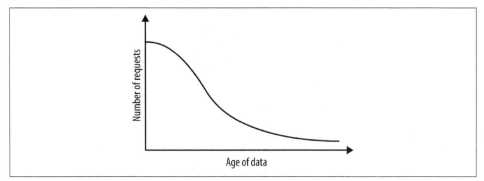

Figure 22-5. A plot of data accesses by age of data

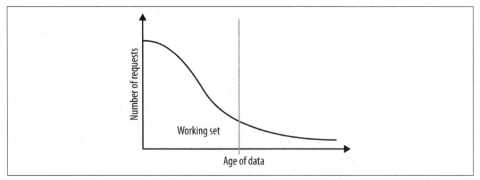

Figure 22-6. The working set is data used in the requests before the cutoff of "frequent requests" (indicated by the vertical line in the graph)

Some Working Set Examples

Suppose that you have a 40 GB working set. A total of 90% of requests hit the working set, and 10% hit other data. If you have 500 GB of data and 50 GB of RAM, your working set fits entirely in RAM. Once your application has accessed the data it usually accesses (a process called *preheating*), it should never have to go to disk again for the working set. It then has 10 GB of space available for the 460 GB of less-frequently-accessed data. Obviously, MongoDB will almost always have to go to disk for the non-working set data.

On the other hand, suppose your working set does not fit in RAM—say, if you have only 35 GB of RAM. Then the working set will generally take up most of the RAM. The working set has a higher probability of staying in RAM because it's accessed more frequently, but at some point the less-frequently-accessed data will have to be paged in, evicting the working set (or other less-frequently-accessed data). Thus, there is a constant churn back and forth from disk: accessing the working set does not have predictable performance anymore.

Tracking Performance

Performance of queries is often important to track and keep consistent. There are several ways to track if MongoDB is having trouble with the current request load.

CPU can be I/O bound with MongoDB (indicated by a high I/O wait). The WiredTiger storage engine is multithreaded and can take advantage of additional CPU cores. This can be seen in a higher level of usage across CPU metrics when compared with the older MMAP storage engine. However, if user or system time is approaching 100% (or 100% multiplied by the number of CPUs you have), the most common cause is that you're missing an index on a frequently used query. It is a good idea to track CPU usage (particularly after deploying a new version of your application) to ensure that all your queries are behaving as they should.

Note that the graph shown in Figure 22-7 is fine: if there is a low number of page faults, I/O wait may be dwarfed by other CPU activities. It is only when the other activities creep up that bad indexes may be a culprit.

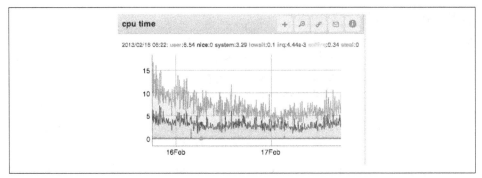

Figure 22-7. A CPU with minimal I/O wait: the top line is user and the lower line is system; the other stats are very close to 0%

A similar metric is queuing: how many requests are waiting to be processed by MongoDB. A request is considered queued when it is waiting for the lock it needs to do a read or a write. Figure 22-8 shows a graph of read and write queues over time. No queues are preferred (basically an empty graph), but this graph is nothing to be alarmed about. In a busy system, it isn't unusual for an operation to have to wait a bit for the correct lock to be available.

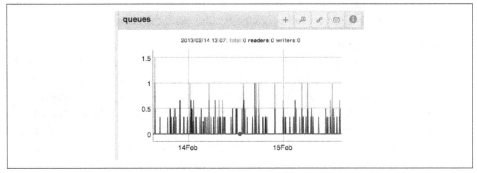

Figure 22-8. Read and write queues over time

The WiredTiger storage engine provides document-level concurrency, which allows for multiple simultaneous writes to the same collection. This has drastically improved the performance of concurrent operations. The ticketing system used controls the number of threads in use to avoid starvation: it issues tickets for read and write operations (128 of each, by default), after which point new read or write operations will queue. The `wiredTiger.concurrentTransactions.read.available` and `wiredTiger.concurrentTransactions.write.available` fields of `serverStatus` can be used to track when the number of available tickets reaches zero, indicating the respective operations are now queuing up.

You can see if requests are piling up by looking at the number of requests enqueued. Generally, the queue size should be low. A large and ever-present queue is an indication that *mongod* cannot keep up with its load. You should decrease the load on that server as fast as possible.

Tracking Free Space

One other metric that is basic but important to monitor is disk usage. Sometimes users wait until their disk runs out of space before they think about how they want to handle it. By monitoring your disk usage and tracking free disk space, you can predict how long your current drive will be sufficient and plan in advance what to do when it is not.

As you run out of space, there are several options:

- If you are using sharding, add another shard.
- If you have unused indexes, remove them. These can be identified using the aggregation $indexStats for a specific collection.
- If you have not run a compaction operation, then do so on a secondary to see if it assists. This is normally only useful in cases where a large amount of data or indexes have been removed from a collection and will not be replaced.
- Shut down each member of the replica set (one at a time) and copy its data to a larger disk, which can then be mounted. Restart the member and proceed to the next.
- Replace members of your replica set with members with a larger drive: remove an old member and add a new member, and allow that one to catch up with the rest of the set. Repeat for each member of the set.
- If you are using the directoryperdb option and you have a particularly fast-growing database, move it to its own drive. Then mount the volume as a directory in your data directory. This way the rest of your data doesn't have to be moved.

Regardless of the technique you choose, plan ahead to minimize the impact on your application. You need time to take backups, modify each member of your set in turn, and copy your data from place to place.

Monitoring Replication

Replication lag and oplog length are important metrics to track. Lag is when the secondaries cannot keep up with the primary. It's calculated by subtracting the time of the last op applied on a secondary from the time of the last op on the primary. For example, if a secondary just applied an op with the timestamp 3:26:00 p.m. and the primary just applied an op with the timestamp 3:29:45 p.m., the secondary is lagging by 3 minutes and 45 seconds. You want lag to be as close to 0 as possible, and it is generally on the order of milliseconds. If a secondary is keeping up with the primary, the replication lag should look something like the graph shown in Figure 22-9: basically 0 all the time.

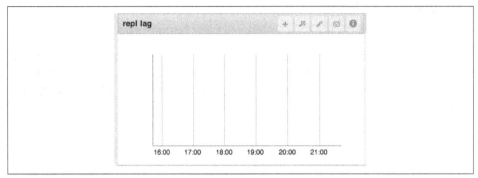

Figure 22-9. A replica set with no lag; this is what you want to see

If a secondary cannot replicate writes as fast as the primary can write, you'll start seeing a nonzero lag. The most extreme case of this is when replication is stuck: the secondary cannot apply any more operations for some reason. At this point, lag will grow by one second per second, creating the steep slope shown in Figure 22-10. This could be caused by network issues or a missing "_id" index, which is required on every collection for replication to function properly.

 If a collection is missing an "_id" index, take the server out of the replica set, start it as a standalone server, and build the "_id" index. Make sure you create the "_id" index as a *unique* index. Once created, the "_id" index cannot be dropped or changed (other than by dropping the whole collection).

If a system is overloaded, a secondary may gradually fall behind. Some replication will still be happening, so you generally won't see the characteristic "one second per second" slope in the graph. Still, it's important to be aware if the secondaries cannot keep up with peak traffic or are gradually falling further behind.

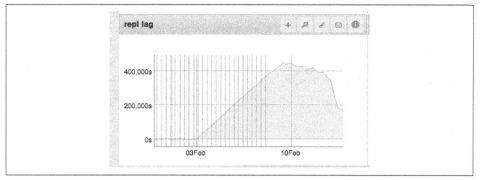

Figure 22-10. Replication getting stuck and, just before February 10, beginning to recover; the vertical lines are server restarts

Primaries do not throttle writes to "help" secondaries catch up, so it's common for secondaries to fall behind on overloaded systems (particularly as MongoDB tends to prioritize writes over reads, which means replication can be starved on the primary). You can force throttling of the primary to some extent by using "w" with your write concern. You also might want to try removing load from the secondary by routing any requests it was handling to another member.

If you are on an extremely *underloaded* system, you may see another interesting pattern: sudden spikes in replication lag, as shown in Figure 22-11. The spikes shown are not actually lag—they are caused by variations in sampling. The *mongod* is processing one write every couple of minutes. Because lag is measured as the difference between timestamps on the primary and secondary, measuring the timestamp of the secondary right before a write on the primary makes it look minutes behind. If you increase the write rate, these spikes should disappear.

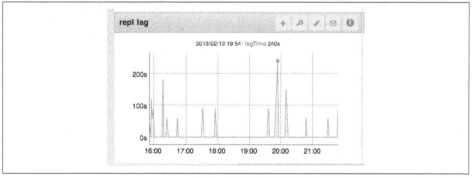

Figure 22-11. A low-write system can cause "phantom" lag

The other important replication metric to track is the length of each member's oplog. Every member that might become primary should have an oplog longer than a day. If a member may be a sync source for another member, it should have an oplog longer than the time an initial sync takes to complete. Figure 22-12 shows what a standard oplog-length graph looks like. This oplog has an excellent length: 1,111 hours is over a month of data! In general, oplogs should be as long as you can afford the disk space to make them. Given the way they're used, they take up basically no memory, and a long oplog can mean the difference between a painful ops experience and an easy one.

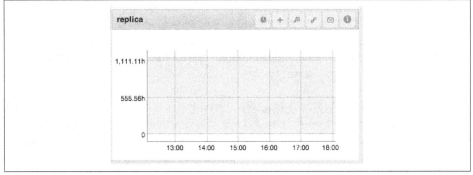

Figure 22-12. A typical oplog-length graph

Figure 22-13 shows a slightly unusual variation caused by a fairly short oplog and variable traffic. This is still healthy, but the oplog on this machine is probably too short (between 6 and 11 hours of maintenance). The administrator may want to make the oplog longer when they get a chance.

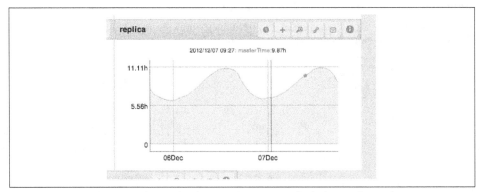

Figure 22-13. Oplog-length graph of an application with daily traffic peaks

## CHAPTER 23

Making Backups

It is important to make regular backups of your system. Backups are good protection against most types of failure, and very little can't be solved by restoring from a clean backup. This chapter covers the common options for making backups:

- Single-server backups, including snapshot backup and restore procedure
- Special considerations for backing up replica sets
- Baking up a sharded cluster

Backups are only useful if you are confident about deploying them in an emergency. Thus, for any backup technique you choose, be sure to practice both making backups and restoring from them until you are comfortable with the restore procedure.

Backup Methods

There are a number of options for backing up clusters in MongoDB. MongoDB Atlas, the official MongoDB cloud service, provides both continuous backups and cloud provider snapshots. Continuous backups take incremental backups of data in your cluster, ensuring your backups are typically just a few seconds behind the operating system. Cloud provider snapshots provide localized backup storage using the snapshot functionality of the cluster's cloud service provider (e.g., Amazon Web Services, Microsoft Azure, or Google Cloud Platform). The best backup solution for the majority of scenarios is continuous backups.

MongoDB also provides backup capability through Cloud Manager and Ops Manager. Cloud Manager is a hosted backup, monitoring, and automation service for MongoDB. Ops Manager is an on-premise solution that has similar functionality to Cloud Manager.

For individuals and teams managing MongoDB clusters directly, there are several backup strategies. We will outline these strategies in the rest of this chapter.

Backing Up a Server

There are a variety of ways to create backups. Regardless of the method, making a backup can cause strain on a system: it generally requires reading all your data into memory. Thus, backups should generally be done on replica set secondaries (as opposed to the primary) or, for standalone servers, at an off time.

The techniques in this section apply to any *mongod*, whether a standalone server or a member of a replica set, unless otherwise noted.

Filesystem Snapshot

Filesystem snapshots use system-level tools to create copies of the device that holds MongoDB's data files. These methods complete quickly and work reliably, but require additional system configuration outside of MongoDB.

MongoDB 3.2 added support for volume-level backup of MongoDB instances using the WiredTiger storage engine when those instances' data files and journal files reside on separate volumes. However, to create a coherent backup, the database must be locked and all writes to the database must be suspended during the backup process.

Prior to MongoDB 3.2, creating volume-level backups of MongoDB instances using WiredTiger required that the data files and journal reside on the same volume.

Snapshots work by creating pointers between the live data and a special snapshot volume. These pointers are theoretically equivalent to "hard links." As the working data diverges from the snapshot, the snapshot process uses a copy-on-write strategy. As a result, the snapshot only stores modified data.

After making the snapshot, you mount the snapshot image on your filesystem and copy data from the snapshot. The resulting backup contains a full copy of all data.

The database must be valid when the snapshot takes place. This means that all writes accepted by the database need to be fully written to disk: either to the journal or to data files. If there are writes that are not on disk when the backup occurs, the backup will not reflect these changes.

For the WiredTiger storage engine, the data files reflect a consistent state as of the last checkpoint. Checkpoints occur every minute.

Snapshots create an image of an entire disk or volume. Unless you need to back up your entire system, consider isolating your MongoDB data files, journal (if applicable), and configuration on one logical disk that doesn't contain any other data.

Alternatively, store all MongoDB data files on a dedicated device so that you can make backups without duplicating extraneous data.

Ensure that you copy data from snapshots onto other systems. This ensures that data is safe from site failures.

If your *mongod* instance has journaling enabled, then you can use any kind of filesystem or volume/block-level snapshot tool to create backups.

If you manage your own infrastructure on a Linux-based system, configure your system using the Linux Logical Volume Manager (LVM) to provide your disk packages and provide snapshot capability. LVM allows for the flexible combination and division of physical disk partitions, enabling dynamically resizable filesystems. You can also use LVM-based setups within a cloud/virtualized environment.

In the initial setup of LVM, first we assign disk partitions to physical volumes (pvcreate), then one or more of these are then assigned to a volume group (vgcreate), and then we create logical volumes (lvcreate) referring to the volume groups. We can build a filesystem on the logical volume (mkfs), which when created can be mounted for use (mount).

Snapshot backup and restore procedure

This section provides an overview of a simple backup process using LVM on a Linux system. While the tools, commands, and paths may be (slightly) different on your system, the following steps provide a high-level overview of the backup operation.

Only use the following procedure as a guideline for a backup system and infrastructure. Production backup systems must consider a number of application-specific requirements and factors unique to specific environments.

To create a snapshot with LVM, issue a command as root in the following format:

```
# lvcreate --size 100M --snapshot --name mdb-snap01 /dev/vg0/mongodb
```

This command creates an LVM snapshot (with the --snapshot option) named mdb-snap01 of the mongodb volume in the vg0 volume group, which will be located at /dev/vg0/mdb-snap01. The location and paths to your systems, volume groups, and devices may vary slightly depending on your operating system's LVM configuration.

The snapshot has a cap of 100 MB, because of the parameter --size 100M. This size does not reflect the total amount of the data on the disk, but rather the amount of differences between the current state of */dev/vg0/mongodb* and the snapshot (*/dev/vg0/mdb-snap01*).

The snapshot will exist when the command returns. You can restore directly from the snapshot at any time, or create a new logical volume and restore from the snapshot to the alternate image.

While snapshots are great for creating high-quality backups quickly, they are not ideal as a format for storing backup data. Snapshots typically depend and reside on the same storage infrastructure as the original disk images. Therefore, it's crucial that you archive these snapshots and store them elsewhere.

After creating a snapshot, mount the snapshot and copy the data to separate storage. Alternatively, take a block-level copy of the snapshot image, such as with the following procedure:

```
# umount /dev/vg0/mdb-snap01
# dd if=/dev/vg0/mdb-snap01 | gzip > mdb-snap01.gz
```

This command sequence does the following:

- Ensures that the */dev/vg0/mdb-snap01* device is not mounted
- Performs a block-level copy of the entire snapshot image using the dd command and compresses the result in a gzipped file in the current working directory

> The dd command will create a large *.gz* file in your current working directory. Make sure that you run *this command* in a filesystem that has enough free space.

To restore a snapshot created with LVM, issue the following sequence of commands:

```
# lvcreate --size 1G --name mdb-new vg0
# gzip -d -c mdb-snap01.gz | dd of=/dev/vg0/mdb-new
# mount /dev/vg0/mdb-new /srv/mongodb
```

This sequence does the following:

- Creates a new logical volume named *mdb-new*, in the */dev/vg0* volume group. The path to the new device will be */dev/vg0/mdb-new*. You can use a different name, and change 1G to your desired volume size.
- Uncompresses and unarchives the *mdb-snap01.gz* file into the *mdb-new* disk image.

- Mounts the *mdb-new* disk image to the */srv/mongodb* directory. Modify the mount point to correspond to your MongoDB data file location or other location as needed.

The restored snapshot will have a stale `mongod.lock` file. If you do not remove this file from the snapshot, MongoDB may assume that the stale lock file indicates an unclean shutdown. If you're running with `storage.journal.enabled` enabled and you do not use `db.fsyncLock()`, you do not need to remove the `mongod.lock` file. If you use `db.fsyncLock()` you will need to remove the lock.

To restore a backup without writing to a compressed *.gz* file, use the following sequence of commands:

```
# umount /dev/vg0/mdb-snap01
```

```
# lvcreate --size 1G --name mdb-new vg0
```

```
# dd if=/dev/vg0/mdb-snap01 of=/dev/vg0/mdb-new
```

```
# mount /dev/vg0/mdb-new /srv/mongodb
```

You can implement off-system backups using the combined process and SSH. This sequence is identical to procedures explained previously, except that it archives and compresses the backup on a remote system using SSH:

```
umount /dev/vg0/mdb-snap01
```

```
dd if=/dev/vg0/mdb-snap01 | ssh username@example.com gzip > /opt/backup/mdb-snap01.gz
```

```
lvcreate --size 1G --name mdb-new vg0
```

```
ssh username@example.com gzip -d -c /opt/backup/mdb-snap01.gz | dd of=/dev/vg0/mdb-new
```

```
mount /dev/vg0/mdb-new /srv/mongodb
```

Starting in MongoDB 3.2, for the purpose of volume-level backup of MongoDB instances using WiredTiger, the data files and the journal are no longer required to reside on a single volume. However, the database must be locked and all writes to the database must be suspended during the backup process to ensure the consistency of the backup.

If your *mongod* instance is either running without journaling or has the journal files on a separate volume, you must flush all writes to disk and lock the database to prevent writes during the backup process. If you have a replica set configuration, then for your backup use a secondary that is not receiving reads (i.e., a hidden member).

To do this, issue the db.fsyncLock() method in the mongo shell:

```
> db.fsyncLock();
```

Then perform the backup operation described previously.

After the snapshot completes, unlock the database by issuing the following command in the mongo shell:

```
> db.fsyncUnlock();
```

This process is described more fully in the following section.

Copying Data Files

Another way of creating single-server backups is to make a copy of everything in the data directory. Because you cannot copy all of the files at the same moment without filesystem support, you must prevent the data files from changing while you are making the copy. This can be accomplished with a command called fsyncLock:

```
> db.fsyncLock()
```

This command locks the database against any further writes and then flushes all dirty data to disk (fsync), ensuring that the files in the data directory have the latest consistent information and are not changing.

Once this command has been run, *mongod* will enqueue all incoming writes. It will not process any further writes until it has been unlocked. Note that this command stops writes to *all* databases (not just the one *db* is connected to).

Once the fsyncLock command returns, copy all of the files in your data directory to a backup location. On Linux, this can be done with a command such as:

```
$ cp -R /data/db/* /mnt/external-drive/backup
```

Make sure that you copy absolutely every file and folder from the data directory to the backup location. Excluding files or directories may make the backup unusable or corrupt.

Once you have finished copying the data, unlock the database to allow it to take writes again:

```
> db.fsyncUnlock()
```

Your database will begin handling writes again normally.

Note that there are some locking issues with authentication and fsyncLock. If you are using authentication, do not close the shell between calling fsyncLock and fsyncUnlock. If you disconnect, you may be unable to reconnect and have to restart mongod. The fsyncLock setting does not persist between restarts; mongod will always start up unlocked.

As an alternative to fsyncLock, you can instead shut down *mongod*, copy the files, and then start *mongod* back up again. Shutting down *mongod* effectively flushes all changes to disk and prevents new writes from occurring during the backup.

To restore from the copy of the data directory, ensure that *mongod* is not running and that the data directory you want to restore into is empty. Copy the backed-up data files to the data directory, and then start *mongod*. For example, the following command would restore the files backed up with the command shown earlier:

```
$ cp -R /mnt/external-drive/backup/* /data/db/
$ mongod -f mongod.conf
```

Despite the warnings about partial data directory copies, you can use this method to back up individual databases if you know what to copy and where they are using the --directoryperdb option. To back up an individual database (called, say, *myDB*), which is only available if you are using the --directoryperdb option, copy the entire *myDB* directory. Partial data directory copies are only possible with the --directoryperdb option.

You can restore specific databases by copying just the files with the correct database name into your data directory. You must be starting from a clean shutdown to restore piecemeal like this. If you had a crash or a hard shutdown, do not attempt to restore a single database from the backup: replace the entire directory and start the *mongod* to allow the journal files to be replayed.

 Never use fsyncLock in conjunction with *mongodump* (described next). Depending on what else your database is doing, *mongodump* may hang forever if the database is locked.

Using mongodump

The final way of making a single-server backup is to use *mongodump*. *mongodump* is mentioned last because it has some downsides. It is slower (both to get the backup and to restore from it) and it has some issues with replica sets, which are discussed in "Specific Considerations for Replica Sets" on page 446. However, it also has some benefits: it is a good way to back up individual databases, collections, and even subsets of collections.

mongodump has a variety of options that you can see by running mongodump --help. Here, we will focus on the most useful ones to use for backing up.

To back up all databases, simply run *mongodump*. If you are running *mongodump* on the same machine as the *mongod*, you can simply specify the port *mongod* is running on:

```
$ mongodump -p 31000
```

mongodump will create a *dump* directory in the current directory, which contains a dump of all your data. This *dump* directory is organized by database and by collection into folders and subfolders. The actual data is stored in *.bson* files, which merely contain every document in a collection in BSON, concatenated together. You can examine *.bson* files using the *bsondump* tool, which comes with MongoDB.

You do not even need to have a server running to use *mongodump*. You can use the --dbpath option to specify your data directory, and *mongodump* will use the data files to copy data:

```
$ mongodump --dbpath /data/db
```

You should not use --dbpath if *mongod* is running.

One issue with *mongodump* is that it is not an instantaneous backup: the system may be taking writes while the backup occurs. Thus, you might end up with a situation where user A begins a backup that causes *mongodump* to dump the database *A*, but while this is happening user B drops *A*. However, *mongodump* has already dumped it, so you'll end up with a snapshot of the data that is inconsistent with the state on the original server.

To avoid this, if you are running *mongod* with --replSet, you can use *mongodump*'s --oplog option. This will keep track of all operations that occur on the server while the dump is taking place, so these operations can be replayed when the backup is restored. This gives you a consistent point-in-time snapshot of data from the source server.

If you pass *mongodump* a replica set connection string (e.g., "*setName/ seed1,seed2,seed3*"), it will automatically select the primary to dump from. If you want to use a secondary, you can specify a read preference. The read preference can be specified by --uri connection string, by the uri readPreferenceTags option, or by the --readPreference command-line option. For more details on the various settings and options, please see the *mongodump* MongoDB documentation page (*https://oreil.ly/GH3-O*).

To restore from a *mongodump* backup, use the *mongorestore* tool:

```
$ mongorestore -p 31000 --oplogReplay dump/
```

If you used the --oplog option to dump the database, you must use the --oplogReplay option with *mongorestore* to get the point-in-time snapshot.

If you are replacing data on a running server, you may (or may not) wish to use the --drop option, which drops a collection before restoring it.

The behavior of *mongodump* and *mongorestore* has changed over time. To prevent compatibility issues, try to use the same version of both utilities (you can see their versions by running mongodump --version and mongorestore --version).

 From MongoDB version 4.2 and up, you cannot use either *mongo-dump* or *mongorestore* as a strategy for backing up a sharded cluster. These tools do not maintain the atomicity guarantees of transactions across shards.

Moving collections and databases with mongodump and mongorestore

You can restore into an entirely different database and collection than you dumped from. This can be useful if different environments use different database names (say, *dev* and *prod*) but the same collection names.

To restore a *.bson* file into a specific database and collection, specify the targets on the command line:

```
$ mongorestore --db newDb --collection someOtherColl dump/oldDB/oldColl.bson
```

It is also possible to use these tools with SSH to perform data migration without any disk I/O using the archive feature of these tools. This simplifies three stages into one operation, when previously you had to back up to disk, then copy those backup files to a target server, and then run *mongorestore* on that server to restore the backups:

```
$ ssh eoin@proxy.server.com mongodump --host source.server.com\ --archive
        | ssh eoin@target.server.com mongorestore --archive
```

Compression can be combined with the archive feature of these tools to further reduce the size of the information sent while performing a data migration. Here is the same SSH data migration example using both the archive and compression features of these tools:

```
$ ssh eoin@proxy.server.com mongodump --host source.server.com\ --archive
        --gzip | ssh eoin@target.server.com mongorestore --archive --gzip
```

Administrative complications with unique indexes

If you have a unique index (other than "_id") on any of your collections, you should consider using a different type of backup than *mongodump*/*mongorestore*. Unique indexes require that the data does not change in ways that would violate the unique index constraint during the copy. The safest way to ensure this is to choose a method that "freezes" the data, then make a backup as described in either of the previous two sections.

If you are determined to use *mongodump*/*mongorestore*, you may need to preprocess your data when you restore from a backup.

Specific Considerations for Replica Sets

The main additional consideration when backing up a replica set is that as well as the data, you must also capture the state of the replica set to ensure an accurate point-in-time snapshot of your deployment is made.

Generally, you should make backups from a secondary: this keeps load off of the primary, and you can lock a secondary without affecting your application (so long as your application isn't sending it read requests). You can use any of the three methods outlined previously to back up a replica set member, but a filesystem snapshot or data file copy is recommended. Either of these techniques can be applied to replica set secondaries with no modification.

mongodump is not quite as simple to use when replication is enabled. First, if you are using *mongodump*, you must take your backups using the --oplog option to get a point-in-time snapshot; otherwise the backup's state won't match the state of any other members in the cluster. You must also create an oplog when you restore from a *mongodump* backup, or the restored member will not know where it was synced to.

To restore a replica set member from a *mongodump* backup, start the target replica set member as a standalone server with an empty data directory and run *mongorestore* on it (as described in the previous section) with the --oplogReplay option. Now it should have a complete copy of the data, but it still needs an oplog. Create an oplog using the createCollection command:

```
> use local
> db.createCollection("oplog.rs", {"capped" : true, "size" : 10000000})
```

Specify the size of the collection in bytes. See "Resizing the Oplog" on page 282 for advice on oplog sizing.

Now you need to populate the oplog. The easiest way to do this is to restore the *oplog.bson* backup file from the dump into the *local.oplog.rs* collection:

```
$ mongorestore -d local -c oplog.rs dump/oplog.bson
```

Note that this is not a dump of the oplog itself (*dump/local/oplog.rs.bson*), but rather of the oplog operations that occurred during the dump. Once this *mongorestore* is complete, you can restart this server as a replica set member.

Specific Considerations for Sharded Clusters

The main additional consideration when backing up a sharded cluster using the approaches in this chapter is that you can only back up the pieces when they are active, and sharded clusters are impossible to "perfectly" back up while active: you can't get a snapshot of the entire state of the cluster at a point in time. However, this limitation is generally sidestepped by the fact that as your cluster gets bigger, it becomes less and less likely that you'd ever have to restore the whole thing from a backup. Thus, when dealing with a sharded cluster, we focus on backing up pieces: the config servers and the replica sets individually. If you need the ability to back up the whole cluster to a particular point in time or would prefer an automated solution, you can avail yourself of MongoDB's Cloud Manager or Atlas backup feature.

Turn off the balancer before performing any of these operations on a sharded cluster (either backup or restore). You cannot get a consistent snapshot of the world with chunks flying around. See "Balancing Data" on page 359 for instructions on turning the balancer on and off.

Backing Up and Restoring an Entire Cluster

When a cluster is very small or in development, you may want to actually dump and restore the entire thing. You can accomplish this by turning off the balancer and then running *mongodump* through the *mongos*. This creates a backup of all of the shards on whatever machine *mongodump* is running on.

To restore from this type of backup, run *mongorestore* connected to a *mongos*.

Alternatively, after turning off the balancer you can take filesystem or data directory backups of each shard and the config servers. However, you will inevitably get copies from each at slightly different times, which may or may not be a problem. Also, as soon as you turn on the balancer and a migrate occurs, some of the data you backed up from one shard will no longer be there.

Backing Up and Restoring a Single Shard

Most often, you'll only need to restore a single shard in a cluster. If you are not too picky, you can restore from a backup of that shard using one of the single-server methods just described.

There is one important issue to be aware of, however. Suppose you make a backup of your cluster on Monday. On Thursday, your disk melts down and you have to restore from the backup. In the intervening days, new chunks may have moved to this shard. Your backup of the shard from Monday will not contain these new chunks. You may be able to use a config server backup to figure out where the disappearing chunks lived on Monday, but it is a lot more difficult than simply restoring the shard. In most cases, restoring the shard and losing the data in those chunks is the preferable route.

You can connect directly to a shard to restore from a backup (instead of going through *mongos*).

## CHAPTER 24

Deploying MongoDB

This chapter gives recommendations for setting up a server to go into production. In particular, it covers:

- Choosing what hardware to buy and how to set it up
- Using virtualized environments
- Important kernel and disk I/O settings
- Network setup: who needs to connect to whom

Designing the System

You generally want to optimize for data safety and the quickest access you can afford. This section discusses the best way to accomplish these goals when choosing disks, RAID configuration, CPUs, and other hardware and low-level software components.

Choosing a Storage Medium

In order of preference, we would like to store and retrieve data from:

1. RAM
2. SSD
3. Spinning disk

Unfortunately, most people have limited budgets or enough data that storing everything in RAM is impractical and SSDs are too expensive. Thus, the typical deployment is a small amount of RAM (relative to total data size) and a lot of space on a spinning disk. If you are in this camp, the important thing is that your working set is smaller than RAM, and you should be ready to scale out if the working set gets bigger.

If you are able to spend what you like on hardware, buy a lot of RAM and/or SSDs.

Reading data from RAM takes a few nanoseconds (say, 100). Conversely, reading from disk takes a few milliseconds (say, 10). It can be hard to picture the difference between these two numbers, so let's scale them up to more relatable numbers: if accessing RAM took 1 second, accessing the disk would take over a day!

100 nanoseconds × 10,000,000 = 1 second

10 milliseconds × 10,000,000 = 1.16 days

These are very back-of-the-envelope calculations (your disk might be a bit faster or your RAM a bit slower), but the magnitude of this difference doesn't change much. Thus, we want to access the disk as seldom as possible.

Recommended RAID Configurations

RAID is hardware or software that lets you treat multiple disks as though they were a single disk. It can be used for reliability, performance, or both. A set of disks using RAID is referred to as a RAID array (somewhat redundantly, as RAID stands for redundant *array* of inexpensive disks).

There are a number of ways to configure RAID, depending on the features you're looking for—generally some combination of speed and fault tolerance. These are the most common varieties:

RAID0
> Striping disks for improved performance. Each disk holds part of the data, similar to MongoDB's sharding. Because there are multiple underlying disks, lots of data can be written to disk at the same time. This improves throughput on writes. However, if a disk fails and data is lost, there are no copies of it. It also can cause slow reads, as some data volumes may be slower than others.

RAID1
> Mirroring for improved reliability. An identical copy of the data is written to each member of the array. This has lower performance than RAID0, as a single member with a slow disk can slow down all writes. However, if a disk fails, you will still have a copy of the data on another member of the array.

RAID5
> Striping disks, plus keeping an extra piece of data about the other data that's been stored to prevent data loss on server failure. Basically, RAID5 can handle one

disk going down and hide that failure from the user. However, it is slower than any of the other varieties listed here because it needs to calculate this extra piece of information whenever data is written. This is particularly expensive with MongoDB, as a typical workload does many small writes.

RAID10

A combination of RAID0 and RAID1: data is striped for speed and mirrored for reliability.

We recommend using RAID10: it is safer than RAID0 and can smooth out performance issues that can occur with RAID1. However, some people feel that RAID1 on top of replica sets is overkill and opt for RAID0. It is a matter of personal preference: how much risk are you willing to trade for performance?

Do not use RAID5: it is very, very slow.

CPU

MongoDB historically was very light on CPU, but with the use of the WiredTiger storage engine this is no longer the case. The WiredTiger storage engine is multithreaded and can take advantage of additional CPU cores. You should therefore balance your investment between memory and CPU.

When choosing between speed and number of cores, go with speed. MongoDB is better at taking advantage of more cycles on a single processor than increased parallelization.

Operating System

64-bit Linux is the operating system MongoDB runs best on. If possible, use some flavor of that. CentOS and Red Hat Enterprise Linux are probably the most popular choices, but any flavor should work (Ubuntu and Amazon Linux are also common). Be sure to use the most recent stable version of the operating system, because old, buggy packages or kernels can sometimes cause issues.

64-bit Windows is also well supported.

Other flavors of Unix are not as well supported: proceed with caution if you're using Solaris or one of the BSD variants. Builds for these systems have, at least historically, had a lot of issues. MongoDB explicitly stopped supporting Solaris in August 2017, noting a lack of adoption among users.

One important note on cross-compatibility: MongoDB uses the same wire protocol and lays out data files identically on all systems, so you can deploy on a combination of operating systems. For example, you could have a *mongos* process running on Windows and the *mongod*s that are its shards running on Linux. You can also copy data files from Windows to Linux or vice versa with no compatibility issues.

Since version 3.4, MongoDB no longer supports 32-bit x86 platforms. Do not run any type of MongoDB server on a 32-bit machine.

MongoDB works with little-endian architectures and one big-endian architecture: IBM's zSeries. Most drivers support both little- and big-endian systems, so you can run clients on either. However, the server will typically be run on a little-endian machine.

Swap Space

You should allocate a small amount of swap in case memory limits are reached to prevent the kernel from killing MongoDB. It doesn't usually use any swap space, but in extreme circumstances the WiredTiger storage engine might use some. If this occurs, then you should consider increasing the memory capacity of your machine or reviewing your workload to avoid this problematic situation for performance and for stability.

The majority of memory MongoDB uses is "slippery": it'll be flushed to disk and replaced with other memory as soon as the system requests the space for something else. Therefore, database data should never be written to swap space: it'll be flushed back to disk first.

However, occasionally MongoDB will use swap for operations that require ordering data: either building indexes or sorting. It attempts not to use too much memory for these types of operations, but by performing many of them at the same time you may be able to force swapping.

If your application is managing to make MongoDB use swap space, you should look into redesigning the application or reducing load on the swapping server.

Filesystem

For Linux, only the XFS filesystem is recommended for your data volumes with the WiredTiger storage engine. It is possible to use the ext4 filesystem with WiredTiger, but be aware there are known performance issues (specifically, that it may stall on WiredTiger checkpoints).

On Windows, either NTFS or FAT is fine.

 Do not use Network File Storage (NFS) directly mounted for MongoDB storage. Some client versions lie about flushing, randomly remount and flush the page cache, and do not support exclusive file locking. Using NFS can cause journal corruption and should be avoided at all costs.

Virtualization

Virtualization is a great way to get cheap hardware and be able to expand fast. However, there are some downsides—particularly unpredictable network and disk I/O. This section covers virtualization-specific issues.

Memory Overcommitting

The memory overcommit Linux kernel setting controls what happens when processes request too much memory from the operating system. Depending on how it's set, the kernel may give memory to processes even if that memory is not actually available (in the hopes that it'll become available by the time the process needs it). That's called *overcommitting*: the kernel promises memory that isn't actually there. This operating system kernel setting does not work well with MongoDB.

The possible values for vm.overcommit_memory are 0 (the kernel guesses about how much to overcommit); 1 (memory allocation always succeeds); or 2 (don't commit more virtual address space than swap space plus a fraction of the overcommit ratio). The value 2 is complicated, but it's the best option available. To set this, run:

```
$ echo 2 > /proc/sys/vm/overcommit_memory
```

You do not need to restart MongoDB after changing this operating system setting.

Mystery Memory

Sometimes the virtualization layer does not handle memory provisioning correctly. Thus, you may have a virtual machine that claims to have 100 GB of RAM available but only ever allows you to access 60 GB of it. Conversely, we've seen people that were supposed to have 20 GB of memory end up being able to fit an entire 100 GB dataset into RAM!

Assuming you don't end up on the lucky side, there isn't much you can do. If your operating system readahead is set appropriately and your virtual machine just won't use all the memory it should, you may just have to switch virtual machines.

Handling Network Disk I/O Issues

One of the biggest problems with using virtualized hardware is that you are generally sharing a disk with other tenants, which exacerbates the disk slowness mentioned previously because everyone is competing for disk I/O. Thus, virtualized disks can have very unpredictable performance: they can work fine while your neighbors aren't busy and suddenly slow down to a crawl if someone else starts hammering the disks.

The other issue is that this storage is often not physically attached to the machine MongoDB is running on, so even when you have a disk all to yourself I/O will be slower than it would be with a local disk. There is also the unlikely-but-possible scenario of your MongoDB server losing its network connection to your data.

Amazon has what is probably the most widely used networked block store, called Elastic Block Store (EBS). EBS volumes can be connected to Elastic Compute Cloud (EC2) instances, allowing you to give a machine almost any amount of disk immediately. If you are using EC2, you should also enable AWS Enhanced Networking if it's available for the instance type, as well as disable the dynamic voltage and frequency scaling (DVFS) and CPU power-saving modes plus hyperthreading. On the plus side, EBS makes backups very easy (take a snapshot from a secondary, mount the EBS drive on another instance, and start up *mongod*). On the downside, you may encounter variable performance.

If you require more predictable performance, there are a couple of options. One is to host MongoDB on your own servers—that way, you know no one else is slowing things down. However, that's not an option for a lot of people, so the next best thing is to get an instance in the cloud that guarantees a certain number of I/O Operations Per Second (IOPS). See *http://docs.mongodb.org* for up-to-date recommendations on hosted offerings.

If you can't pursue either of these options and you need more disk I/O than an overloaded EBS volume can sustain, there is a way to hack around it. Basically, what you can do is keep monitoring the volume MongoDB is using. If and when that volume slows down, immediately kill that instance and bring up a new one with a different data volume.

There are a couple of statistics to watch for:

- Spiking I/O utilization ("IO wait" on Cloud Manager/Atlas), for obvious reasons.
- Page fault rates spiking. Note that changes in application behavior could also cause working set changes: you should disable this assassination script before deploying new versions of your application.
- The number of lost TCP packets going up (Amazon is particularly bad about this: when performance starts to fall, it drops TCP packets all over the place).
- MongoDB's read and write queues spiking (this can be seen in Cloud Manager/ Atlas or in *mongostat*'s qr/qw column).

If your load varies over the day or week, make sure your script takes that into account: you don't want a rogue cron job killing off all of your instances because of an unusually heavy Monday morning rush.

This hack relies on you having recent backups or relatively quick-to-sync datasets. If you have each instance holding terabytes of data, you might want to pursue an alternative approach. Also, this is only *likely* to work: if your new volume is also being hammered, it will be just as slow as the old one.

Using Non-Networked Disks

 This section uses Amazon-specific vocabulary. However, it may apply to other providers.

Ephemeral drives are the actual disks attached to the physical machine your VM is running on. They don't have a lot of the problems networked storage does. Local disks can still be overloaded by other users on the same box, but with a large box you can be reasonably sure you're not sharing disks with too many others. Even with a smaller instance, often an ephemeral drive will give better performance than a net-worked drive so long as the other tenants aren't doing tons of IOPS.

The downside is in the name: these disks are ephemeral. If your EC2 instance goes down, there's no guarantee you'll end up on the same box when you restart the instance, and then your data will be gone.

Thus, ephemeral drives should be used with care. You should make sure that you do not store any important or unreplicated data on these disks. In particular, do not put the journal on these ephemeral drives, or your database on network storage. In gen-eral, think of ephemeral drives as a slow cache rather than a fast disk and use them accordingly.

Configuring System Settings

There are several system settings that can help MongoDB run more smoothly, which are mostly related to disk and memory access. This section covers each of these options and how you should tweak them.

Turning Off NUMA

When machines had a single CPU, all RAM was basically the same in terms of access time. As machines started to have more processors, engineers realized that having all memory be equally far from each CPU (as shown in Figure 24-1) was less efficient than having each CPU have some memory that is especially close to it and fast for that particular CPU to access (Figure 24-2). This architecture, where each CPU has its own "local" memory, is called *nonuniform memory architecture* (NUMA).

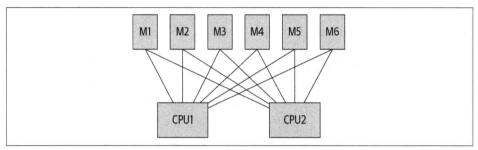

Figure 24-1. Uniform memory architecture: all memory has the same access cost for each CPU

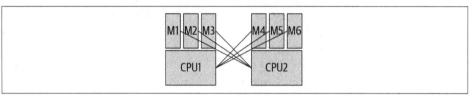

Figure 24-2. Nonuniform memory architecture: certain memory is attached to a CPU, giving the CPU faster access to that memory; CPUs can still access other CPUs' memory, but it is more expensive than accessing their own

For lots of applications, NUMA works well: the processors often need different data because they're running different programs. However, this works terribly for databases in general and MongoDB in particular because databases have such different memory access patterns than other types of applications. MongoDB uses a massive amount of memory and needs to be able to access memory that is "local" to other CPUs. However, the default NUMA settings on many systems make this difficult.

CPUs favor using the memory that is attached to them, and processes tend to favor one CPU over the others. This means that memory often fills up unevenly, potentially leaving you with one processor using 100% of its local memory and the other processors using only a fraction of their memory, as shown in Figure 24-3.

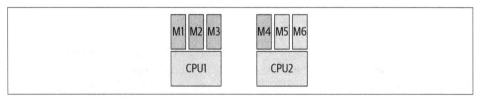

Figure 24-3. Sample memory usage in a NUMA system

In the scenario in Figure 24-3, suppose CPU1 needs some data that isn't in memory yet. It must use its local memory for data that doesn't have a "home" yet, but its local memory is full. Thus, it has to evict some of the data in its local memory to make room for the new data, even though there's plenty of space left in the memory attached to CPU2! This process tends to cause MongoDB to run much slower than expected, as it only has a fraction of the memory available that it should have. MongoDB vastly prefers semiefficient access to more data over extremely efficient access to less data.

When running MongoDB servers and clients on NUMA hardware, you should configure a memory interleave policy so that the host behaves in a non-NUMA fashion. MongoDB checks NUMA settings on startup when deployed on Linux and Windows machines. If the NUMA configuration may degrade performance, MongoDB prints a warning.

On Windows, memory interleaving must be enabled through the machine's BIOS. Consult your system documentation for details.

When running MongoDB on Linux, you should disable zone reclaim in the *sysctl* settings using one of the following commands:

```
echo 0 | sudo tee /proc/sys/vm/zone_reclaim_mode
    sudo sysctl -w vm.zone_reclaim_mode=0
```

Then, you should use *numactl* to start your *mongod* instances, including the config servers, *mongos* instances, and any clients. If you do not have the `numactl` command, refer to the documentation for your operating system to install the *numactl* package.

The following command demonstrates how to start a MongoDB instance using *numactl*:

```
    numactl --interleave=all <path> <options>
```

The `<path>` is the path to the program you are starting and the `<options>` are any optional arguments to pass to the program.

To fully disable NUMA behavior, you must perform both operations. For more information, see the documentation (*https://oreil.ly/cm-_D*).

Setting Readahead

Readahead is an optimization where the operating system reads more data from disk than was actually requested. This is useful because most workloads that computers handle are sequential: if you load the first 20 MB of a video, you are probably going to want the next couple of megabytes of it. Thus, the system will read more from disk than you actually request and store it in memory, just in case you need it soon.

For the WiredTiger storage engine, you should set readahead to between 8 and 32 regardless of the storage media type (spinning disk, SSD, etc.). Setting it higher benefits sequential I/O operations, but since MongoDB disk access patterns are typically random, a higher readahead value provides limited benefit and may even result in performance degradation. For most workloads, a readahead of between 8 and 32 provides optimal MongoDB performance.

In general, you should set the readahead within this range unless testing shows that a higher value is measurably, repeatably, and reliably beneficial. MongoDB Professional Support can provide advice and guidance on nonzero readahead configurations.

Disabling Transparent Huge Pages (THP)

THP causes similar issues to high readahead. Do not use this feature unless:

- All of your data fits into memory.
- You have no plans for it to ever grow beyond memory.

MongoDB needs to page in lots of tiny pieces of memory, so using THP can result in more disk I/O.

Systems move data from disk to memory and back by the page. Pages are generally a couple of kilobytes (x86 defaults to 4,096-byte pages). If a machine has many gigabytes of memory, keeping track of each of these (relatively tiny) pages can be slower than just tracking a few larger-granularity pages. THP is a solution that allows you to have pages that are up to 256 MB (on IA-64 architectures). However, using it means that you are keeping megabytes of data from one section of disk in memory. If your data does not fit in RAM, then swapping in larger pieces from disk will just fill up your memory quickly with data that will need to be swapped out again. Also, flushing any changes to disk will be slower, as the disk must write megabytes of "dirty" data, instead of a few kilobytes.

THP was actually developed to benefit databases, so this may be surprising to experienced database admins. However, MongoDB tends to do a lot less sequential disk access than relational databases do.

 On Windows these are called Large Pages, not Huge Pages. Some versions of Windows have this feature enabled by default and some do not, so check and make sure it is turned off.

Choosing a Disk Scheduling Algorithm

The disk controller receives requests from the operating system and processes them in an order determined by a scheduling algorithm. Sometimes changing this algorithm can improve disk performance. For other hardware and workloads, it may not make a difference. The best way to decide which algorithm to use is to test them out yourself on your workload. Deadline and completely fair queueing (CFQ) both tend to be good choices.

There are a couple of situations where the noop scheduler (a contraction of "no-op") is the best choice. If you're in a virtualized environment, use the noop scheduler. This scheduler basically passes the operations through to the underlying disk controller as quickly as possible. It is fastest to do this and let the real disk controller handle any reordering that needs to happen.

Similarly, on SSDs, the noop scheduler is generally the best choice. SSDs don't have the same locality issues that spinning disks do.

Finally, if you're using a RAID controller with caching, use noop. The cache behaves like an SSD and will take care of propagating the writes to the disk efficiently.

If you are on a physical server that is not virtualized, the operating system should use the deadline scheduler. The deadline scheduler caps maximum latency per request and maintains a reasonable disk throughput that is best for disk-intensive database applications.

You can change the scheduling algorithm by setting the `--elevator` option in your boot configuration.

The option is called "elevator" because the scheduler behaves like an elevator, picking up people (I/O requests) from different floors (processes/times) and dropping them off where they want to go in an arguabley optimal way.

Often all of the algorithms work pretty well; you may not see much of a difference between them.

Disabling Access Time Tracking

By default, the system tracks when files were last accessed. As the data files used by MongoDB are very high-traffic, you can get a performance boost by disabling this tracking. You can do this on Linux by changing `atime` to `noatime` in */etc/fstab*:

```
/dev/sda7 /data xfsf rw,noatime 1  2
```

You must remount the device for the changes to take effect.

`atime` is more of an issue on older kernels (e.g., ext3); newer ones use `relatime` as a default, which is less aggressively updated. Also, be aware that setting `noatime` can affect other programs using the partition, such as *mutt* or backup tools.

Similarly, on Windows you should set the `disablelastaccess` option. To turn off last access time recording, run:

```
C:\> fsutil behavior set disablelastaccess 1
```

You must reboot for this setting to take effect. Setting this may affect the remote storage service, but you probably shouldn't be using a service that automatically moves your data to other disks anyway.

Modifying Limits

There are two limits that MongoDB tends to blow by: the number of threads a process is allowed to spawn and the number of file descriptors a process is allowed to open. Both of these should generally be set to unlimited.

Whenever a MongoDB server accepts a connection, it spawns a thread to handle all activity on that connection. Therefore, if you have 3,000 connections to the database, the database will have 3,000 threads running (plus a few other threads for non-client-related tasks). Depending on your application server configuration, your client may spawn anywhere from a dozen to thousands of connections to MongoDB.

If your client will dynamically spawn more child processes as traffic increases (most application servers will do this), it is important to make sure that these child processes are not so numerous that they can max out MongoDB's limits. For example, if you have 20 application servers, each one of which is allowed to spawn 100 child processes, and each child process can spawn 10 threads that all connect to MongoDB, that could result in the spawning of $20 \times 100 \times 10 = 20{,}000$ connections at peak traffic. MongoDB is probably not going to be very happy about spawning tens of thousands of threads and, if you run out of threads per process, will simply start refusing new connections.

The other limit to modify is the number of file descriptors MongoDB is allowed to open. Every incoming and outgoing connection uses a file descriptor, so the client connection storm just mentioned would create 20,000 open filehandles.

mongos in particular tends to create connections to many shards. When a client connects to a *mongos* and makes a request, the *mongos* opens connections to any and all shards necessary to fulfill that request. Thus, if a cluster has 100 shards and a client connects to a *mongos* and tries to query for all of its data, the *mongos* must open 100 connections: one connection to each shard. This can quickly lead to an explosion in the number of connections, as you can imagine from the previous example. Suppose a liberally configured app server made a hundred connections to a *mongos* process. This could get translated to 100 inbound connections × 100 shards = 10,000 connections to shards! (This assumes a nontargeted query on each connection, which would be a bad design, so this is a somewhat extreme example.)

Thus, there are a few adjustments to make. Many people purposefully configure *mongos* processes to only allow a certain number of incoming connections by using the maxConns option. This is a good way to enforce that your client is behaving well.

You should also increase the limit on the number of file descriptors, as the default (generally 1,024) is simply too low. Set the max number of file descriptors to unlimited (*https://oreil.ly/oTGLL*) or, if you're nervous about that, 20,000. Each system has a different way of changing these limits, but in general, make sure that you change both the hard and soft limits. A hard limit is enforced by the kernel and can only be changed by an administrator, whereas a soft limit is user-configurable.

If the maximum number of connections is left at 1,024, Cloud Manager will warn you by displaying the host in yellow in the host list. If low limits are the issue that triggered the warning, the Last Ping tab should display a message similar to that shown in Figure 24-4.

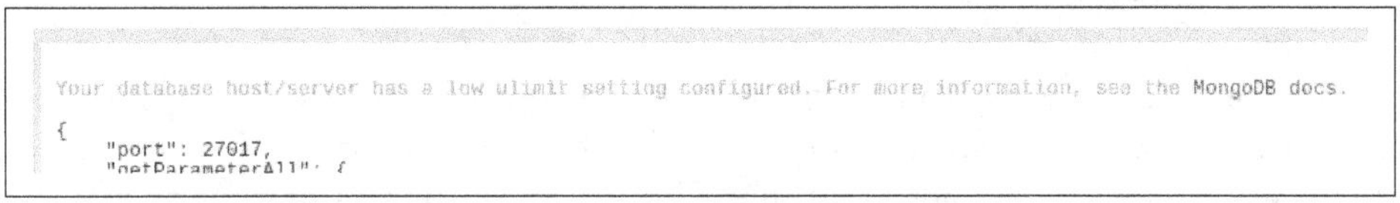

Figure 24-4. Cloud Manager low ulimit (file descriptors) setting warning

Even if you have a nonsharded setup and an application that only uses a small number of connections, it's a good idea to increase the hard and soft limits to at least 4,096. That will stop MongoDB from warning you about them and give you some breathing room, just in case.

Configuring Your Network

This section covers which servers should have connectivity to which other servers. Often, for reasons of network security (and sensibility), you may want to limit the connectivity of MongoDB servers. Note that multiserver MongoDB deployments should handle networks being partitioned or down, but it isn't recommended as a general deployment strategy.

For a standalone server, clients must be able to make connections to the *mongod*.

Members of a replica set must be able to make connections to every other member. Clients must be able to connect to all nonhidden, nonarbiter members. Depending on network configuration, members may also attempt to connect to themselves, so you should allow *mongod*s to create connections to themselves.

Sharding is a bit more complicated. There are four components: *mongos* servers, shards, config servers, and clients. Connectivity can be summarized in the following three points:

- A client must be able to connect to a *mongos*.
- A *mongos* must be able to connect to the shards and config servers.

- A shard must be able to connect to the other shards and the config servers.

The full connectivity chart is described in Table 24-1.

Table 24-1. Sharding connectivity

Connectivity to server type	from server type *mongos*	Shard	Config server	Client
mongos	Not required	Not required	Not required	Required
Shard	Required	Required	Not required	Not recommended
Config server	Required	Required	Not required	Not recommended
Client	Not required	Not required	Not required	Not MongoDB-related

There are three possible values in the table. "Required" means that connectivity between these two components is required for sharding to work as designed. MongoDB will attempt to degrade gracefully if it loses these connections due to network issues, but you shouldn't purposely configure it that way.

"Not required" means that these two elements never talk in the direction specified, so no connectivity is needed.

"Not recommended" means that these two elements should never talk, but due to user error they could. For example, it is recommended that clients only make connections to the *mongos*, not the shards, so that clients do not inadvertently make requests directly to shards. Similarly, clients should not be able to directly access config servers so that they cannot accidentally modify config data.

Note that *mongos* processes and shards talk to config servers, but config servers don't make connections to anyone, even one another.

Shards must communicate during migrates: shards connect to one another directly to transfer data.

As mentioned earlier, replica set members that compose shards should be able to connect to themselves.

System Housekeeping

This section covers some common issues you should be aware of before deploying.

Synchronizing Clocks

In general, it's safest to have your systems' clocks within a second of each other. Replica sets should be able to handle nearly any clock skew. Sharding can handle some skew (if it gets beyond a few minutes, you'll start seeing warnings in the logs), but it's best to minimize it. Having in-sync clocks also makes figuring out what's happening from logs easier.

You can keep clocks synchronized using the *w32tm* tool on Windows and the *ntp* daemon on Linux.

The OOM Killer

Very occasionally, MongoDB will allocate enough memory that it will be targeted by the out-of-memory (OOM) killer. This particularly tends to happen during index builds, as that is one of the only times when MongoDB's resident memory should put any strain on the system.

If your MongoDB process suddenly dies with no errors or exit messages in the logs, check */var/log/messages* (or wherever your kernel logs such things) to see if it has any messages about terminating *mongod*.

If the kernel has killed MongoDB for memory overuse, you should see something like this in the kernel log:

```
kernel: Killed process 2771 (mongod)
kernel: init invoked oom-killer: gfp_mask=0x201d2, order=0, oomkilladj=0
```

If you were running with journaling, you can simply restart *mongod* at this point. If you were not, restore from a backup or resync the data from a replica.

The OOM killer gets particularly nervous if you have no swap space and start running low on memory, so a good way to prevent it from going on a spree is to configure a modest amount of swap. As mentioned earlier, MongoDB should never use it, but it makes the OOM killer happy.

If the OOM killer kills a *mongos*, you can simply restart it.

Turn Off Periodic Tasks

Check that there aren't any cron jobs, antivirus scanners, or daemons that might periodically pop to life and steal resources. One culprit we've seen is package managers' automatic update. These programs will come to life, consume a ton of RAM and CPU, and then disappear. This is not something you want running on your production server.

Installing MongoDB

MongoDB binaries are available for Linux, macOS, Windows, and Solaris. This means that, on most platforms, you can download an archive from the MongoDB Download Center page (*https://www.mongodb.com/download-center*), inflate it, and run the binary.

The MongoDB server requires a directory it can write database files to and a port it can listen for connections on. This section covers the entire install on the two variants of system: Windows and everything else (Linux/Unix/macOS).

When we speak of "installing MongoDB," generally what we are talking about is setting up *mongod*, the core database server. *mongod* can be used as a standalone server or as a member of a replica set. Most of the time, this will be the MongoDB process you are using.

Choosing a Version

MongoDB uses a fairly simple versioning scheme: even-point releases are stable, and odd-point releases are development versions. For example, anything starting with 4.2 is a stable release, such as 4.2.0, 4.2.1, and 4.2.8. Anything starting with 4.3 is a development release, such as 4.3.0, 4.3.2, or 4.3.12. Let's take the 4.2/4.3 release as a sample case to demonstrate how the versioning timeline works:

1. MongoDB 4.2.0 is released. This is a major release and will have an extensive changelog.

2. After the developers start working on the milestones for 4.4 (the next major stable release), they release 4.3.0. This is the new development branch, which is fairly similar to 4.2.0 but probably with an extra feature or two and maybe some bugs.

3. As the developers continue to add features, they will release 4.3.1, 4.3.2, and so on. These releases should not be used in production.

4. Some minor bug fixes may be backported to the 4.2 branch, which will cause releases of 4.2.1, 4.2.2, and so on. Developers are conservative about what is backported; few new features are ever added to a stable release. Generally, only bug fixes are ported.

5. After all of the major milestones have been reached for 4.4.0, 4.3.7 (or whatever the latest development release is) will be turned into 4.4.0-rc0.

6. After extensive testing of 4.4.0-rc0, usually there are a couple minor bugs that need to be fixed. Developers fix these bugs and release 4.4.0-rc1.

7. Developers repeat step 6 until no new bugs are apparent, and then 4.4.0-rc2 (or whatever the latest release ended up being) is renamed 4.4.0.

8. Developers start over from step 1, incrementing all versions by 0.2.

You can see how close a production release is by browsing the core server roadmap on the MongoDB bug tracker (*http://jira.mongodb.org*).

If you are running in production, you should use a stable release. If you are planning to use a development release in production, ask about it first on the mailing list or IRC to get the developers' advice.

If you are just starting development on a project, using a development release may be a better choice. By the time you deploy to production, there will probably be a stable release with the features you're using (MongoDB attempts to stick to a regular cycle of stable releases every 12 months). However, you must balance this against the possibility that you may run into server bugs, which can be discouraging to a new user.

Windows Install

To install MongoDB on Windows, download the Windows *.msi* from the MongoDB Download Center page (*https://oreil.ly/nZZd0*). Use the advice in the previous section to choose the correct version of MongoDB. When you click the link, it will download the *.msi*. Double-click the *.msi* file icon to launch the installer program.

Now you need to make a directory in which MongoDB can write database files. By default, MongoDB tries to use the *\data\db* directory on the current drive as its data directory (e.g., if you're running *mongod* on *C:* on Windows, it'll use *C:\Program Files \MongoDB\Server\&<VERSION>\data*). This will be created automatically for you by the installer. If you chose to use a directory other than *\data\db*, you'll need to specify the path when you start MongoDB, which is covered in a moment.

Now that you have a data directory, open the command prompt (*cmd.exe*). Navigate to the directory where you unzipped the MongoDB binaries and run the following:

```
$ C:\Program Files\MongoDB\Server\&<VERSION>\bin\mongod.exe
```

If you chose a directory other than *C:\Program Files\MongoDB\Server\&<VERSION>\data*, you'll have to specify it here, with the --dbpath argument:

```
$ C:\Program Files\MongoDB\Server\&<VERSION>\bin\mongod.exe \
      --dbpath C:\Documents and Settings\Username\My Documents\db
```

See Chapter 21 for more common options, or run mongod.exe --help to see all the options.

Installing as a Service

MongoDB can also be installed as a service on Windows. To do this, simply run it with the full path, escape any spaces, and use the --install option. For example:

```
$ C:\Program Files\MongoDB\Server\4.2.0\bin\mongod.exe \
      --dbpath "\"C:\Documents and Settings\Username\My Documents\db\"" \
      --install
```

It can then be started and stopped from the Control Panel.

POSIX (Linux and Mac OS X) Install

Choose a version of MongoDB, based on the advice in the section "Choosing a Version" on page 465. Go to the MongoDB Download Center (*https://oreil.ly/XEScg*) and select the correct version for your OS.

> If you are using a Mac and are running macOS Catalina 10.15+, you should use */System/Volumes/Data/db* instead of */data/db*. This version made a change that renders the root folder read-only and resets upon reboot, which would result in the loss of your MongoDB data folder.

You must create a directory for the database to put its files in. By default the database will use */data/db*, although you can specify any other directory. If you create the default directory, make sure it has the correct write permissions. You can create the directory and set the permissions by running the following commands:

```
$ mkdir -p /data/db
$ chown -R $USER:$USER /data/db
```

mkdir -p creates the directory and all its parents, if necessary (i.e., if the */data* directory doesn't exist, it will create the */data* directory and then the */data/db* directory). chown changes the ownership of */data/db* so that your user can write to it. Of course, you can also just create a directory in your home folder and specify that MongoDB should use that when you start the database, to avoid any permissions issues.

Decompress the *.tar.gz* file you downloaded from the MongoDB Download Center:

```
$ tar zxf mongodb-linux-x86_64-enterprise-rhel62-4.2.0.tgz
$ cd mongodb-linux-x86_64-enterprise-rhel62-4.2.0
```

Now you can start the database:

```
$ bin/mongod
```

Or, if you'd like to use an alternate database path, specify it with the --dbpath option:

```
$ bin/mongod --dbpath ~/db
```

You can run `mongod.exe --help` to see all the possible options.

Installing from a Package Manager

There are also many package managers that can be used to install MongoDB. If you prefer using one of these, there are official packages for Red Hat, Debian, and Ubuntu as well as unofficial packages for many other systems. If you use an unofficial version, make sure it installs a relatively recent version.

On macOS, there are unofficial packages for Homebrew and MacPorts. To use the MongoDB Homebrew tap (*https://oreil.ly/9xoTe*), you first install the tap and then install the required version of MongoDB via Homebrew. The following example highlights how to install the latest production version of MongoDB Community Edition. You can add the custom tap in a macOS terminal session using:

```
$ brew tap mongodb/brew
```

Then install the latest available production release of MongoDB Community Server (including all command-line tools) using:

```
$ brew install mongodb-community
```

If you go for the MacPorts version, be forewarned: it takes hours to compile all the Boost libraries, which are MongoDB prerequisites. Start the download and leave it overnight.

Regardless of the package manager you use, it is a good idea to figure out where it is putting the MongoDB log files before you have a problem and need to find them. It's important to make sure they're being saved properly in advance of any possible issues.

MongoDB Internals

It is not necessary to understand MongoDB's internals to use it effectively, but they may be of interest to developers who wish to work on tools, contribute, or simply understand what's happening under the hood. This appendix covers some of the basics. The MongoDB source code is available at *https://github.com/mongodb/mongo*.

BSON

Documents in MongoDB are an abstract concept—the concrete representation of a document varies depending on the driver/language being used. Because documents are used extensively for communication in MongoDB, there also needs to be a representation of documents that is shared by all drivers, tools, and processes in the MongoDB ecosystem. That representation is called Binary JSON, or BSON (no one knows where the J went).

BSON is a lightweight binary format capable of representing any MongoDB document as a string of bytes. The database understands BSON, and BSON is the format in which documents are saved to disk.

When a driver is given a document to insert, use as a query, and so on, it will encode that document to BSON before sending it to the server. Likewise, documents being returned to the client from the server are sent as BSON strings. This BSON data is decoded by the driver to its native document representation before being returned to the client.

The BSON format has three primary goals:

Efficiency

BSON is designed to represent data efficiently, without using much extra space. In the worst case BSON is slightly less efficient than JSON, and in the best case (e.g., when storing binary data or large numerics), it is much more efficient.

Traversability

In some cases, BSON does sacrifice space efficiency to make the format easier to traverse. For example, string values are prefixed with a length rather than relying on a terminator to signify the end of a string. This traversability is useful when the MongoDB server needs to introspect documents.

Performance

Finally, BSON is designed to be fast to encode to and decode from. It uses C-style representations for types, which are fast to work with in most programming languages.

For the exact BSON specification, see *http://www.bsonspec.org*.

Wire Protocol

Drivers access the MongoDB server using a lightweight TCP/IP wire protocol. The protocol is documented on the MongoDB documentation site (*https://oreil.ly/rVJAr*) but basically consists of a thin wrapper around BSON data. For example, an insert message consists of 20 bytes of header data (which includes a code telling the server to perform an insert and the message length), the collection name to insert into, and a list of BSON documents to insert.

Data Files

Inside the MongoDB data directory, which is */data/db/* by default, a separate file will be stored for each collection and each index. The filenames do not correspond to the names of the collections or indexes, but you can use the stats within the *mongo* shell to identify the related file for a specific collection. The "wiredTiger.uri" field will contain the name of the file to look for in the MongoDB data directory.

Using stats on the *sample_mflix* database for the *movies* collection provides "collection-14--2146526997547809066" as result in the "wiredTiger.uri" field:

```
>db.movies.stats()
{
    "ns" : "sample_mflix.movies",
    "size" : 65782298,
    "count" : 45993,
    "avgObjSize" : 1430,
    "storageSize" : 45445120,
    "capped" : false,
```

```
"wiredTiger" : {
    "metadata" : {
        "formatVersion" : 1
    },
    "creationString" : "access_pattern_hint=none,allocation_size=4KB,\
app_metadata=(formatVersion=1),assert=(commit_timestamp=none,\
read_timestamp=none),block_allocation=best,\
block_compressor=snappy,cache_resident=false,checksum=on,\
colgroups=,collator=,columns=,dictionary=0,\
encryption=(keyid=,name=),exclusive=false,extractor=,format=btree,\
huffman_key=,huffman_value=,ignore_in_memory_cache_size=false,\
immutable=false,internal_item_max=0,internal_key_max=0,\
internal_key_truncate=true,internal_page_max=4KB,key_format=q,\
key_gap=10,leaf_item_max=0,leaf_key_max=0,leaf_page_max=32KB,\
leaf_value_max=64MB,log=(enabled=true),lsm=(auto_throttle=true,\
bloom=true,bloom_bit_count=16,bloom_config=,bloom_hash_count=8,\
bloom_oldest=false,chunk_count_limit=0,chunk_max=5GB,\
chunk_size=10MB,merge_custom=(prefix=,start_generation=0,suffix=),\
merge_max=15,merge_min=0),memory_page_image_max=0,\
memory_page_max=10m,os_cache_dirty_max=0,os_cache_max=0,\
prefix_compression=false,prefix_compression_min=4,source=,\
split_deepen_min_child=0,split_deepen_per_child=0,split_pct=90,\
type=file,value_format=u",
    "type" : "file",
    "uri" : "statistics:table:collection-14--2146526997547809066",
    ...
}
```

The file's details can then be verified within the MongoDB data directory:

```
ls -alh collection-14--2146526997547809066.wt
-rw-------  1 braz  staff  43M 28 Sep 23:33 collection-14--2146526997547809066.wt
```

It's possible to use the aggregation framework to find the URI for each index in a specific collection using the following:

```
db.movies.aggregate([{
    $collStats:{storageStats:{}}}]).next().storageStats.indexDetails
{
    "_id_" : {
    "metadata" : {
        "formatVersion" : 8,
        "infoObj" : "{ \"v\" : 2, \"key\" : { \"_id\" : 1 },\
        \"name\" : \"_id_\", \"ns\" : \"sample_mflix.movies\" }"
    },
    "creationString" : "access_pattern_hint=none,allocation_size=4KB,\
app_metadata=(formatVersion=8,infoObj={ \"v\" : 2, \"key\" : \
{ \"_id\" : 1 },\"name\" : \"_id_\", \"ns\" : \"sample_mflix.movies\" }),\
assert=(commit_timestamp=none,read_timestamp=none),block_allocation=best,\
block_compressor=,cache_resident=false,checksum=on,colgroups=,collator=,\
columns=,dictionary=0,encryption=(keyid=,name=),exclusive=false,extractor=,\
format=btree,huffman_key=,huffman_value=,ignore_in_memory_cache_size=false,\
immutable=false,internal_item_max=0,internal_key_max=0,\
```

```
        internal_key_truncate=true,internal_page_max=16k,key_format=u,key_gap=10,\
        leaf_item_max=0,leaf_key_max=0,leaf_page_max=16k,leaf_value_max=0,\
        log=(enabled=true),lsm=(auto_throttle=true,bloom=true,bloom_bit_count=16,\
        bloom_config=,bloom_hash_count=8,bloom_oldest=false,chunk_count_limit=0,\
        chunk_max=5GB,chunk_size=10MB,merge_custom=(prefix=,start_generation=0,\
        suffix=),merge_max=15,merge_min=0),memory_page_image_max=0,\
        memory_page_max=5MB,os_cache_dirty_max=0,os_cache_max=0,\
        prefix_compression=true,prefix_compression_min=4,source=,\
        split_deepen_min_child=0,split_deepen_per_child=0,split_pct=90,type=file,\
        value_format=u",
        "type" : "file",
        "uri" : "statistics:table:index-17--2146526997547809066",
    ...
        "$**_text" : {
    ...
        "uri" : "statistics:table:index-29--2146526997547809066",
    ...
        "genres_1_imdb.rating_1_metacritic_1" : {
    ...
        "uri" : "statistics:table:index-30--2146526997547809066",
    ...
    }
```

WiredTiger stores each collection or index in a single arbitrarily large file. The only limits that impact the potential maximum size of this file are filesystem size limits.

WiredTiger writes a new copy of the full document whenever that document is updated. The old copy on disk is flagged for reuse and will eventually be overwritten at a future point, typically during the next checkpoint. This recycles the space used within the WiredTiger file. The `compact` command can be run to move the data within this file to the start, leaving empty space at the end. At regular intervals, WiredTiger removes this excess empty space by truncating the file. At the end of the compaction process, the excess space is returned to the filesystem.

Namespaces

Each database is organized into *namespaces*, which are mapped to WiredTiger files. This abstraction separates the storage engine's internal details from the MongoDB query layer.

WiredTiger Storage Engine

The default storage engine for MongoDB is the WiredTiger storage engine. When the server starts up, it opens the data files and begins the checkpointing and journaling processes. It works in conjunction with the operating system, whose responsibility is focused on paging data in and out as well as flushing data to disk. This storage engine has several important properties:

- Compression is on by default for collections and for indexes. The default compression algorithm is Google's snappy. Other options include Facebook's Zstandard (zstd) and zlib, or indeed no compression. This minimizes storage use in the database at the expense of additional CPU requirements.

- Document-level concurrency allows for updates on different documents from multiple clients in a collection as the same time. WiredTiger uses MultiVersion Concurrency Control (MVCC) to isolate read and write operations to ensure clients see a consistent point-in-time view of the data at the start of an operation.

- Checkpointing creates a consistent point-in-time snapshot of the data and occurs every 60 seconds. It involves writing all the data in the snapshot to disk and updating the related metadata.

- Journaling with checkpointing ensures there is no point in time where data might be lost if there was a failure of a *mongod* process. WiredTiger uses a write-ahead log (journal) that stores modifications before they are applied.

Index

networking
for replica sets, 229
tracking network connections, 348
new Date(), 18
new Mongo("hostname"), 22
new users, adding, 391
$nin operator, 56
--nodb option, 22, 291
non-networked disks, 455
nonuniform memory architecture (NUMA),
455
--norc options, 291
normalization and denormalization
benefits and drawbacks of, 213
cardinality, 216
data representation examples, 212
defined, 211
embedding versus references, 215
social graph data and, 216
update operators, 215
Wil Wheaton effect, 218
--noscripting, 421
$not operator, 57, 105
--nounixsocket, 421
null type
querying on, 57
uses for, 17
number type, 17

O

object ID type, 18
Object.bsonsize(), 379
ObjectIDs
basics of, 20
storing _ids as, 379
objects, indexing, 114
one-to-many relationships, 216
one-to-one relationships, 216
operating system, selecting, 451
operations, killing, 375
(see also application operations)
oplogs
avoiding out-of-sync secondaries, 253
changing size of, 251
defining size of, 292
purpose of, 249
resizing, 282
size limits, 206, 250
statement-based replication, 406

syncing, 249
oplogSizeMB option, 251
Ops Manager, 228, 290, 437
$or operator, 56, 112
$out operator, 198
out-of-memory (OOM) killer, 463
outlier schema design pattern, 209
overcommitting, 453

P

page faults, tracking, 427, 431
partialFilterExpression, 126, 128
partitioning, 289
passive members, 244
performance, tracking, 431
(see also monitoring)
periodic tasks, turning off, 463
Perl Compatible Regular Expression (PCRE)
library, 58
permissions, 390
phantom operations, 375
ping time, 279
polymorphic schema design pattern, 209
$pop operator, 44
--port, 416
position operator ($), 45
preallocation schema design pattern, 211
primary shards, 294
primary-secondary-arbiter (PSA) architecture,
247
problematic operations, 374
production set up
checking log, 417
data encryption, 422
file-based configuration, 419
logging, 423
security, 421
(see also security considerations)
servers, 449
SSL connections, 423
starting from command line, 415-420
stopping MongoDB, 420
--profile level, 379
$project operator, 169-174
public key infrastructure (PKI) standard, 390
publication/subscription systems, 216
$pull operator, 44
$push operator, 41, 186, 196
PyMongo, 157

About the Authors

Shannon Bradshaw is VP of education at MongoDB. Shannon manages the MongoDB Documentation and MongoDB University teams. These teams develop and maintain the majority of MongoDB learning resources used by the MongoDB community. Shannon holds a PhD in computer science from Northwestern University. Prior to MongoDB, Shannon was a computer science professor specializing in information systems and human-information interaction.

Eoin Brazil is a senior curriculum engineer at MongoDB. He works on online and instructor-led training products delivered through MongoDB University and previously held various positions in the technical services support organization within MongoDB. Eoin holds a PhD and a MSc in computer science from the University of Limerick and a PgDip in technology commercialization from the National University of Ireland, Galway. Prior to MongoDB, he led teams in mobile services and in high-performance computing in the academic research sector.

Kristina Chodorow is a software engineer who worked on the MongoDB core for five years. She led MongoDB's replica set development as well as writing the PHP and Perl drivers. She has given talks on MongoDB at meetups and conferences around the world and maintains a blog on technical topics at *http://www.kchodorow.com*. She currently works at Google.

Colophon

The animal on the cover of *MongoDB: The Definitive Guide, Third Edition*, is a mongoose lemur, a member of a highly diverse group of primates endemic to Madagascar. Ancestral lemurs are believed to have inadvertently traveled to Madagascar from Africa (a trip of at least 350 miles) by raft some 65 million years ago. Freed from competition with other African species (such as monkeys and squirrels), lemurs adapted to fill a wide variety of ecological niches, branching into the almost 100 species known today. These animals' otherworldly calls, nocturnal activity, and glowing eyes earned them their name, which comes from the lemures (specters) of Roman myth. Malagasy culture also associates lemurs with the supernatural, variously considering them the souls of ancestors, the source of taboo, or spirits bent on revenge. Some villages identify a particular species of lemur as the ancestor of their group.

Mongoose lemurs (*Eulemur mongoz*) are medium-sized lemurs, about 12 to 18 inches long and 3 to 4 pounds. The bushy tail adds an additional 16 to 25 inches. Females and young lemurs have white beards, while males have red beards and cheeks. Mongoose lemurs eat fruit and flowers and they act as pollinators for some plants; they are particularly fond of the nectar of the kapok tree. They may also eat leaves and insects.

Mongoose lemurs inhabit the dry forests of northwestern Madagascar. One of the two species of lemur found outside of Madagascar, they also live in the Comoros Islands (where they are believed to have been introduced by humans). They have the unusual quality of being cathemeral (alternately wakeful during the day and at night), changing their activity patterns to suit the wet and dry seasons. Mongoose lemurs are threatened by habitat loss and they are classified as a vulnerable species.

Many of the animals on O'Reilly covers are endangered; all of them are important to the world.

The cover illustration is by Karen Montgomery, based on a black and white engraving from Lydekker's *Royal Natural History*. The cover fonts are Gilroy Semibold and Guardian Sans. The text font is Adobe Minion Pro; the heading font is Adobe Myriad Condensed; and the code font is Dalton Maag's Ubuntu Mono.

O'REILLY®

There's much more where this came from.

Experience books, videos, live online training courses, and more from O'Reilly and our 200+ partners—all in one place.

Learn more at oreilly.com/online-learning

CPSIA information can be obtained
at www.ICGtesting.com
Printed in the USA
JSHW030558170522
25979JS00004B/61